The Girl Who Sang

A Holocaust Memoir of Hope and Survival

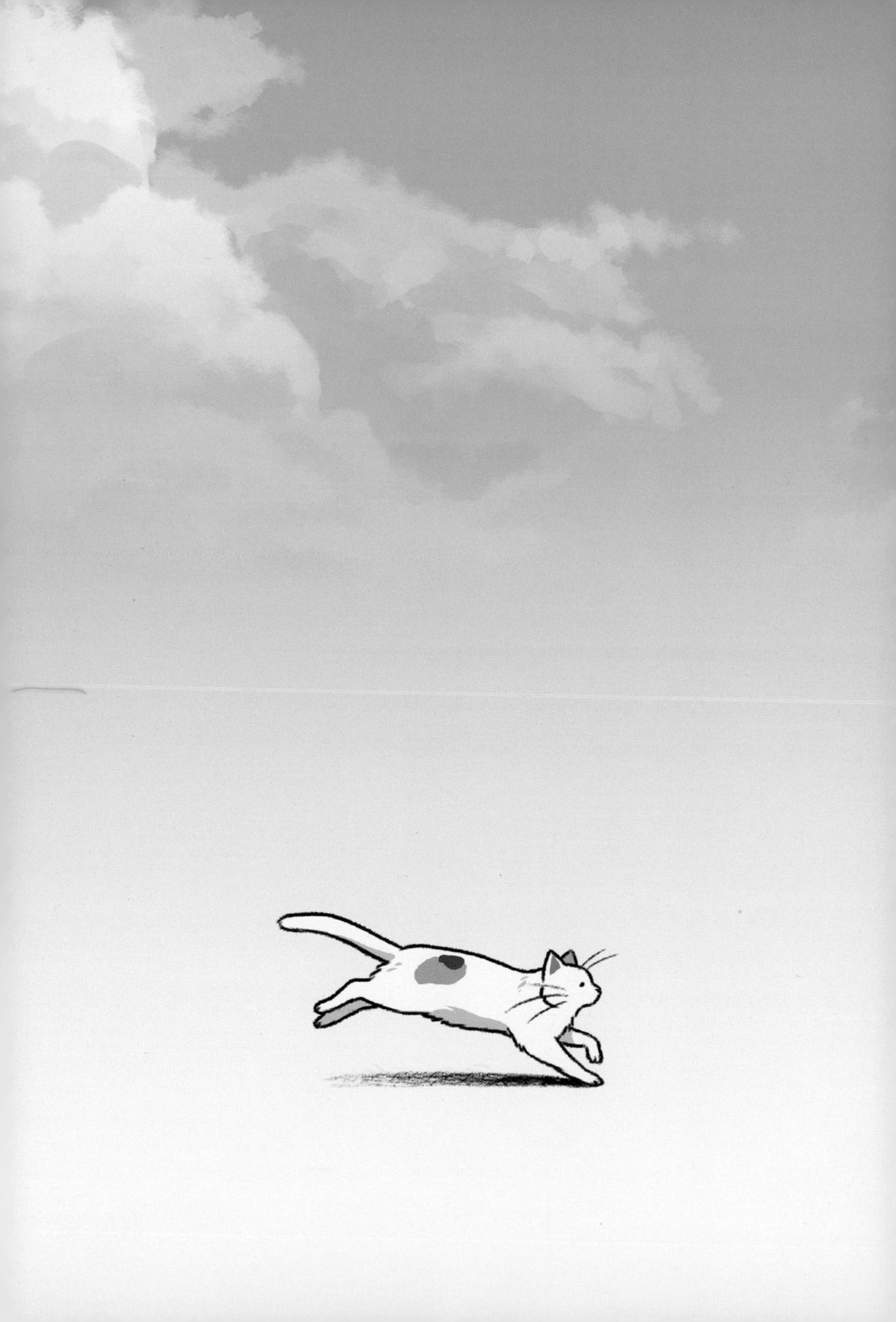

The Girl Who Sang

A Holocaust Memoir of Hope and Survival

written by
Estelle Nadel with
Sammy Savos and
Bethany Strout

art by
Sammy Savos

Roaring Brook Press
New York

The Feld Family

Enia Feld

Minashe Feld
Enia's brother
(seven years older)

Shia Feld
Enia's brother
(eight years older)

Moishe Feld
Enia's brother
(twelve years older)

Sonjia Feld
Enia's sister
(thirteen years older)

Chaya Feld
Enia's mother

Reuven Feld
Enia's Father

The Reiss Family

Józef Reiss
Enia's uncle

Hinda Reiss
Enia's aunt

mala Reiss
Enia's cousin

The Rescuers

Maria Kurowska

Emilia "Milcha"
Kurowska

Jan Kurowski

Pudlina

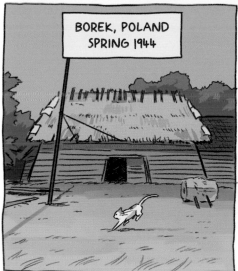

BOREK, POLAND
SPRING 1944

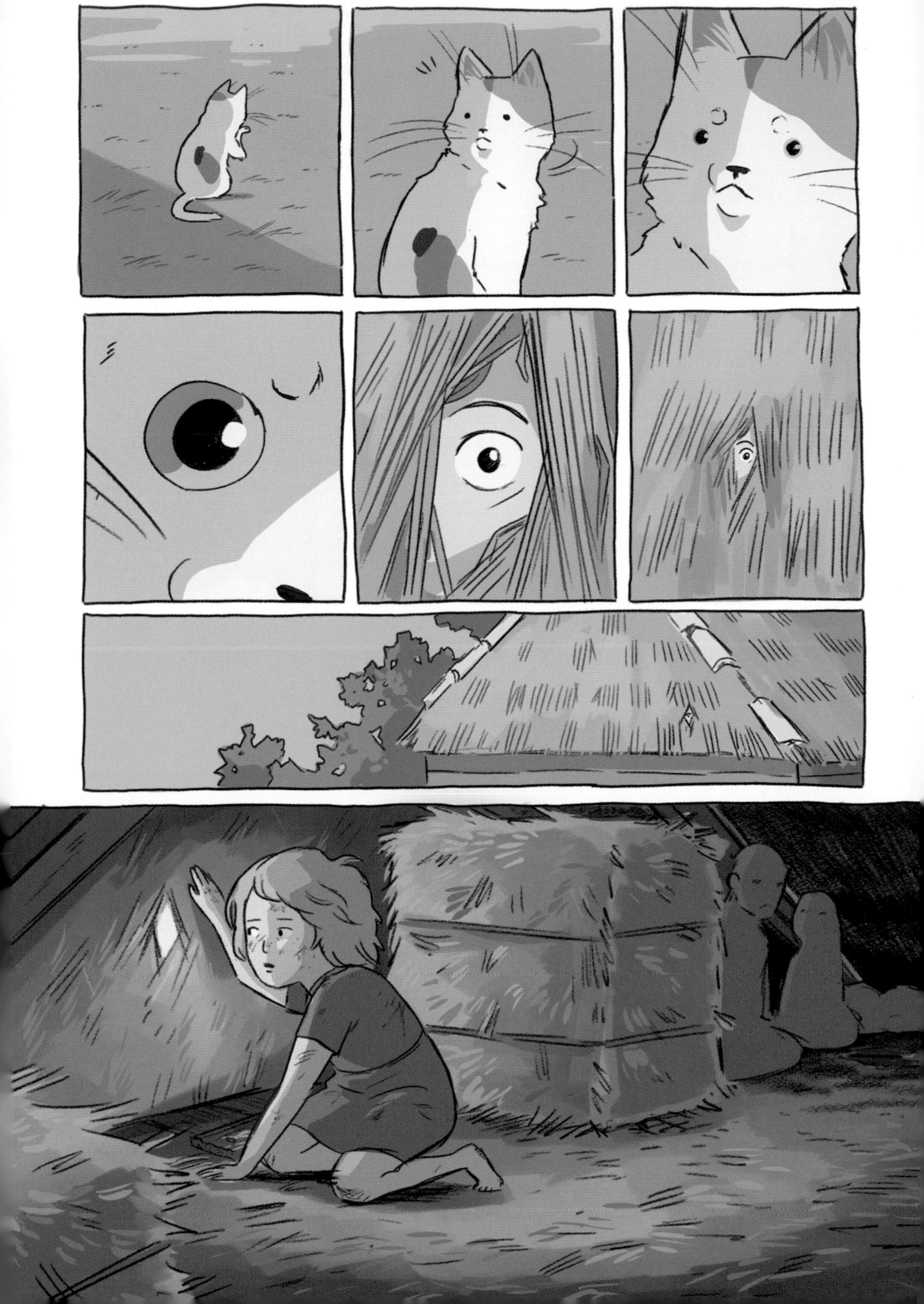

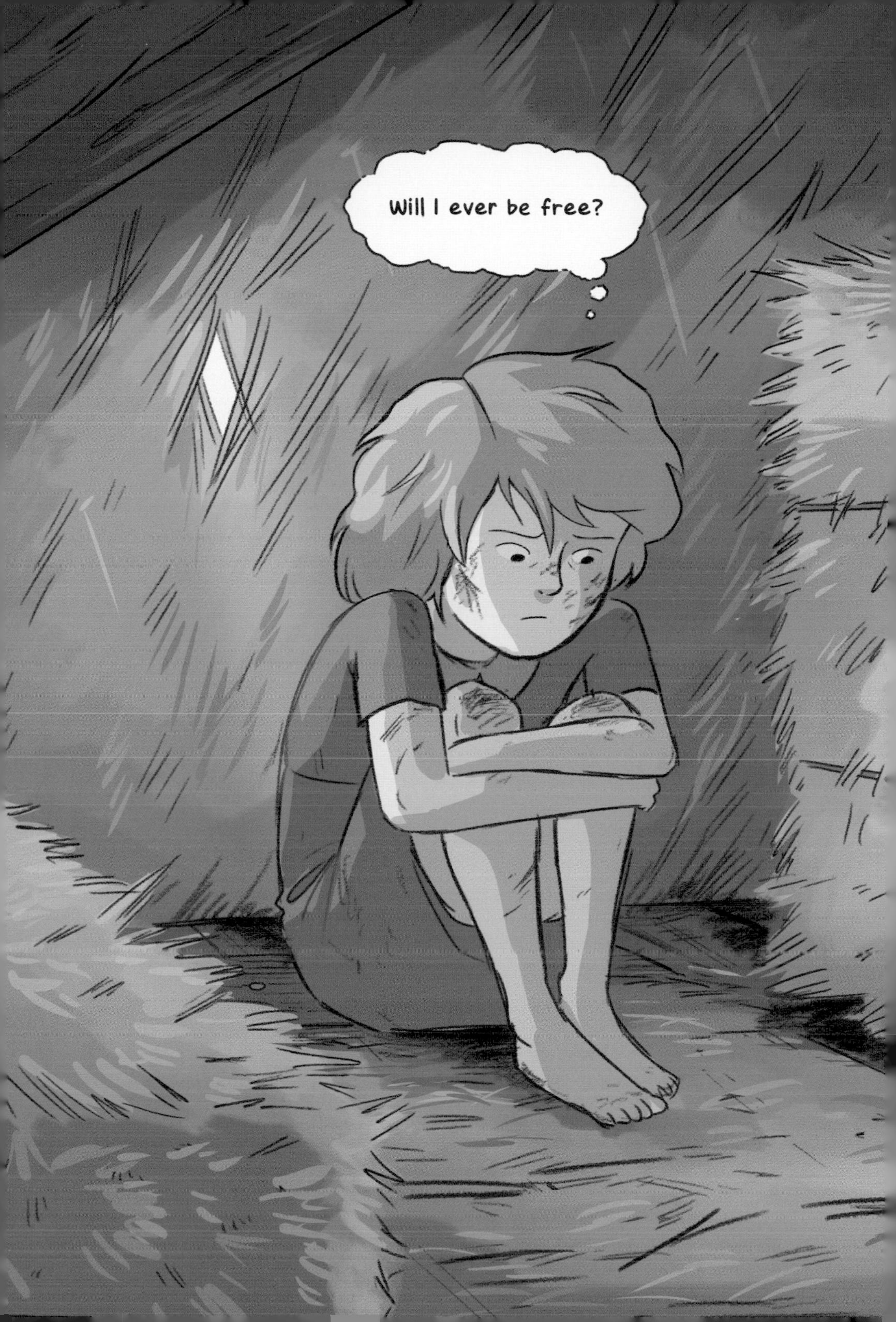
Will I ever be free?

PART 1:

INNOCENCE
1939–1942

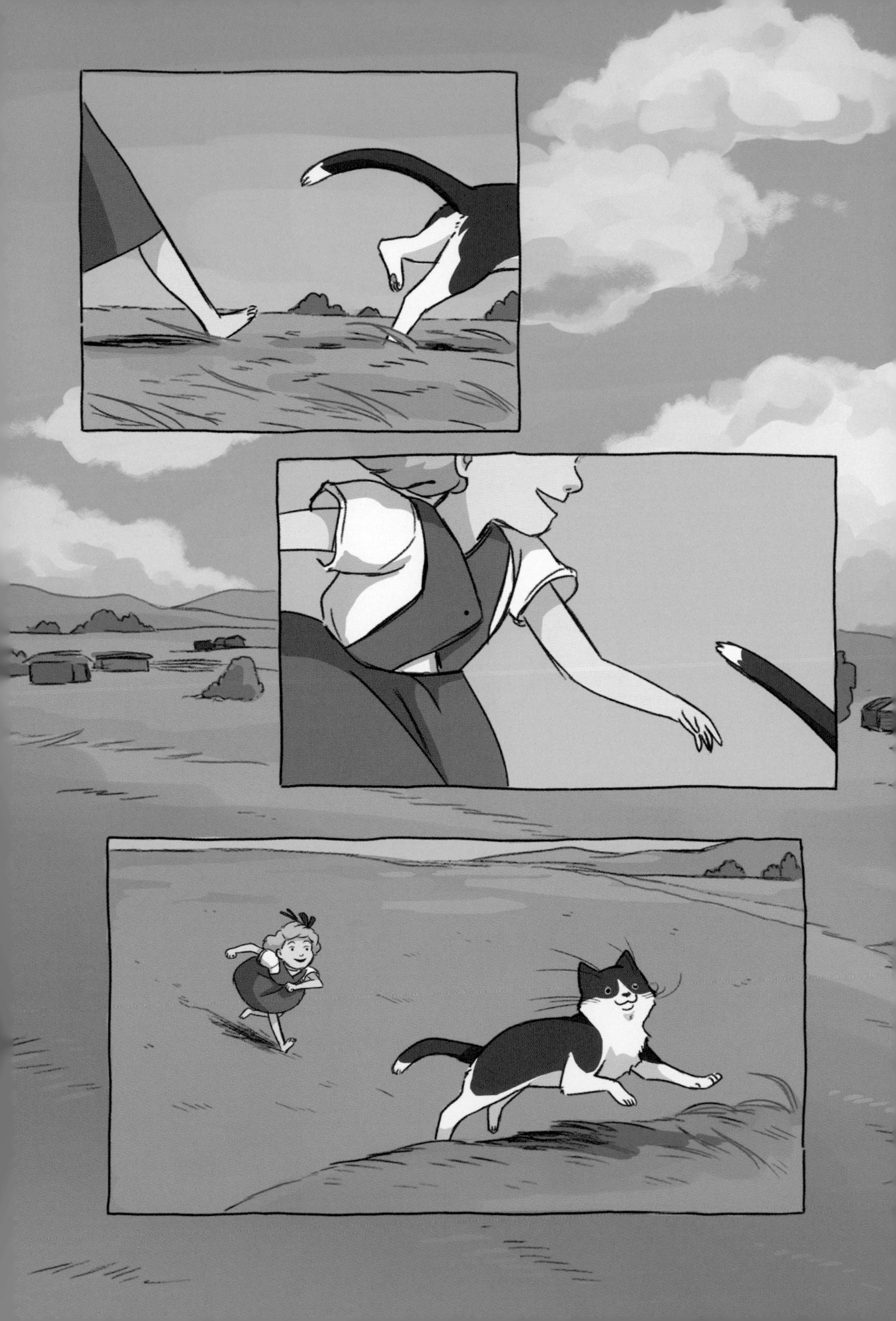

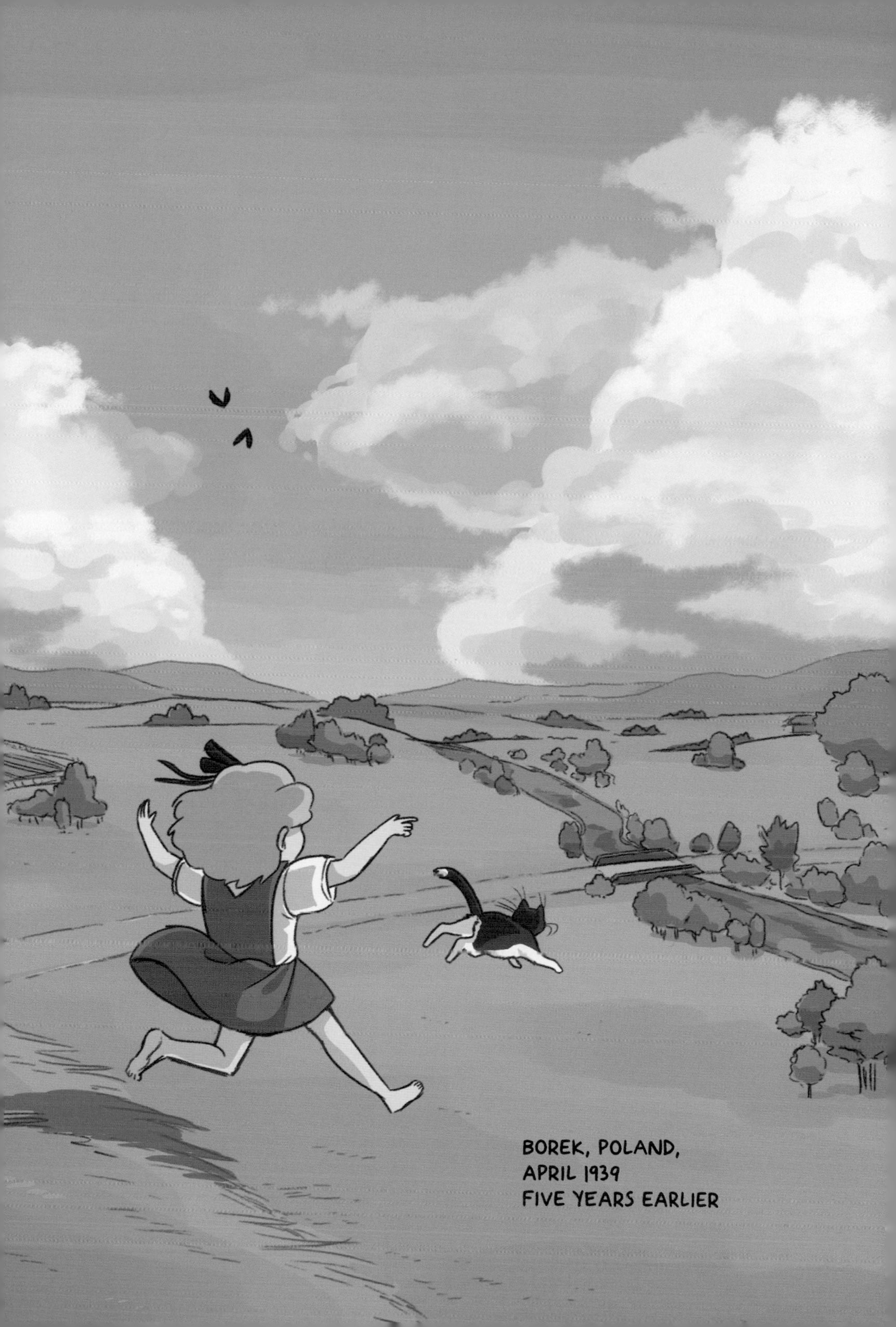
BOREK, POLAND,
APRIL 1939
FIVE YEARS EARLIER

I see the birds fly, fly away...

I hear the river rush on by.

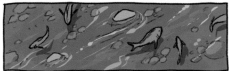

Enia! Enia, come back! It's time to make the matzah!

Coming, Mamchu!*

*This is what we called our mother.

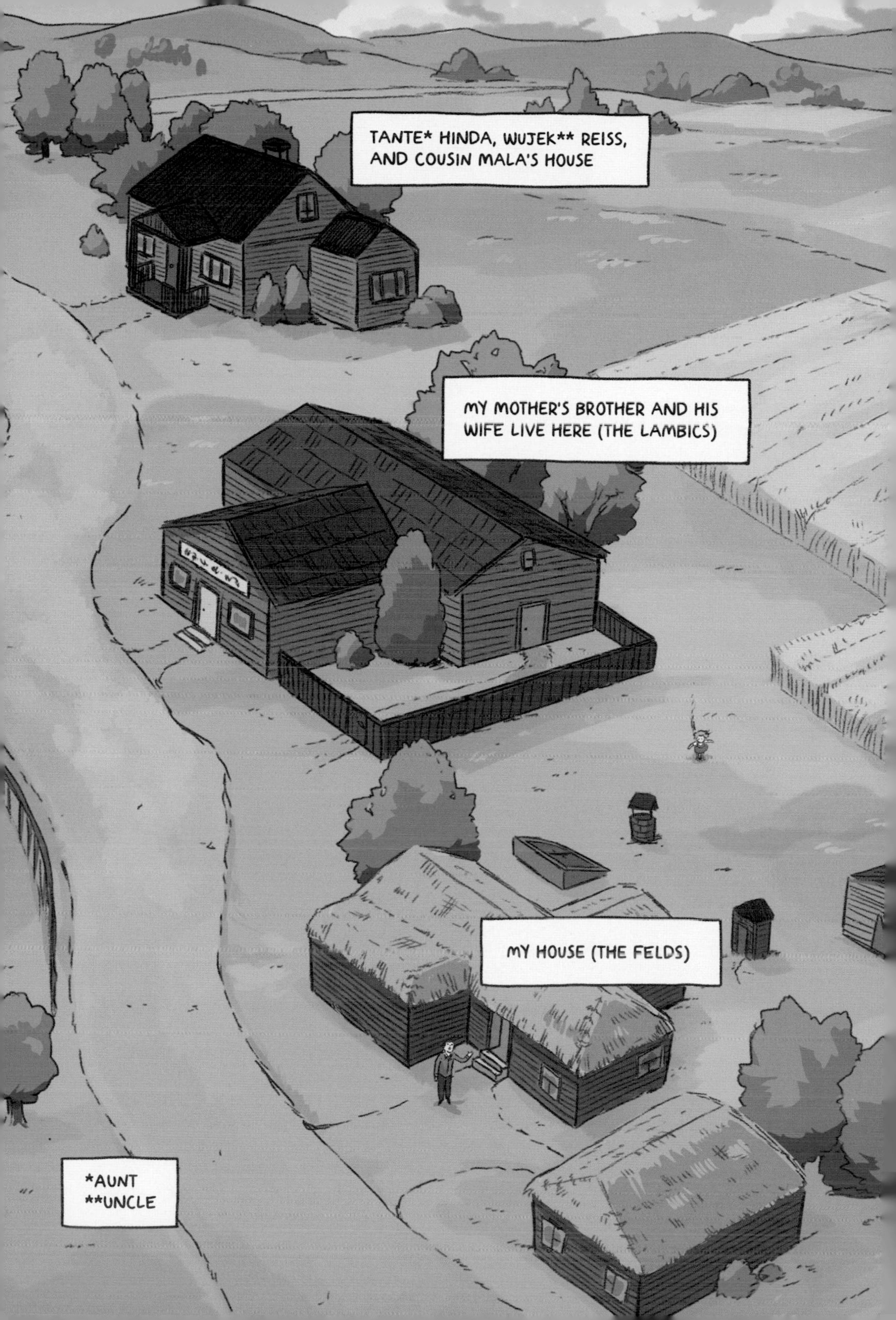
TANTE* HINDA, WUJEK** REISS, AND COUSIN MALA'S HOUSE
MY MOTHER'S BROTHER AND HIS WIFE LIVE HERE (THE LAMBICS)
MY HOUSE (THE FELDS)
*AUNT
**UNCLE

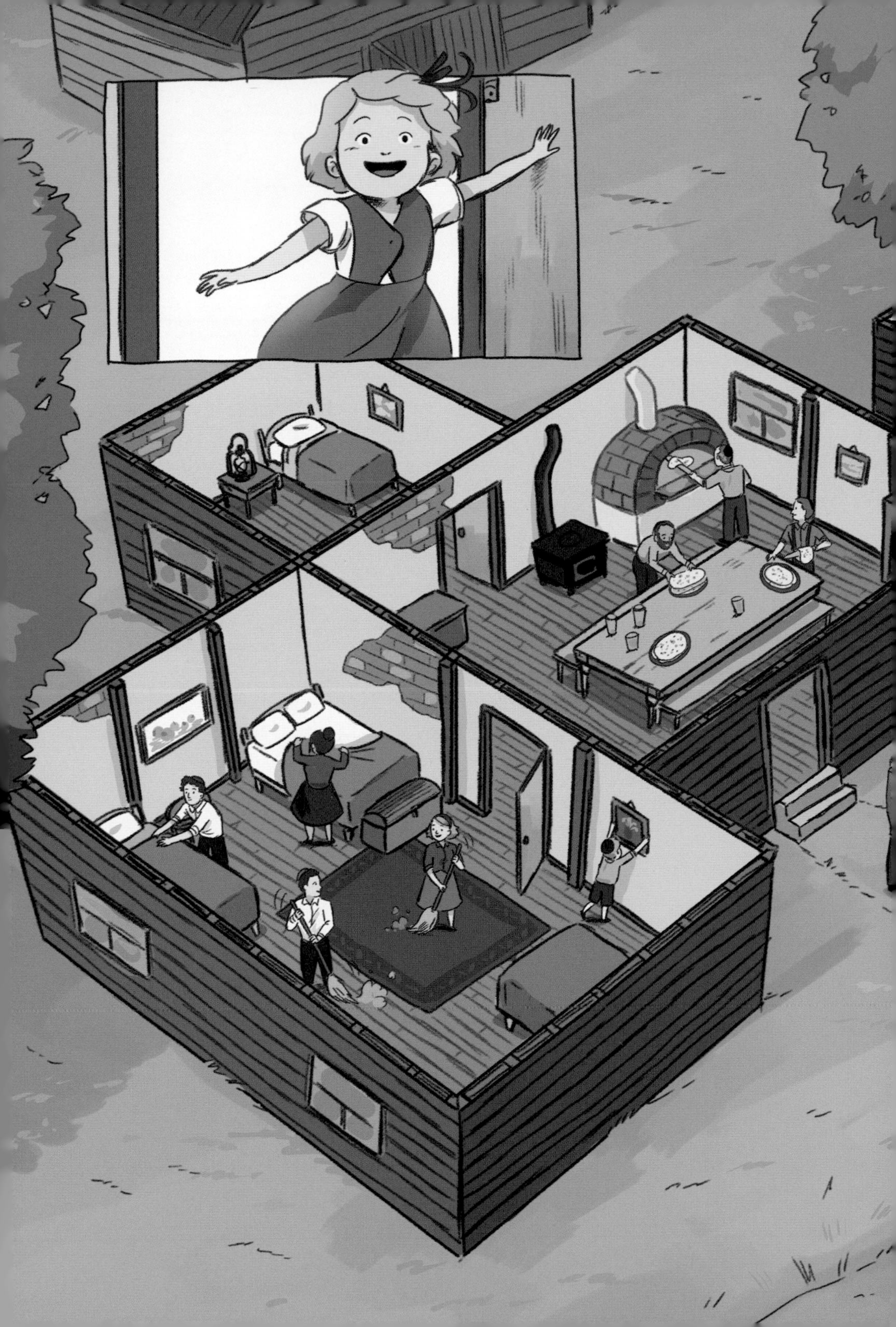

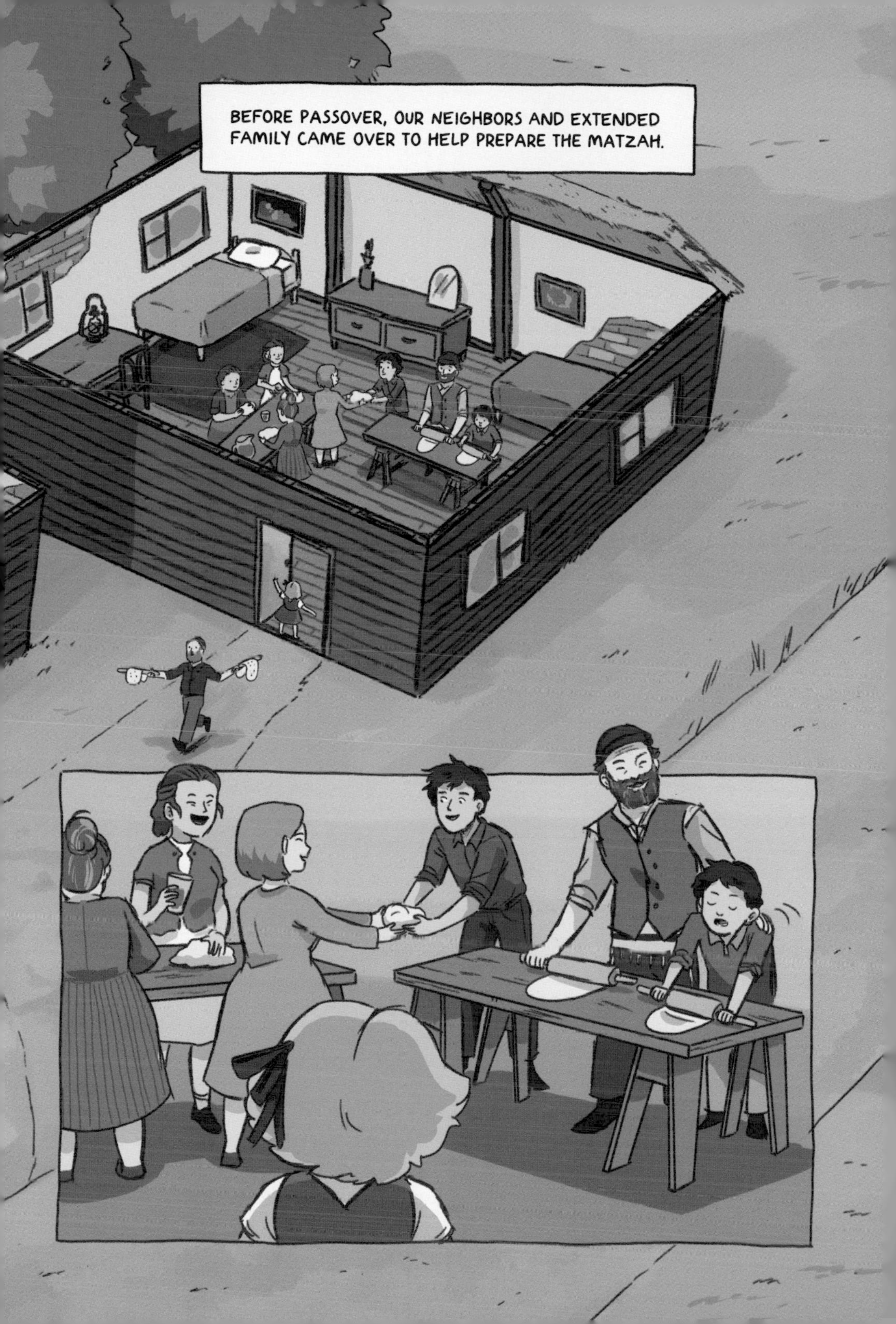
BEFORE PASSOVER, OUR NEIGHBORS AND EXTENDED FAMILY CAME OVER TO HELP PREPARE THE MATZAH.

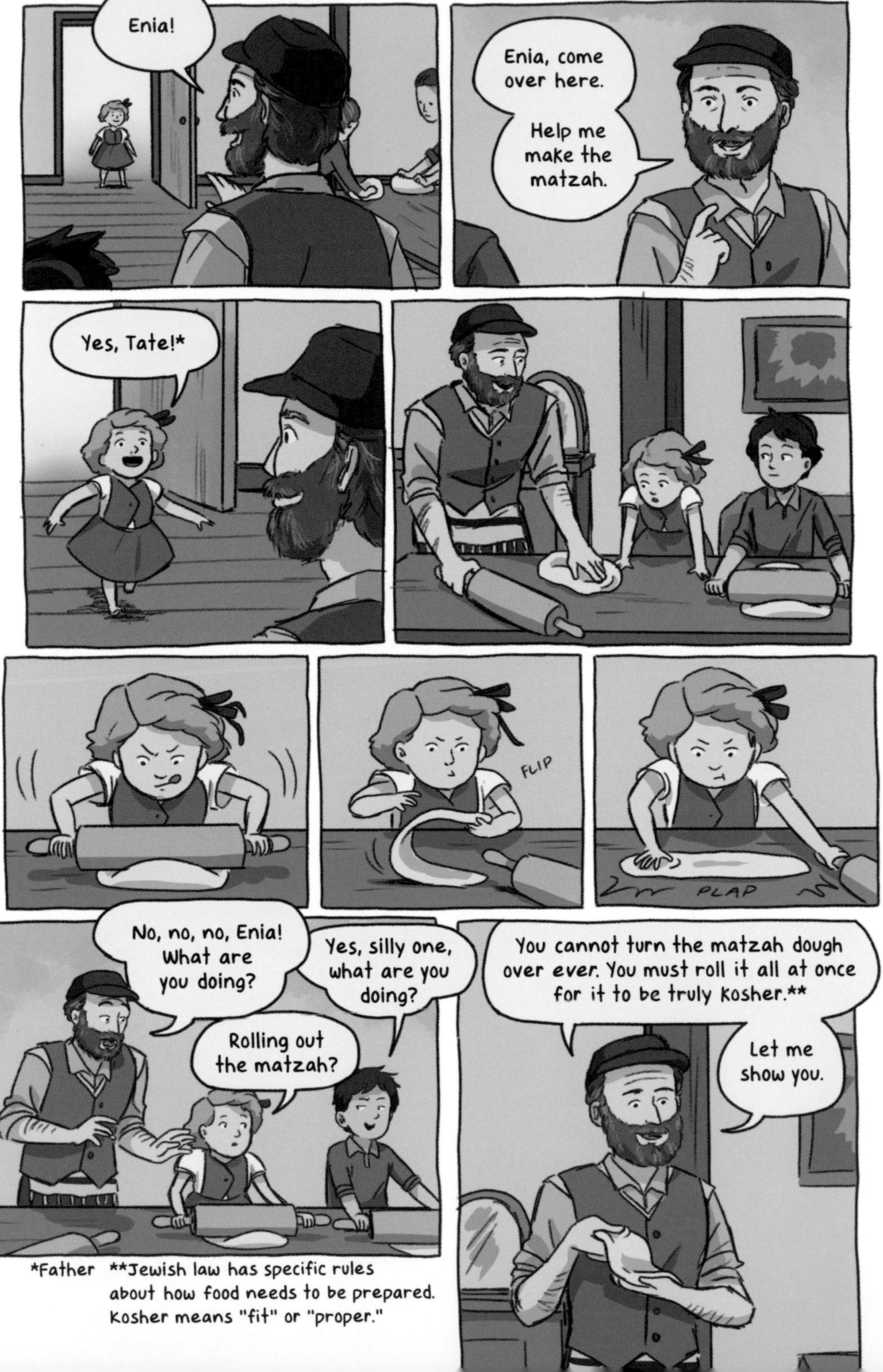

Enia!
Enia, come over here.
Help me make the matzah.
Yes, Tate!*
FLIP
PLAP
No, no, no, Enia! What are you doing?
Yes, silly one, what are you doing?
Rolling out the matzah?
You cannot turn the matzah dough over ever. You must roll it all at once for it to be truly kosher.**
Let me show you.

*Father **Jewish law has specific rules about how food needs to be prepared. Kosher means "fit" or "proper."

HOW TO MAKE MATZAH

STEP 1: MIX TOGETHER FLOUR AND WATER.

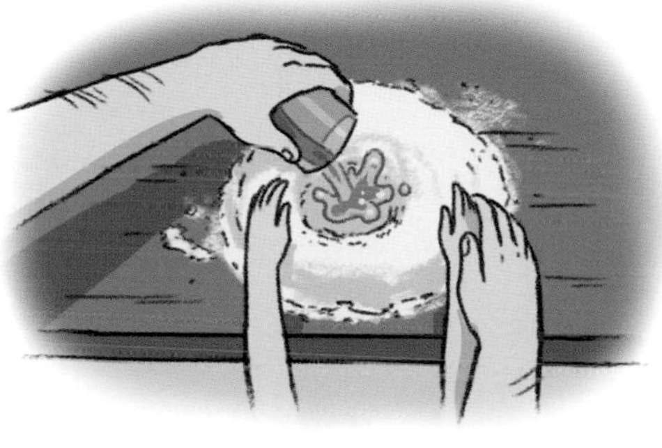

STEP 2: KNEAD THE DOUGH AND THEN DIVIDE IT INTO SMALLER PIECES.

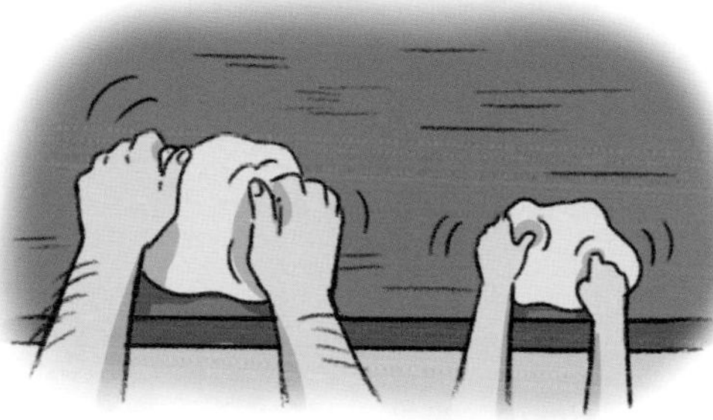

STEP 3: ROLL OUT THE DOUGH SO IT IS VERY THIN. DO *NOT* PICK THE DOUGH UP AND TURN IT OVER.

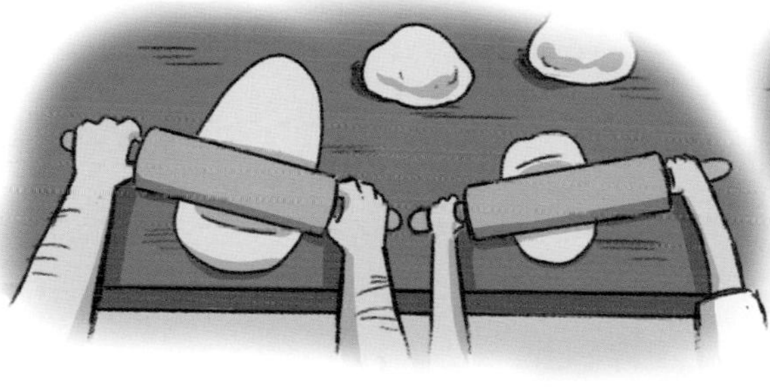

STEP 4: PRICK THE FLAT DOUGH ALL OVER.

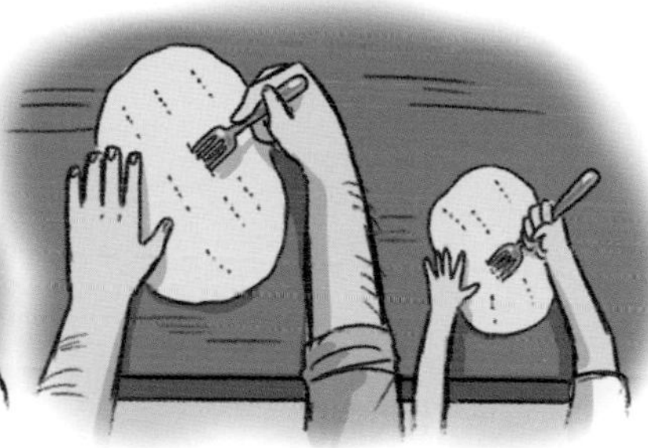

STEP 5: PUT THE MATZAH INTO THE OVEN (VERY HOT!!) AND BAKE FOR 2-3 MINUTES.

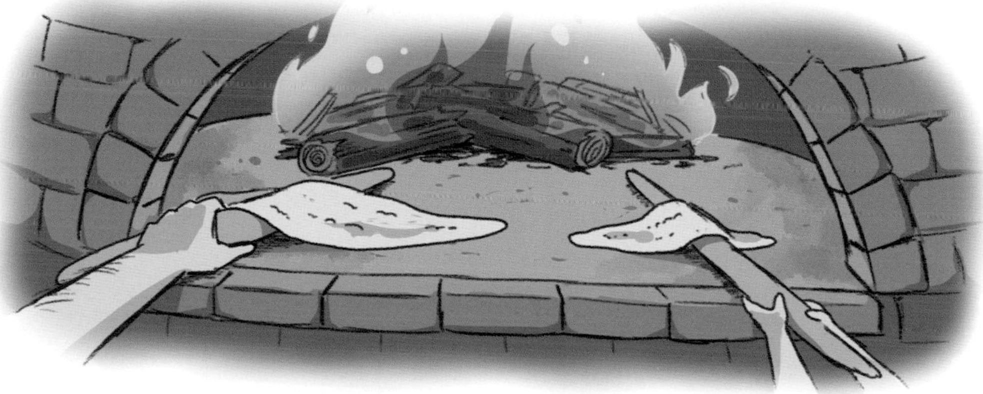

FROM START TO FINISH, IT CAN'T TAKE MORE THAN 18 MINUTES OR IT'S NOT KOSHER AND YOU HAVE TO THROW AWAY THE DOUGH TO START AGAIN!

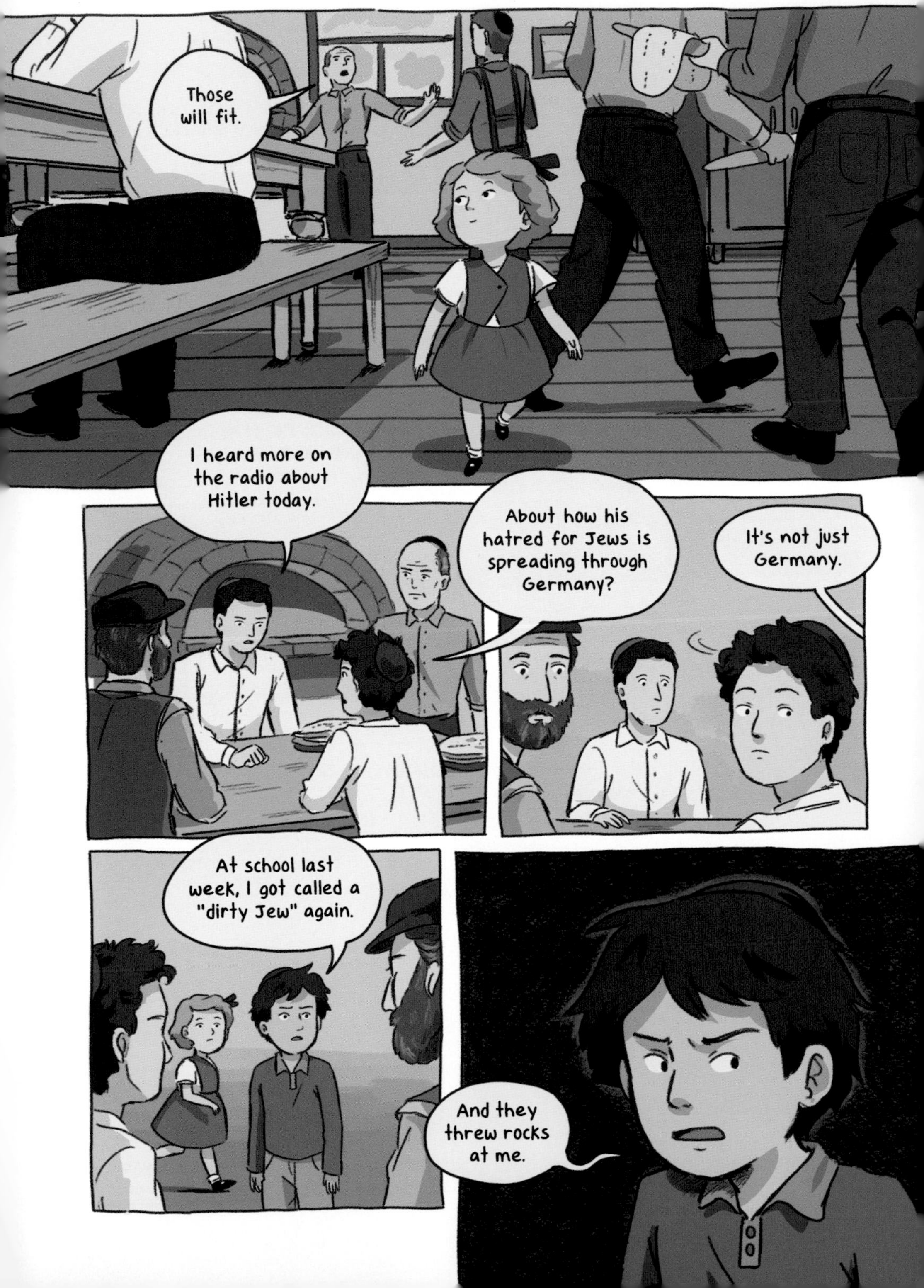
Those will fit.
I heard more on the radio about Hitler today.
About how his hatred for Jews is spreading through Germany?
It's not just Germany.
At school last week, I got called a "dirty Jew" again.
And they threw rocks at me.

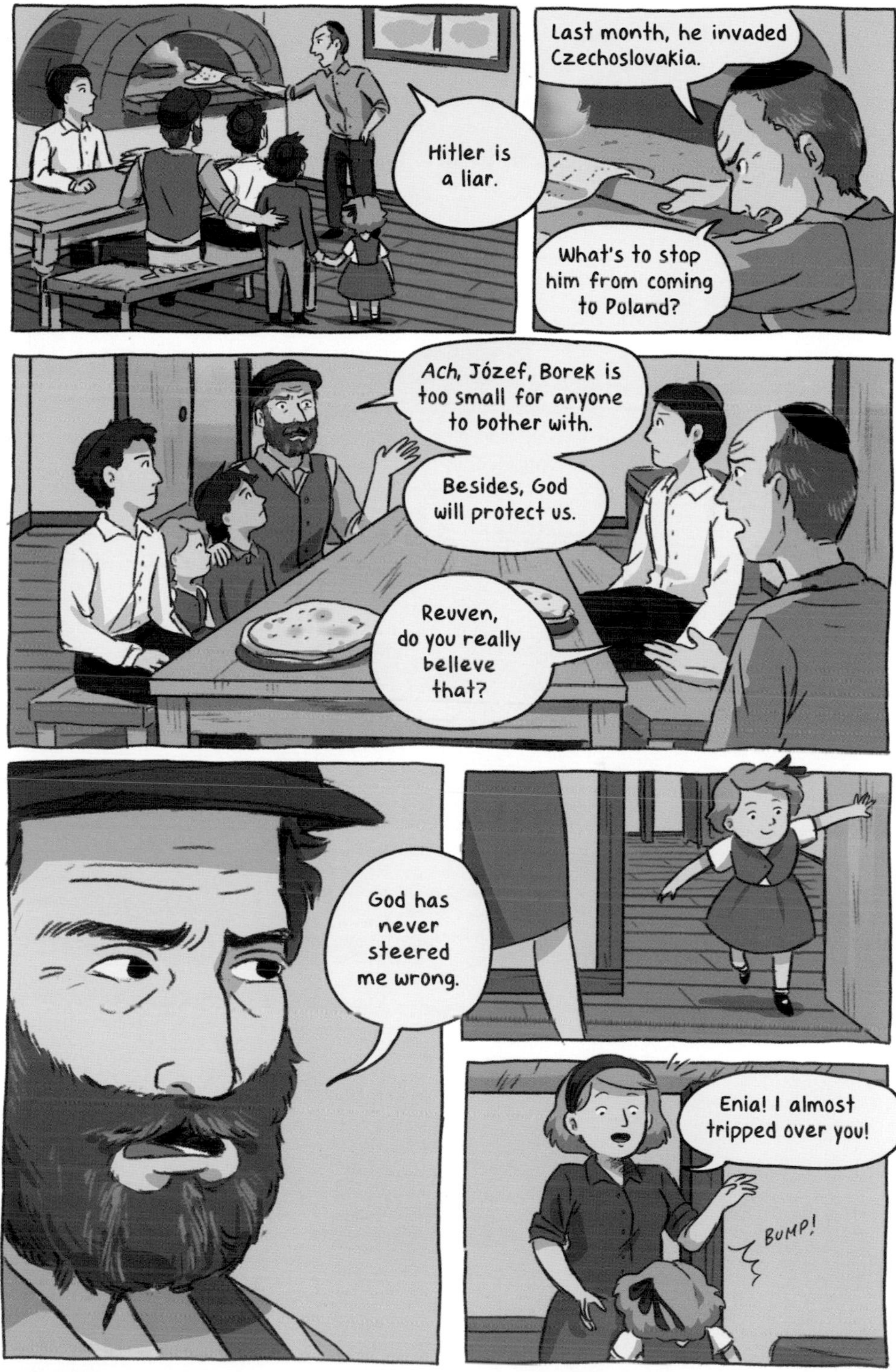
Hitler is a liar.
Last month, he invaded Czechoslovakia.
What's to stop him from coming to Poland?
Ach, Józef, Borek is too small for anyone to bother with.
Besides, God will protect us.
Reuven, do you really belleve that?
God has never steered me wrong.
Enia! I almost tripped over you!
BUMP!

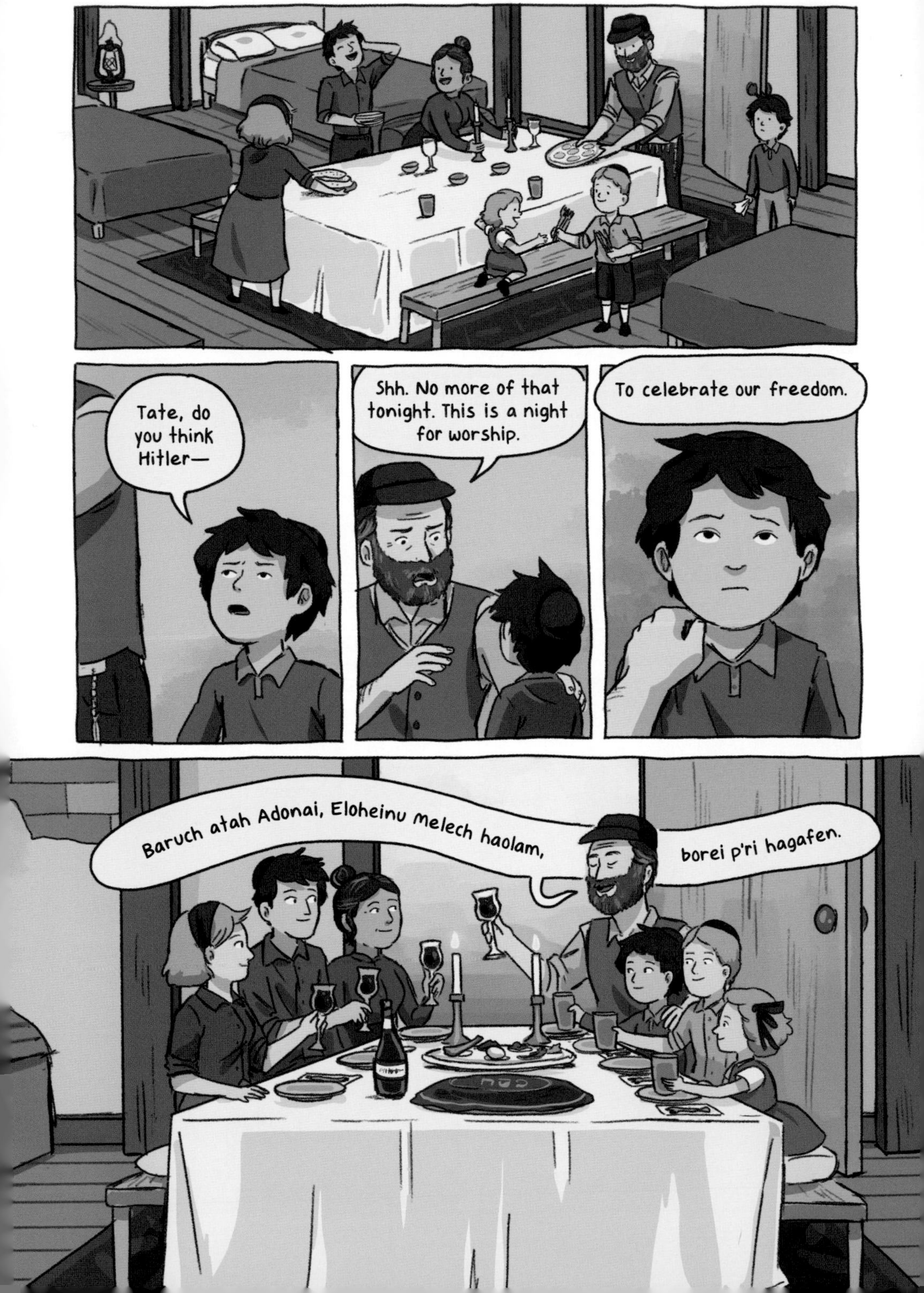
Tate, do you think Hitler—
Shh. No more of that tonight. This is a night for worship.
To celebrate our freedom.
Baruch atah Adonai, Eloheinu melech haolam,
borei p'ri hagafen.

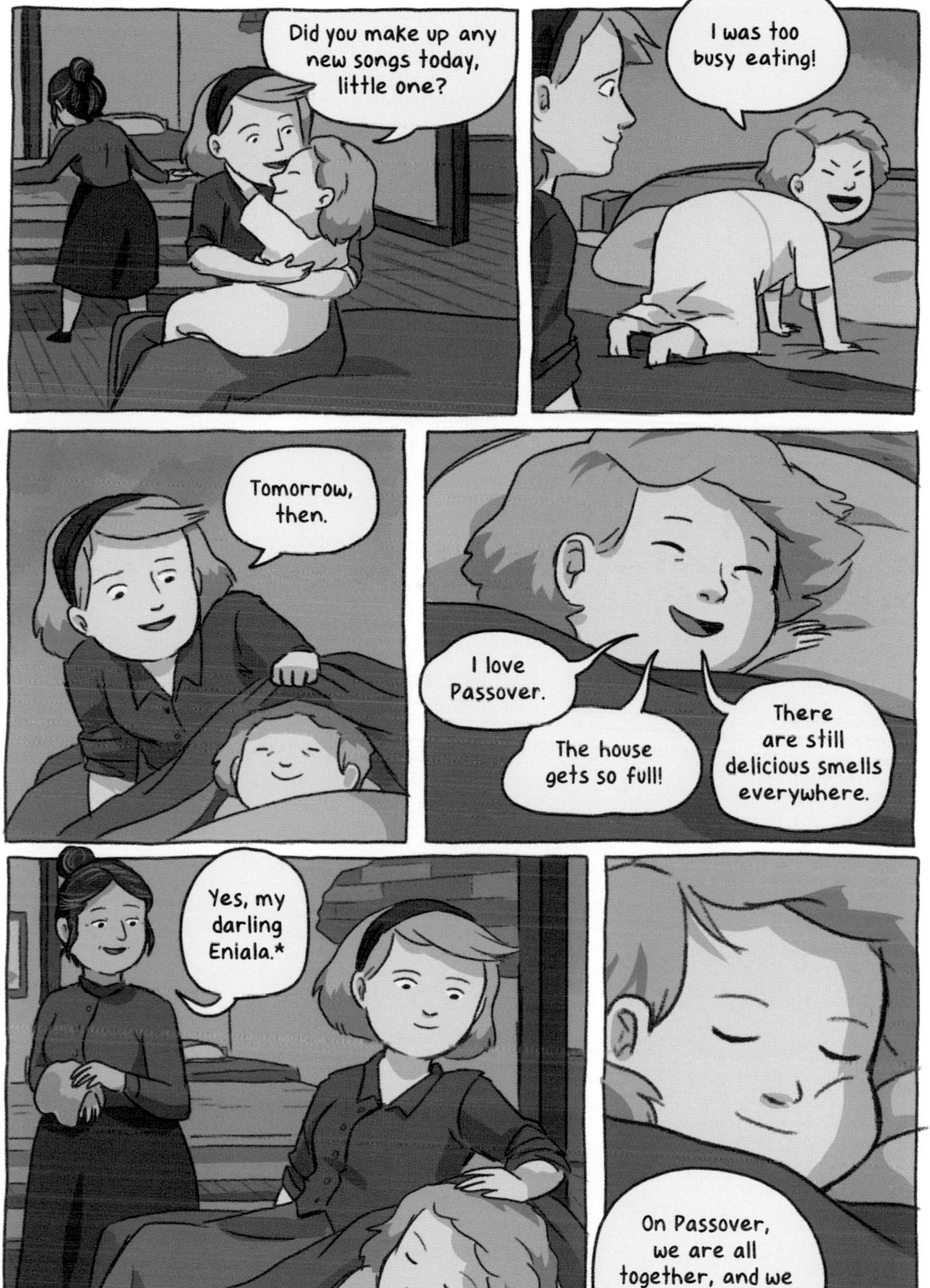

Did you make up any new songs today, little one?
I was too busy eating!
Tomorrow, then.
I love Passover.
The house gets so full!
There are still delicious smells everywhere.
Yes, my darling Eniala.*
On Passover, we are all together, and we have everything we need.

*My mother's pet name for me.

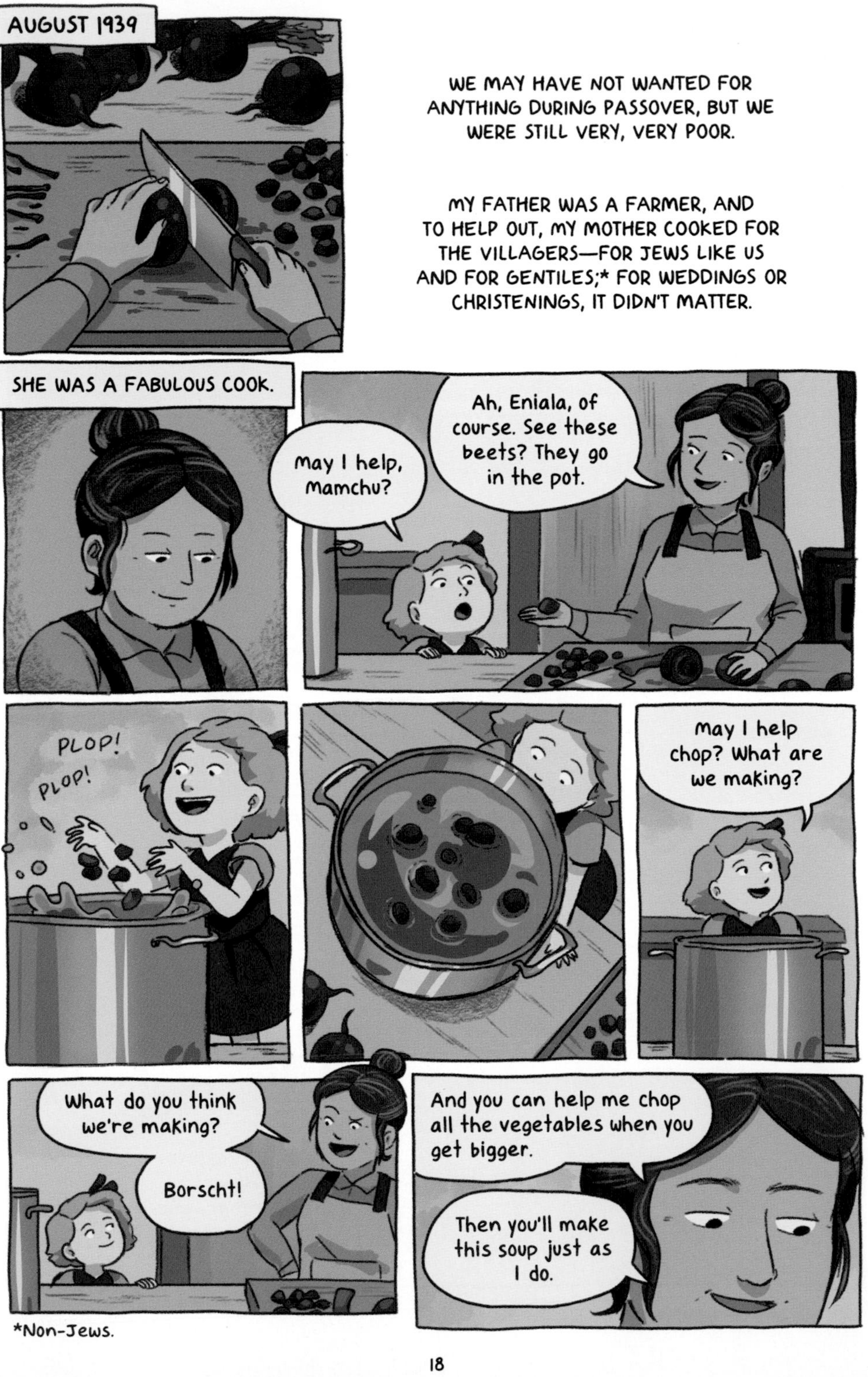
AUGUST 1939
WE MAY HAVE NOT WANTED FOR ANYTHING DURING PASSOVER, BUT WE WERE STILL VERY, VERY POOR.
MY FATHER WAS A FARMER, AND TO HELP OUT, MY MOTHER COOKED FOR THE VILLAGERS—FOR JEWS LIKE US AND FOR GENTILES;* FOR WEDDINGS OR CHRISTENINGS, IT DIDN'T MATTER.
SHE WAS A FABULOUS COOK.
May I help, mamchu?
Ah, Eniala, of course. See these beets? They go in the pot.
PLOP!
PLOP!
May I help chop? What are we making?
What do you think we're making?
Borscht!
And you can help me chop all the vegetables when you get bigger.
Then you'll make this soup just as I do.

*Non-Jews.

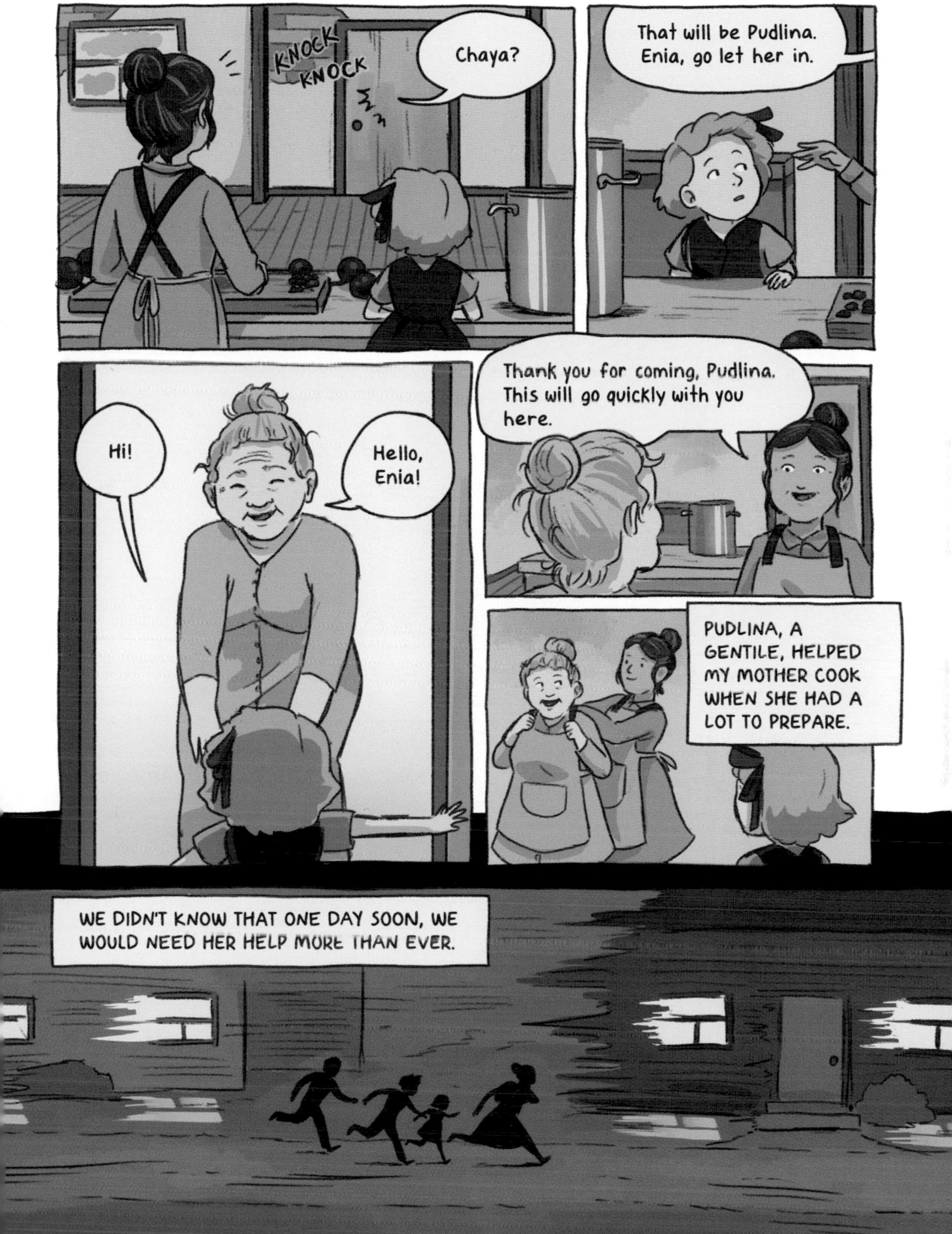
KNOCK
KNOCK
Chaya?
That will be Pudlina.
Enia, go let her in.
Hi!
Hello,
Enia!
Thank you for coming, Pudlina.
This will go quickly with you
here.
PUDLINA, A
GENTILE, HELPED
MY MOTHER COOK
WHEN SHE HAD A
LOT TO PREPARE.
WE DIDN'T KNOW THAT ONE DAY SOON, WE
WOULD NEED HER HELP MORE THAN EVER.

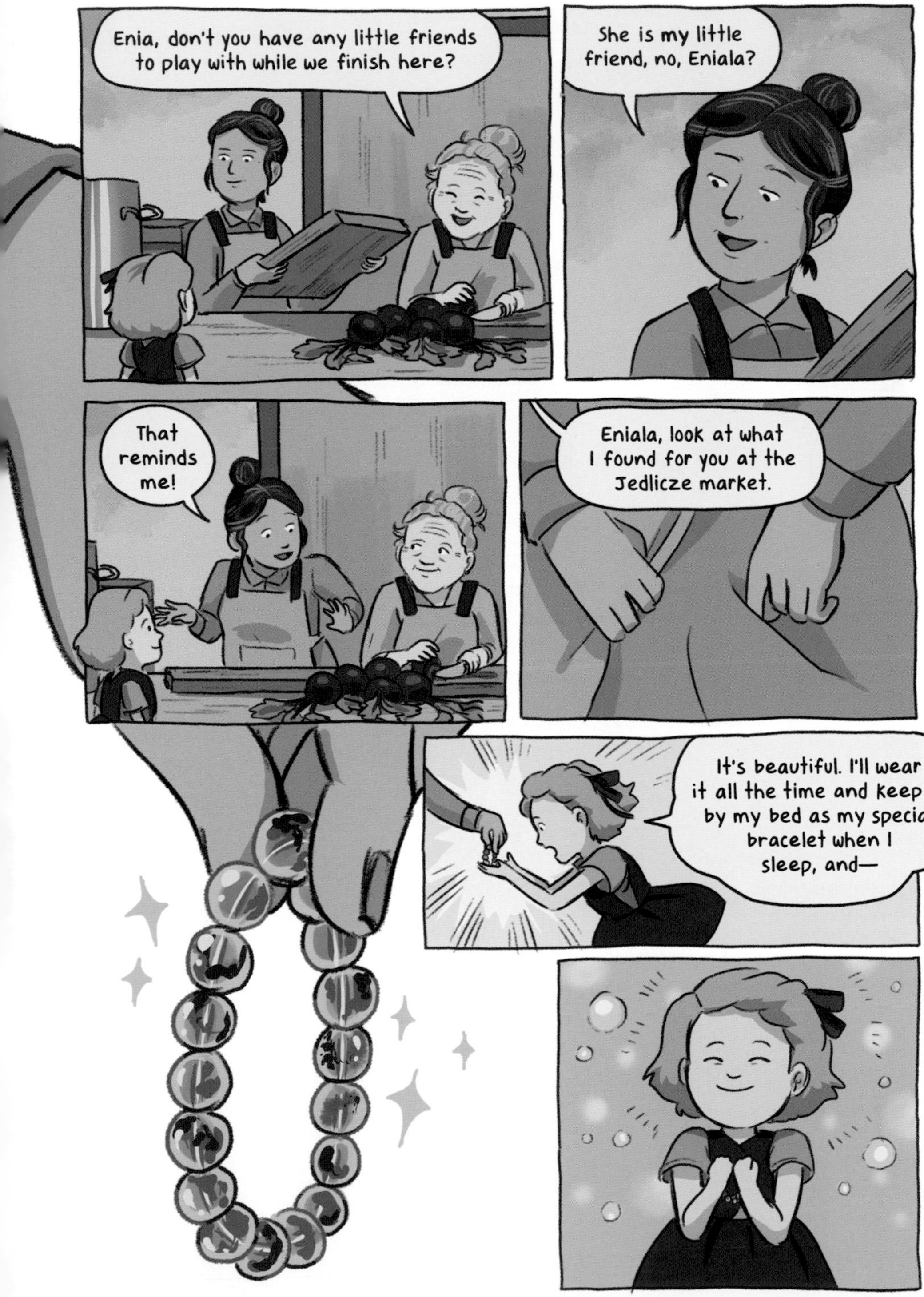
Enia, don't you have any little friends to play with while we finish here?
She is my little friend, no, Eniala?
That reminds me!
Eniala, look at what I found for you at the Jedlicze market.
It's beautiful. I'll wear it all the time and keep it by my bed as my special bracelet when I sleep, and—

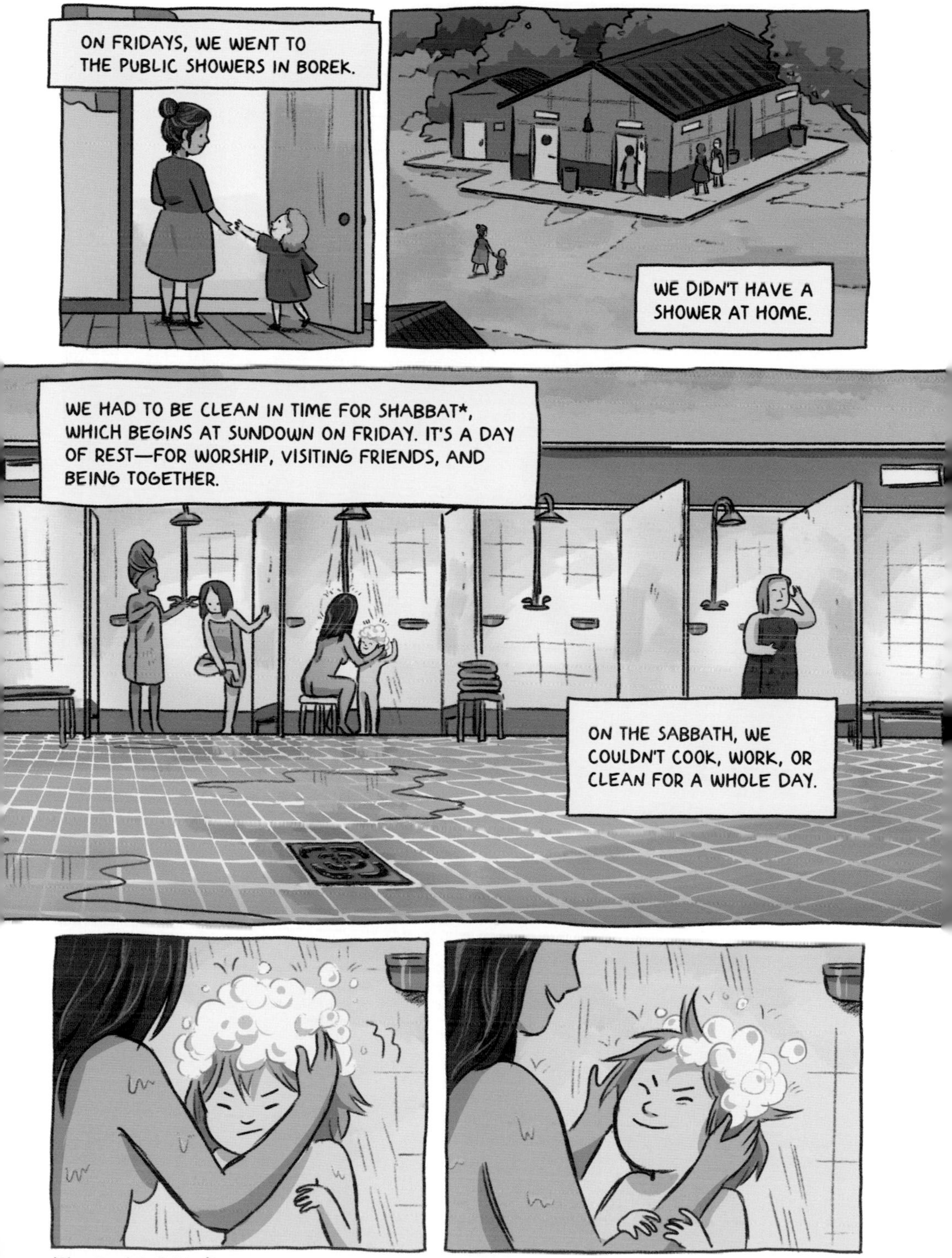
ON FRIDAYS, WE WENT TO THE PUBLIC SHOWERS IN BOREK.
WE DIDN'T HAVE A SHOWER AT HOME.
WE HAD TO BE CLEAN IN TIME FOR SHABBAT*, WHICH BEGINS AT SUNDOWN ON FRIDAY. IT'S A DAY OF REST—FOR WORSHIP, VISITING FRIENDS, AND BEING TOGETHER.
ON THE SABBATH, WE COULDN'T COOK, WORK, OR CLEAN FOR A WHOLE DAY.

*The Jewish Sabbath.

Hurry up, Enia.

EVERY SATURDAY, MY FATHER AND BROTHERS WENT TO SYNAGOGUE.

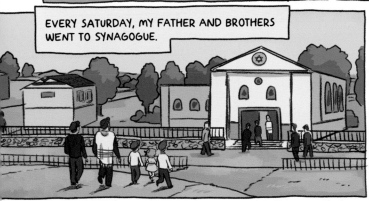

ONLY THE MEN WENT INSIDE THE SANCTUARY, SO I WAITED UNTIL THEY WERE DONE.

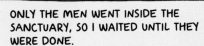

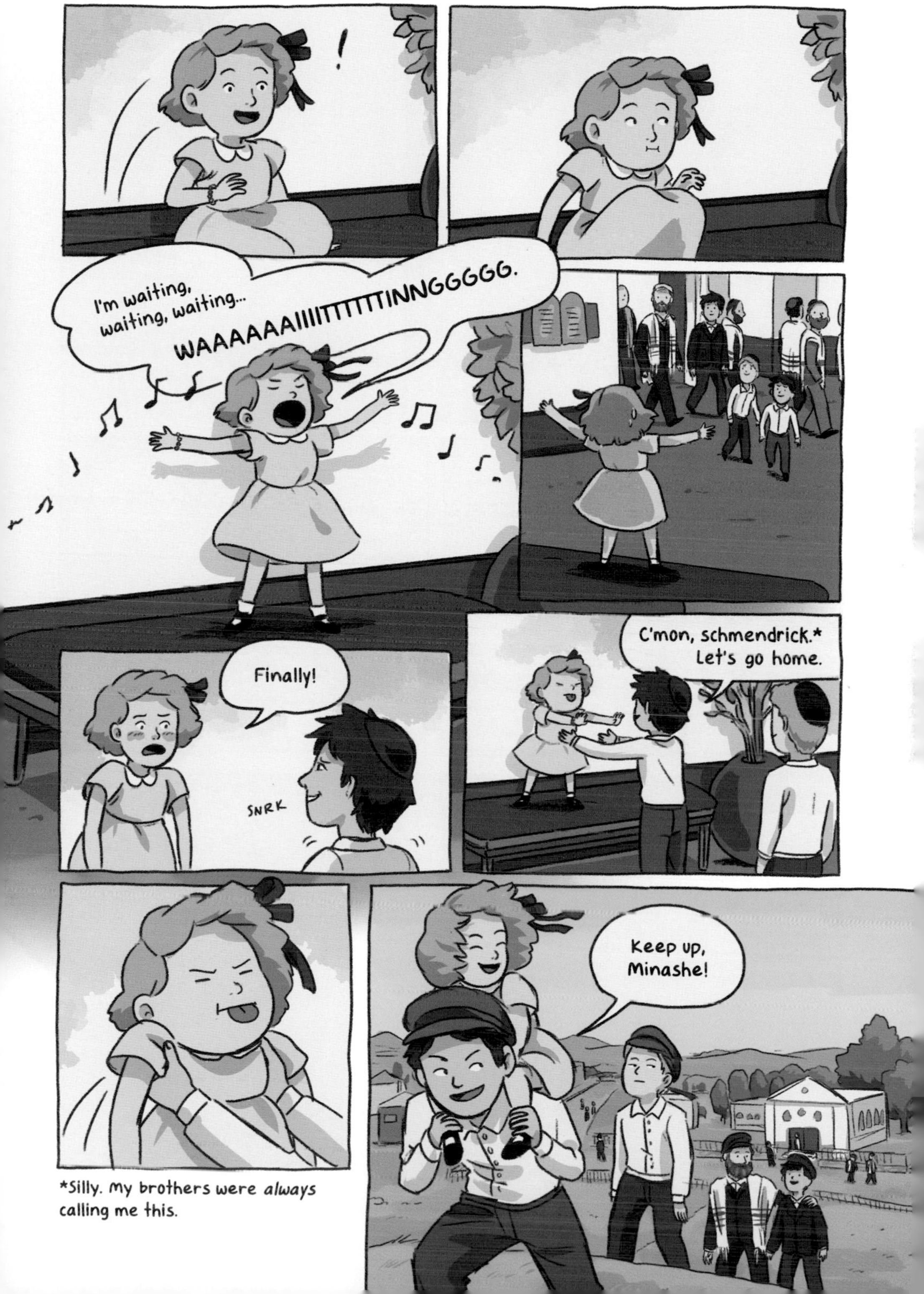
!
I'm waiting, waiting, waiting... WAAAAAAIIIITTTTTTINNGGGGG.
Finally!
SNRK
C'mon, schmendrick.* Let's go home.
Keep up, Minashe!

*Silly. My brothers were *always* calling me this.

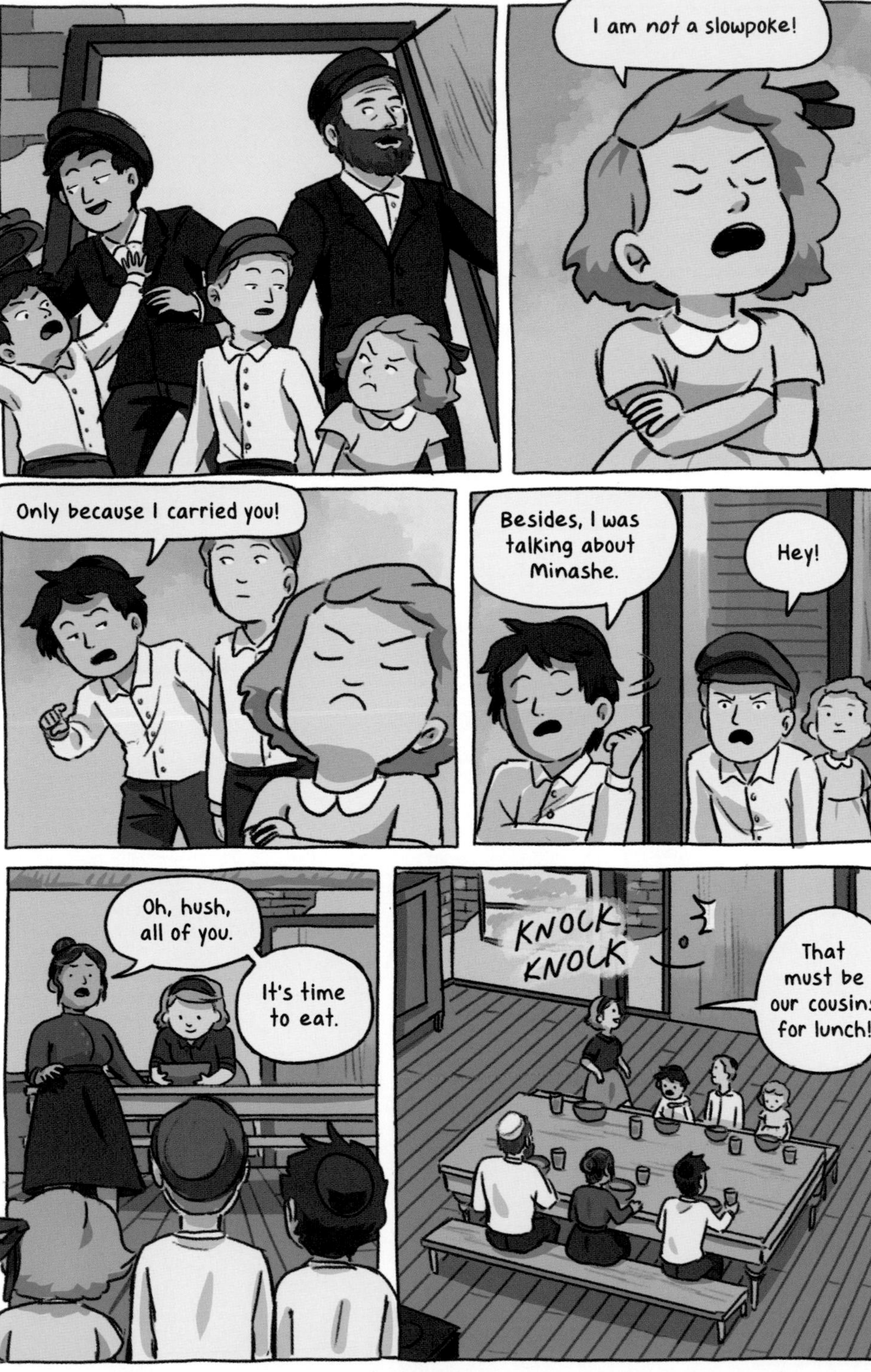
I am not a slowpoke!
Only because I carried you!
Besides, I was talking about Minashe.
Hey!
Oh, hush, all of you.
It's time to eat.
KNOCK KNOCK
That must be our cousins for lunch!

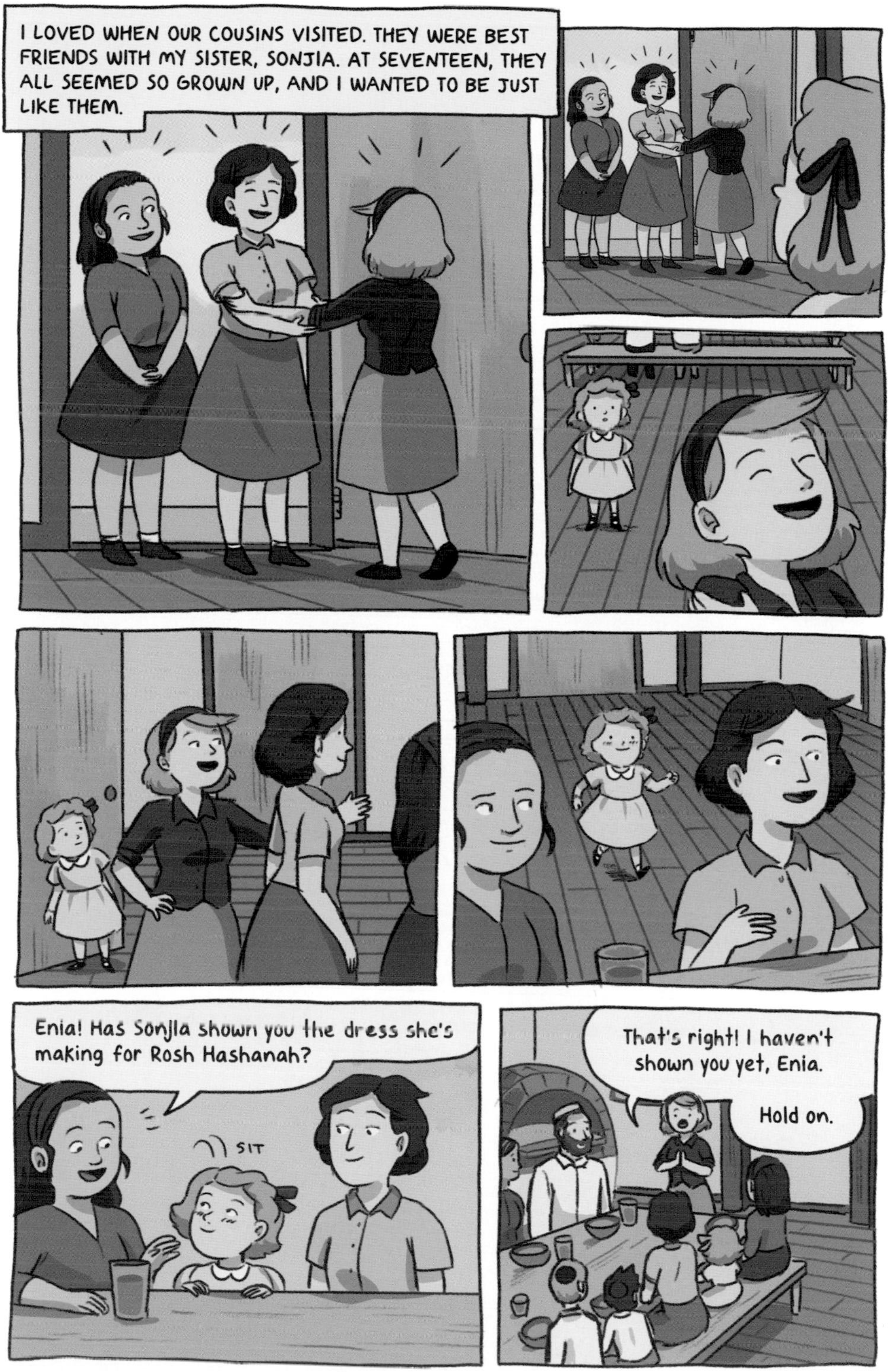
I LOVED WHEN OUR COUSINS VISITED. THEY WERE BEST FRIENDS WITH MY SISTER, SONJIA. AT SEVENTEEN, THEY ALL SEEMED SO GROWN UP, AND I WANTED TO BE JUST LIKE THEM.
Enia! Has Sonjia shown you the dress she's making for Rosh Hashanah?
SIT
That's right! I haven't shown you yet, Enia.
Hold on.

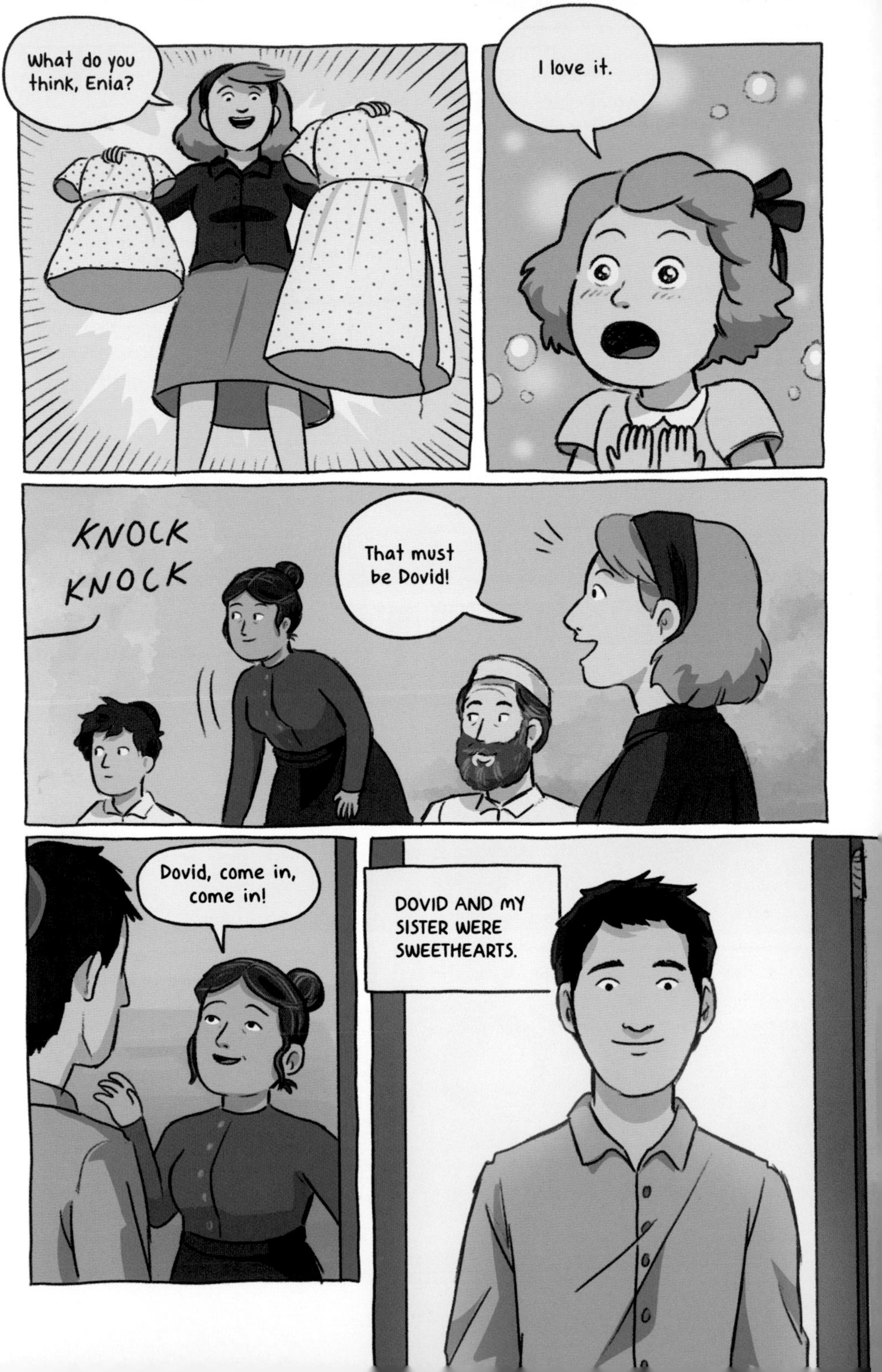
What do you think, Enia?
I love it.
KNOCK KNOCK
That must be Dovid!
Dovid, come in, come in!
DOVID AND MY SISTER WERE SWEETHEARTS.

WE ALL THOUGHT THEY WOULD GET MARRIED.

AND I THOUGHT WE WOULD BE THIS HAPPY FOREVER.

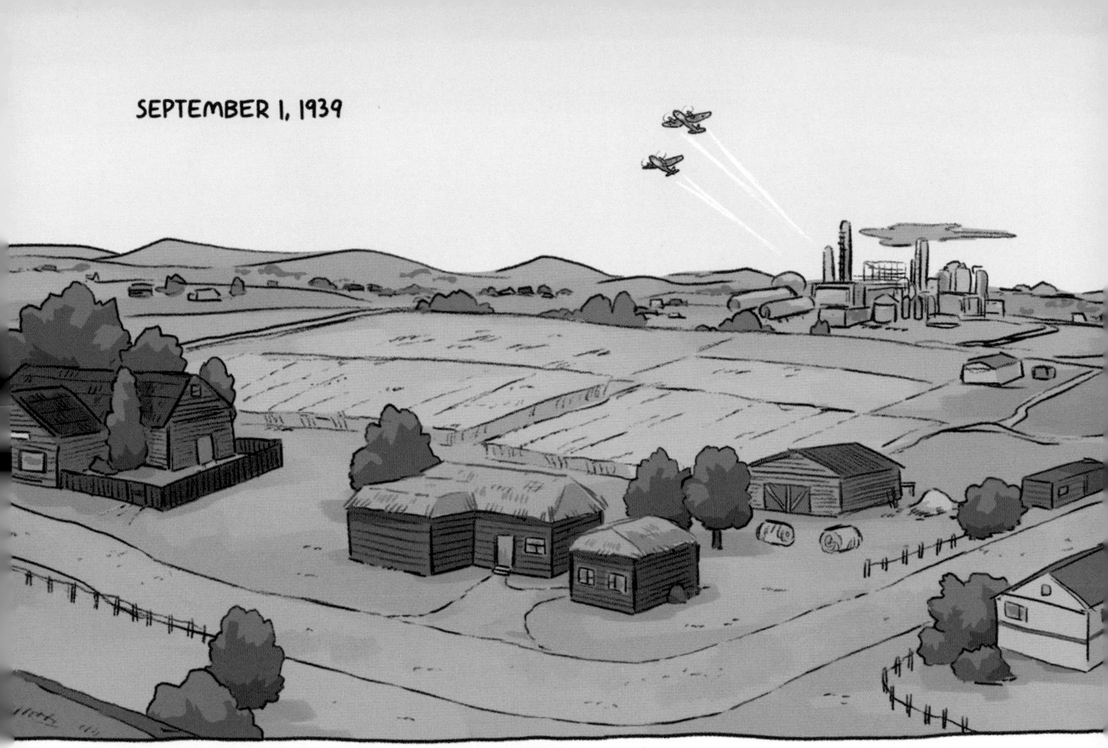
SEPTEMBER 1, 1939

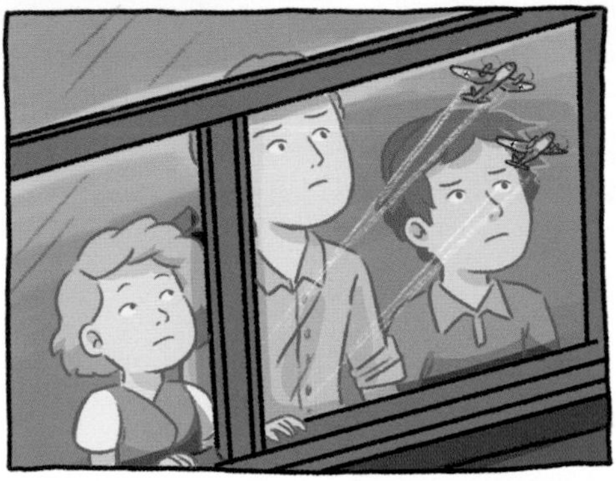

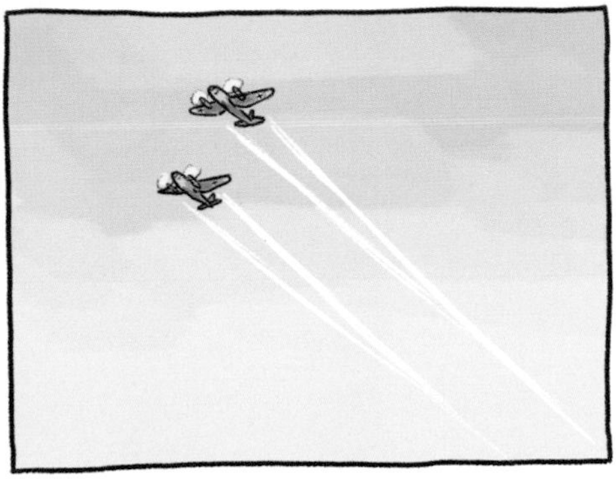

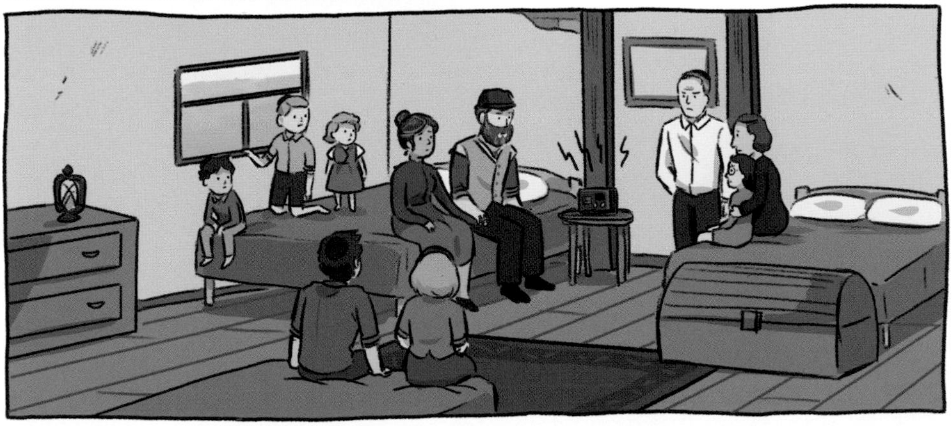

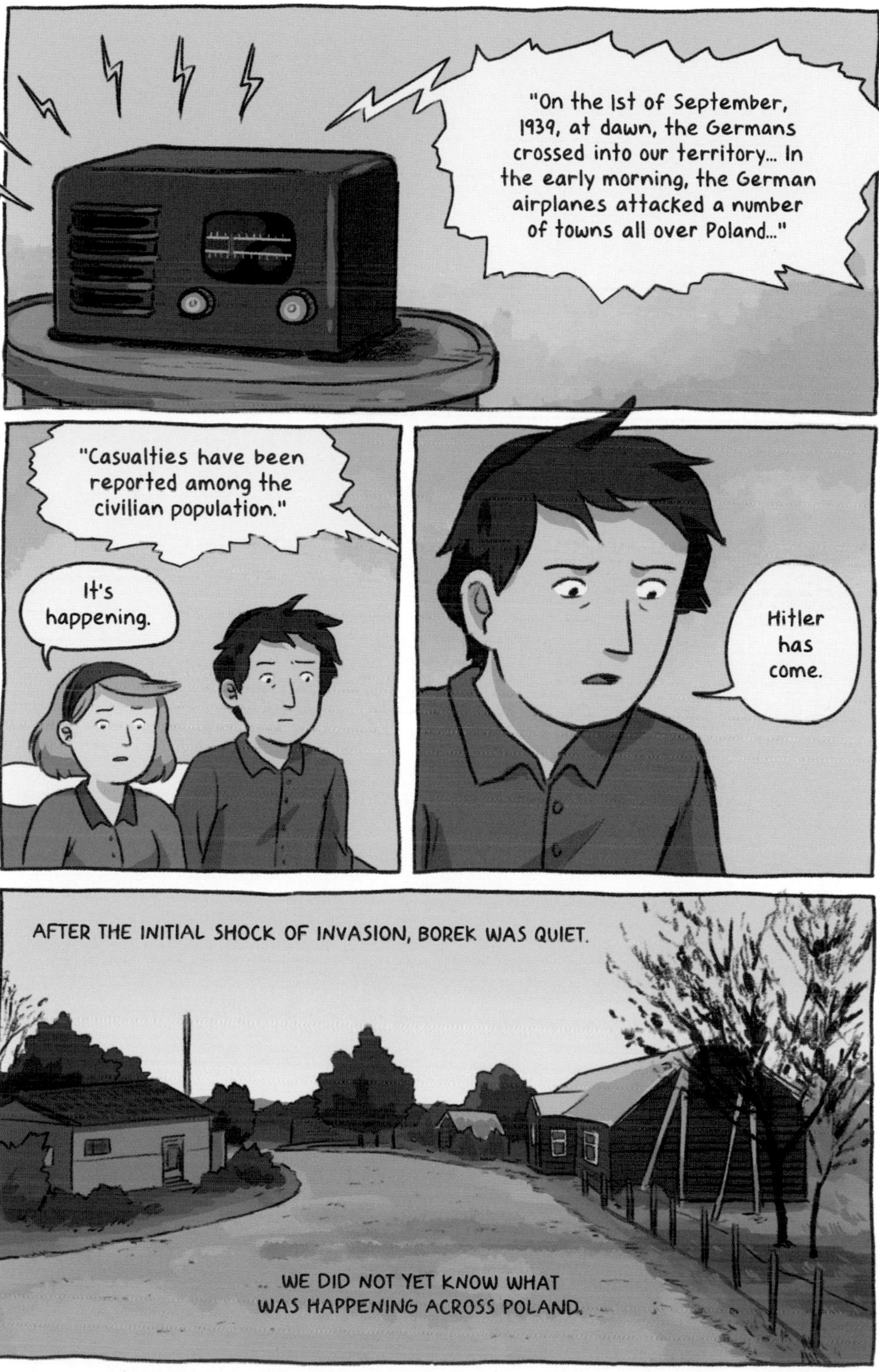

"On the 1st of September, 1939, at dawn, the Germans crossed into our territory... In the early morning, the German airplanes attacked a number of towns all over Poland..."
"Casualties have been reported among the civilian population."
It's happening.
Hitler has come.
AFTER THE INITIAL SHOCK OF INVASION, BOREK WAS QUIET.
.. WE DID NOT YET KNOW WHAT WAS HAPPENING ACROSS POLAND.

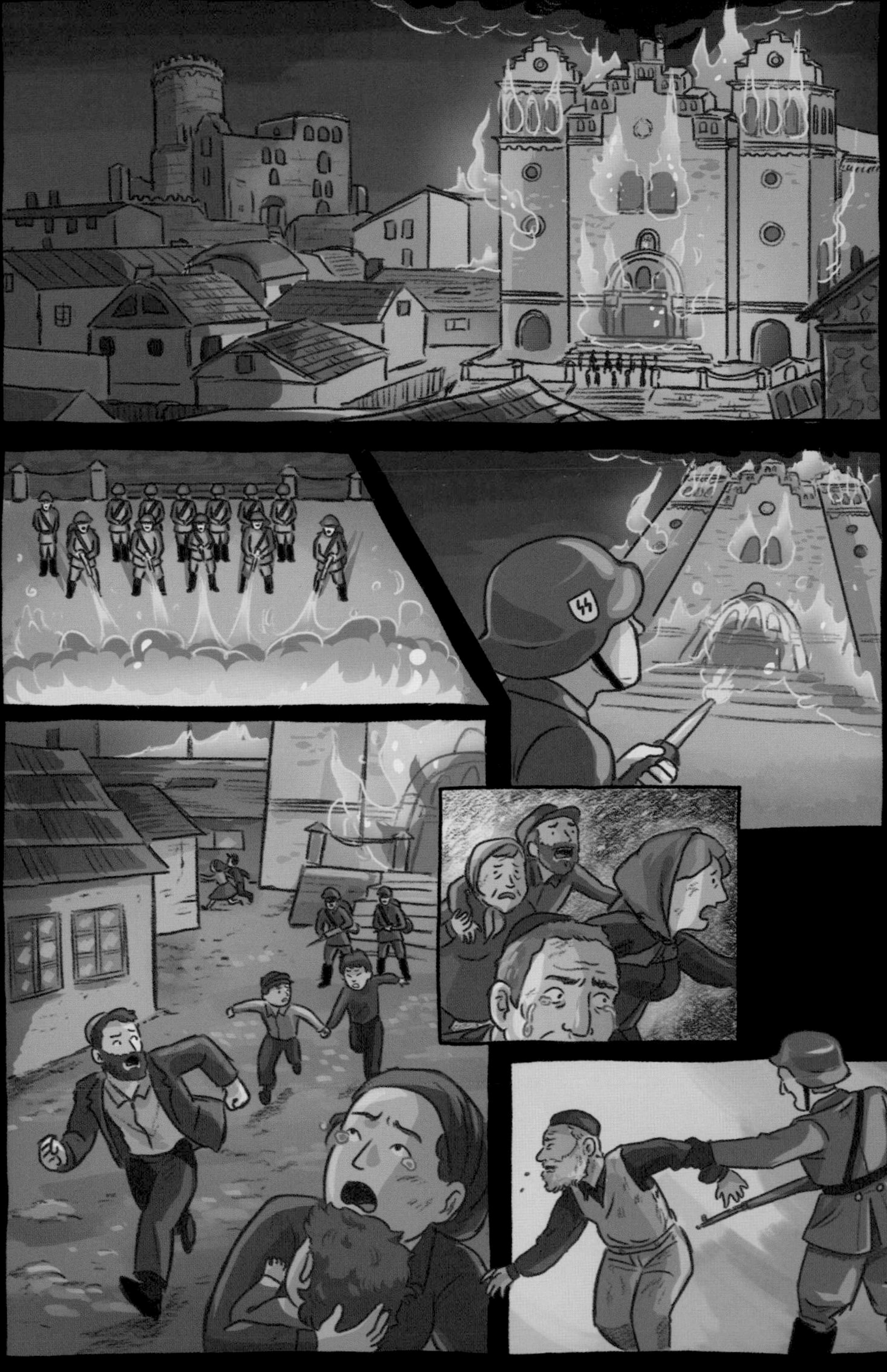

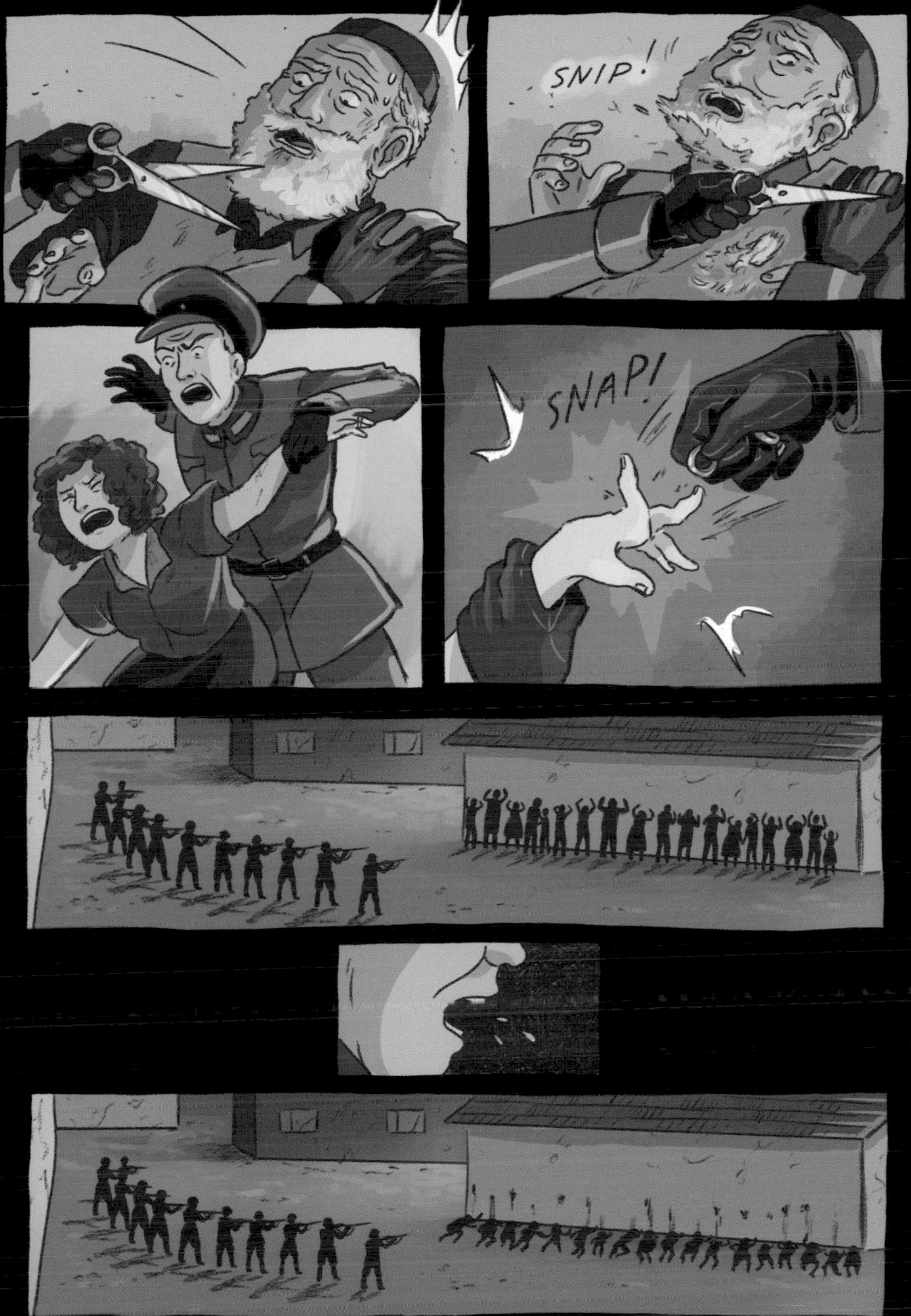
SNIP!
SNAP!

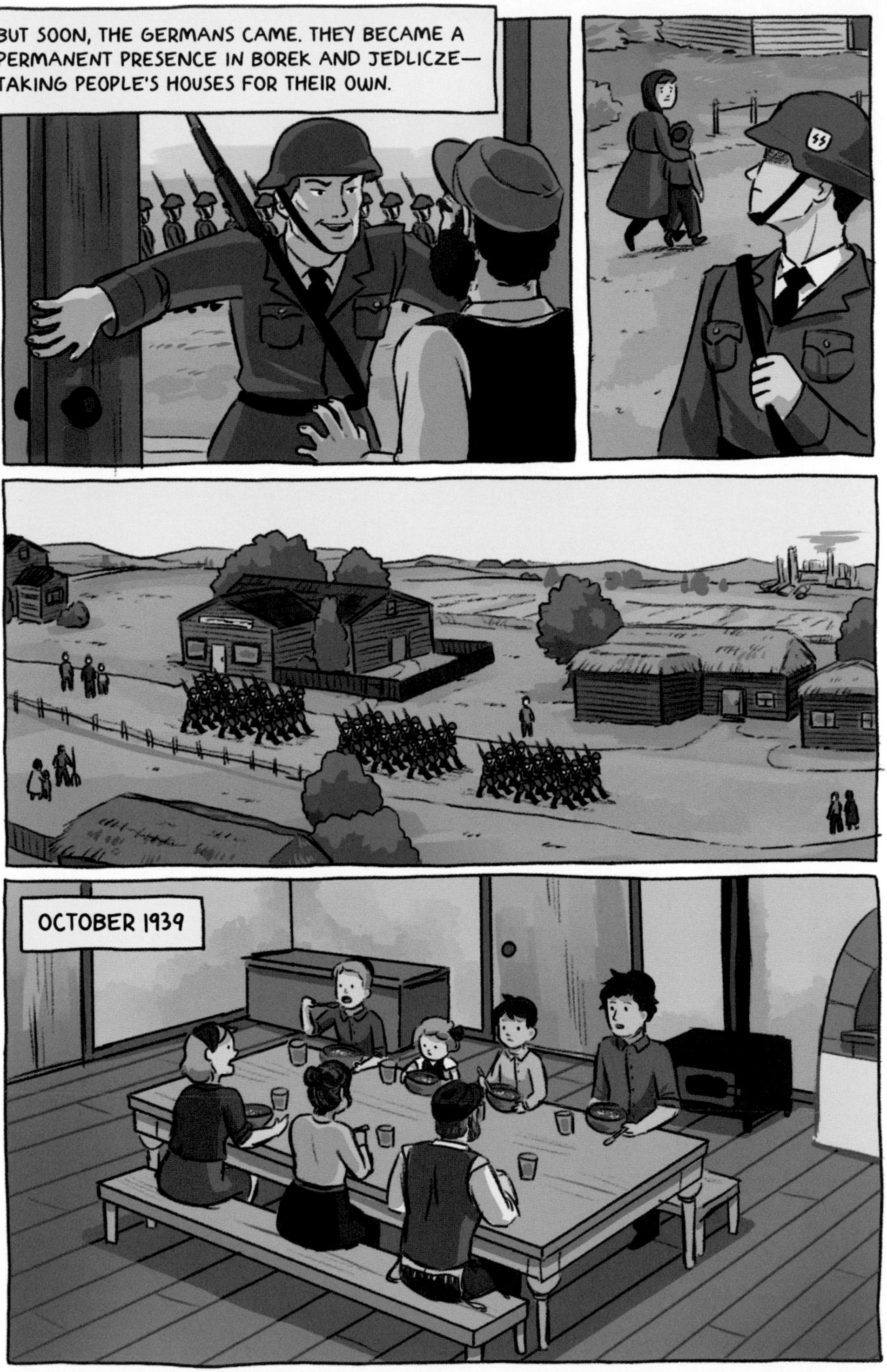
BUT SOON, THE GERMANS CAME. THEY BECAME A PERMANENT PRESENCE IN BOREK AND JEDLICZE—TAKING PEOPLE'S HOUSES FOR THEIR OWN.
OCTOBER 1939

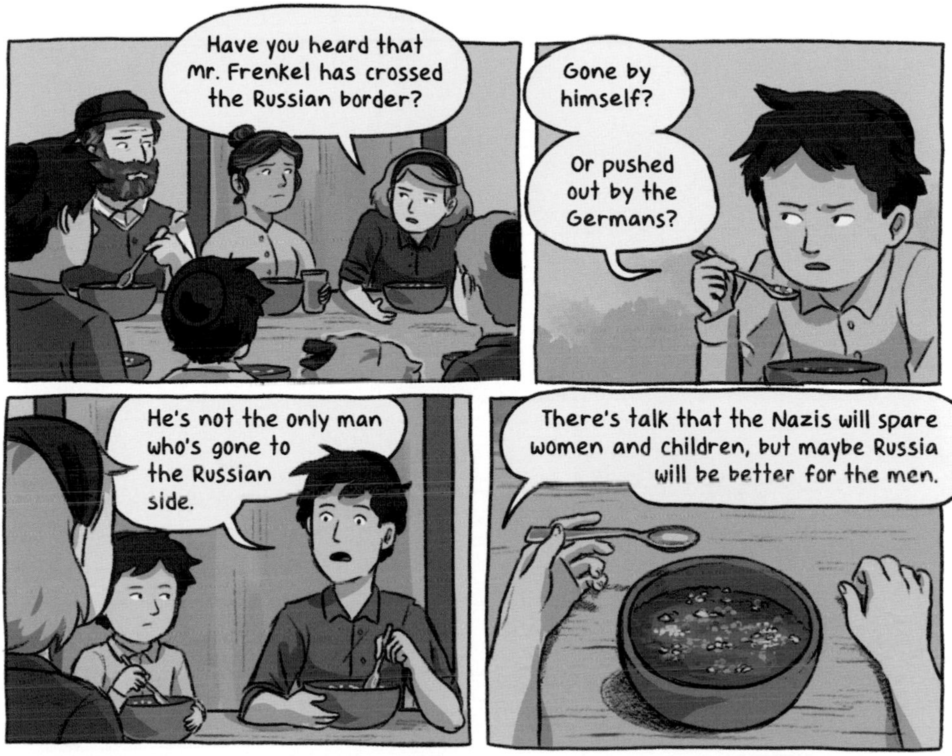
Have you heard that Mr. Frenkel has crossed the Russian border?
Gone by himself?
Or pushed out by the Germans?
He's not the only man who's gone to the Russian side.
There's talk that the Nazis will spare women and children, but maybe Russia will be better for the men.

SOON AFTER THE GERMANS CAME, THE SOVIETS INVADED POLAND FROM THE EAST.

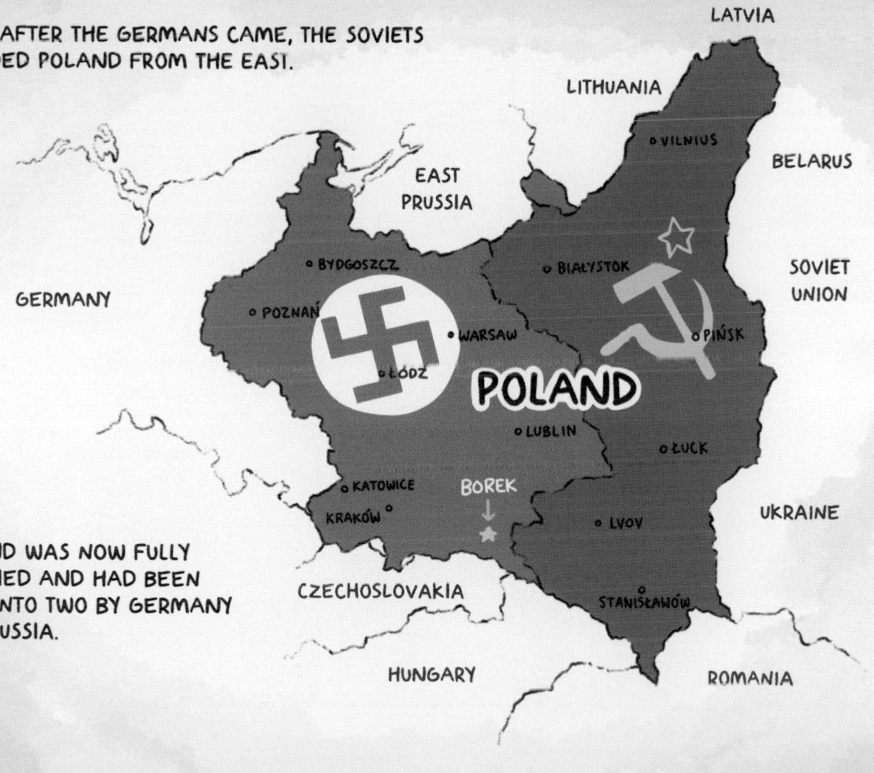
LATVIA
LITHUANIA
VILNIUS
BELARUS
EAST PRUSSIA
BIAŁYSTOK
SOVIET UNION
BYDGOSZCZ
GERMANY
POZNAŃ
WARSAW
PIŃSK
ŁÓDZ
POLAND
LUBLIN
ŁUCK
KATOWICE
BOREK
KRAKÓW
LVOV
UKRAINE
CZECHOSLOVAKIA
STANISŁAWÓW
HUNGARY
ROMANIA

POLAND WAS NOW FULLY OCCUPIED AND HAD BEEN SPLIT INTO TWO BY GERMANY AND RUSSIA.

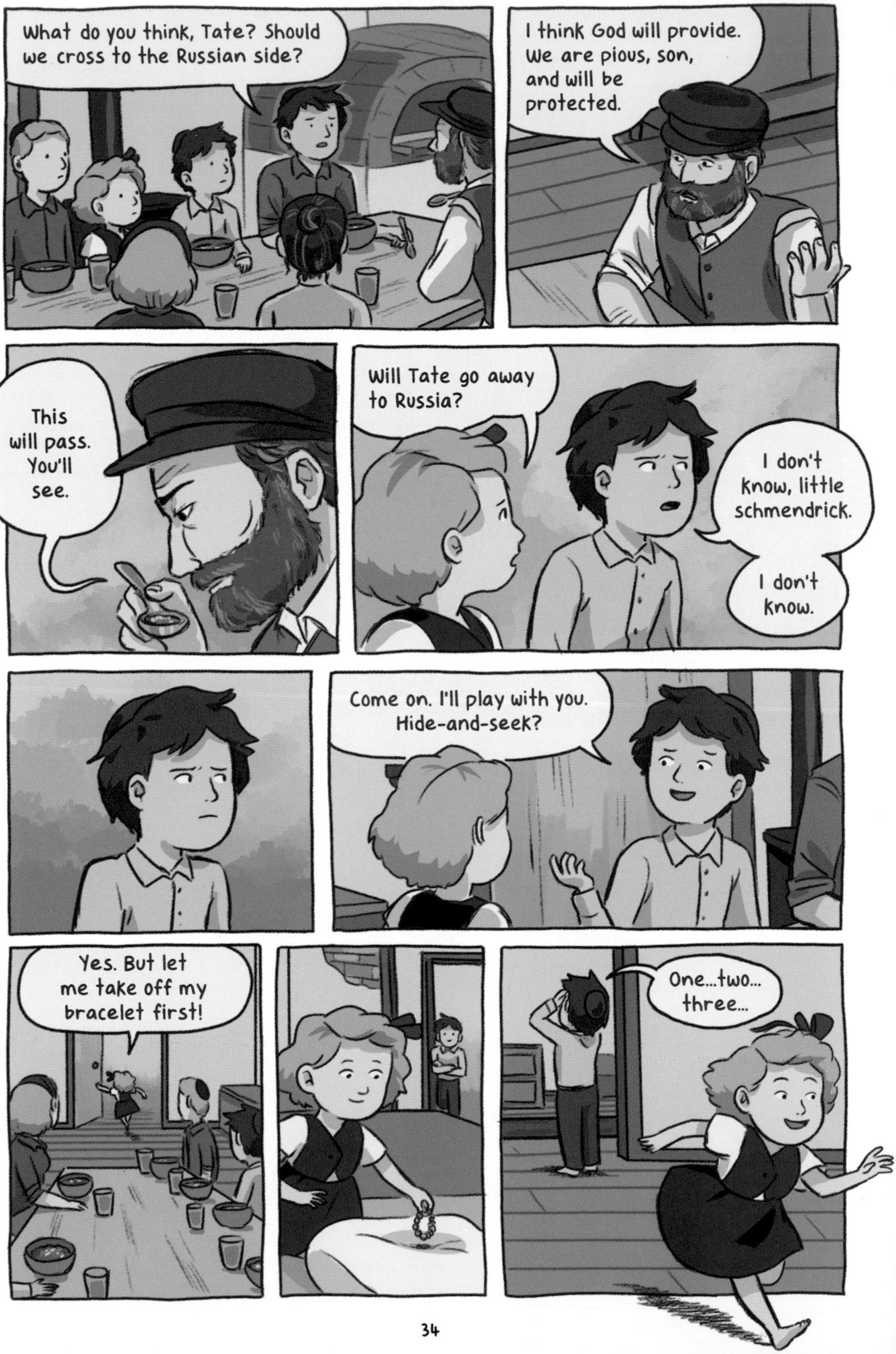
What do you think, Tate? Should we cross to the Russian side?
I think God will provide. We are pious, son, and will be protected.
This will pass. You'll see.
Will Tate go away to Russia?
I don't know, little schmendrick.
I don't know.
Come on. I'll play with you. Hide-and-seek?
Yes. But let me take off my bracelet first!
One...two... three...

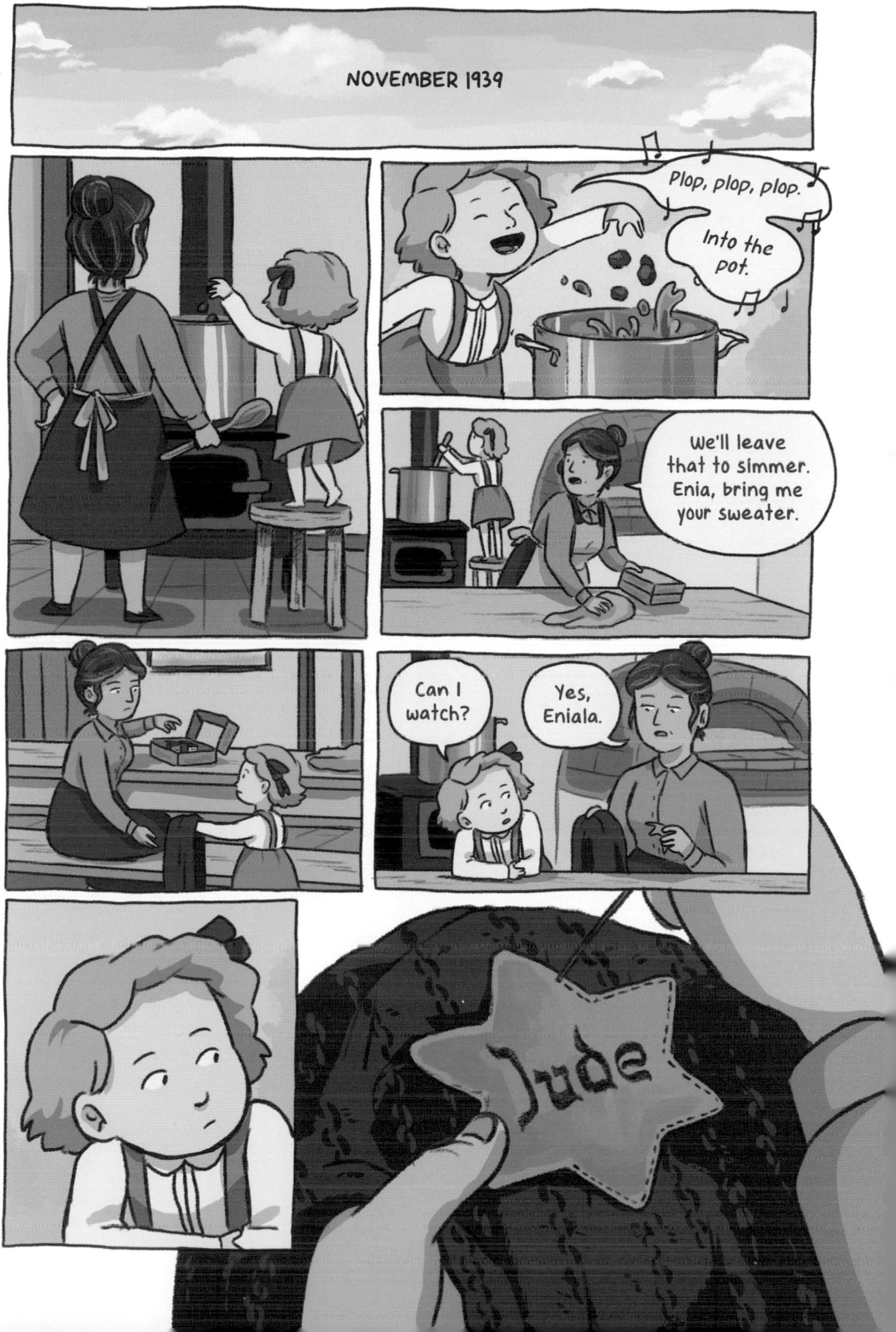
NOVEMBER 1939
Plop, plop, plop.
Into the pot.
We'll leave that to simmer. Enia, bring me your sweater.
Can I watch?
Yes, Eniala.
Jude

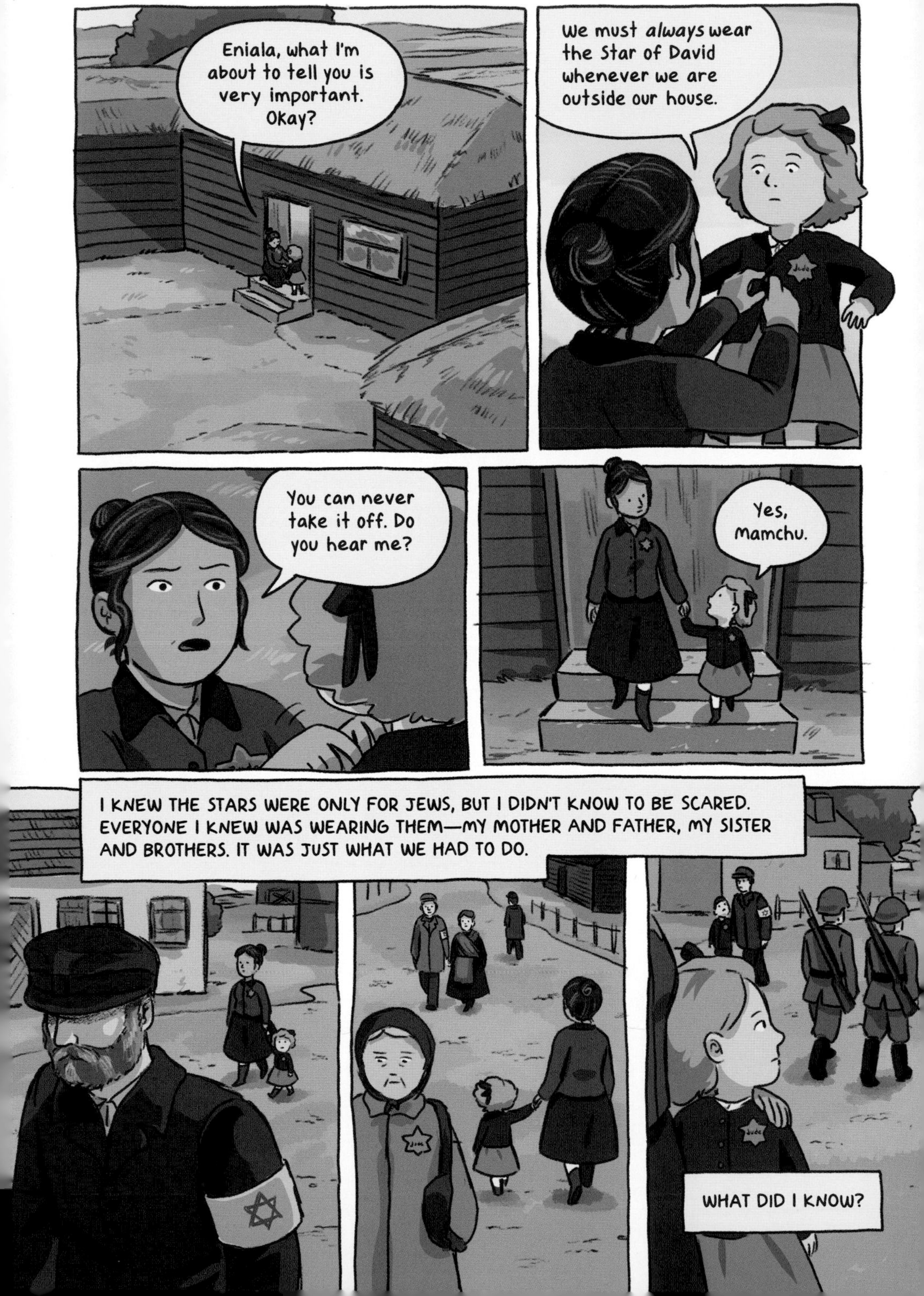
Eniala, what I'm about to tell you is very important. Okay?
We must *always* wear the Star of David whenever we are outside our house.
Jude
You can never take it off. Do you hear me?
Yes, mamchu.
I KNEW THE STARS WERE ONLY FOR JEWS, BUT I DIDN'T KNOW TO BE SCARED. EVERYONE I KNEW WAS WEARING THEM—MY MOTHER AND FATHER, MY SISTER AND BROTHERS. IT WAS JUST WHAT WE HAD TO DO.
WHAT DID I KNOW?

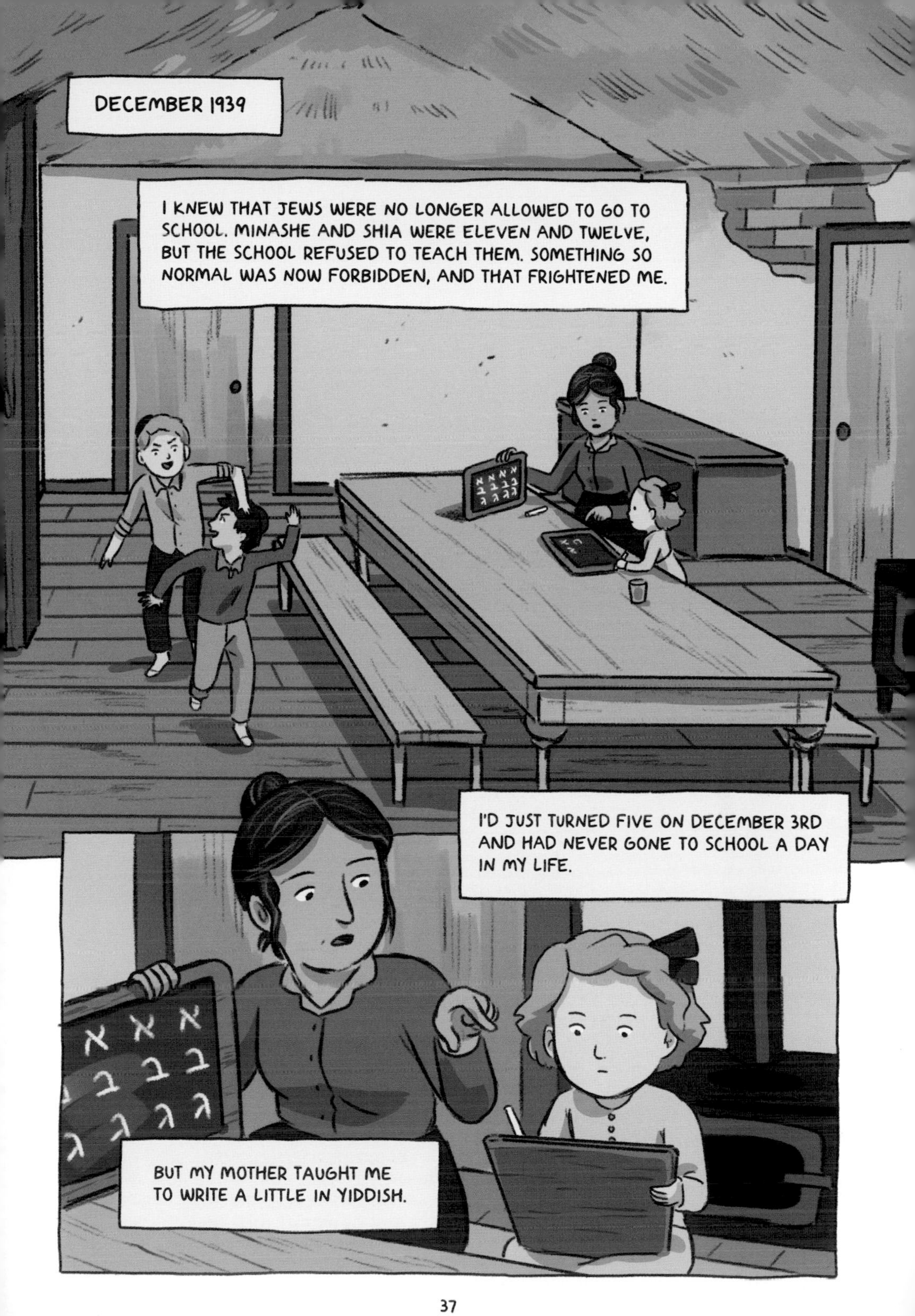

DECEMBER 1939
I KNEW THAT JEWS WERE NO LONGER ALLOWED TO GO TO SCHOOL. MINASHE AND SHIA WERE ELEVEN AND TWELVE, BUT THE SCHOOL REFUSED TO TEACH THEM. SOMETHING SO NORMAL WAS NOW FORBIDDEN, AND THAT FRIGHTENED ME.
I'D JUST TURNED FIVE ON DECEMBER 3RD AND HAD NEVER GONE TO SCHOOL A DAY IN MY LIFE.
BUT MY MOTHER TAUGHT ME TO WRITE A LITTLE IN YIDDISH.

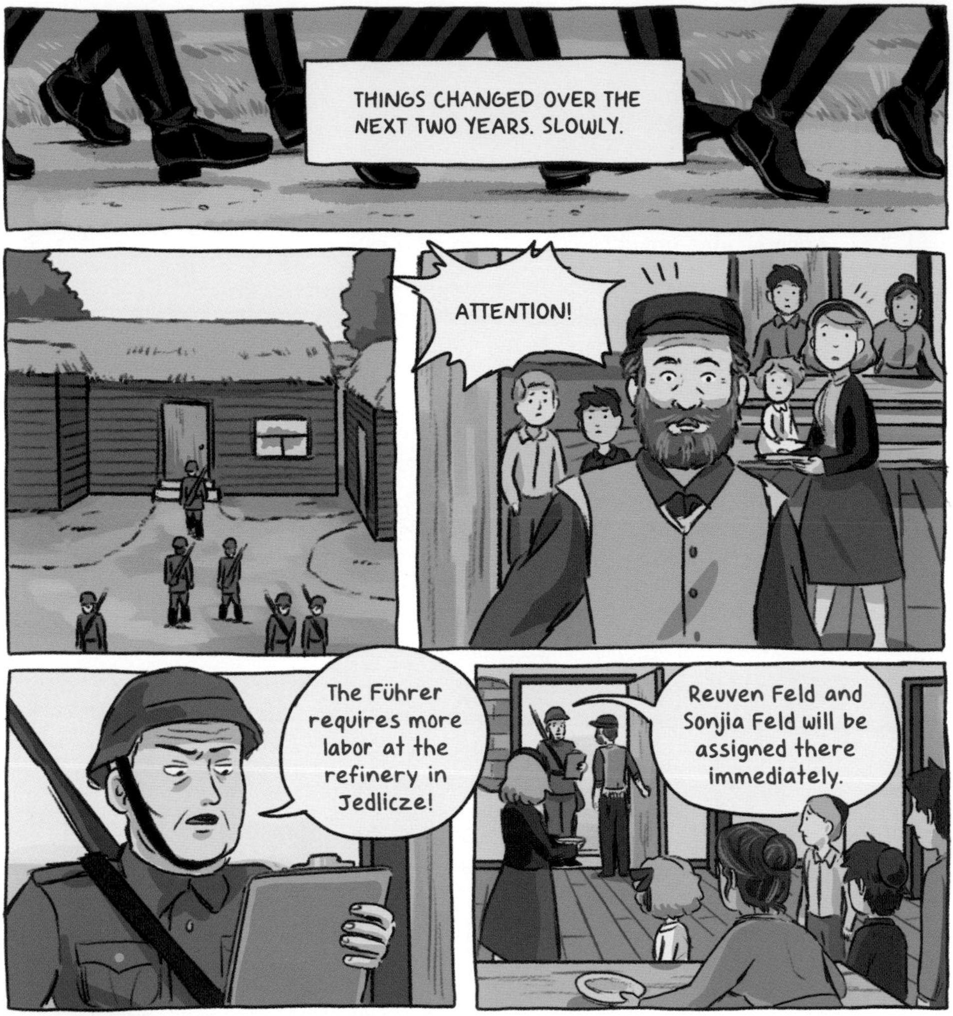
THINGS CHANGED OVER THE NEXT TWO YEARS. SLOWLY.
ATTENTION!
The Führer requires more labor at the refinery in Jedlicze!
Reuven Feld and Sonjia Feld will be assigned there immediately.

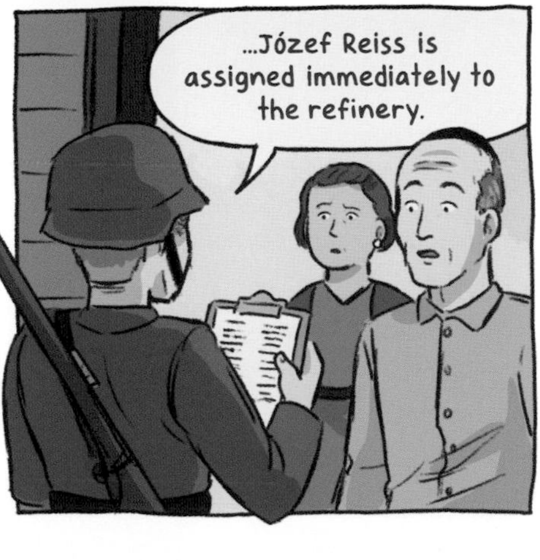
...Józef Reiss is assigned immediately to the refinery.

I KNEW WHAT THE REFINERY WAS; IT HAD BEEN IN OUR VILLAGE FOR A LONG TIME. BUT MY FAMILY HAD NEVER WORKED THERE. MY FATHER WAS A FARMER, AND MY UNCLE HAD AN EGG BUSINESS.

NOW OUR FIELDS WERE ABANDONED, AND MY MOTHER STAYED HOME WITH ME, MINASHE, AND SHIA AS THE REST OF MY FAMILY WAS FORCED TO WORK WHEREVER THE GERMANS TOLD THEM TO GO.

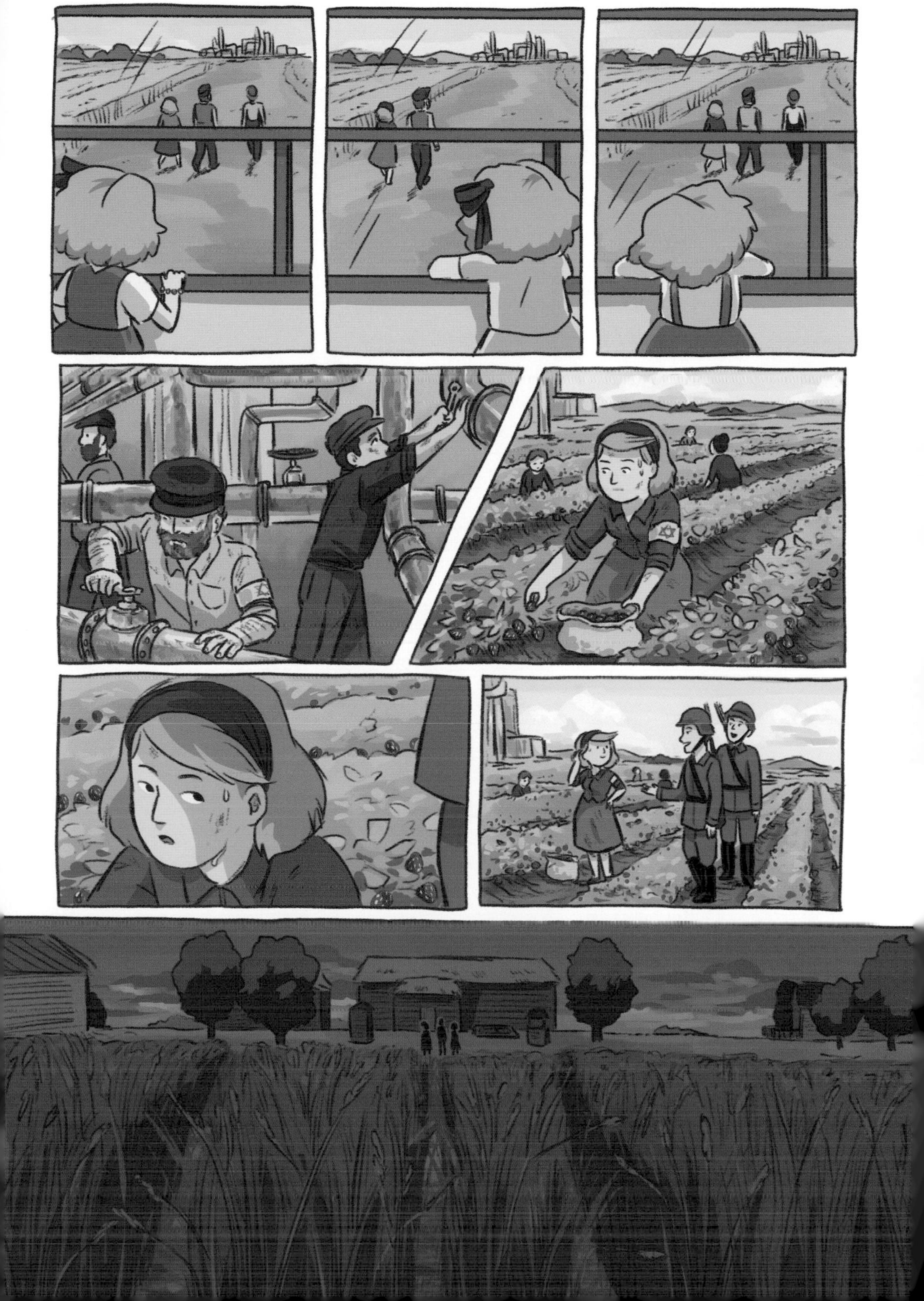

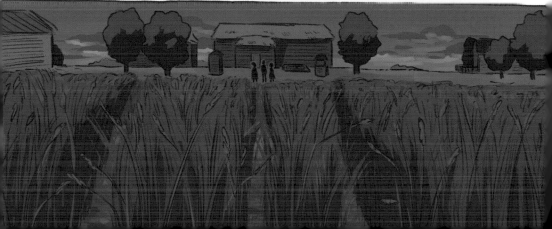

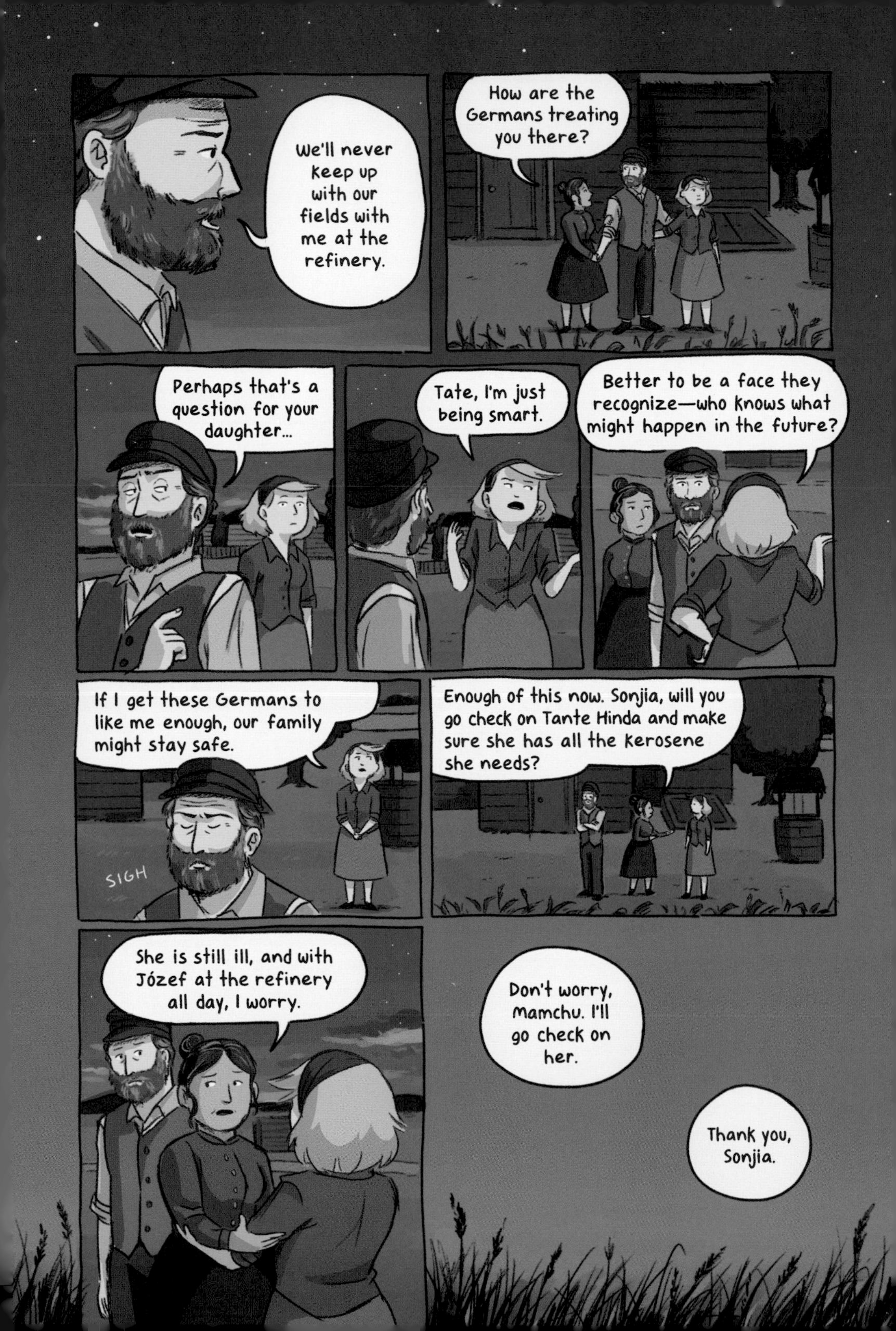
We'll never keep up with our fields with me at the refinery.
How are the Germans treating you there?
Perhaps that's a question for your daughter...
Tate, I'm just being smart.
Better to be a face they recognize—who knows what might happen in the future?
If I get these Germans to like me enough, our family might stay safe.
SIGH
Enough of this now. Sonjia, will you go check on Tante Hinda and make sure she has all the kerosene she needs?
She is still ill, and with Józef at the refinery all day, I worry.
Don't worry, Mamchu. I'll go check on her.
Thank you, Sonjia.

JULY 1942

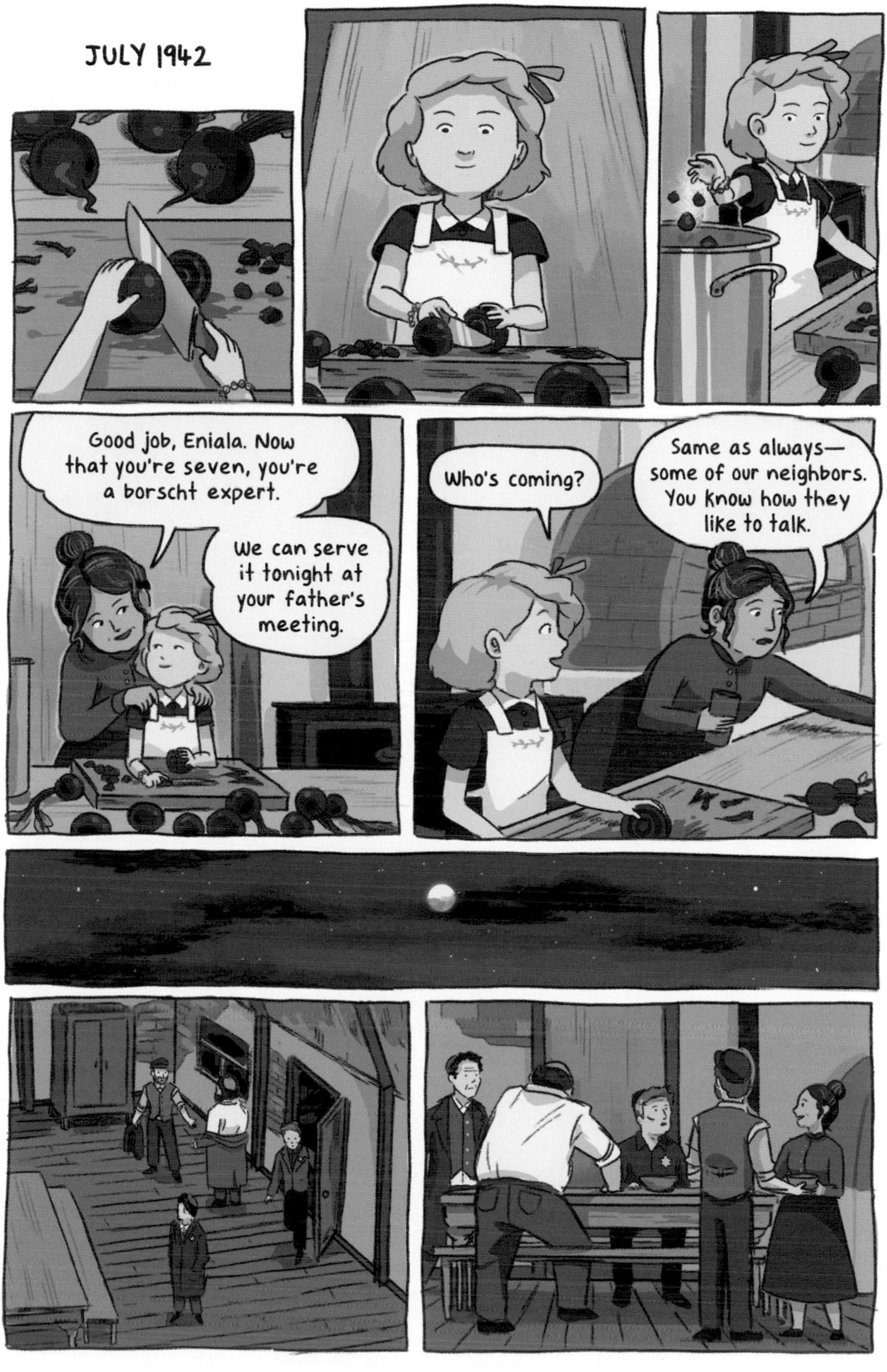
Good job, Eniala. Now that you're seven, you're a borscht expert.
We can serve it tonight at your father's meeting.
Who's coming?
Same as always— some of our neighbors. You know how they like to talk.

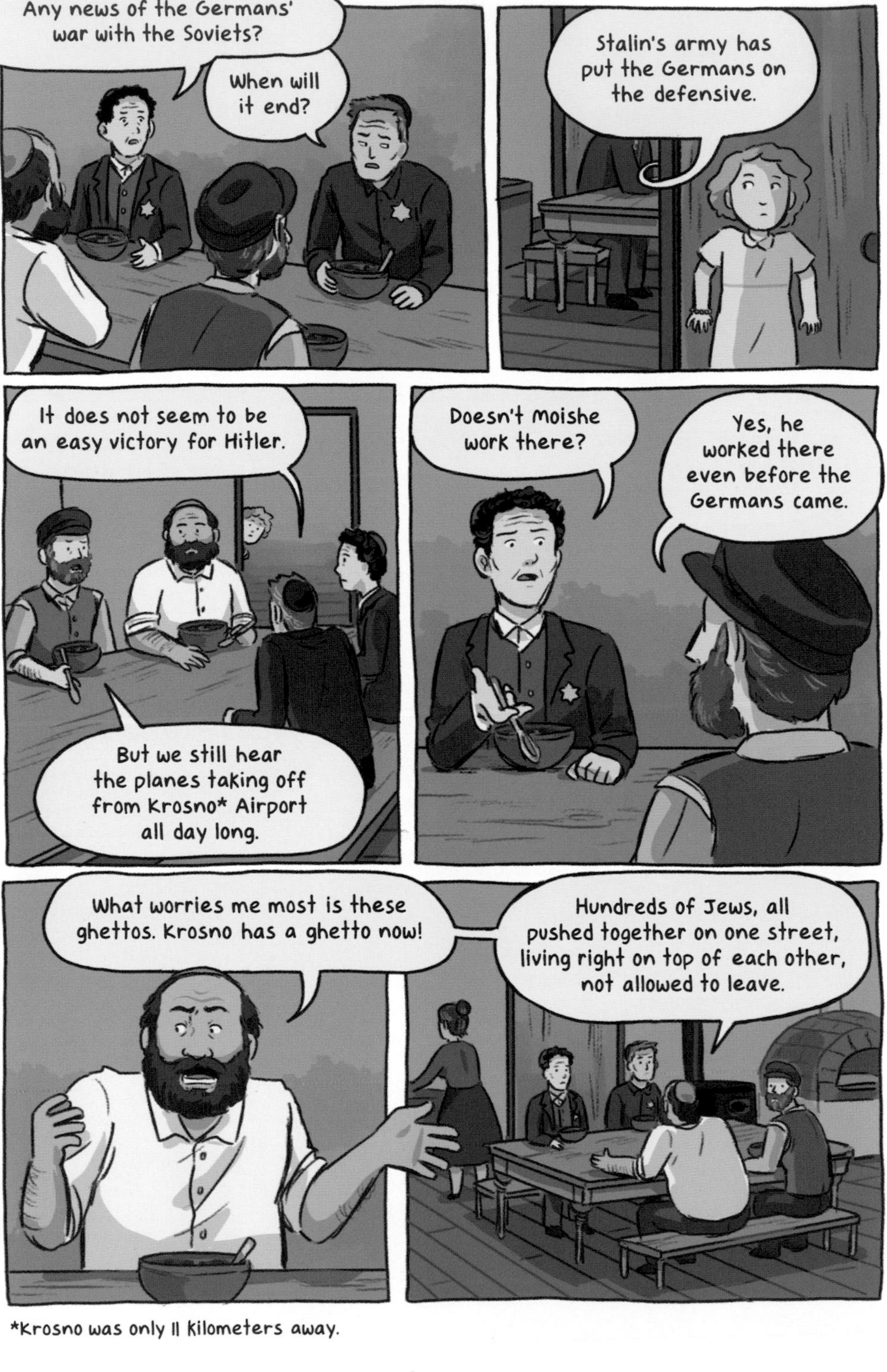

Any news of the Germans' war with the Soviets?
When will it end?
Stalin's army has put the Germans on the defensive.
It does not seem to be an easy victory for Hitler.
But we still hear the planes taking off from Krosno* Airport all day long.
Doesn't Moishe work there?
Yes, he worked there even before the Germans came.
What worries me most is these ghettos. Krosno has a ghetto now!
Hundreds of Jews, all pushed together on one street, living right on top of each other, not allowed to leave.

*Krosno was only 11 kilometers away.

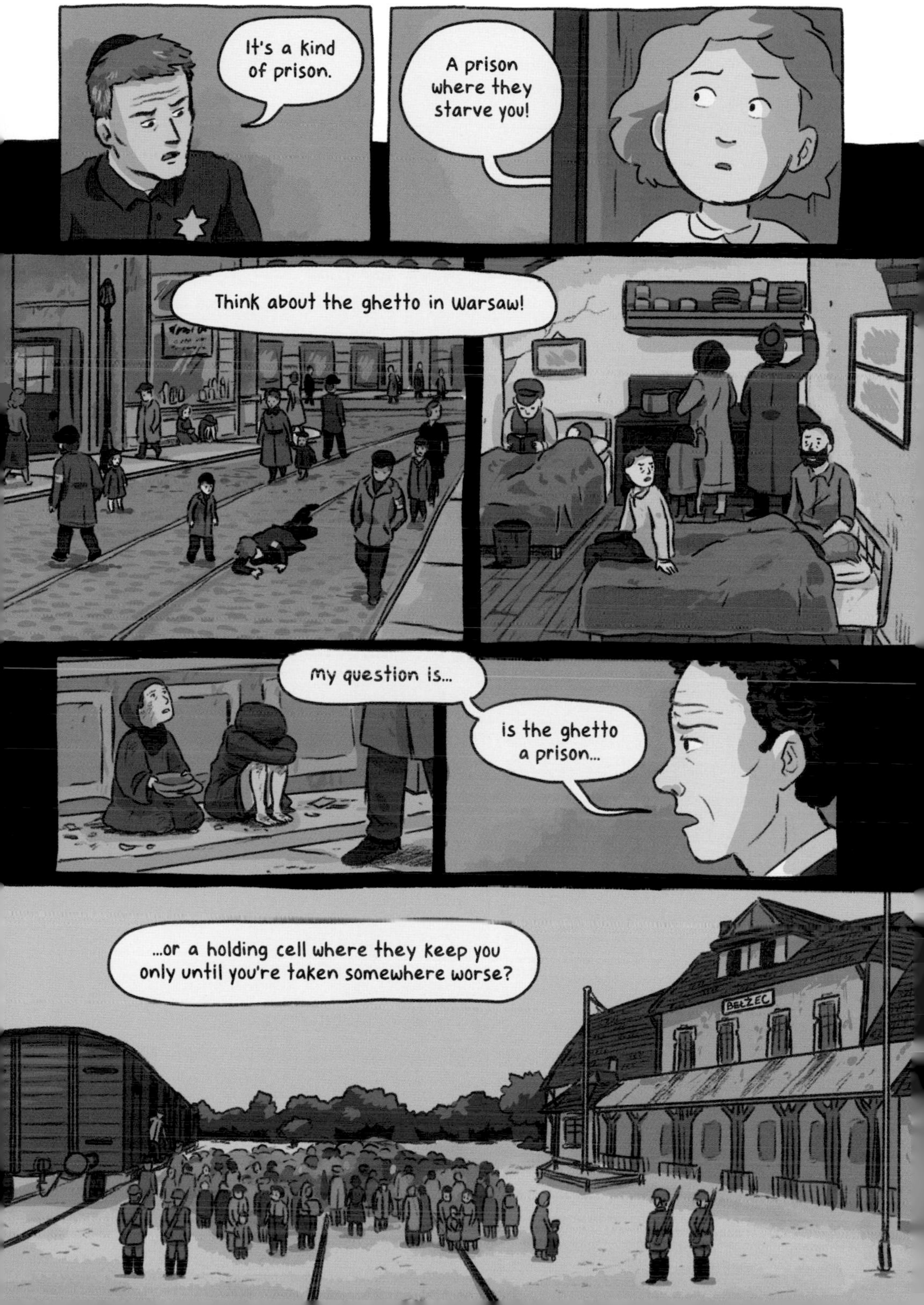
It's a kind of prison.
A prison where they starve you!
Think about the ghetto in Warsaw!
my question is...
is the ghetto a prison...
...or a holding cell where they keep you only until you're taken somewhere worse?
BEŁŻEC

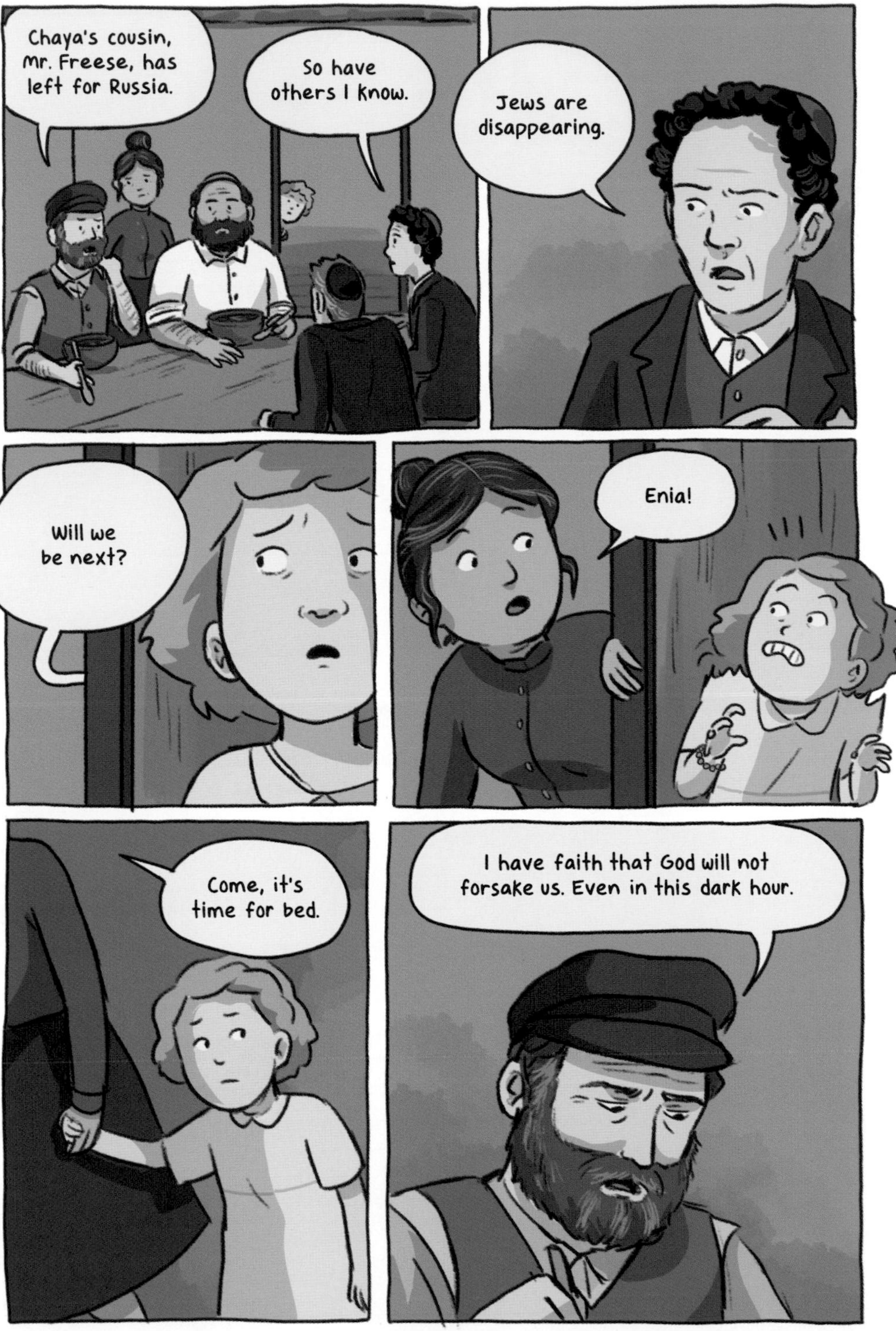
Chaya's cousin, Mr. Freese, has left for Russia.
So have others I know.
Jews are disappearing.
Will we be next?
Enia!
Come, it's time for bed.
I have faith that God will not forsake us. Even in this dark hour.

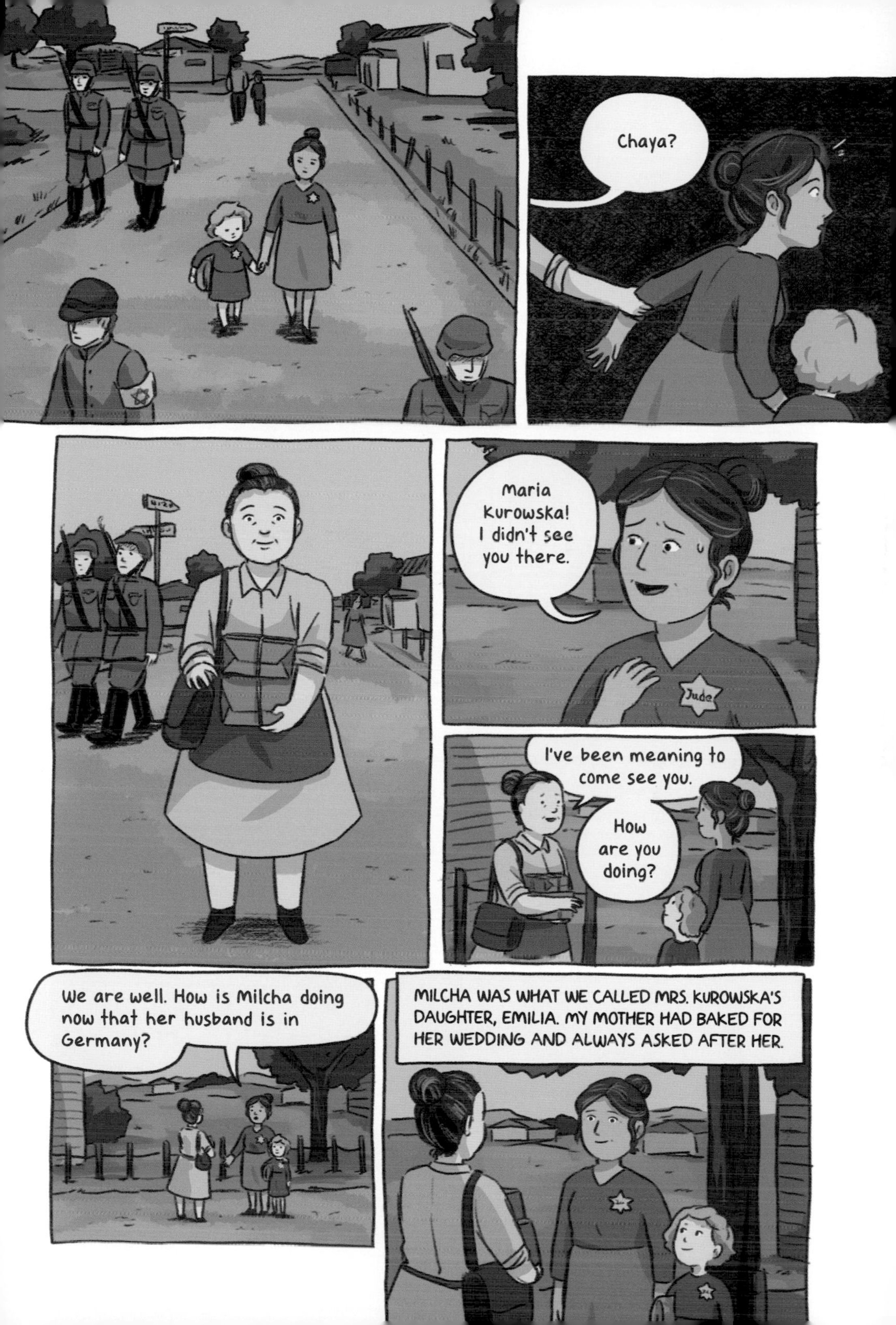
Chaya?
Maria Kurowska! I didn't see you there.
I've been meaning to come see you.
How are you doing?
We are well. How is Milcha doing now that her husband is in Germany?
MILCHA WAS WHAT WE CALLED MRS. KUROWSKA'S DAUGHTER, EMILIA. MY MOTHER HAD BAKED FOR HER WEDDING AND ALWAYS ASKED AFTER HER.

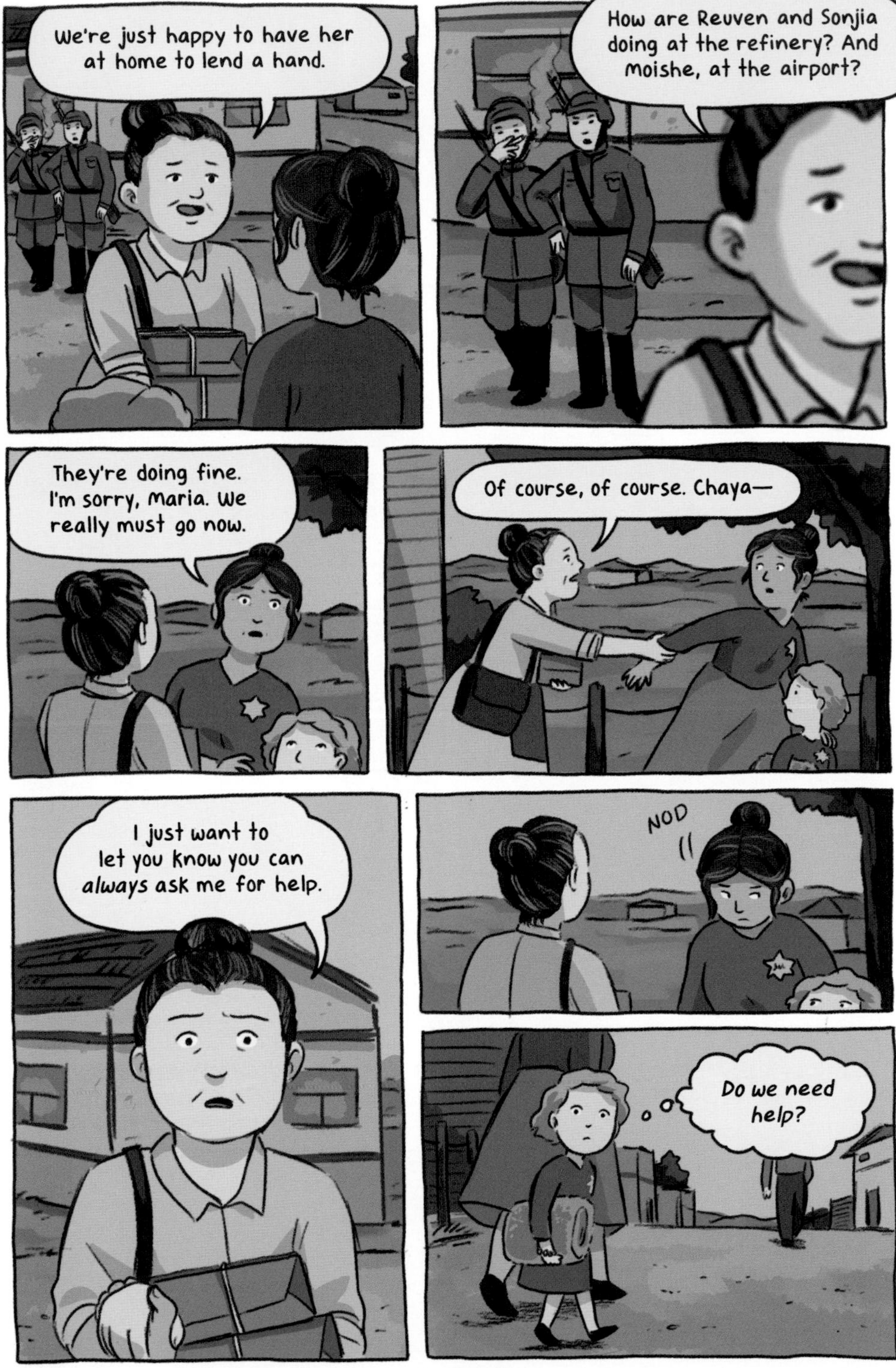
We're just happy to have her at home to lend a hand.
How are Reuven and Sonjia doing at the refinery? And Moishe, at the airport?
They're doing fine. I'm sorry, Maria. We really must go now.
Of course, of course. Chaya—
I just want to let you know you can always ask me for help.
NOD
Do we need help?

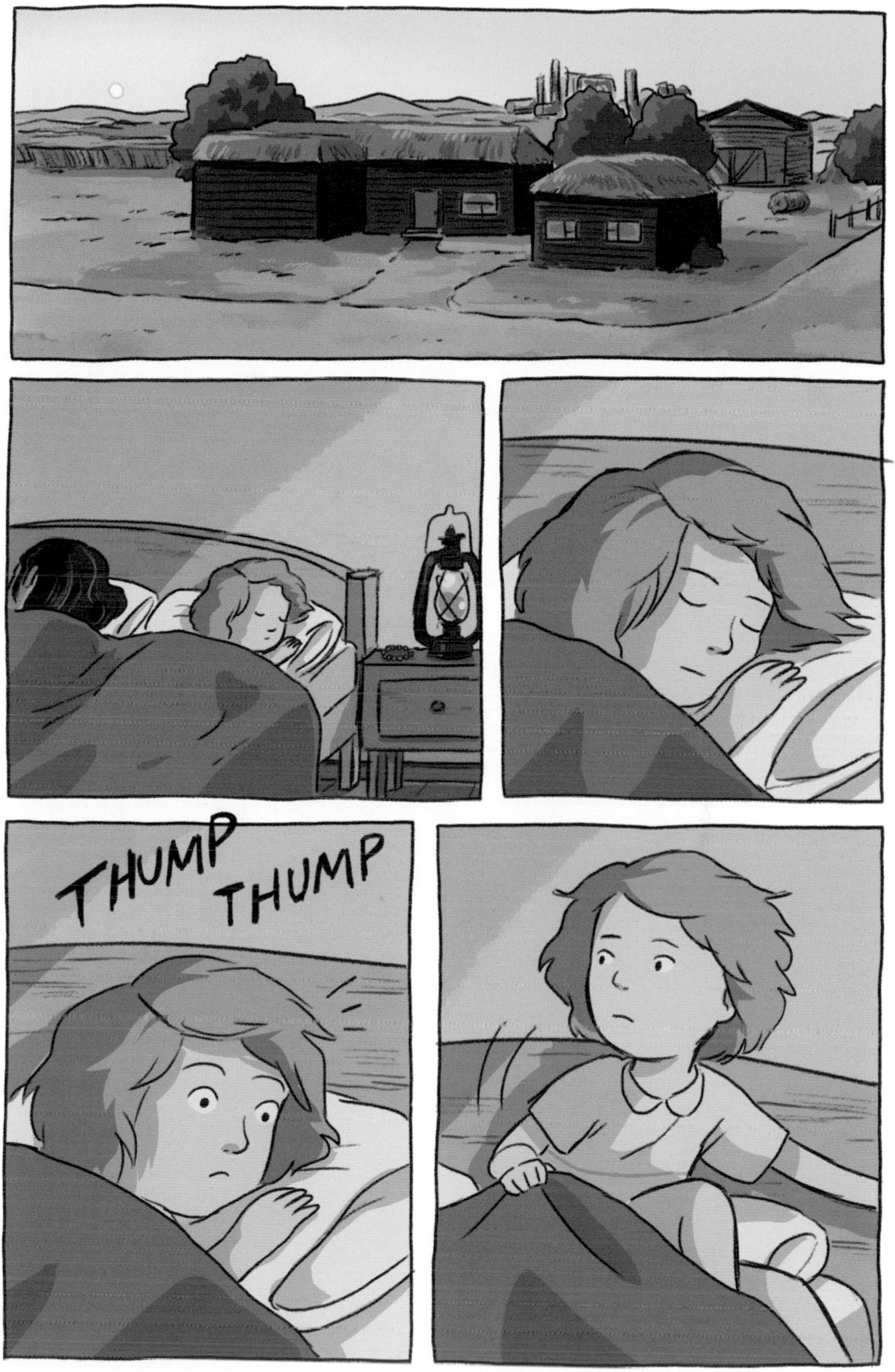
THUMP
THUMP

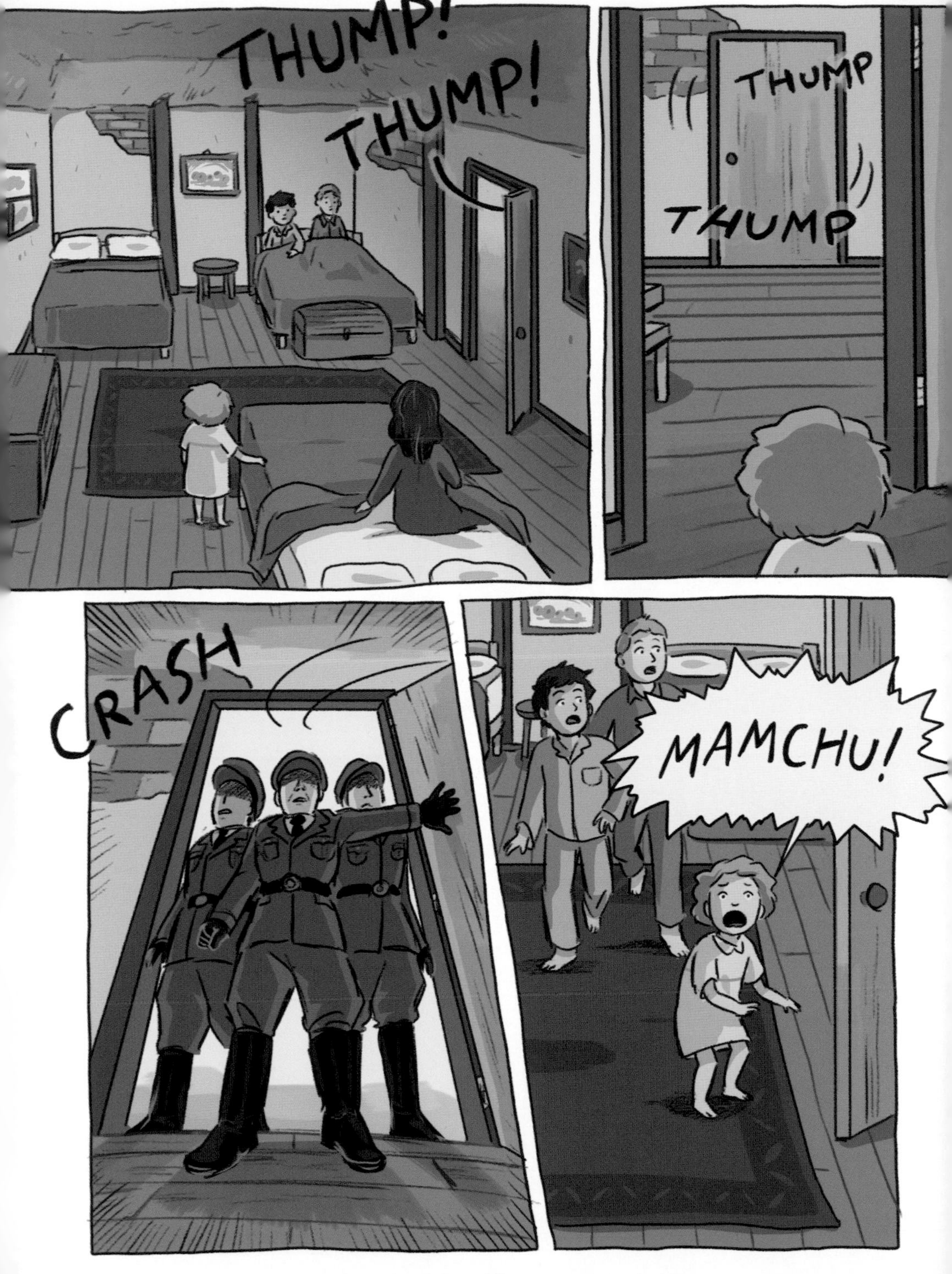
THUMP!
THUMP!
THUMP
THUMP
CRASH
MAMCHU!

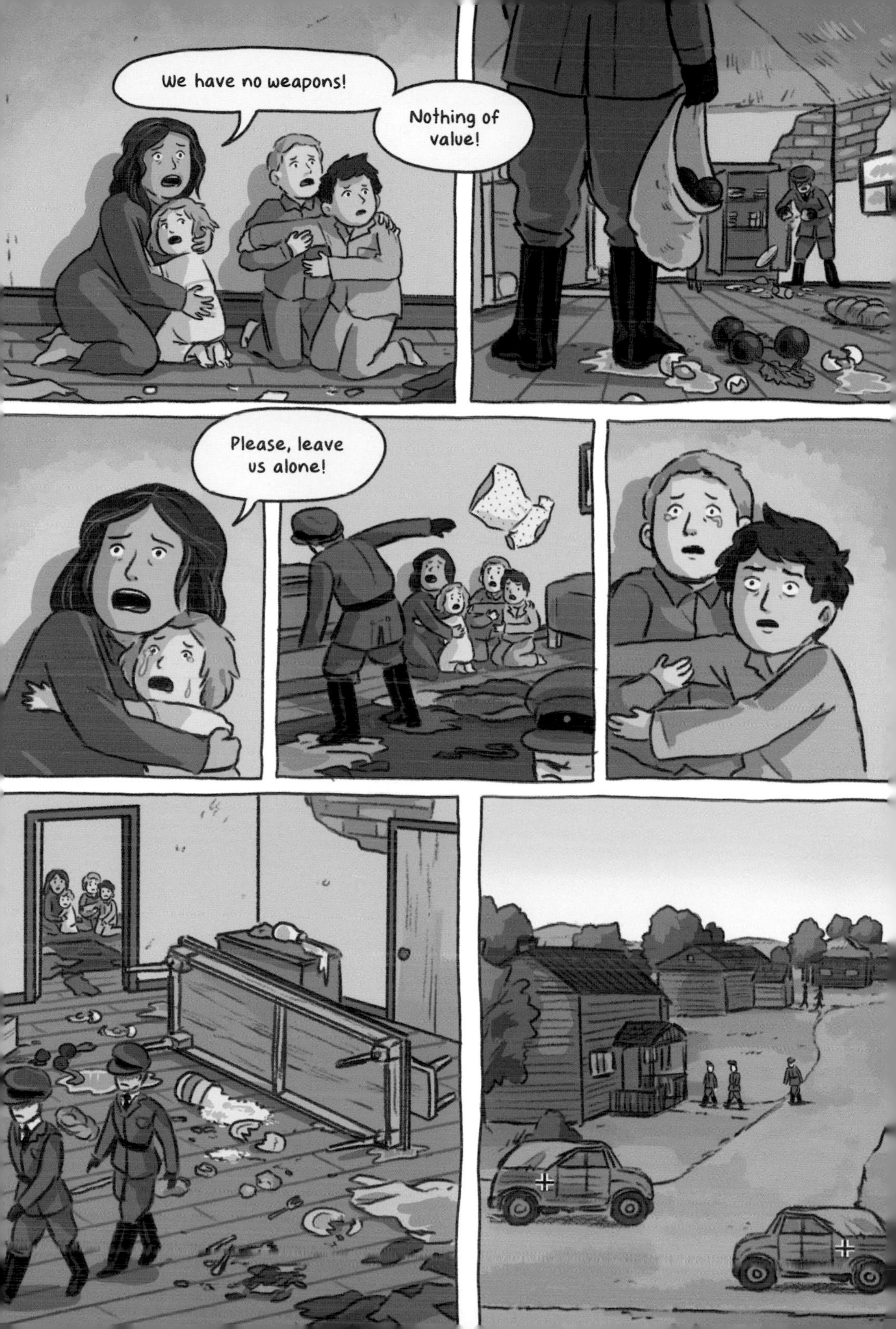
We have no weapons!
Nothing of value!
Please, leave us alone!

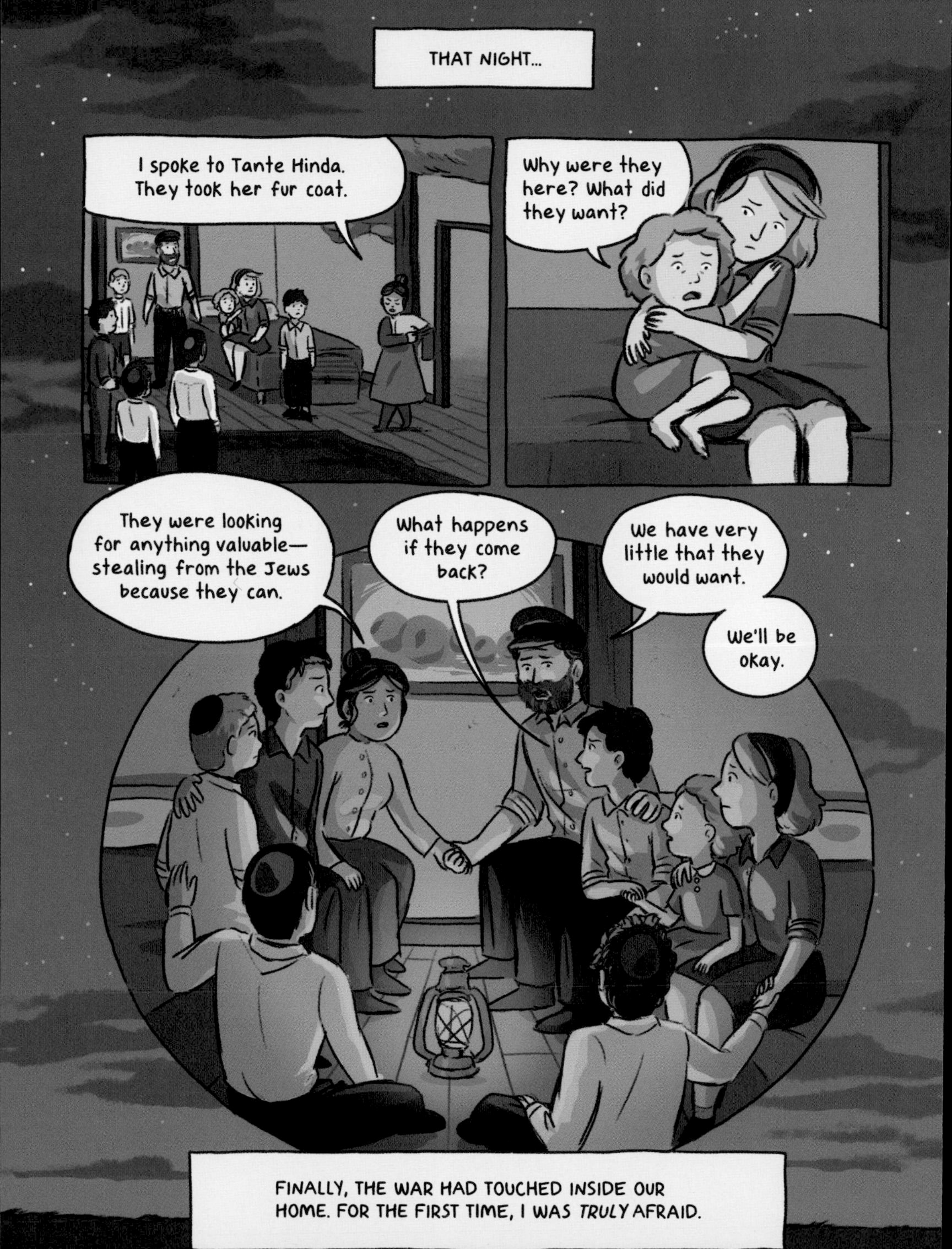
THAT NIGHT...
I spoke to Tante Hinda. They took her fur coat.
Why were they here? What did they want?
They were looking for anything valuable—stealing from the Jews because they can.
What happens if they come back?
We have very little that they would want.
We'll be okay.
FINALLY, THE WAR HAD TOUCHED INSIDE OUR HOME. FOR THE FIRST TIME, I WAS *TRULY* AFRAID.

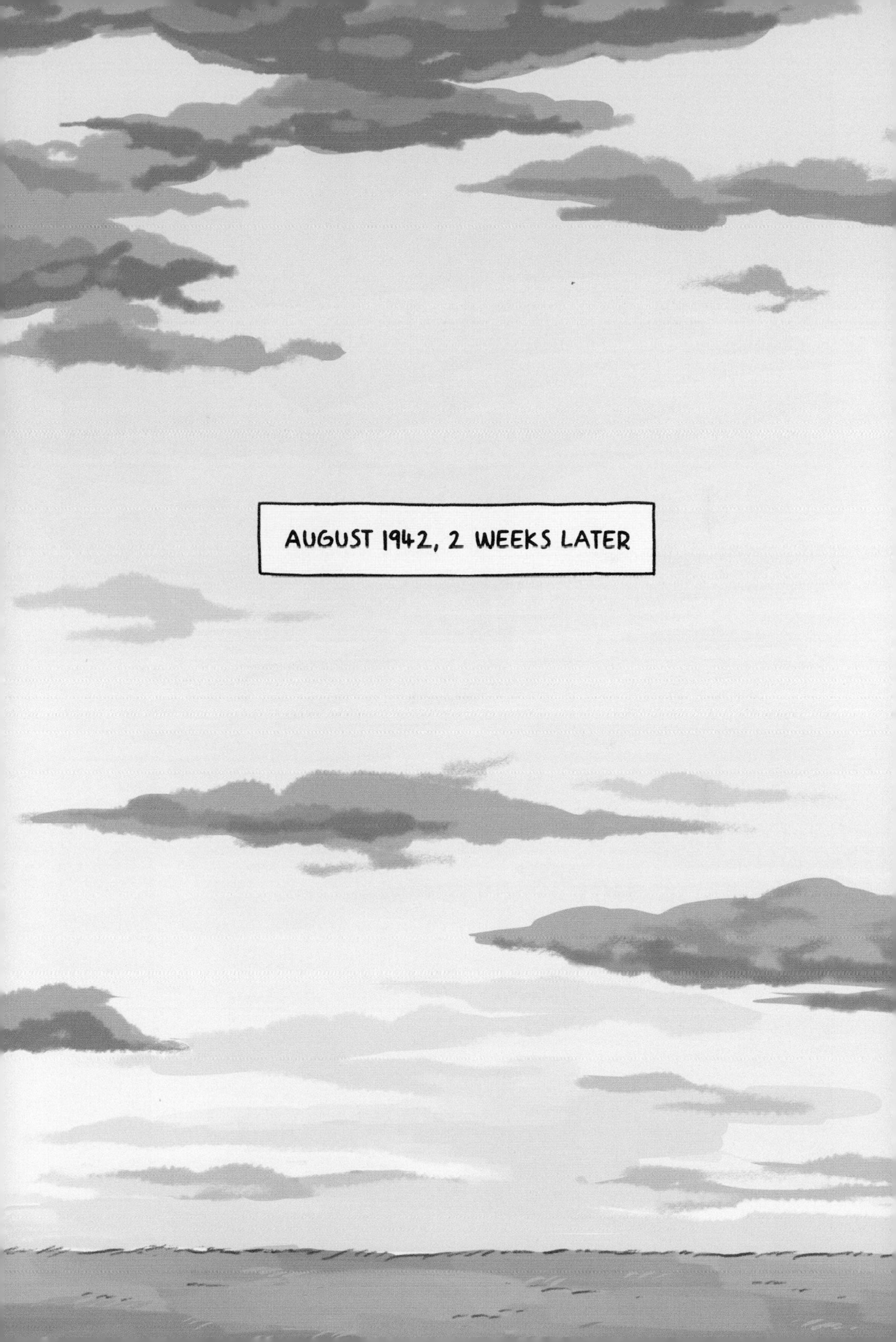
AUGUST 1942, 2 WEEKS LATER

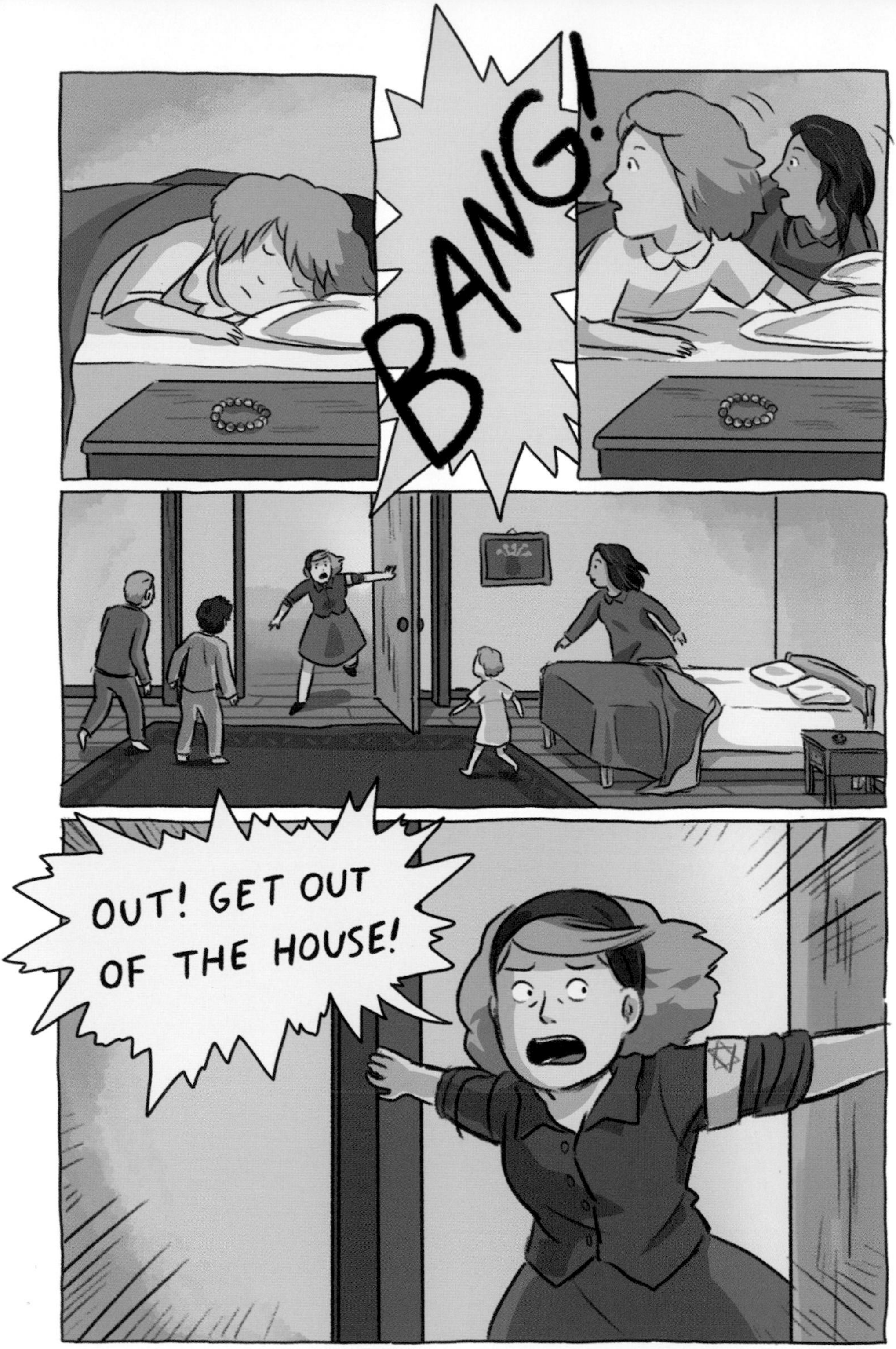
BANG!
OUT! GET OUT OF THE HOUSE!

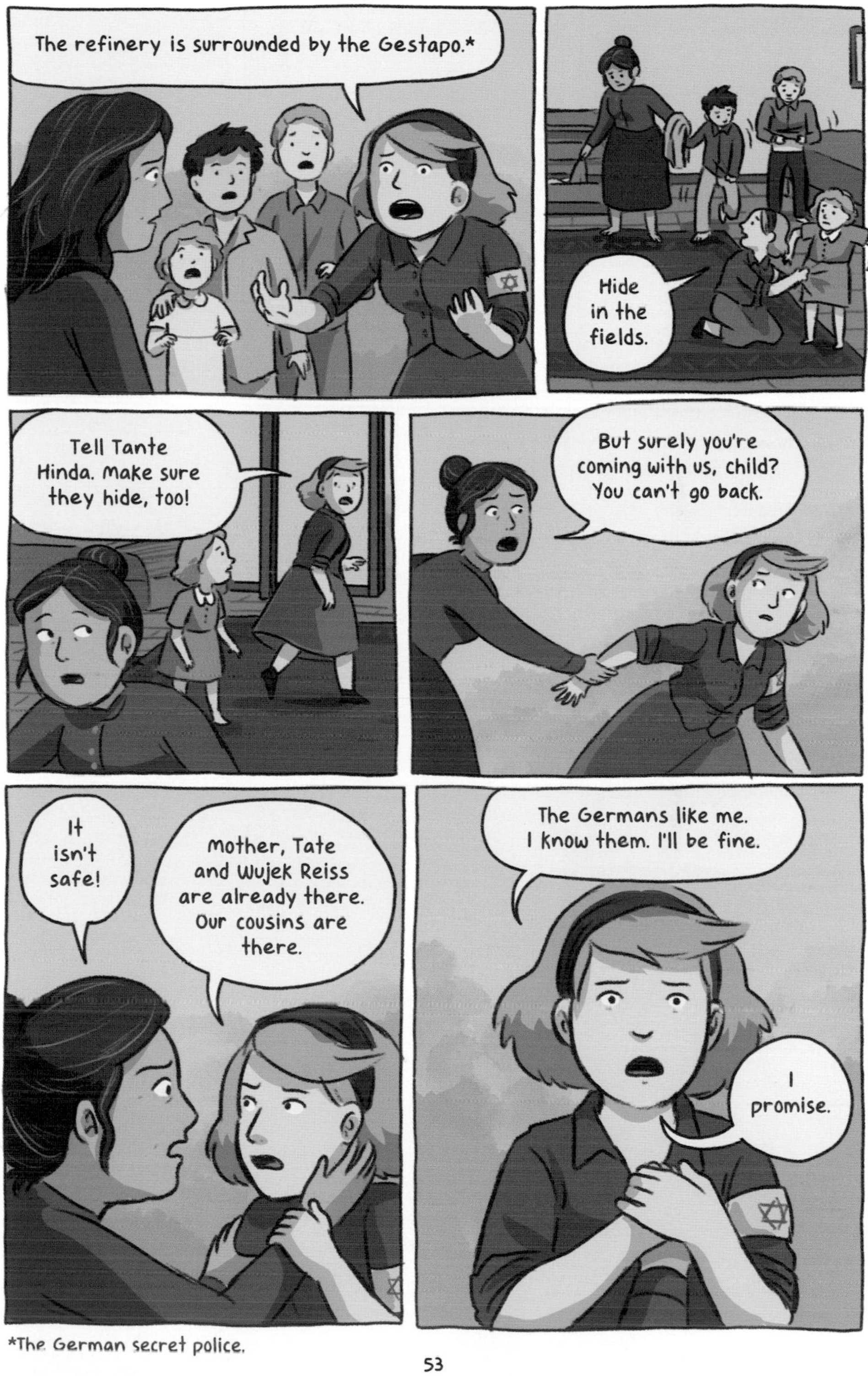
The refinery is surrounded by the Gestapo.*
Hide in the fields.
Tell Tante Hinda. Make sure they hide, too!
But surely you're coming with us, child? You can't go back.
It isn't safe!
Mother, Tate and Wujek Reiss are already there. Our cousins are there.
The Germans like me. I know them. I'll be fine.
I promise.

*The German secret police.

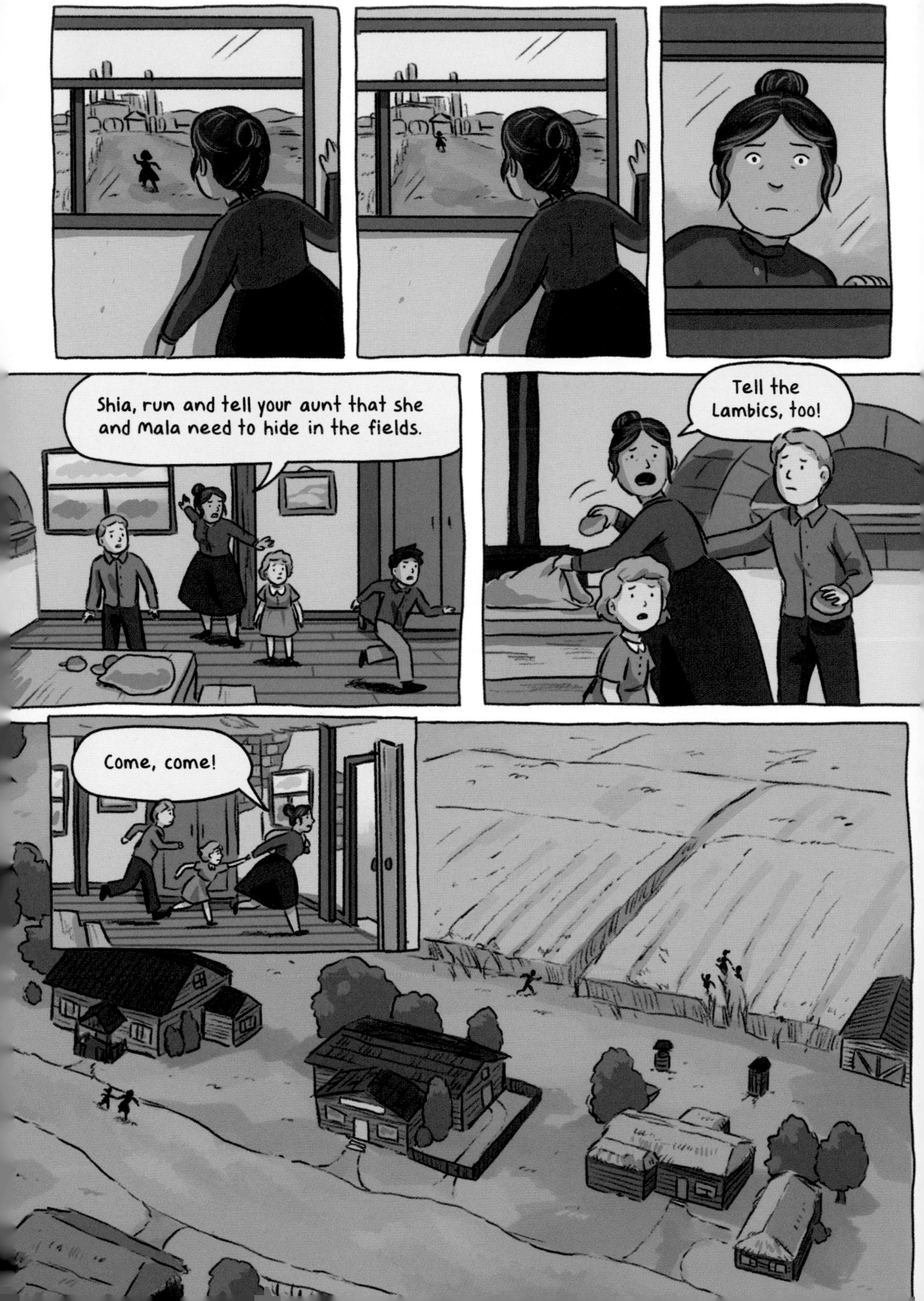
Shia, run and tell your aunt that she and Mala need to hide in the fields.
Tell the Lambics, too!
Come, come!

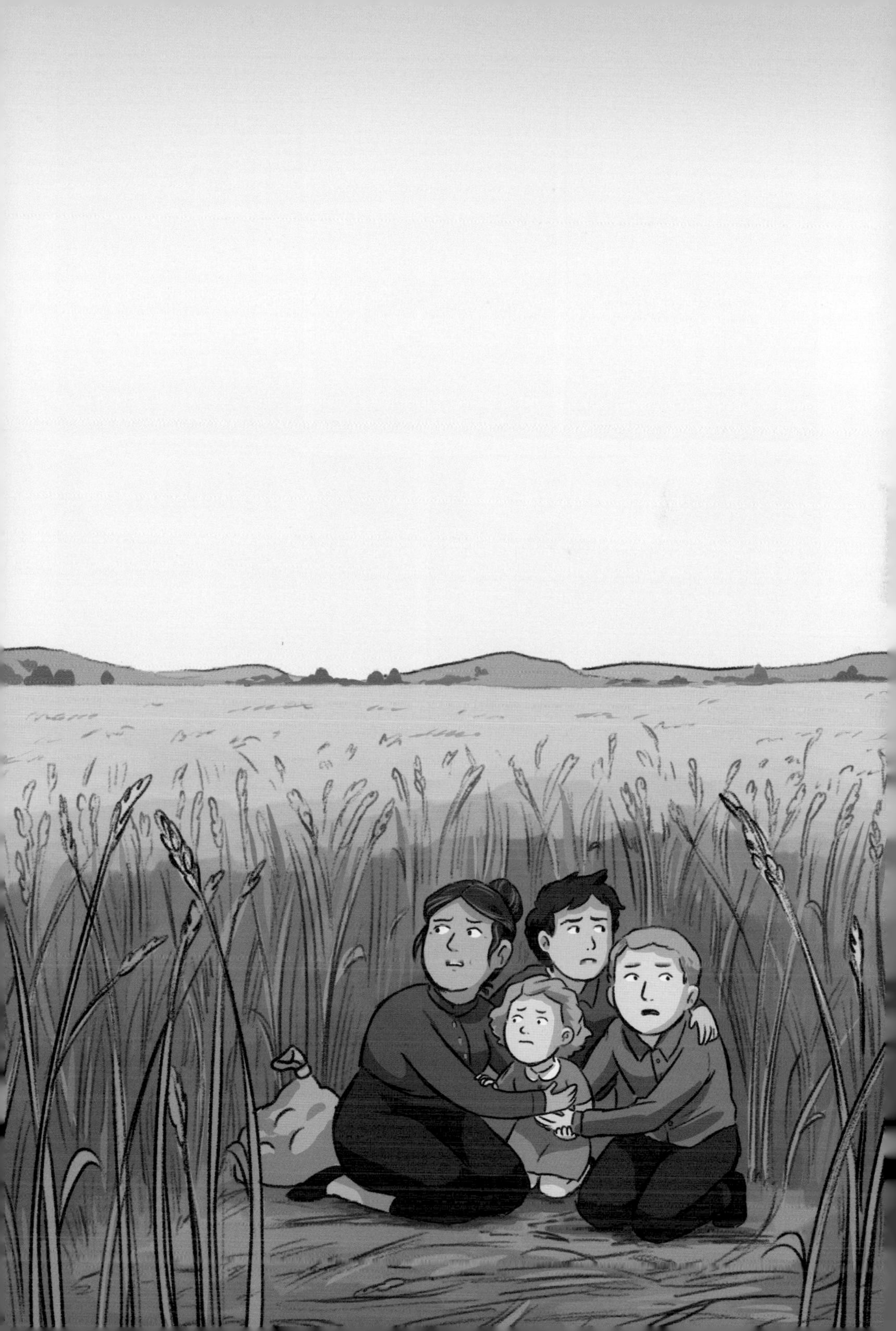

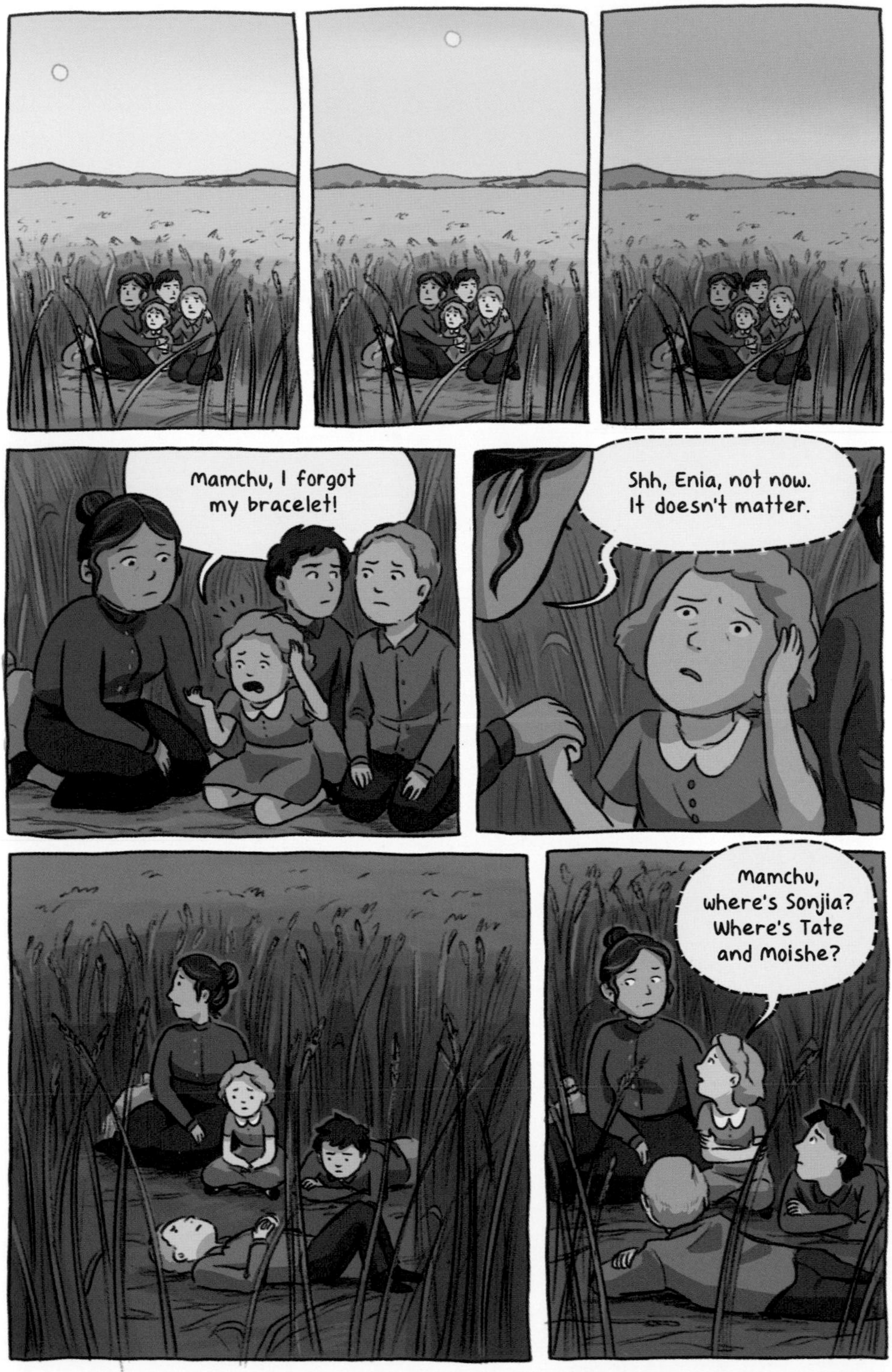
Mamchu, I forgot my bracelet!
Shh, Enia, not now. It doesn't matter.
Mamchu, where's Sonjia? Where's Tate and Moishe?

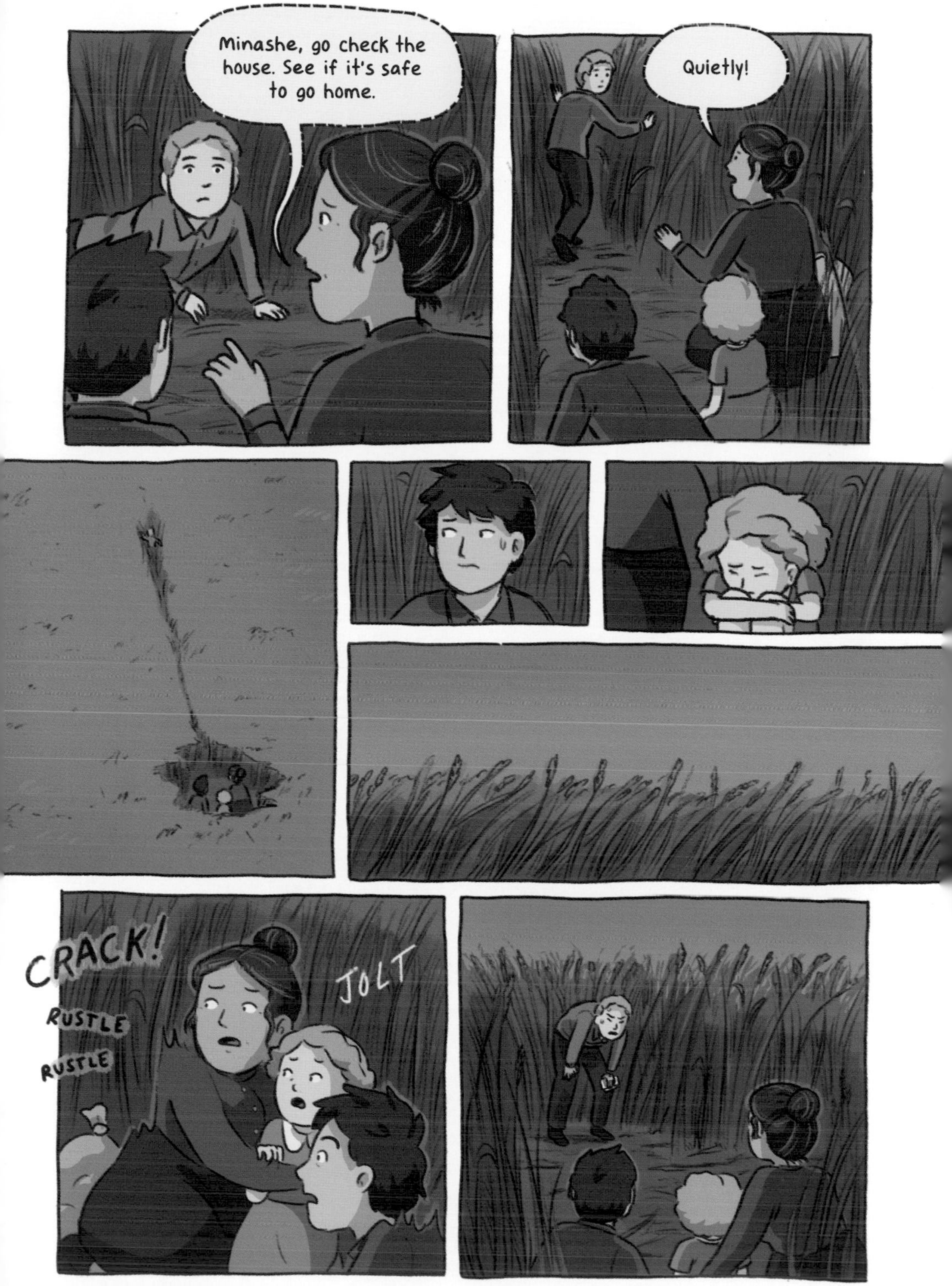
Minashe, go check the house. See if it's safe to go home.
Quietly!
CRACK!
RUSTLE
RUSTLE
JOLT

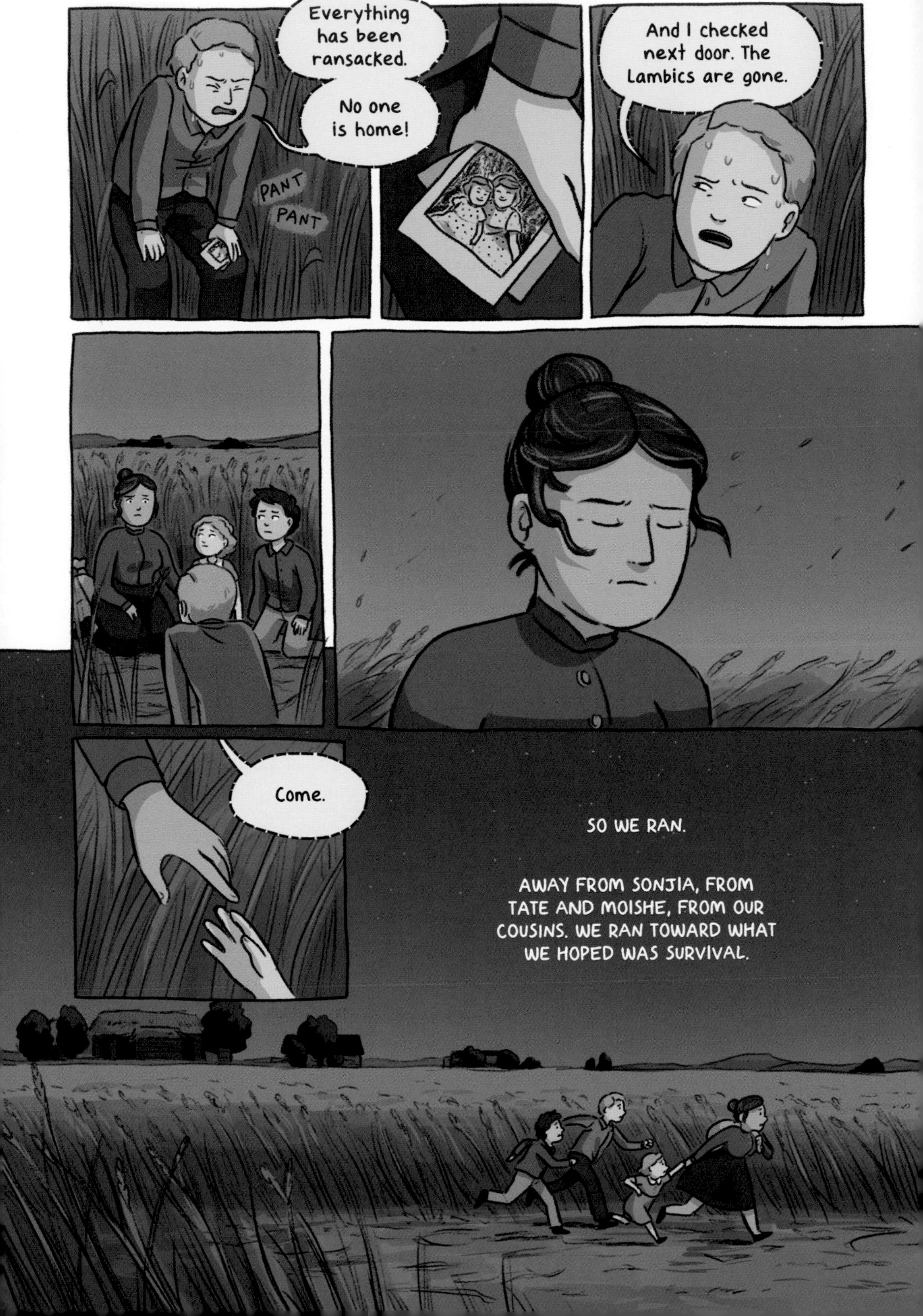
Everything has been ransacked.
No one is home!
PANT
PANT
And I checked next door. The Lambics are gone.
Come.
SO WE RAN.
AWAY FROM SONJIA, FROM TATE AND MOISHE, FROM OUR COUSINS. WE RAN TOWARD WHAT WE HOPED WAS SURVIVAL.

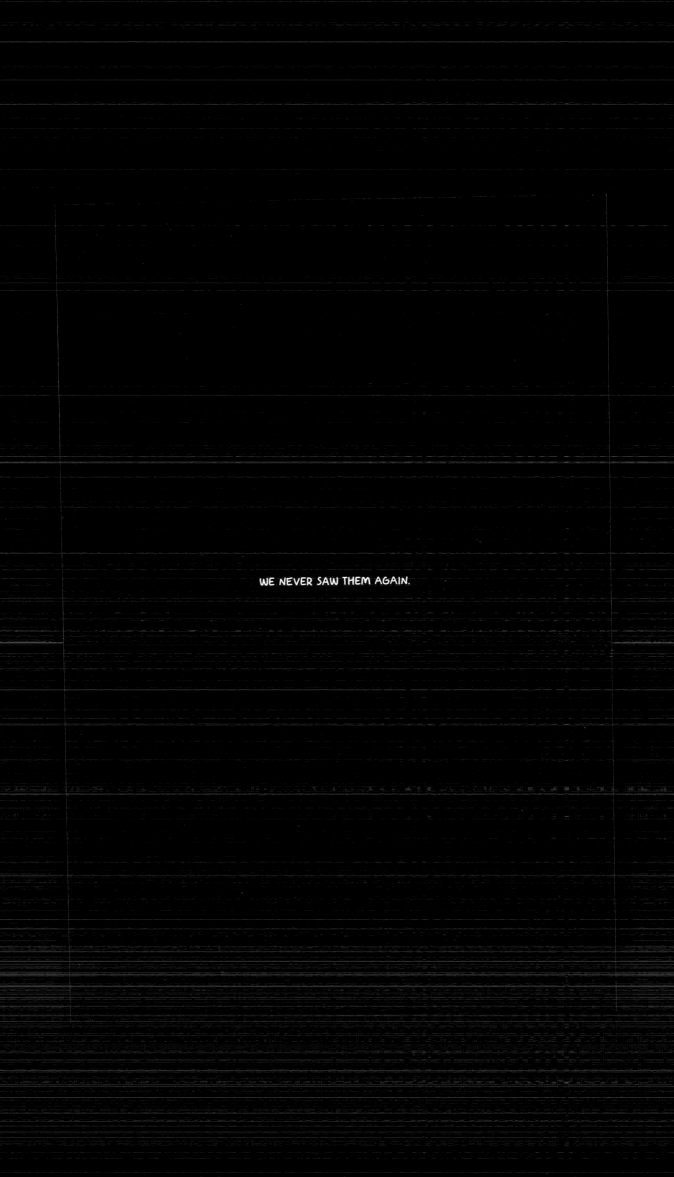

WE NEVER SAW THEM AGAIN.

PART 2:

HIDDEN
1942–1944

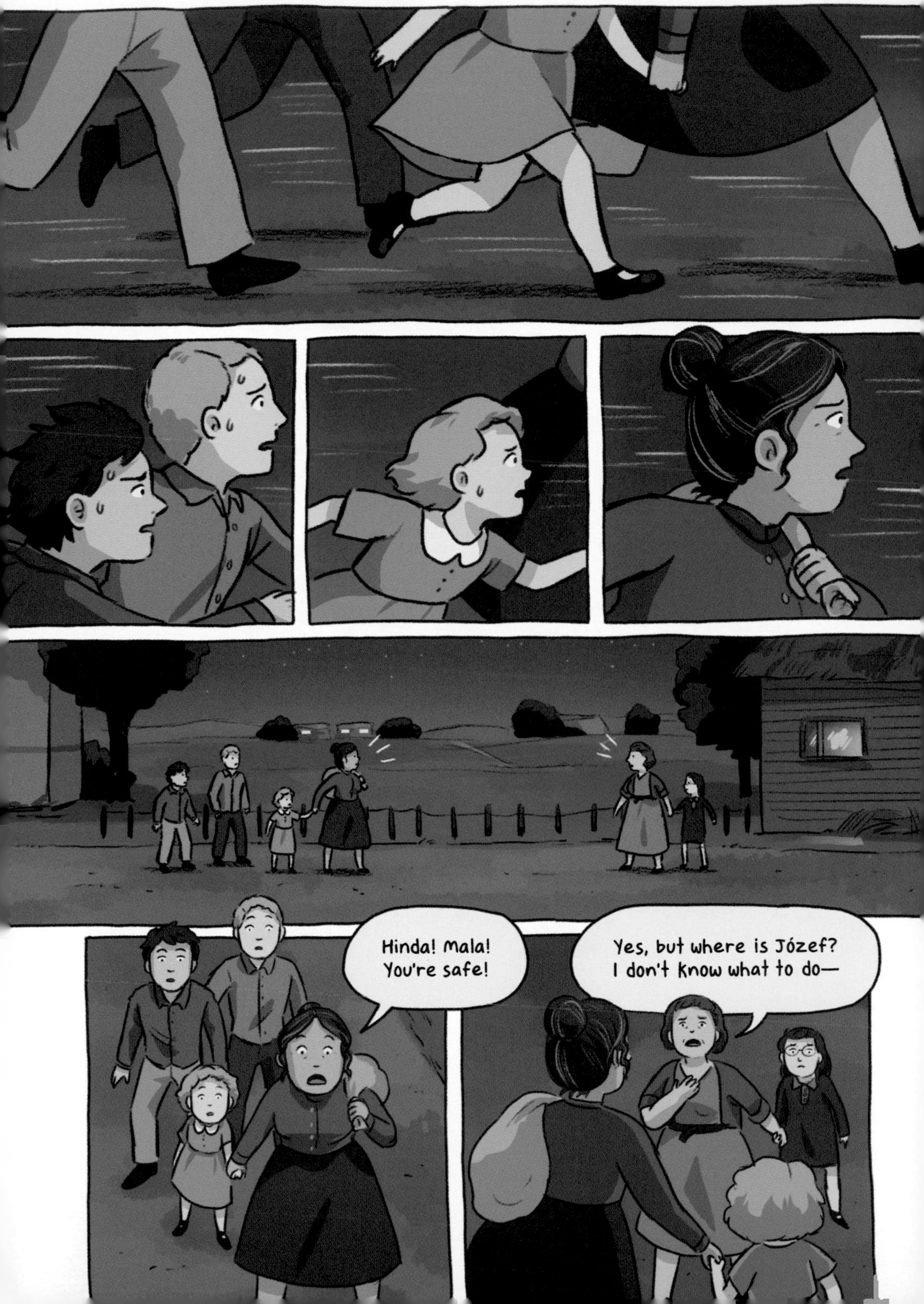
Hinda! Mala!
You're safe!
Yes, but where is Józef?
I don't know what to do—

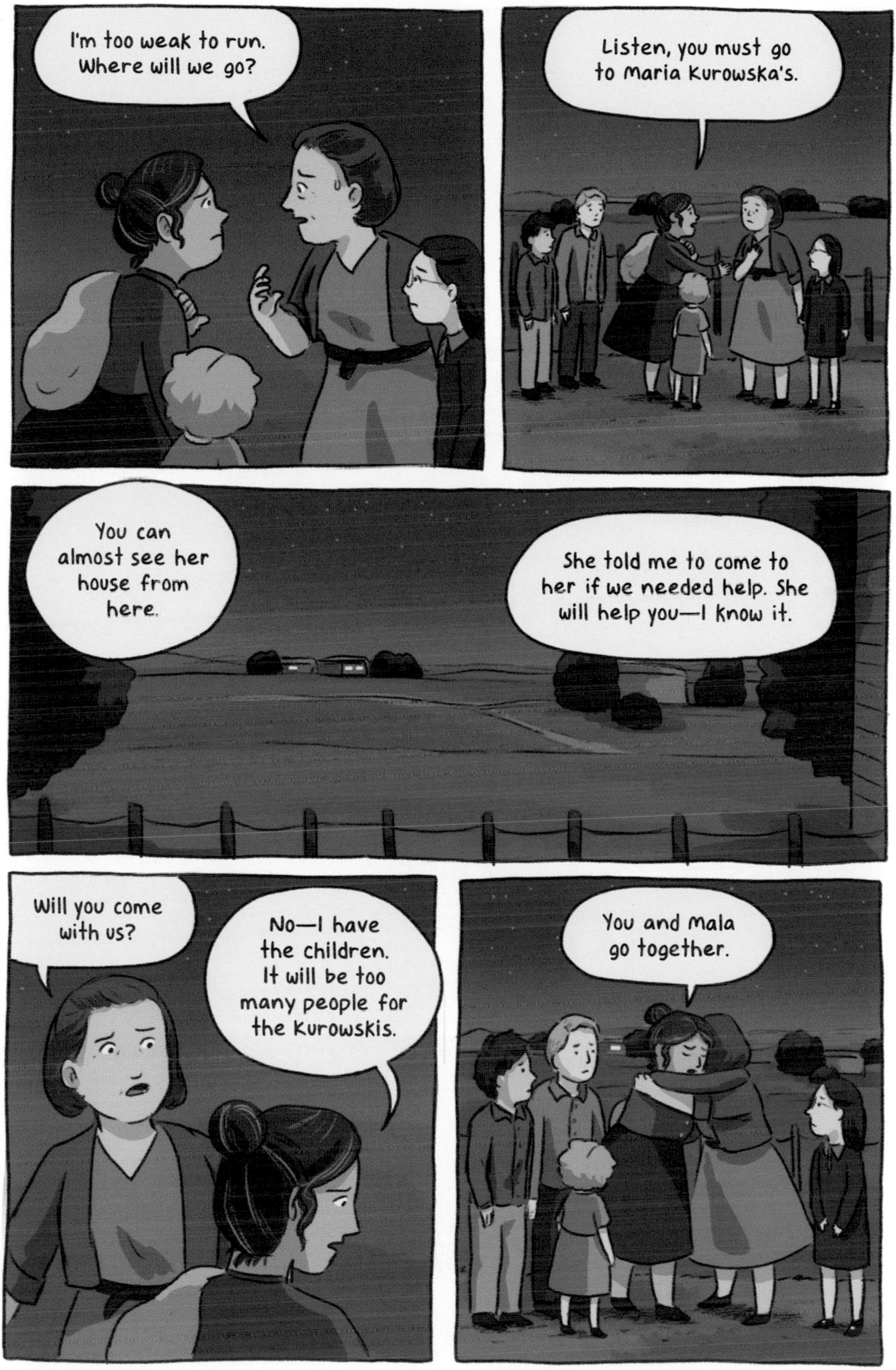
I'm too weak to run. Where will we go?
Listen, you must go to Maria Kurowska's.
You can almost see her house from here.
She told me to come to her if we needed help. She will help you—I know it.
Will you come with us?
No—I have the children. It will be too many people for the Kurowskis.
You and Mala go together.

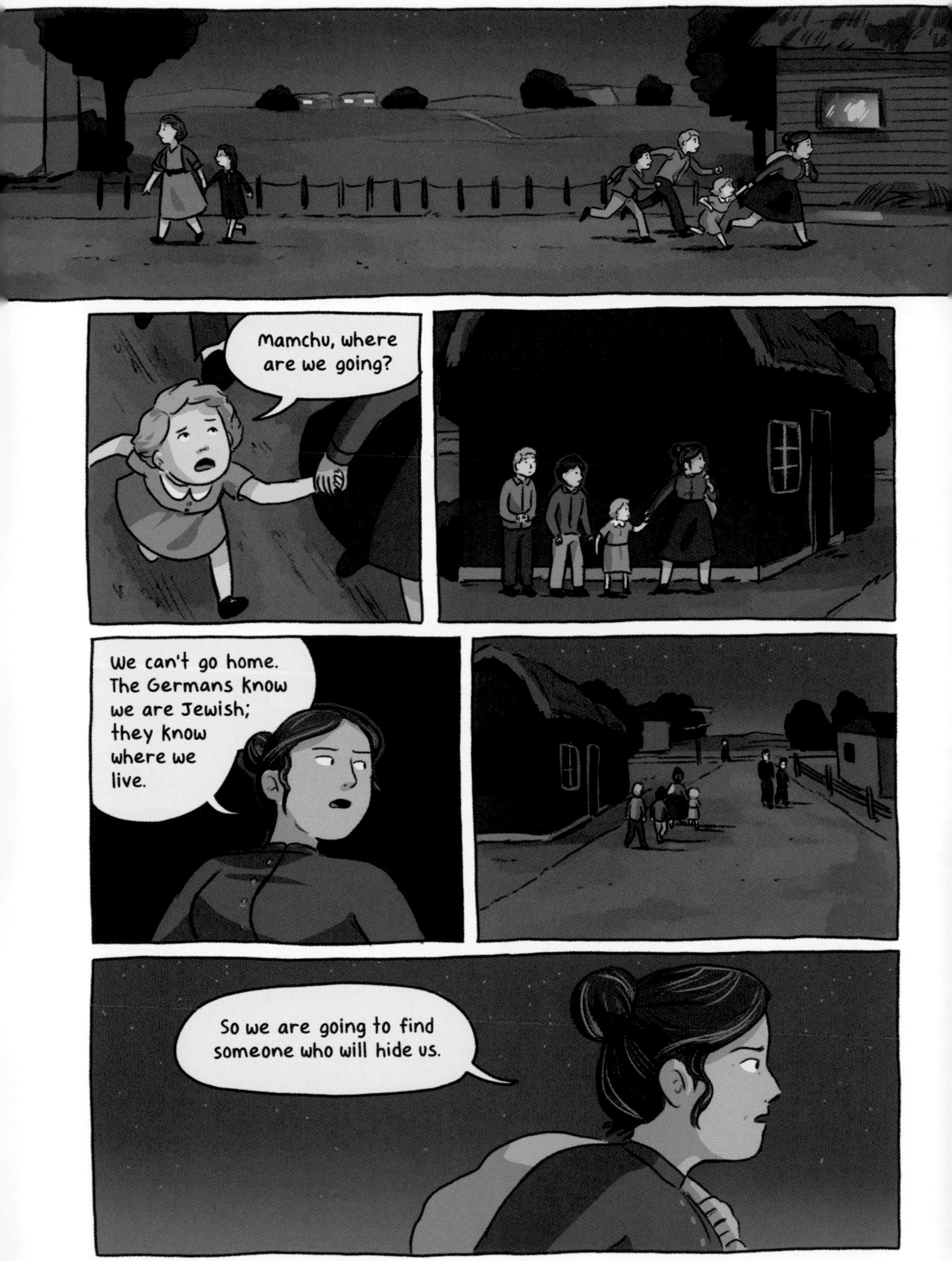
Mamchu, where are we going?
We can't go home. The Germans know we are Jewish; they know where we live.
So we are going to find someone who will hide us.

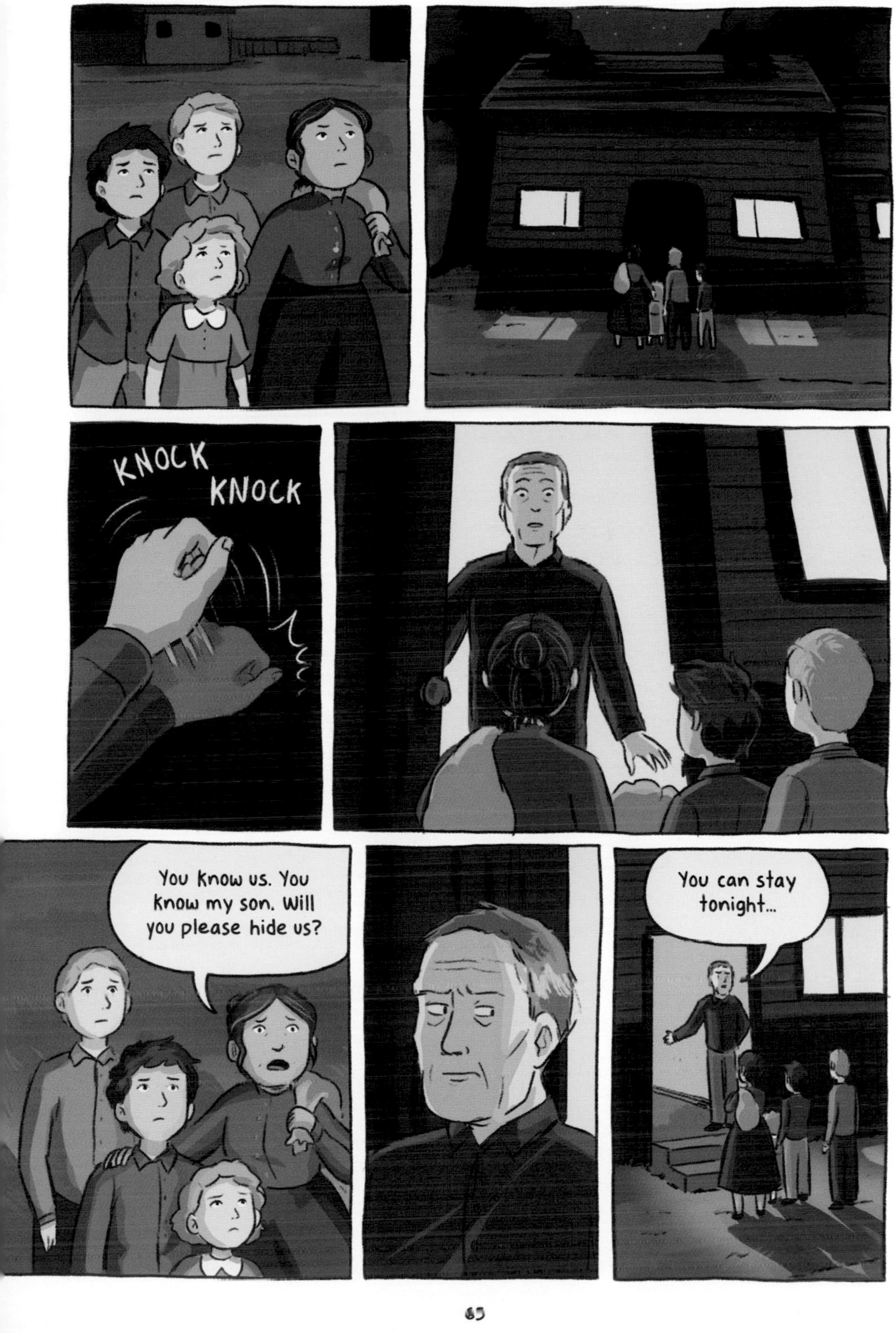
KNOCK
KNOCK
You know us. You know my son. Will you please hide us?
You can stay tonight...

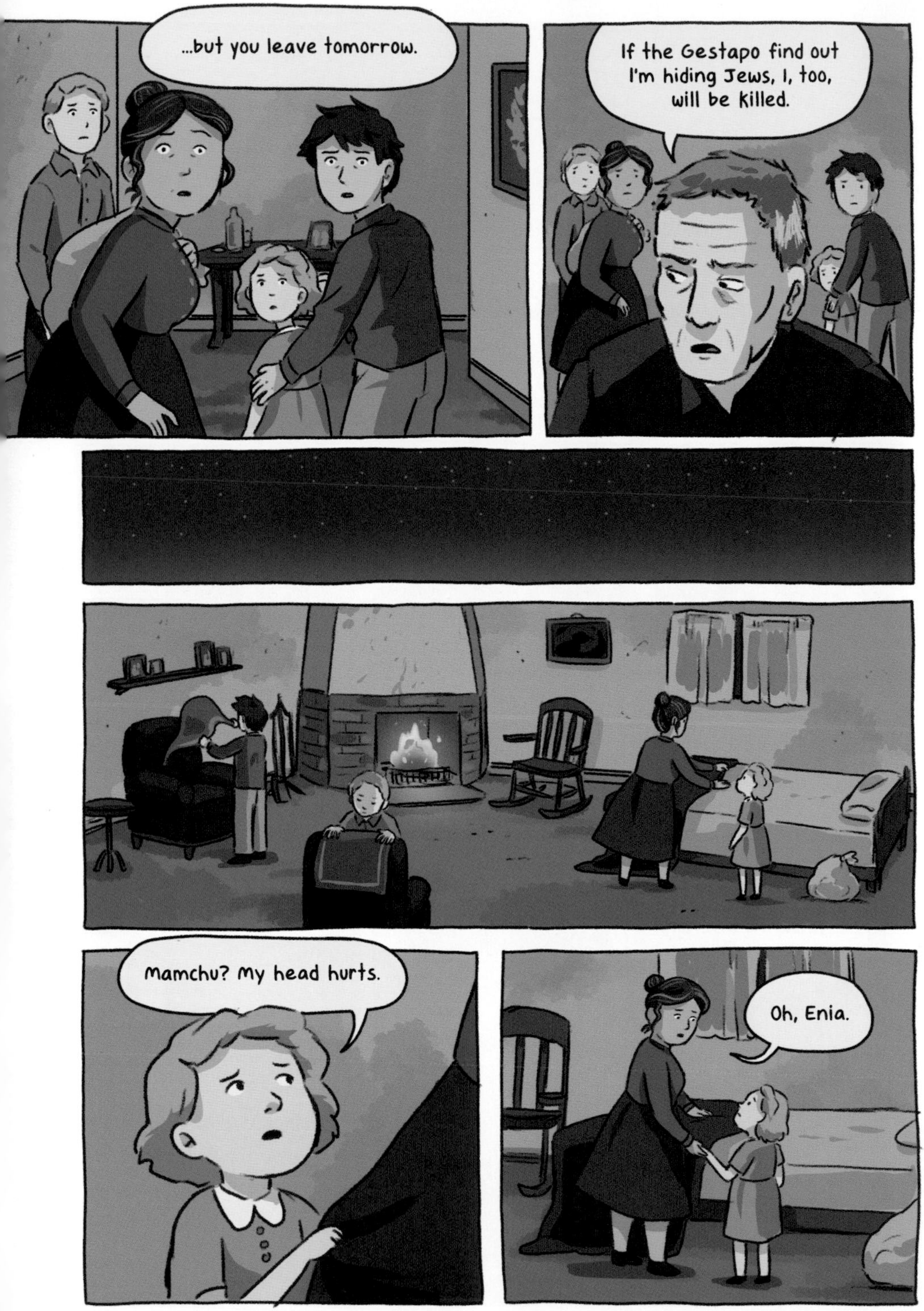
...but you leave tomorrow.
If the Gestapo find out I'm hiding Jews, I, too, will be killed.
Mamchu? My head hurts.
Oh, Enia.

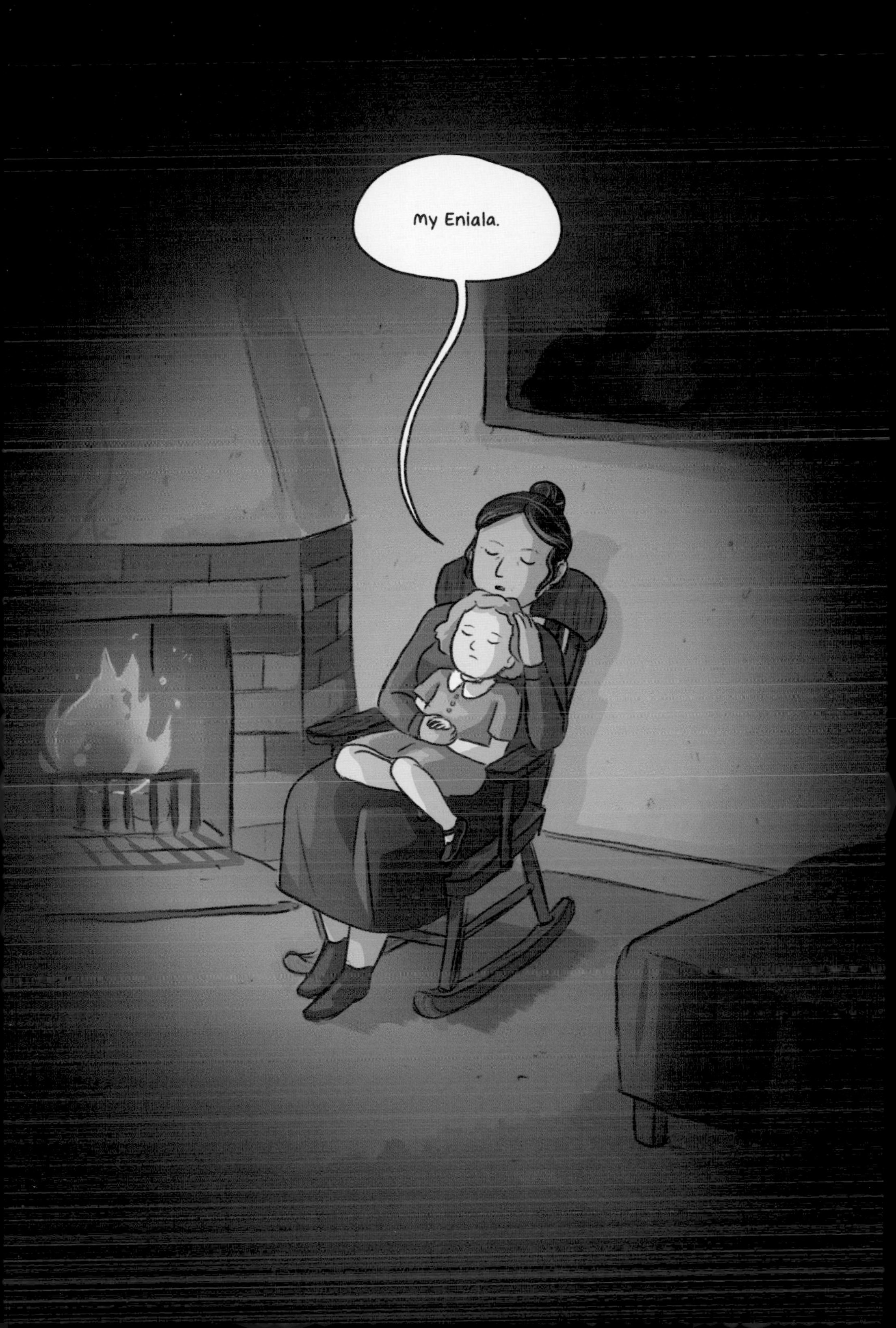
My Eniala.

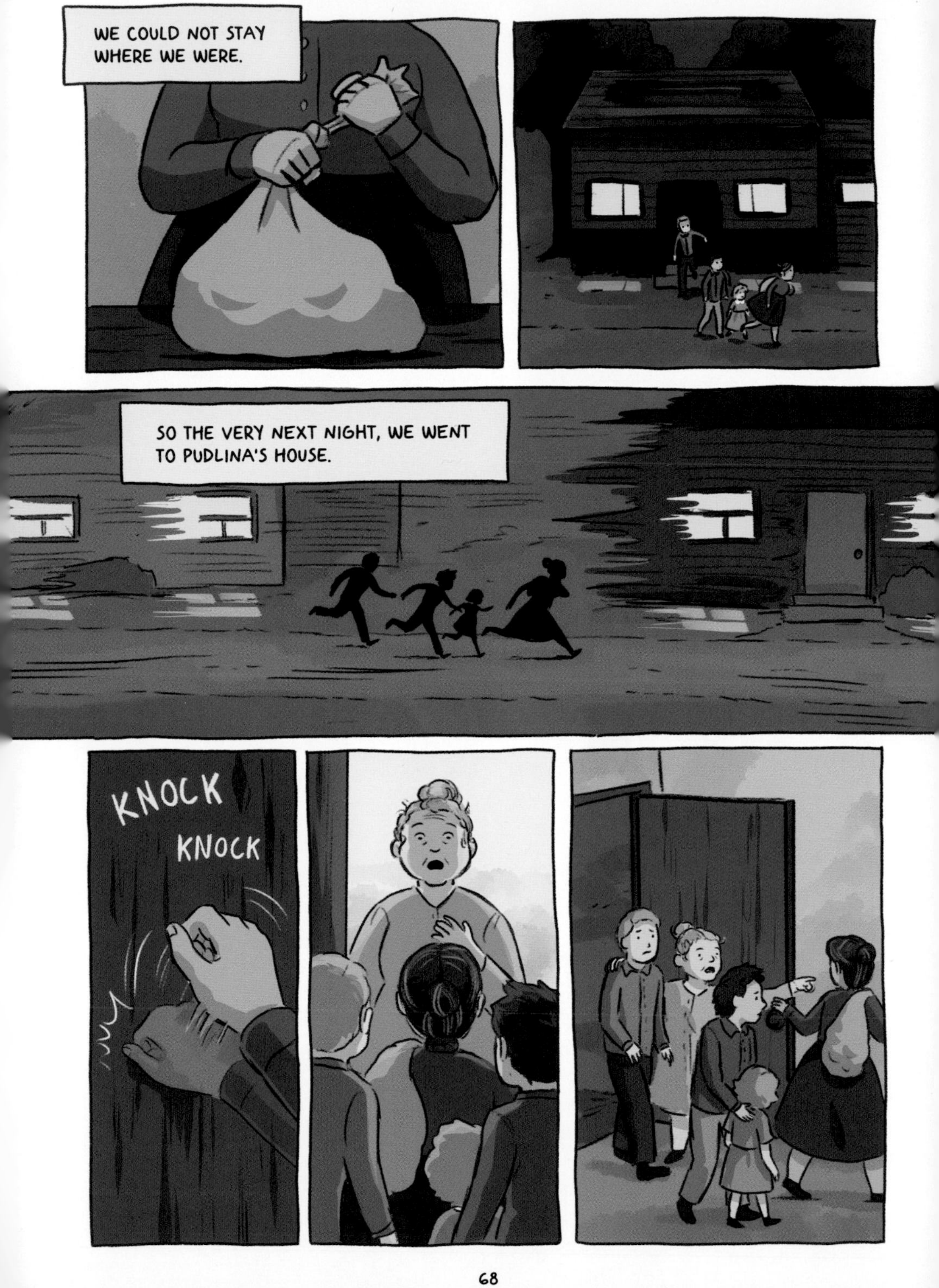

WE COULD NOT STAY WHERE WE WERE.
SO THE VERY NEXT NIGHT, WE WENT TO PUDLINA'S HOUSE.
KNOCK
KNOCK

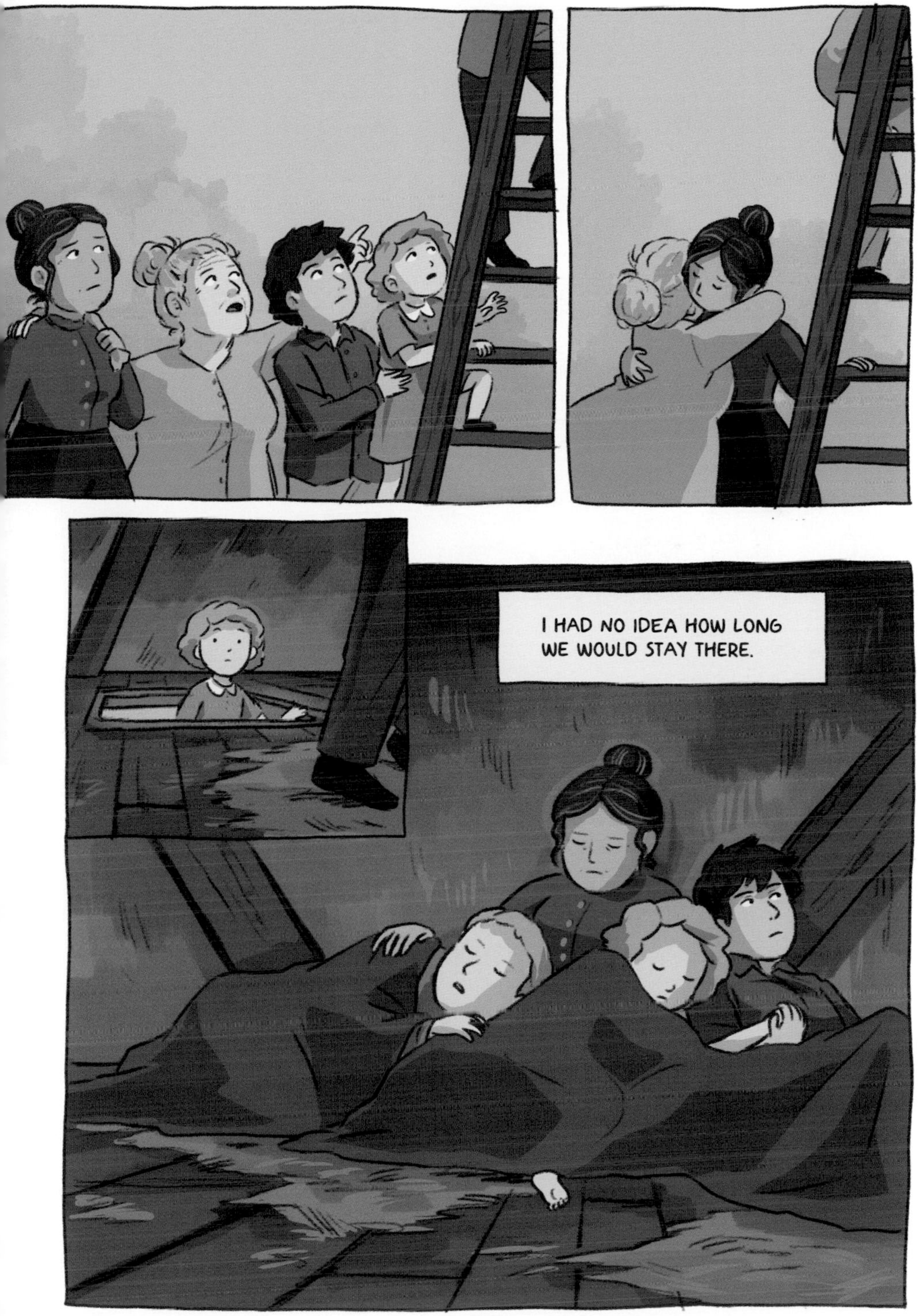
I HAD NO IDEA HOW LONG
WE WOULD STAY THERE.

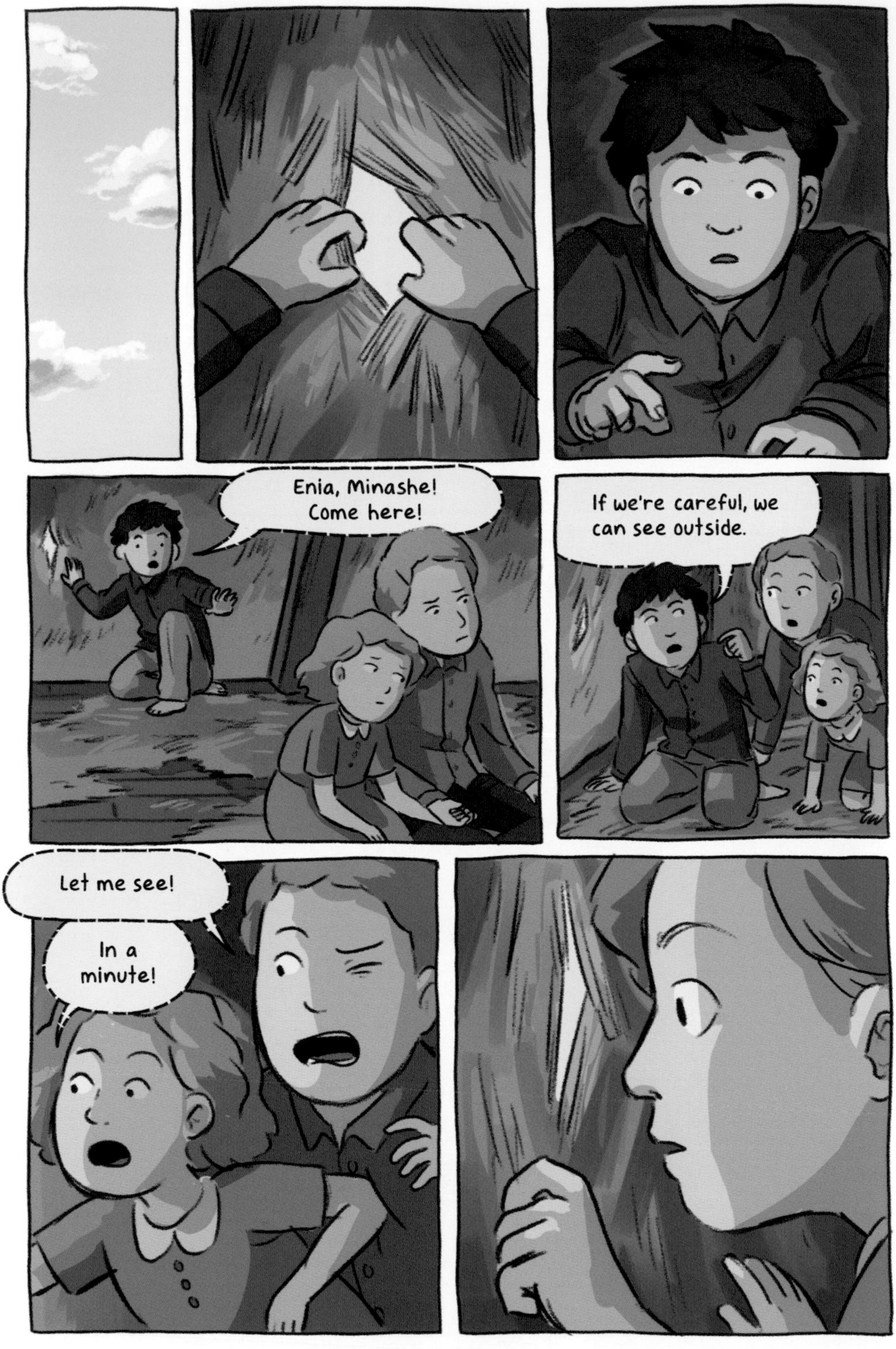
Enia, Minashe! Come here!
If we're careful, we can see outside.
Let me see!
In a minute!

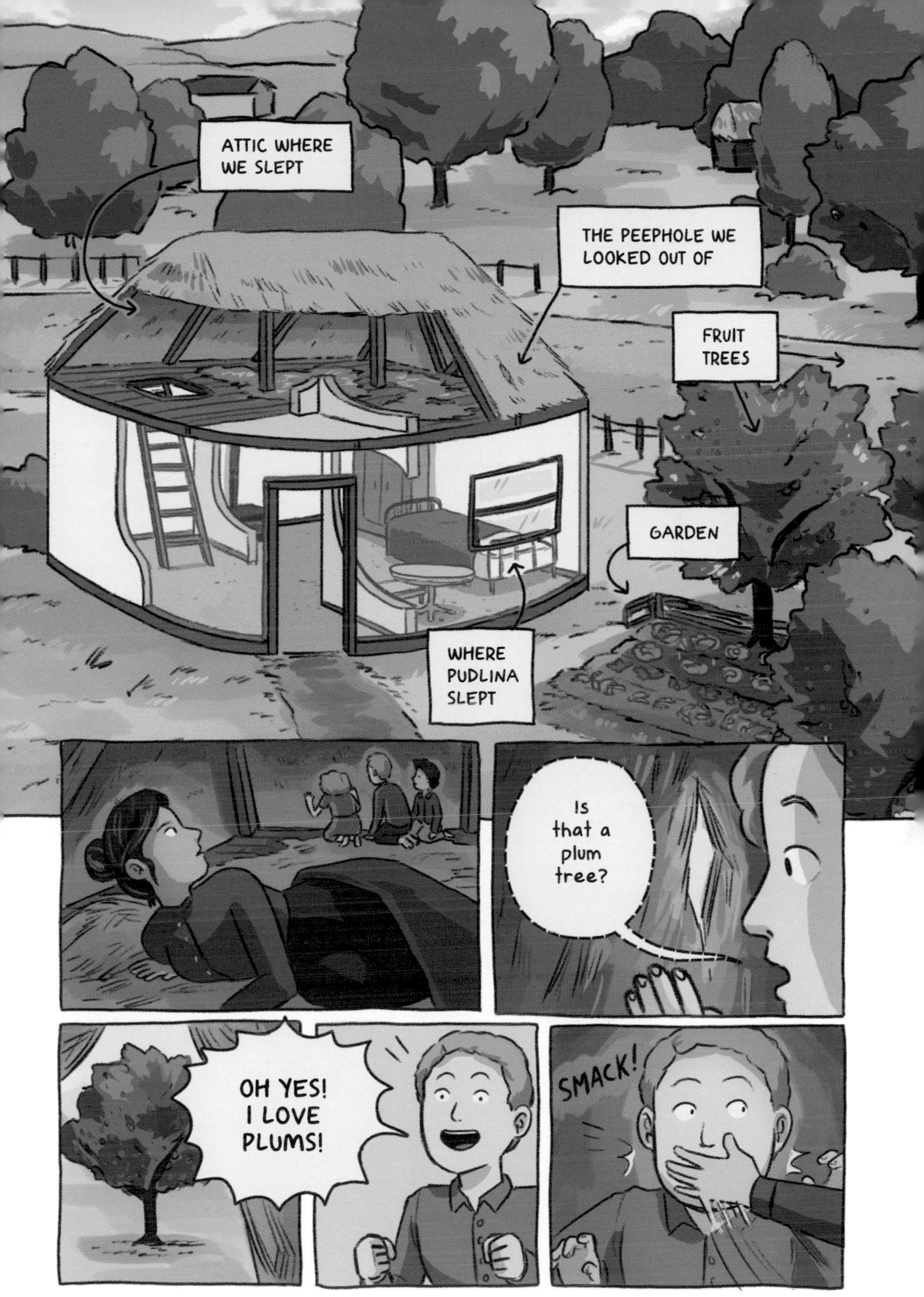
ATTIC WHERE WE SLEPT
THE PEEPHOLE WE LOOKED OUT OF
FRUIT TREES
GARDEN
WHERE PUDLINA SLEPT
Is that a plum tree?
OH YES! I LOVE PLUMS!
SMACK!

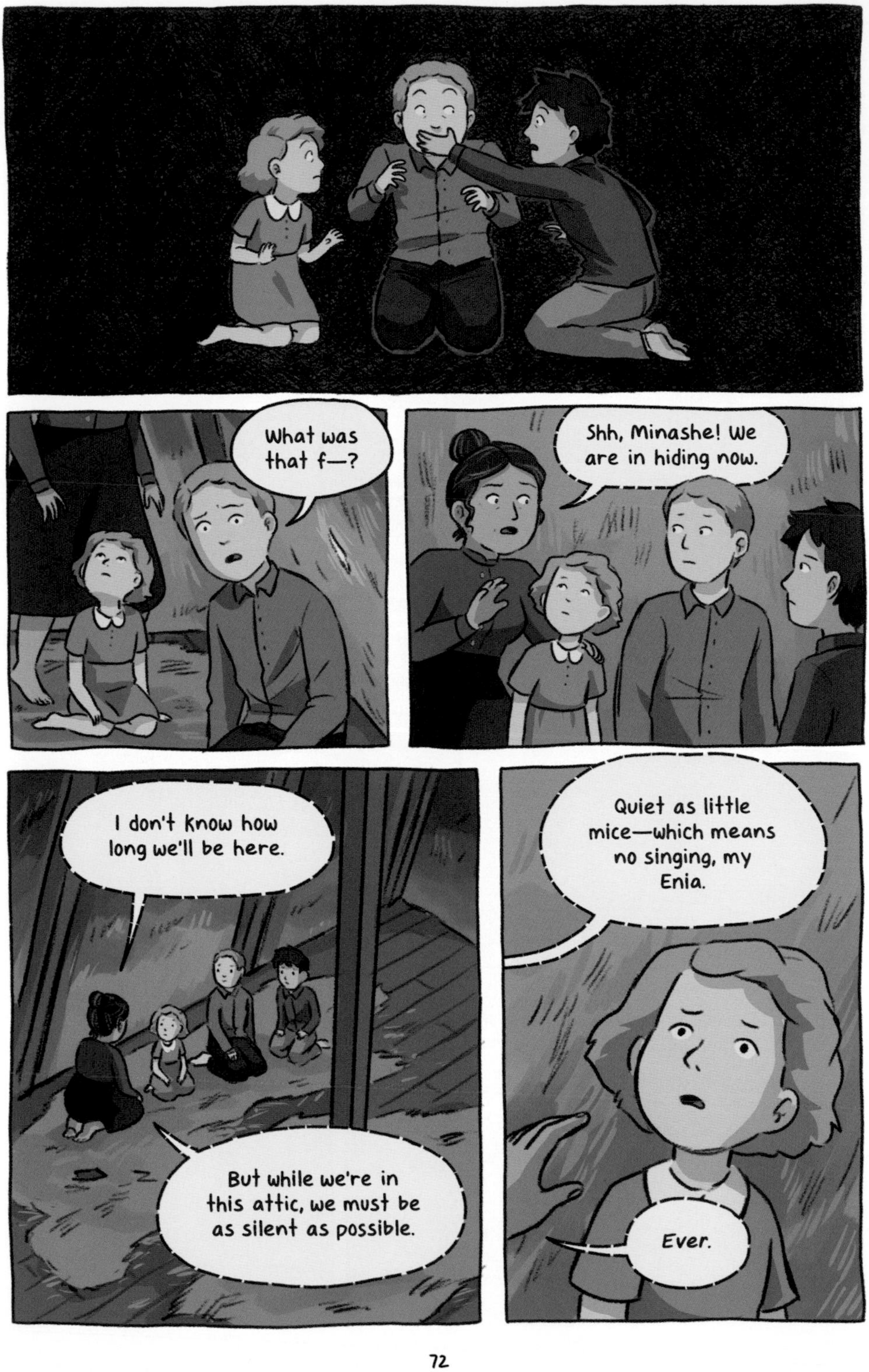
What was that f—?
Shh, Minashe! We are in hiding now.
I don't know how long we'll be here.
But while we're in this attic, we must be as silent as possible.
Quiet as little mice—which means no singing, my Enia.
Ever.

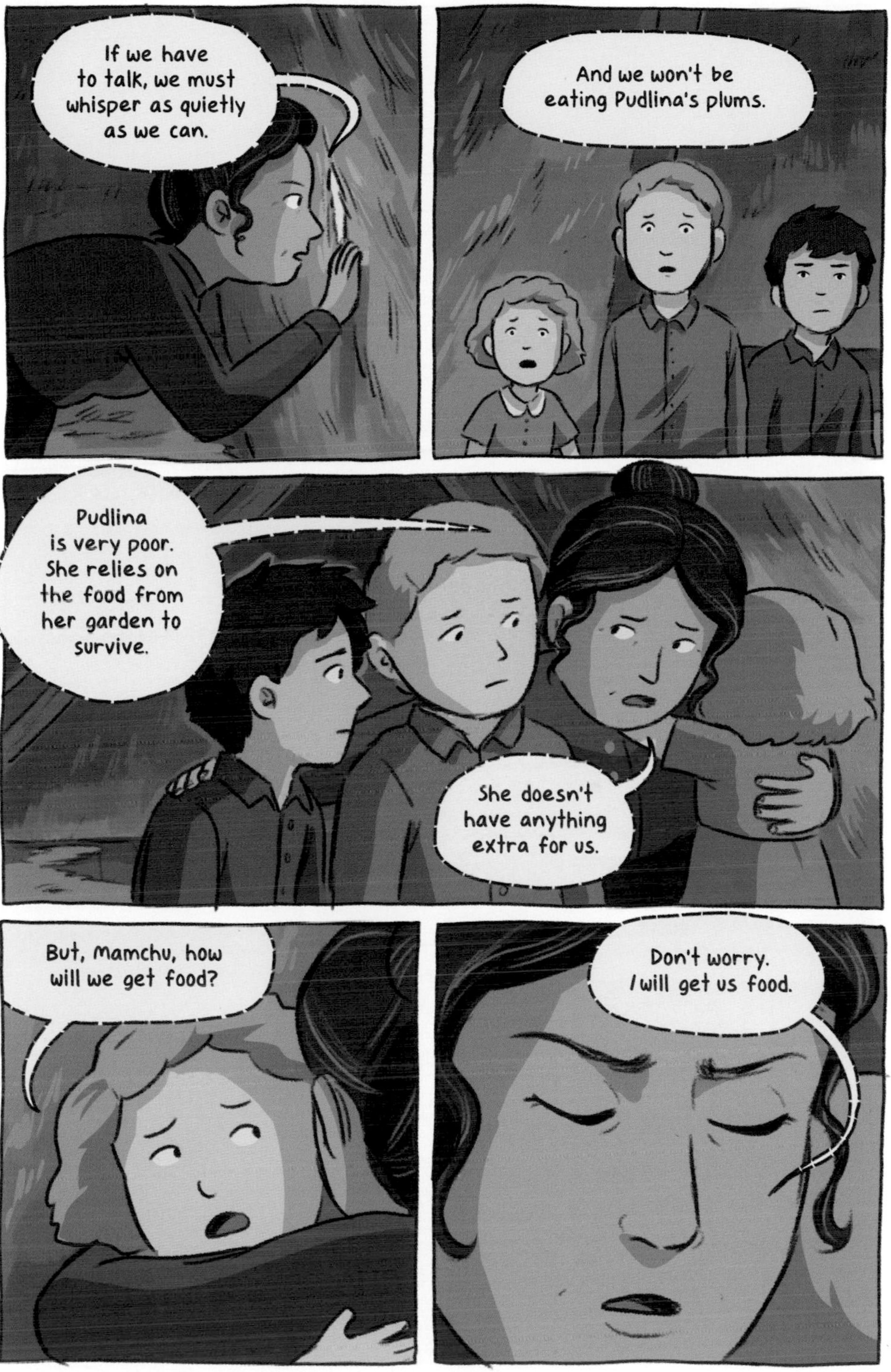
If we have to talk, we must whisper as quietly as we can.
And we won't be eating Pudlina's plums.
Pudlina is very poor. She relies on the food from her garden to survive.
She doesn't have anything extra for us.
But, Mamchu, how will we get food?
Don't worry. I will get us food.

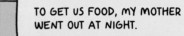
TO GET US FOOD, MY MOTHER WENT OUT AT NIGHT.

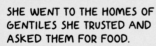
SHE WENT TO THE HOMES OF GENTILES SHE TRUSTED AND ASKED THEM FOR FOOD.

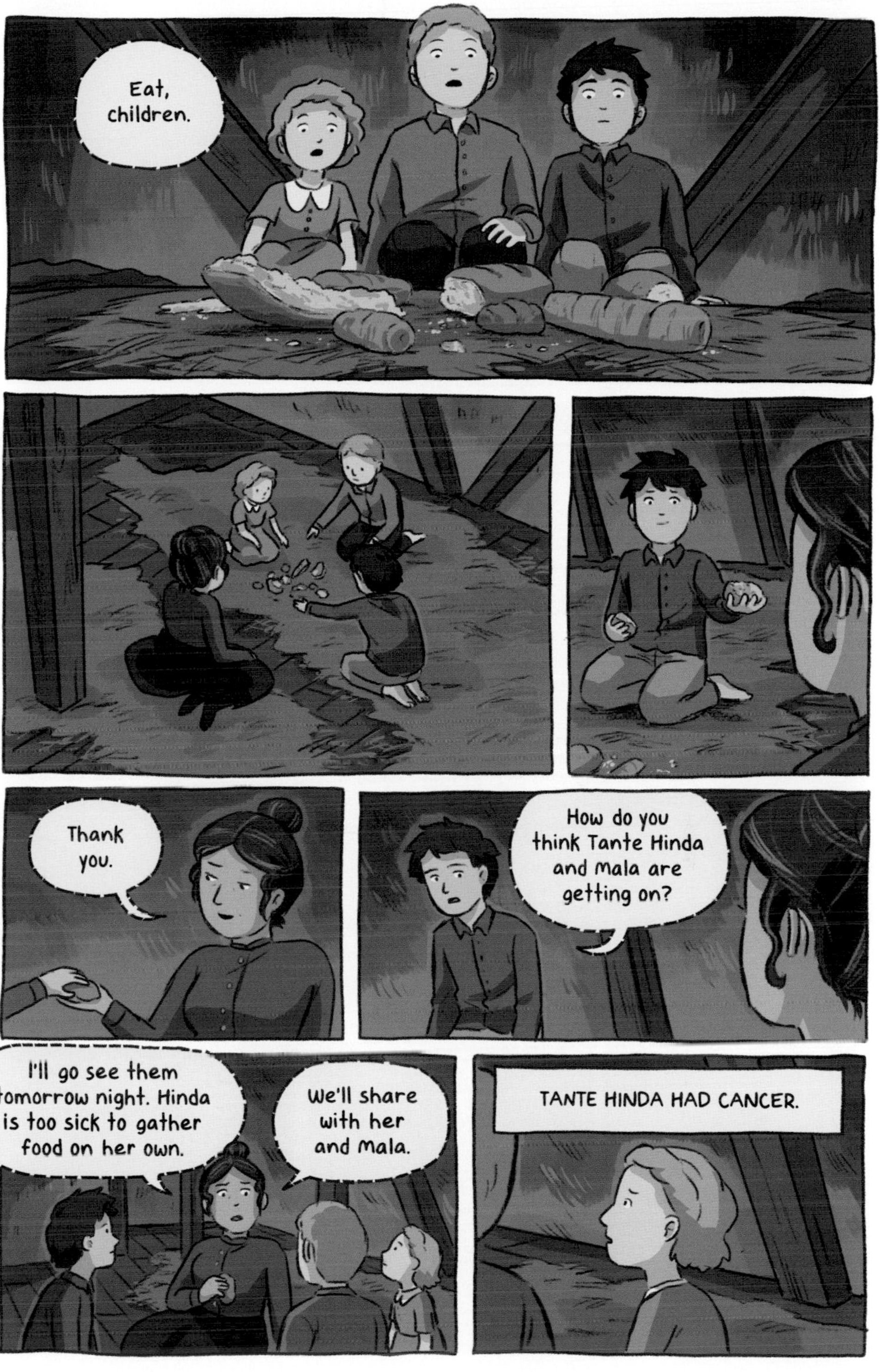
Eat, children.
Thank you.
How do you think Tante Hinda and Mala are getting on?
I'll go see them tomorrow night. Hinda is too sick to gather food on her own.
We'll share with her and Mala.
TANTE HINDA HAD CANCER.

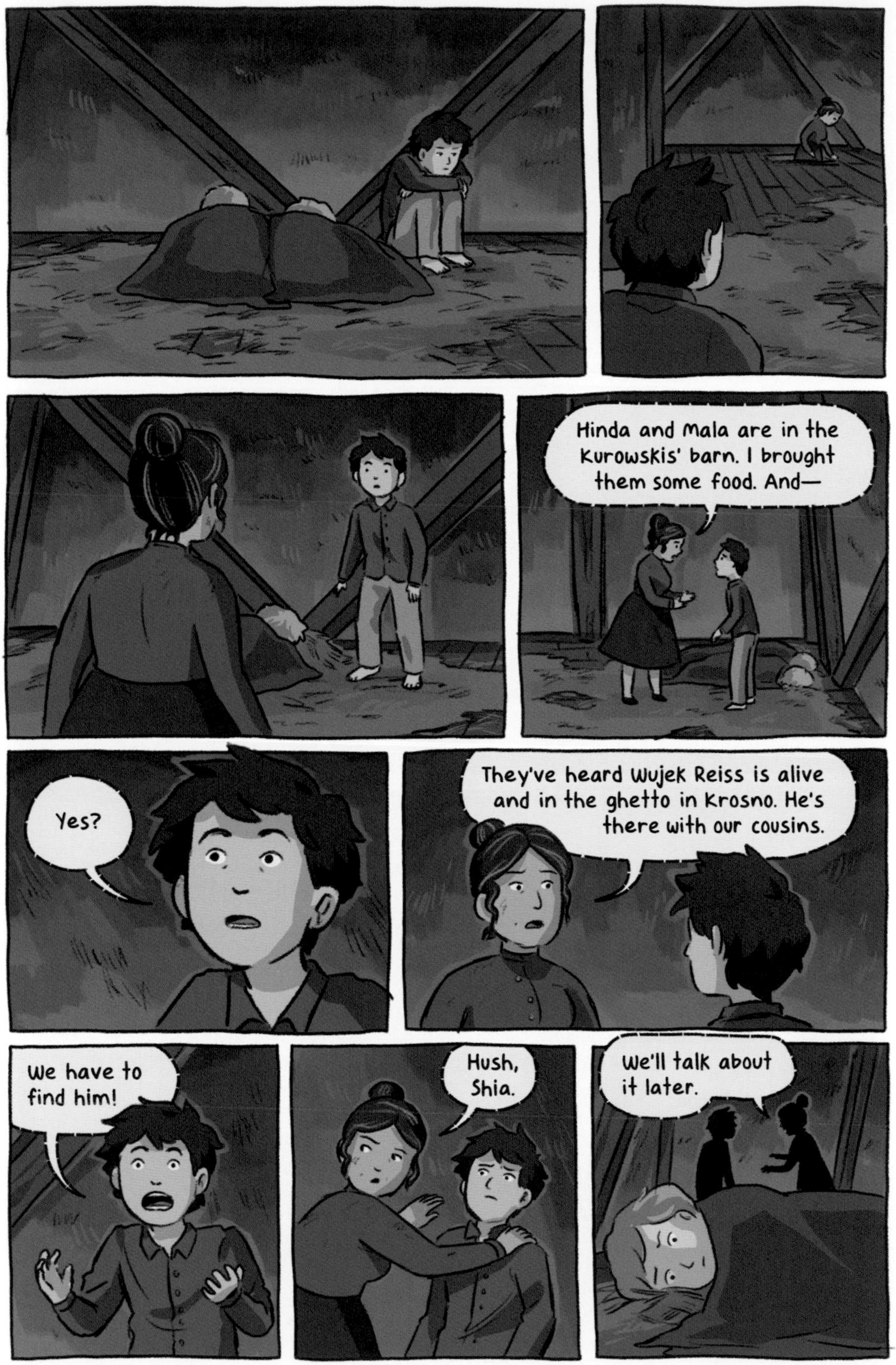
Hinda and Mala are in the Kurowskis' barn. I brought them some food. And—
Yes?
They've heard Wujek Reiss is alive and in the ghetto in Krosno. He's there with our cousins.
We have to find him!
Hush, Shia.
We'll talk about it later.

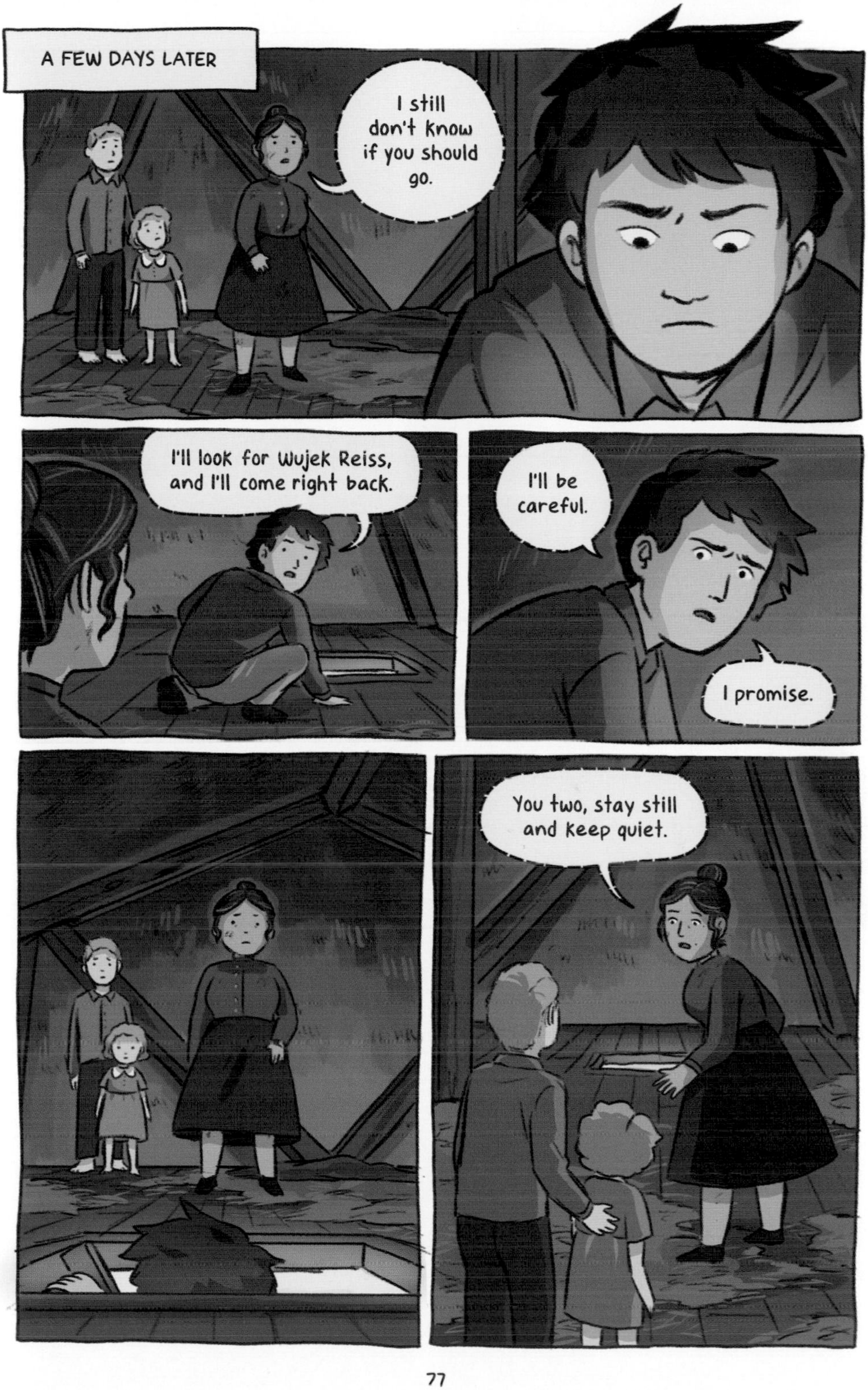
A FEW DAYS LATER
I still don't know if you should go.
I'll look for Wujek Reiss, and I'll come right back.
I'll be careful.
I promise.
You two, stay still and keep quiet.

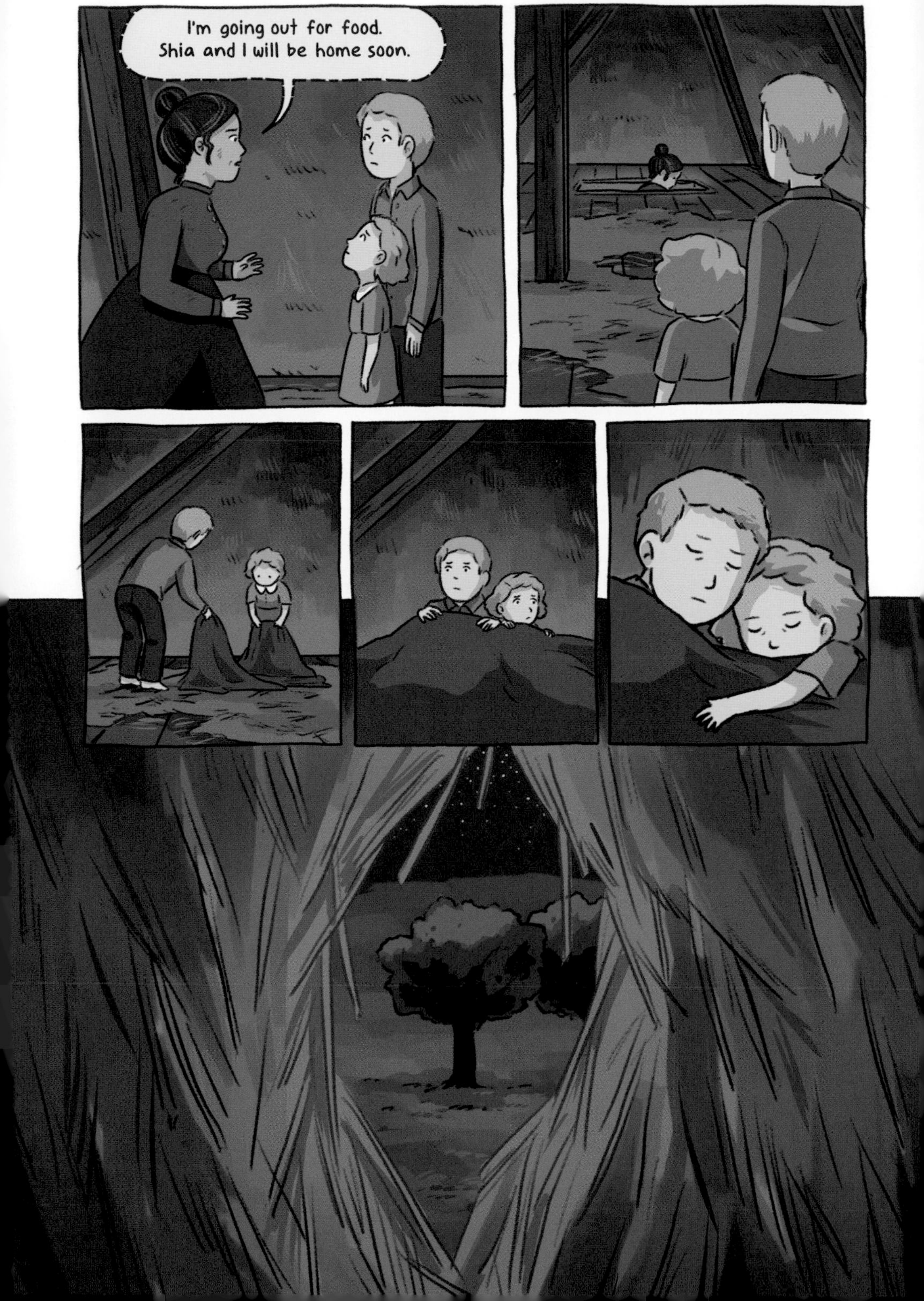
I'm going out for food. Shia and I will be home soon.

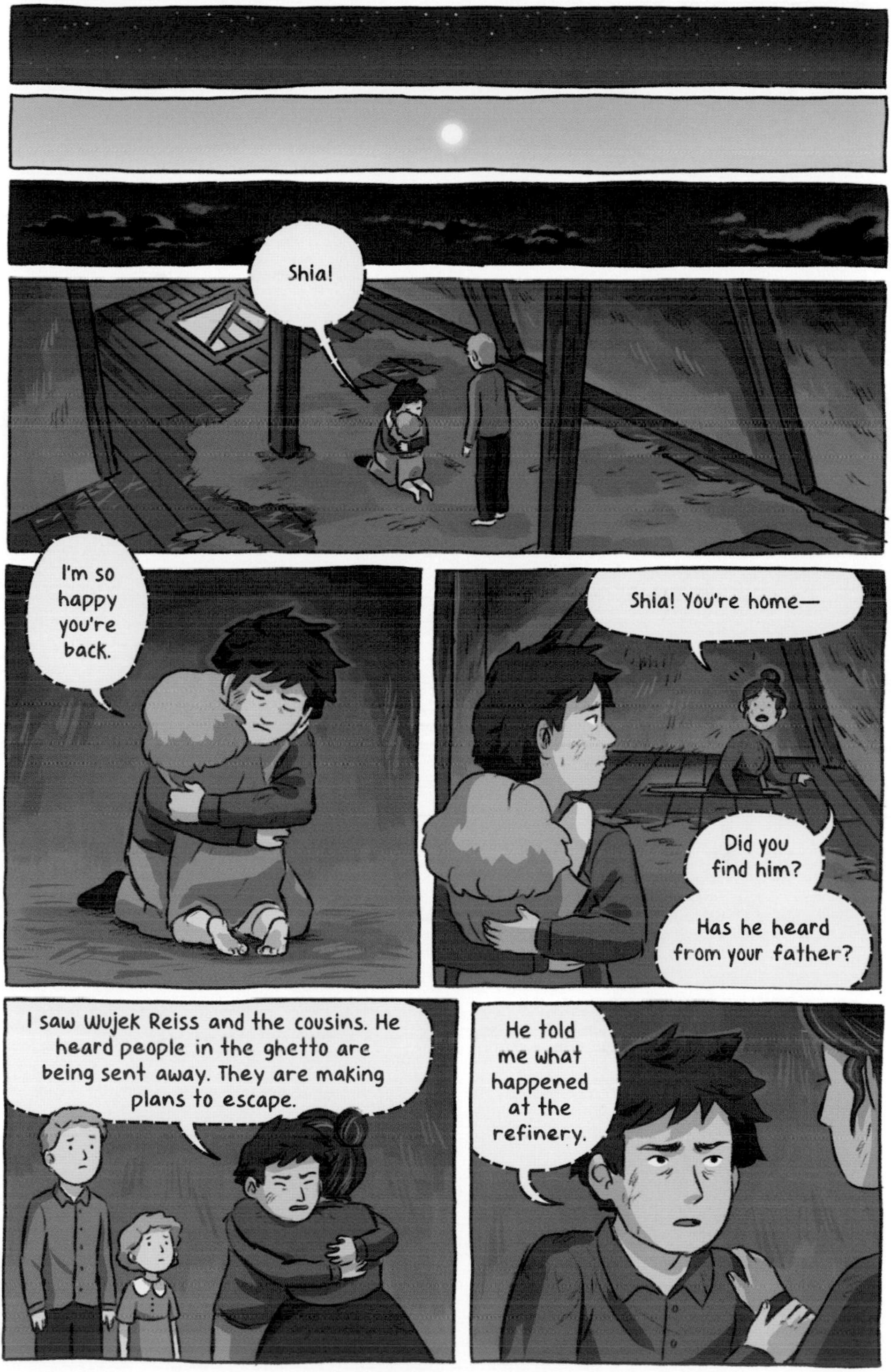
Shia!
I'm so happy you're back.
Shia! You're home—
Did you find him?
Has he heard from your father?
I saw Wujek Reiss and the cousins. He heard people in the ghetto are being sent away. They are making plans to escape.
He told me what happened at the refinery.

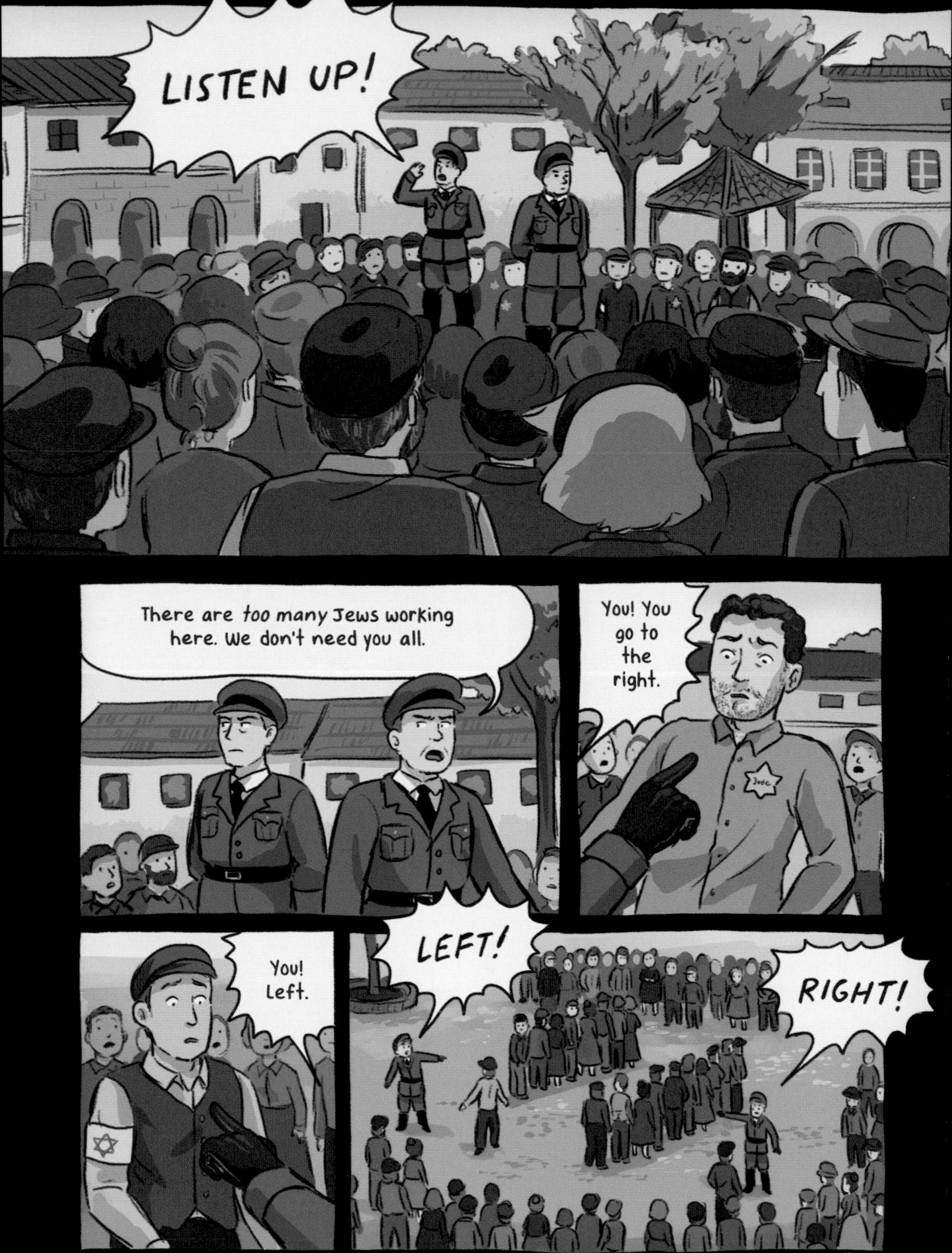
LISTEN UP!
There are *too many* Jews working here. We don't need you all.
You! You go to the right.
Jude
You! Left.
LEFT!
RIGHT!

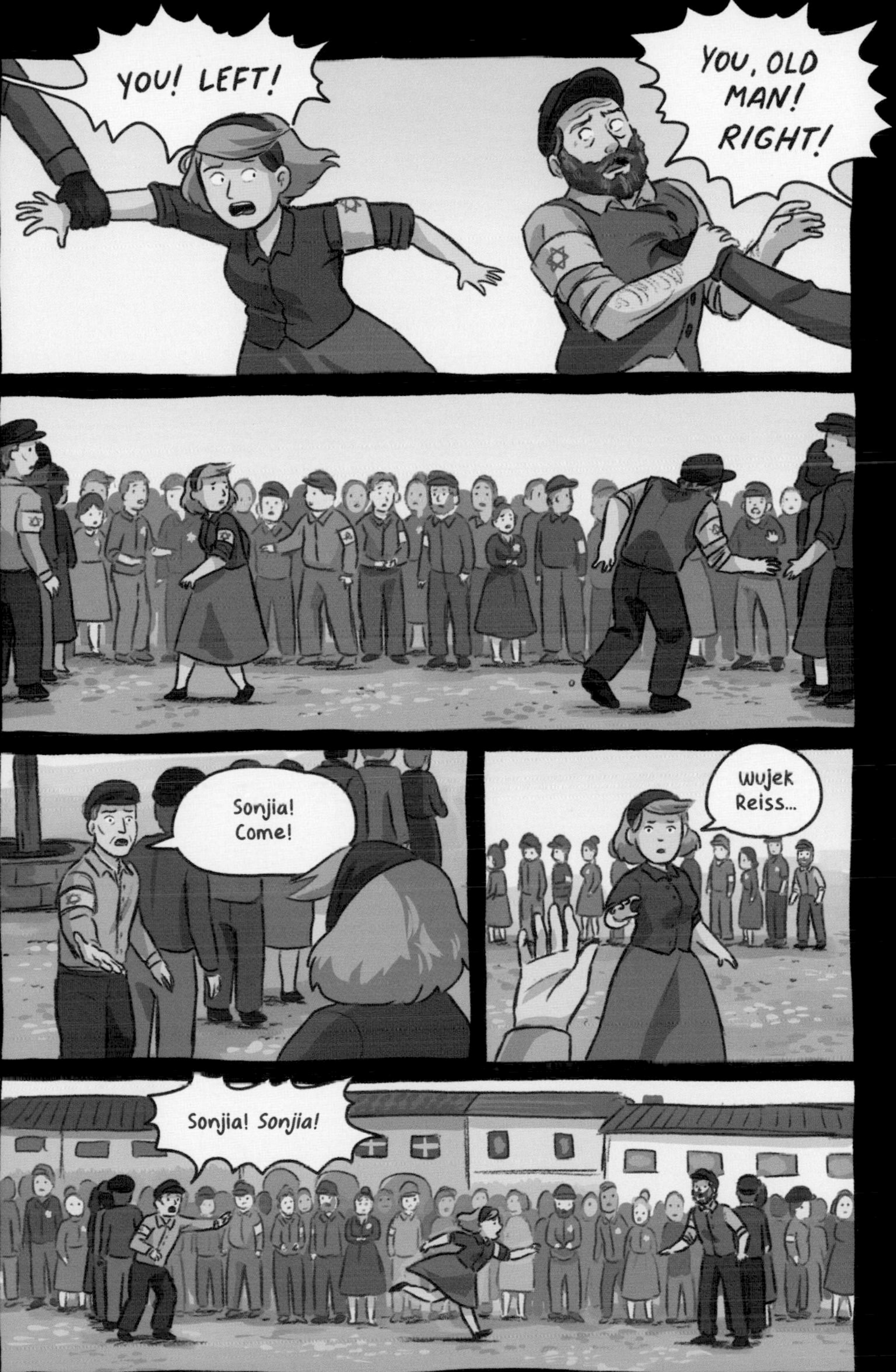
YOU! LEFT!
YOU, OLD MAN! RIGHT!
Sonjia! Come!
Wujek Reiss...
Sonjia! Sonjia!

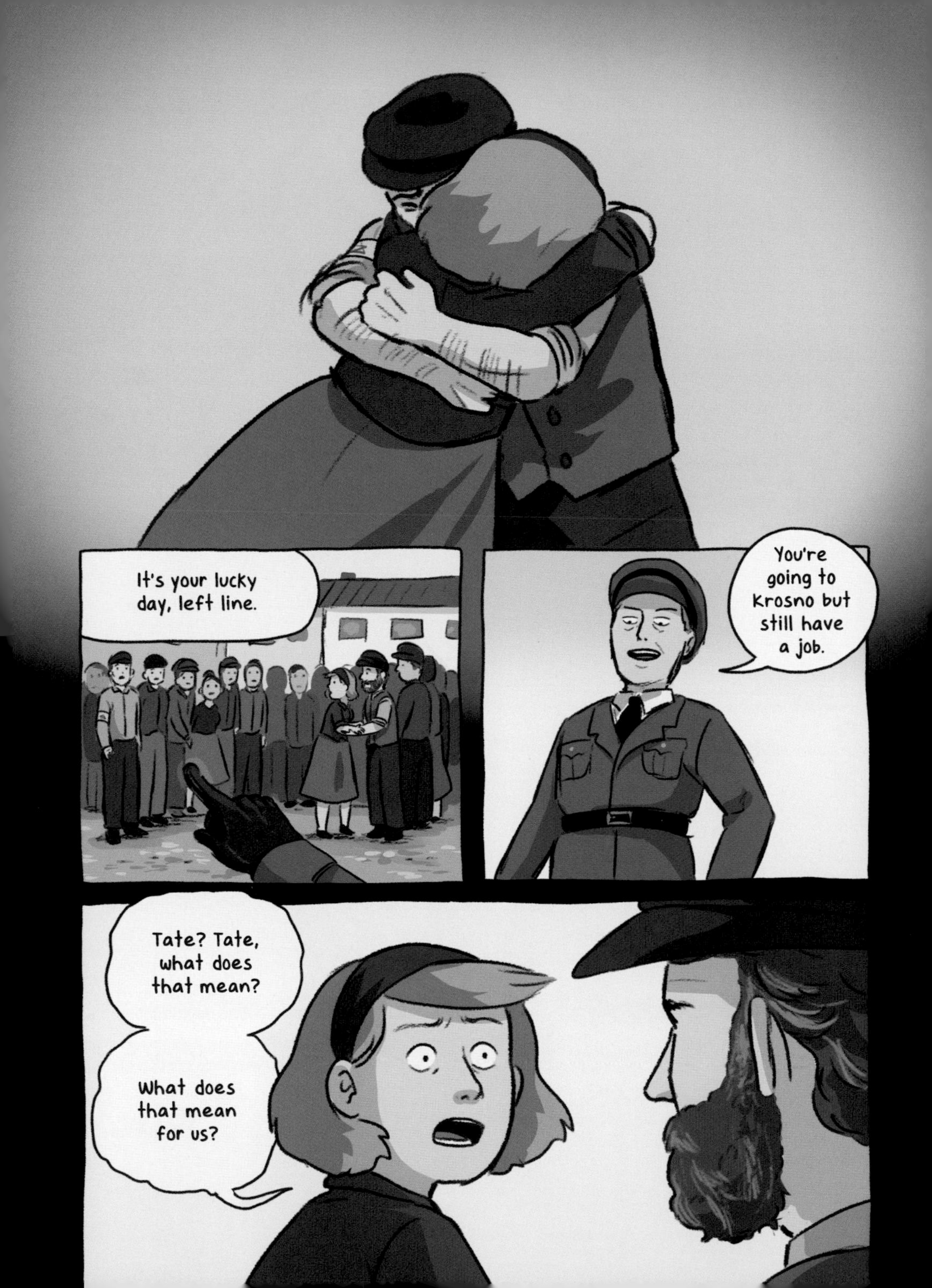
It's your lucky day, left line.
You're going to Krosno but still have a job.
Tate? Tate, what does that mean?
What does that mean for us?

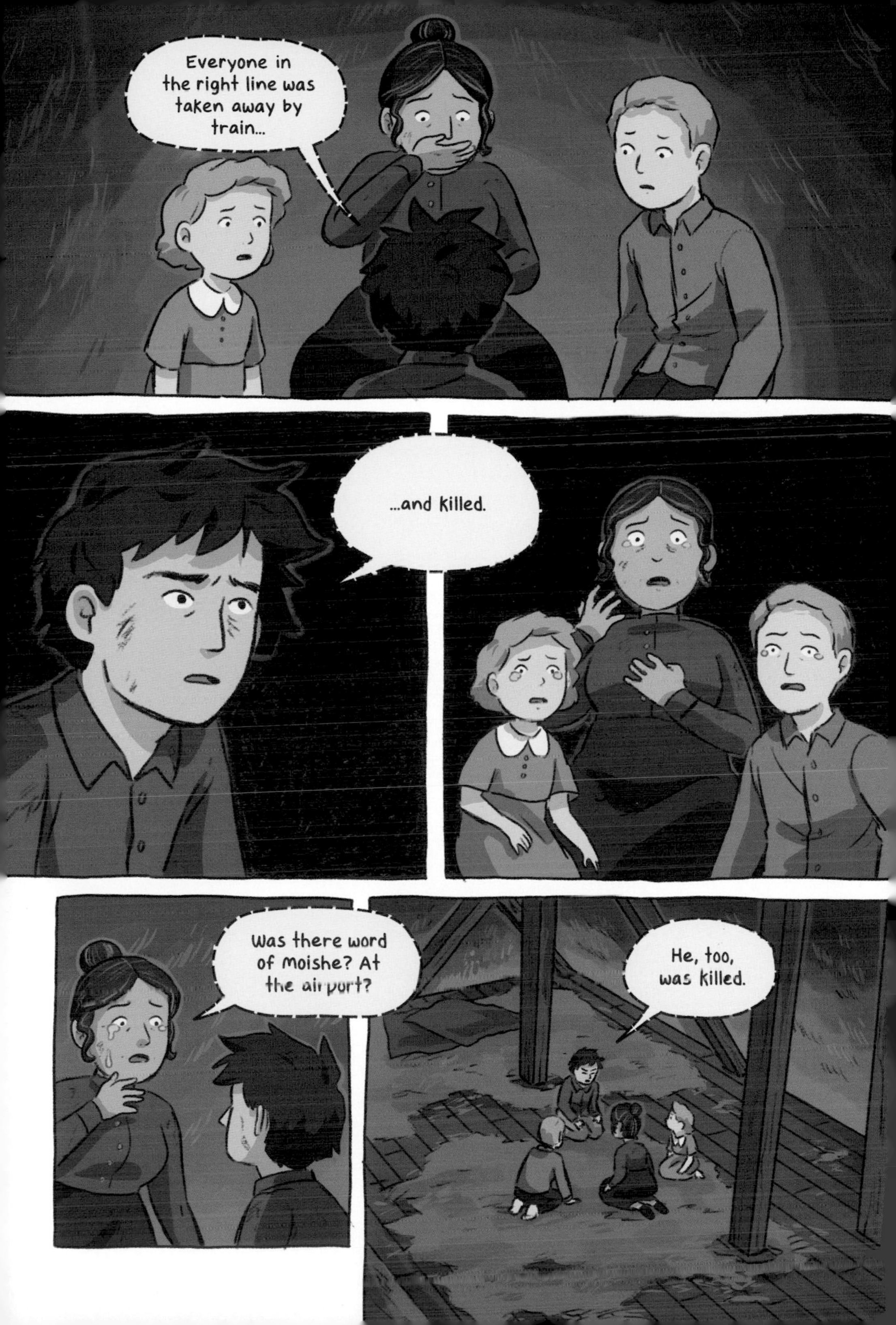
Everyone in the right line was taken away by train...
...and killed.
Was there word of Moishe? At the airport?
He, too, was killed.

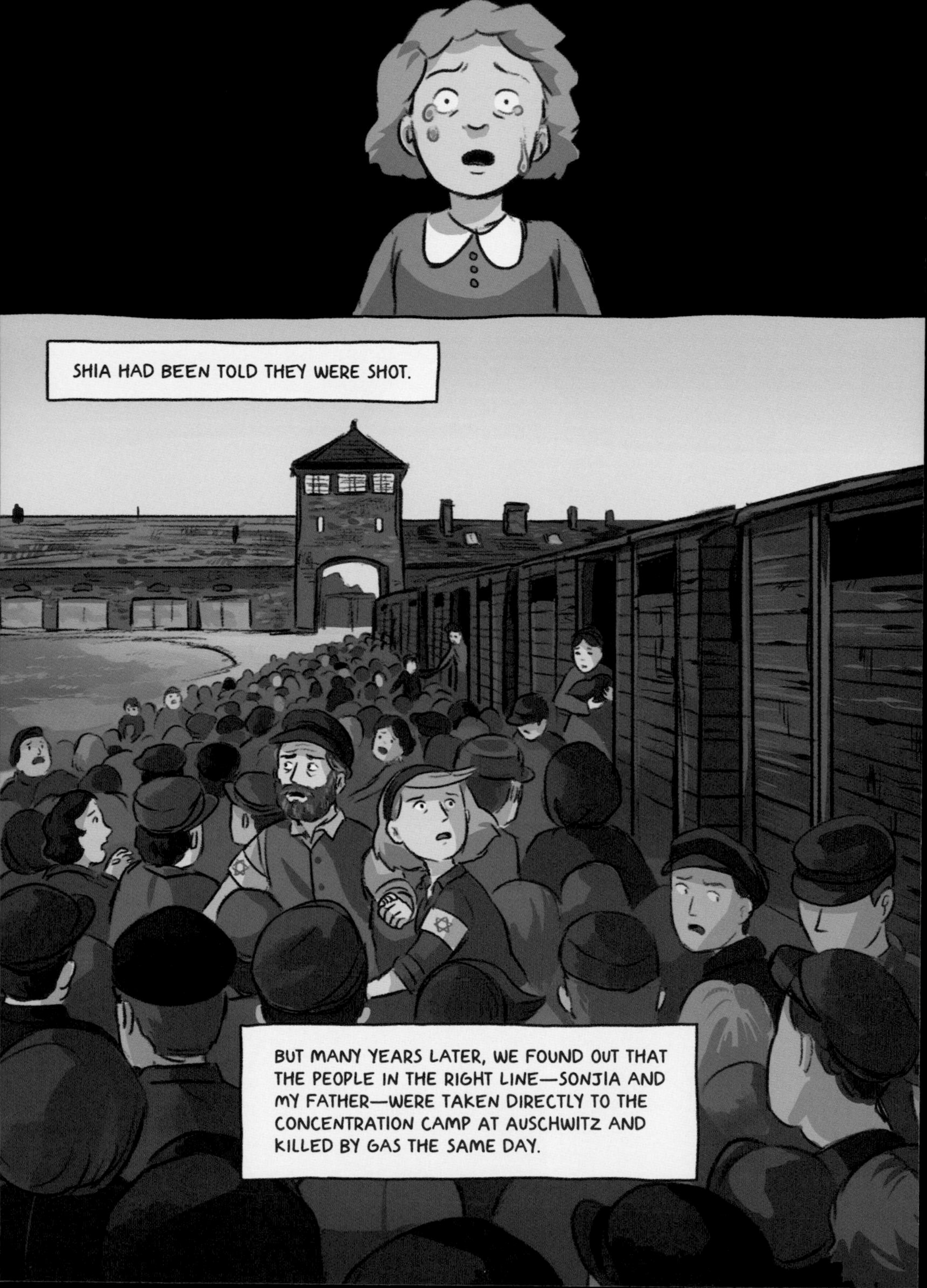
SHIA HAD BEEN TOLD THEY WERE SHOT.
BUT MANY YEARS LATER, WE FOUND OUT THAT THE PEOPLE IN THE RIGHT LINE—SONJIA AND MY FATHER—WERE TAKEN DIRECTLY TO THE CONCENTRATION CAMP AT AUSCHWITZ AND KILLED BY GAS THE SAME DAY.

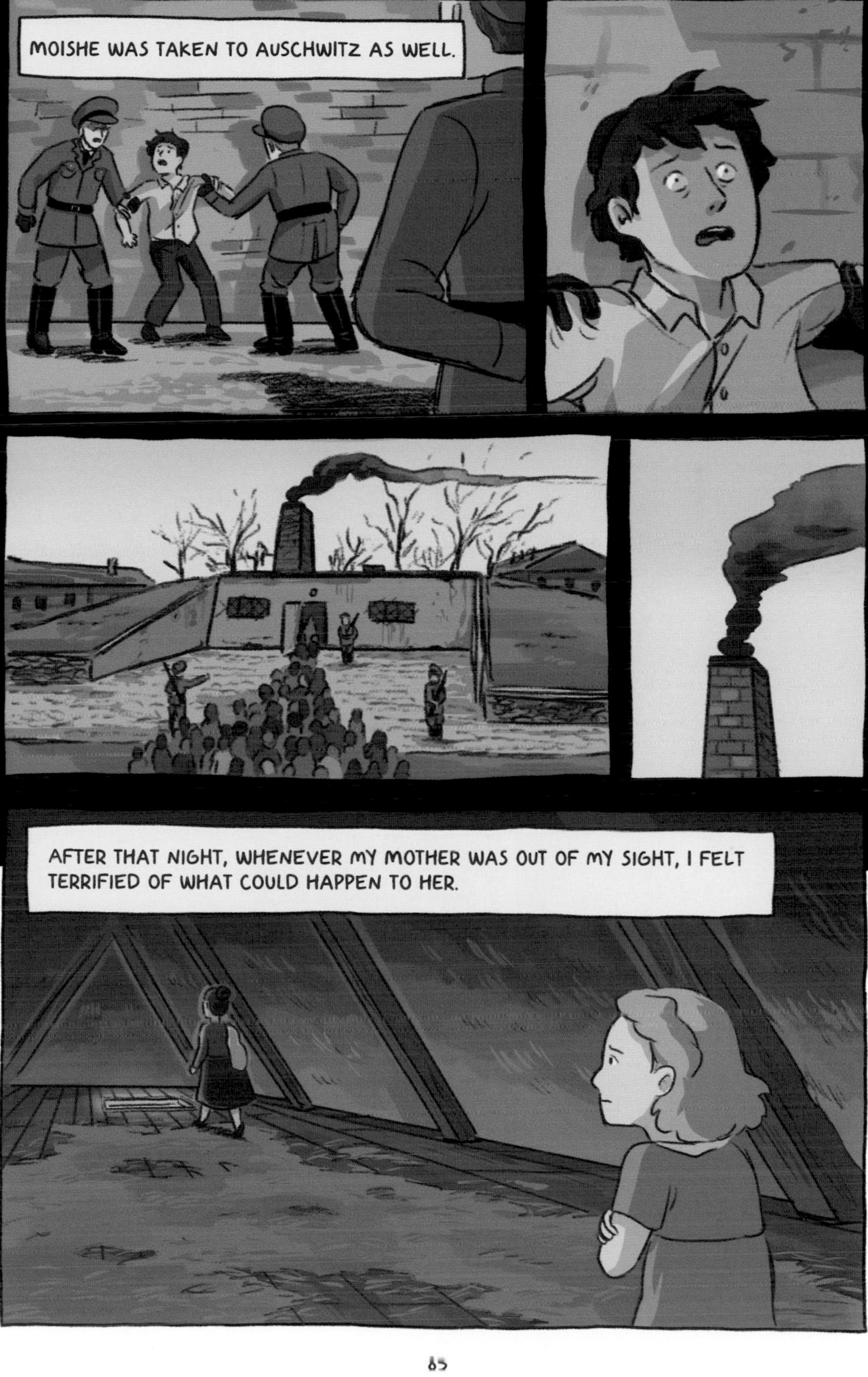
MOISHE WAS TAKEN TO AUSCHWITZ AS WELL.
AFTER THAT NIGHT, WHENEVER MY MOTHER WAS OUT OF MY SIGHT, I FELT TERRIFIED OF WHAT COULD HAPPEN TO HER.

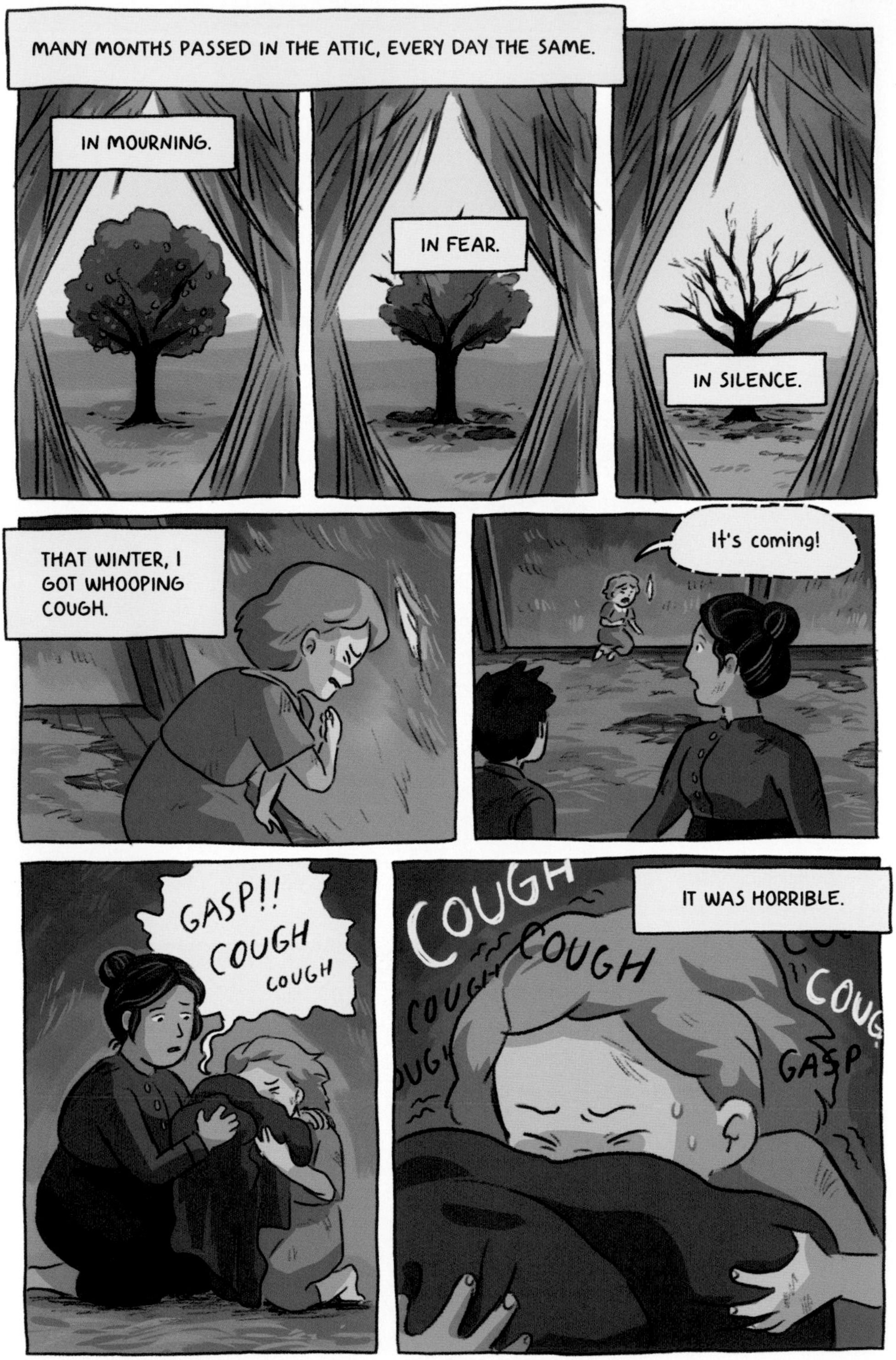
MANY MONTHS PASSED IN THE ATTIC, EVERY DAY THE SAME.
IN MOURNING.
IN FEAR.
IN SILENCE.
THAT WINTER, I GOT WHOOPING COUGH.
It's coming!
GASP!! COUGH COUGH
IT WAS HORRIBLE.
COUGH
COUGH
GASP

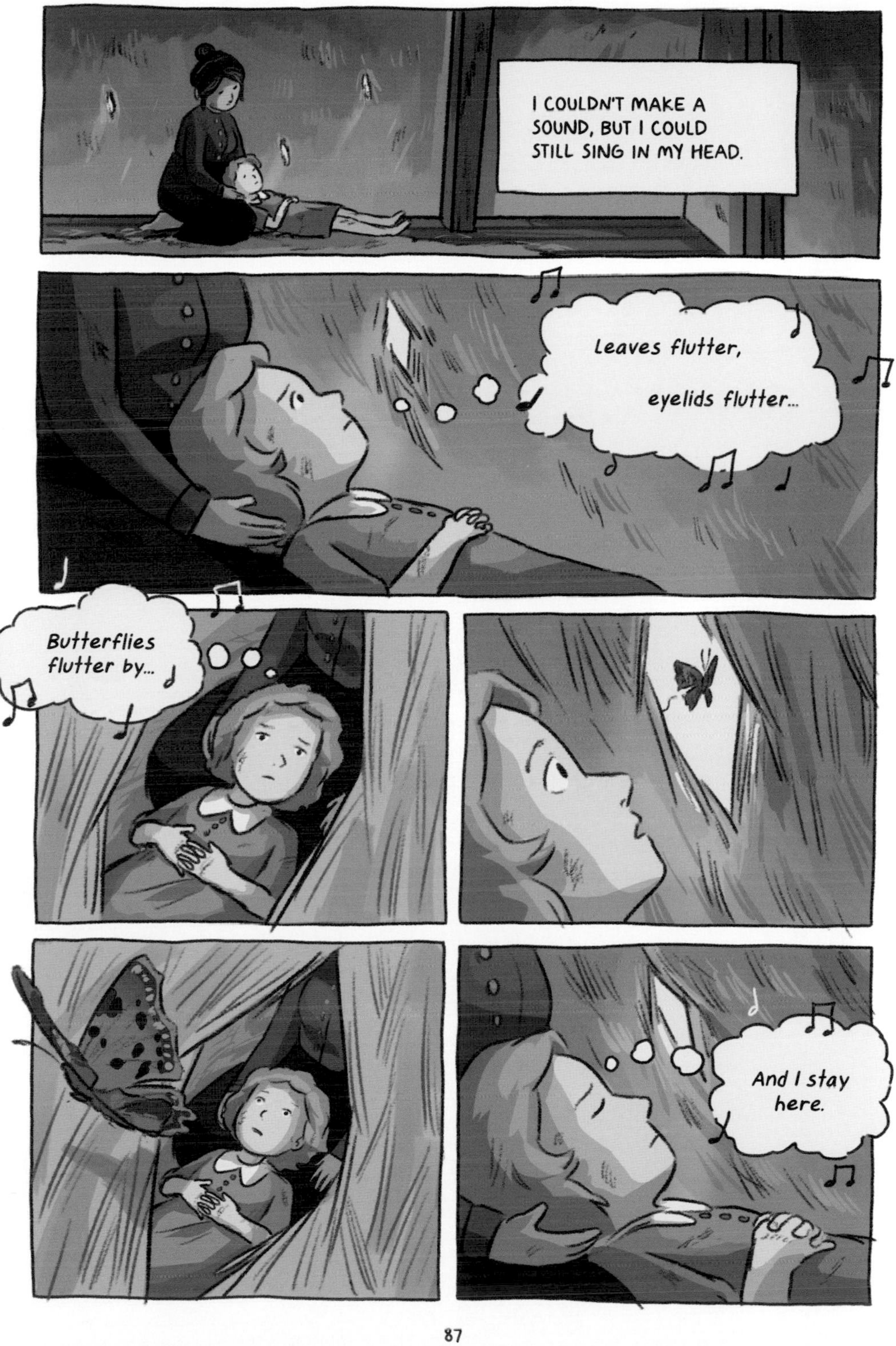
I COULDN'T MAKE A SOUND, BUT I COULD STILL SING IN MY HEAD.
Leaves flutter, eyelids flutter...
Butterflies flutter by...
And I stay here.

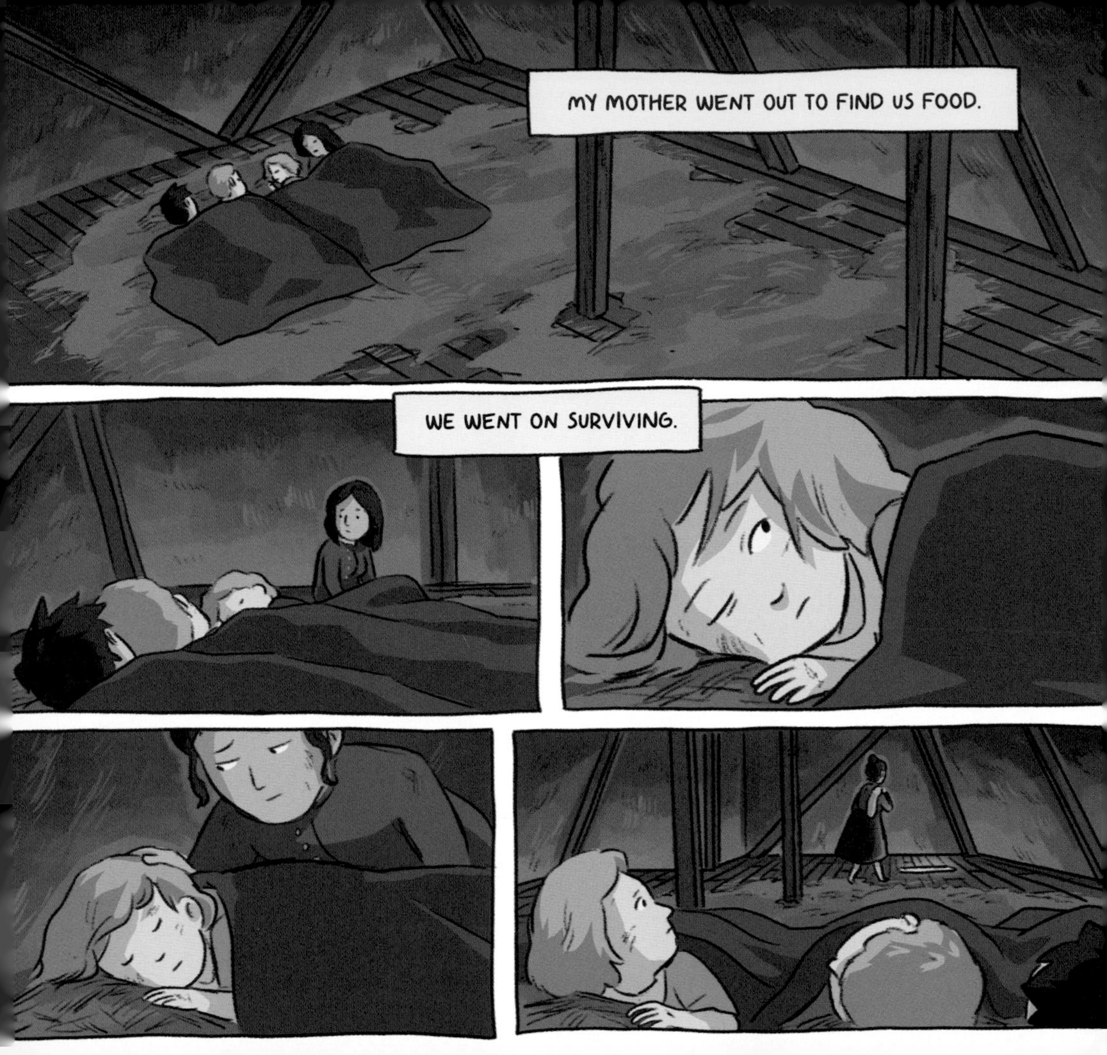
MY MOTHER WENT OUT TO FIND US FOOD.
WE WENT ON SURVIVING.

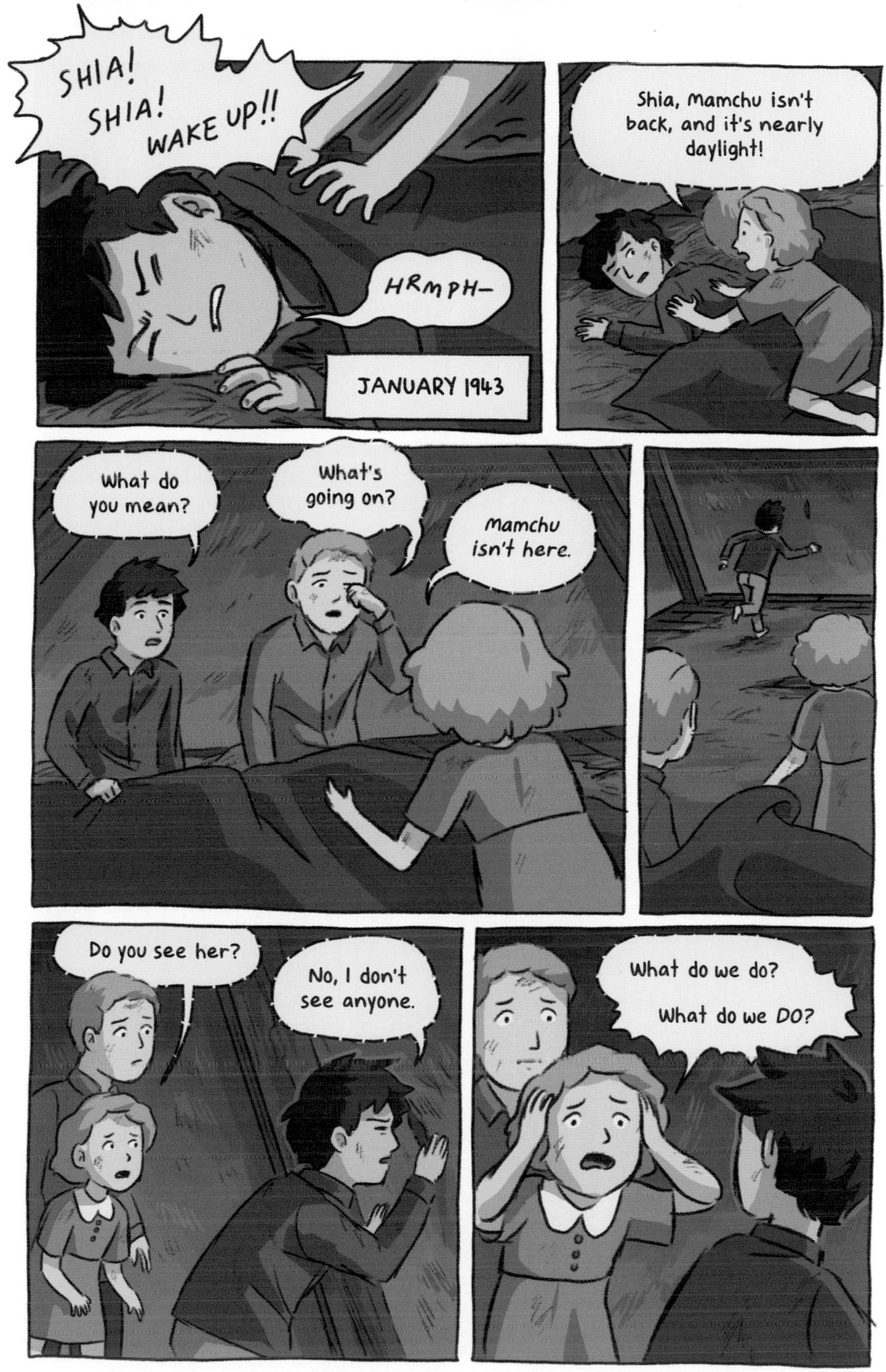
SHIA! SHIA! WAKE UP!!
HRMPH–
JANUARY 1943
Shia, mamchu isn't back, and it's nearly daylight!
What do you mean?
What's going on?
mamchu isn't here.
Do you see her?
No, I don't see anyone.
What do we do?
What do we DO?

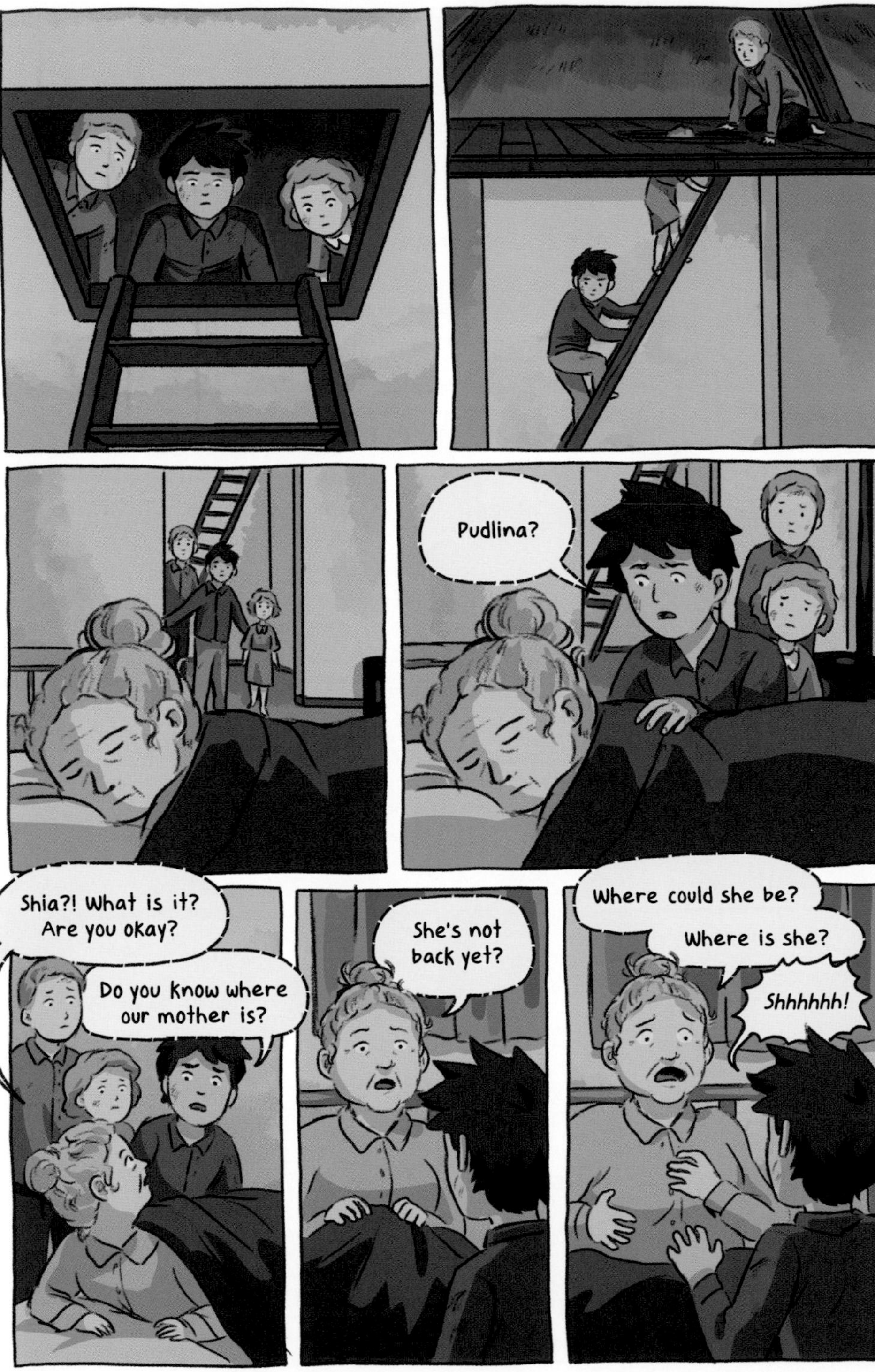
Pudlina?
Shia?! What is it? Are you okay?
Do you know where our mother is?
She's not back yet?
Where could she be?
Where is she?
Shhhhhh!

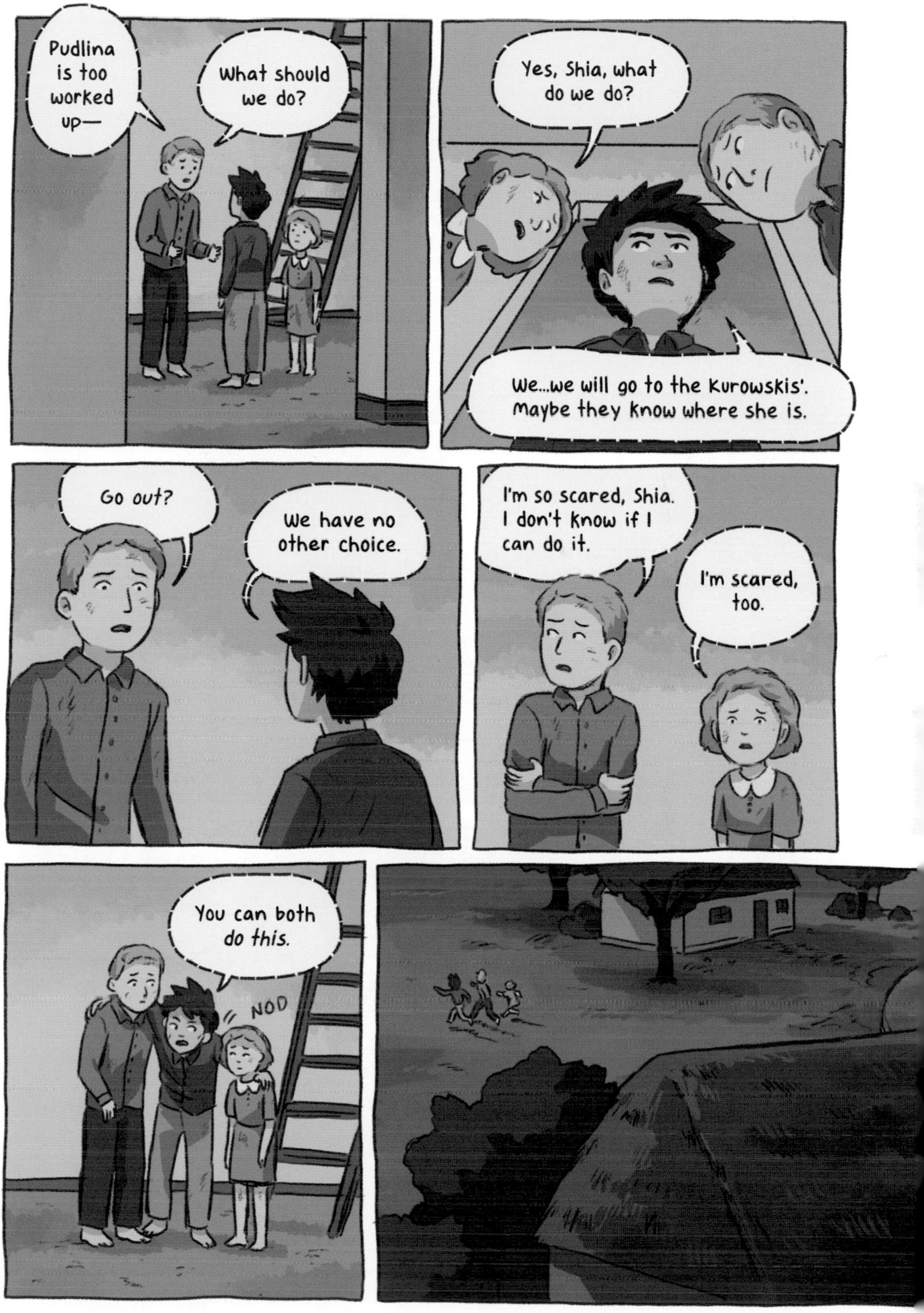
Pudlina is too worked up—
What should we do?
Yes, Shia, what do we do?
We...we will go to the Kurowskis'. Maybe they know where she is.
Go out?
We have no other choice.
I'm so scared, Shia. I don't know if I can do it.
I'm scared, too.
You can both do this.
NOD

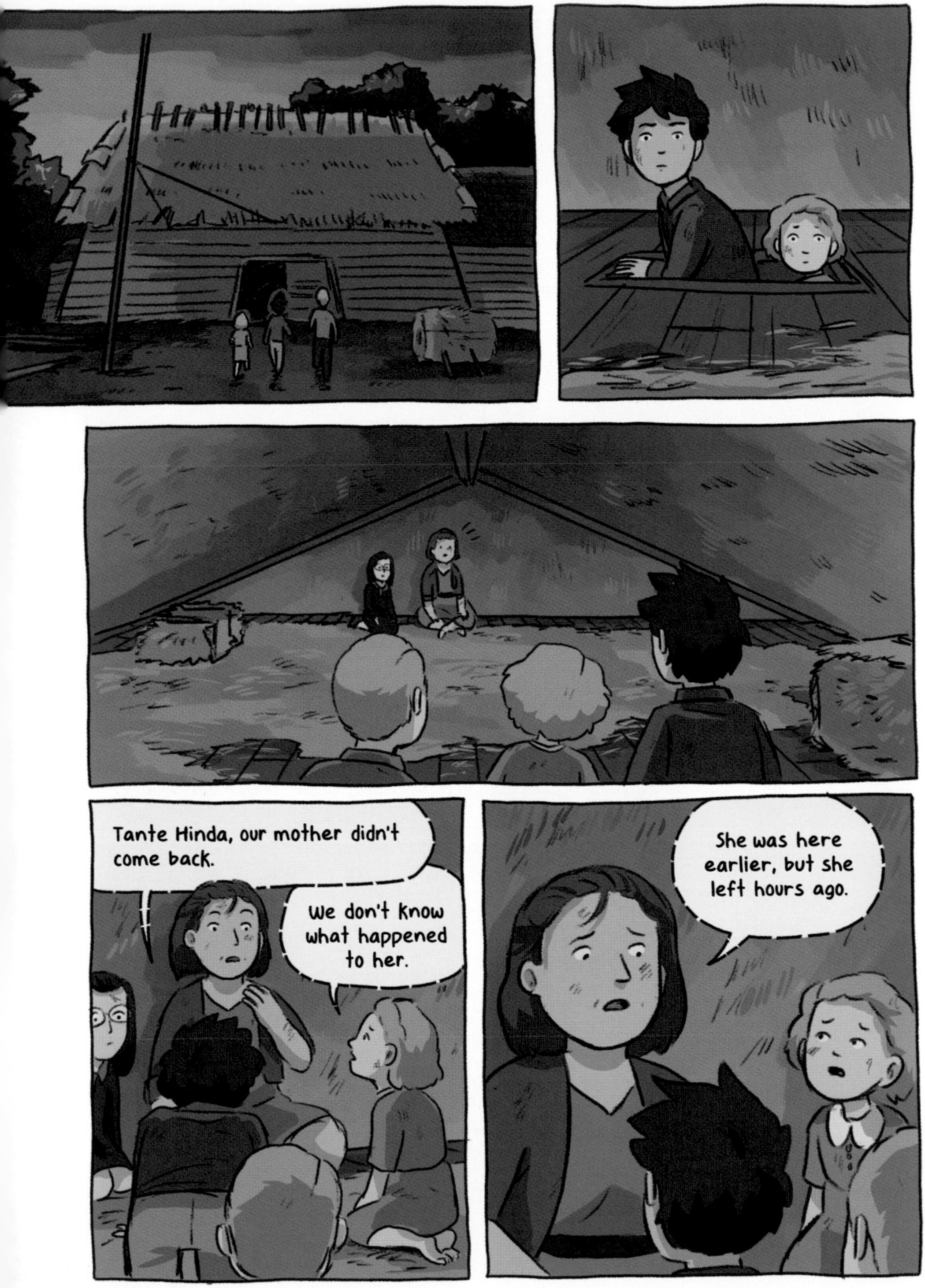
Tante Hinda, our mother didn't come back.
We don't know what happened to her.
She was here earlier, but she left hours ago.

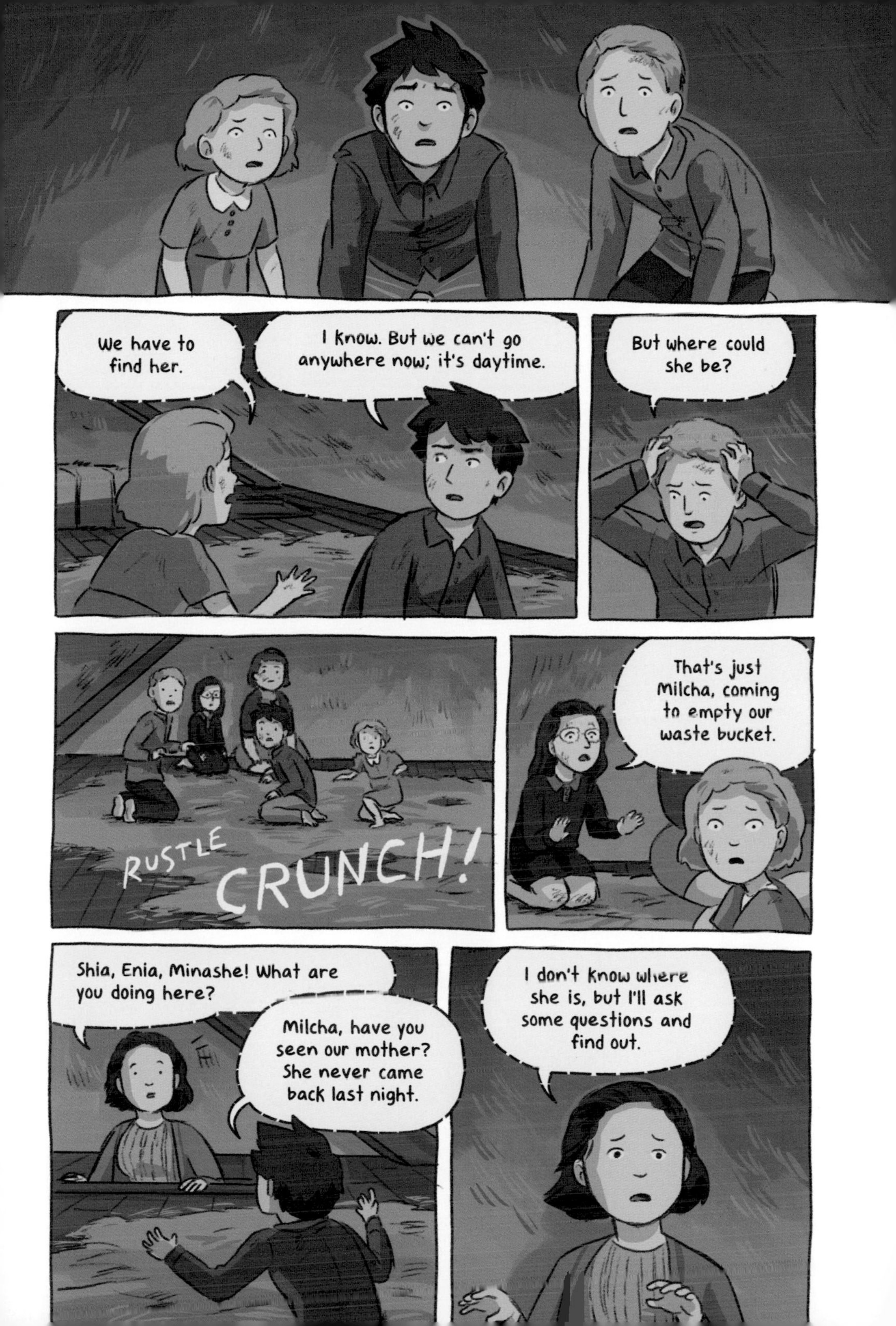
We have to find her.
I know. But we can't go anywhere now; it's daytime.
But where could she be?
RUSTLE
CRUNCH!
That's just Milcha, coming to empty our waste bucket.
Shia, Enia, Minashe! What are you doing here?
Milcha, have you seen our mother? She never came back last night.
I don't know where she is, but I'll ask some questions and find out.

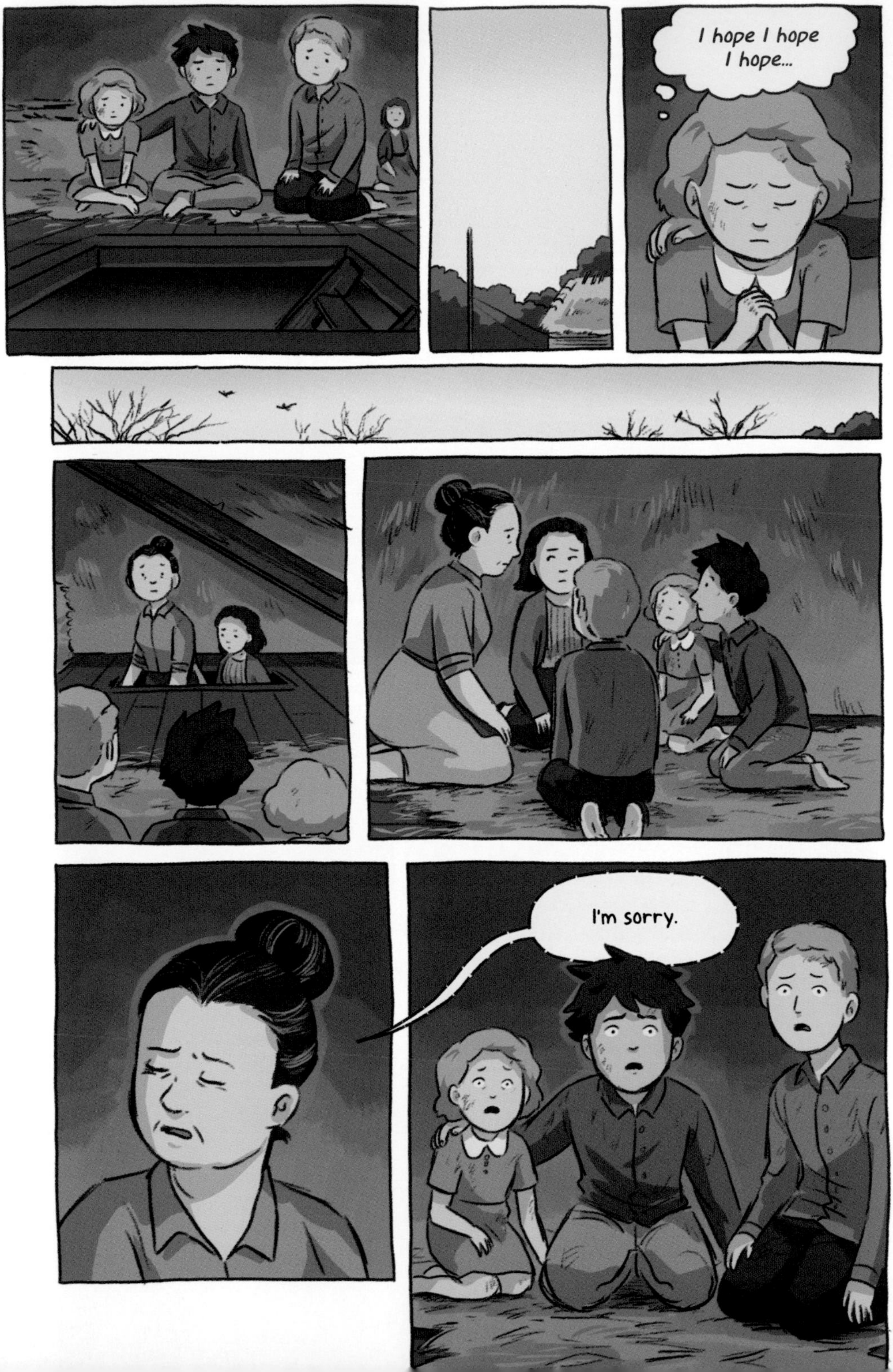
I hope I hope
I hope...
I'm sorry.

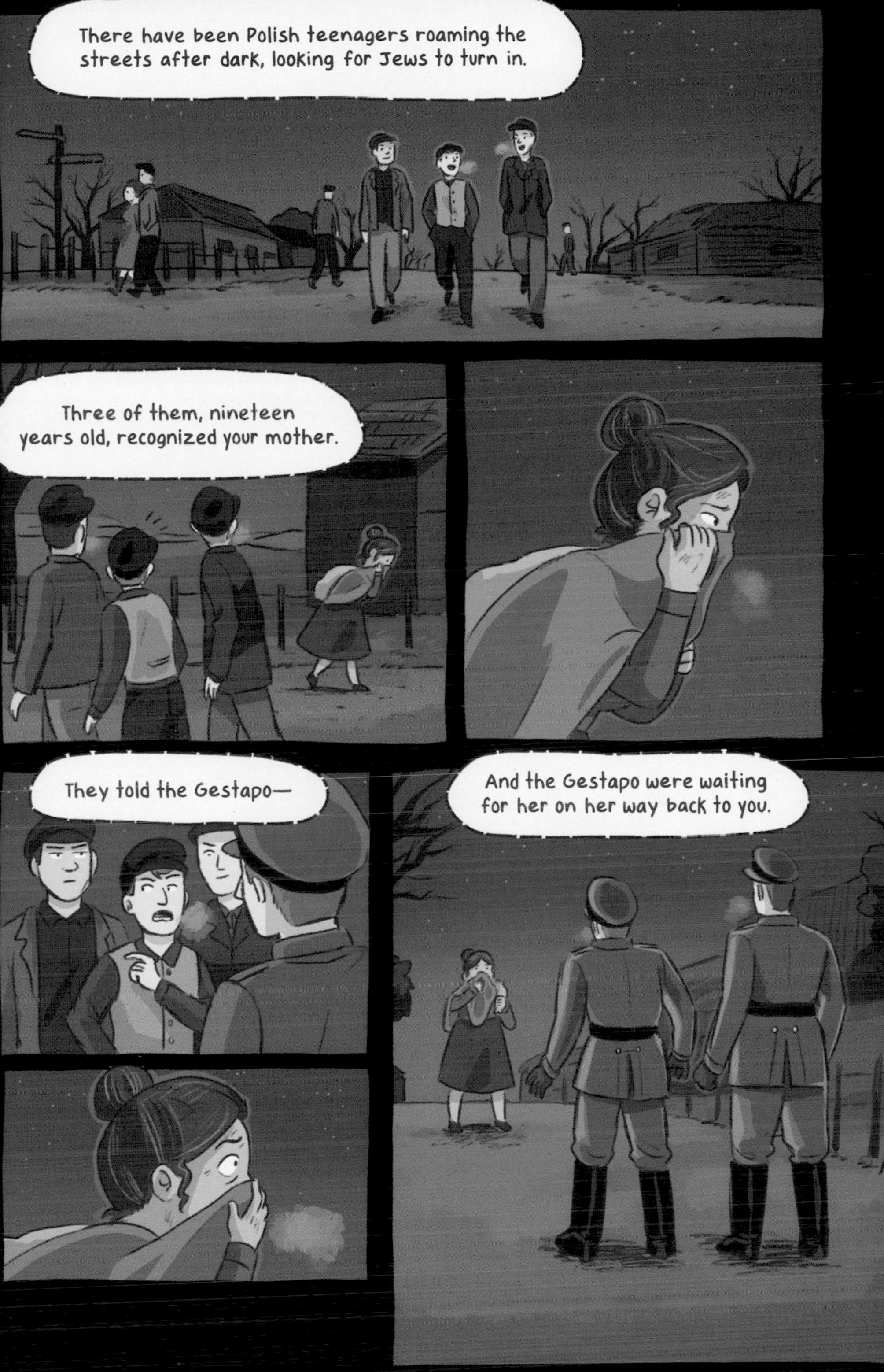
There have been Polish teenagers roaming the streets after dark, looking for Jews to turn in.
Three of them, nineteen years old, recognized your mother.
They told the Gestapo—
And the Gestapo were waiting for her on her way back to you.

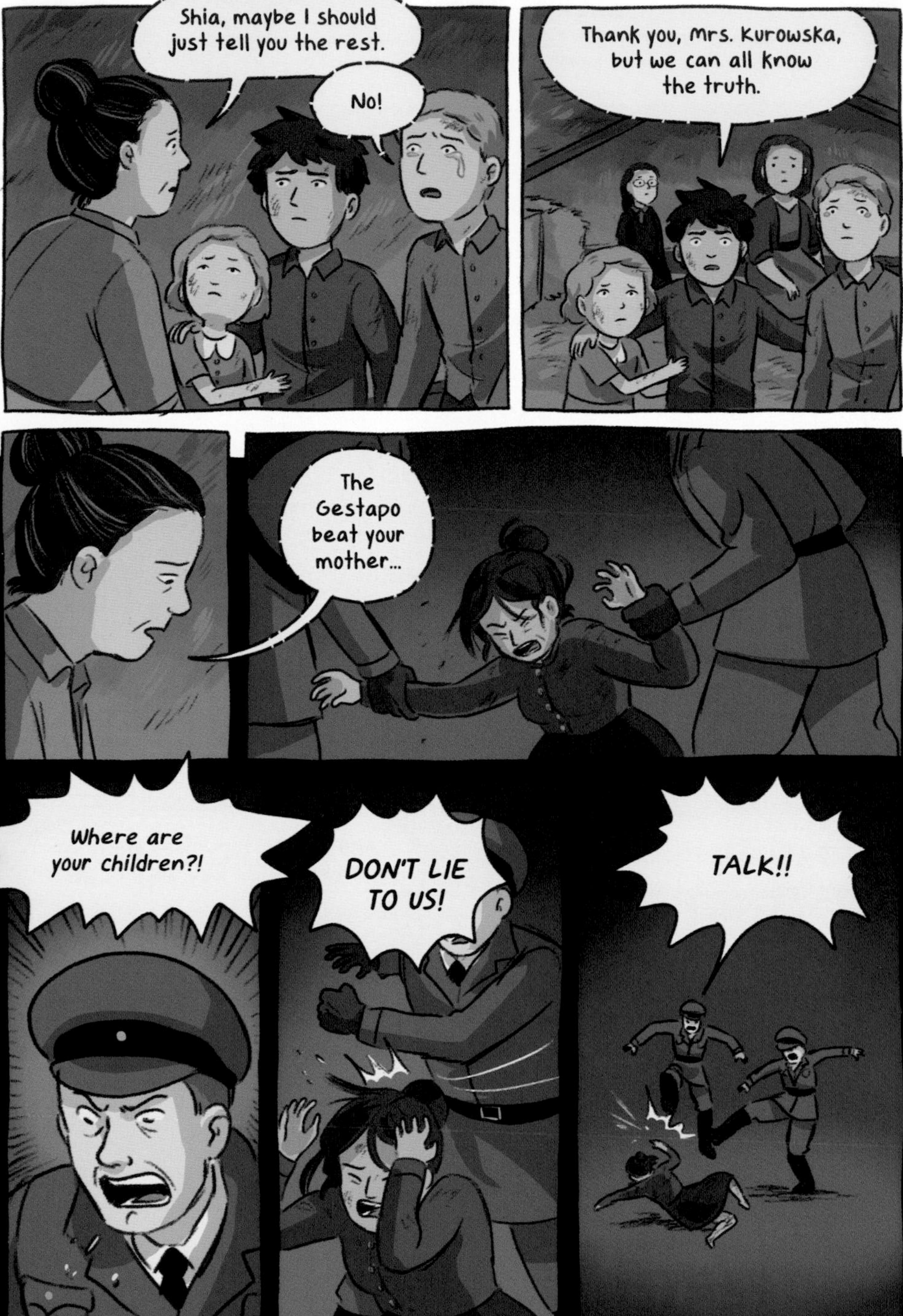
Shia, maybe I should just tell you the rest.
No!
Thank you, Mrs. Kurowska, but we can all know the truth.
The Gestapo beat your mother...
Where are your children?!
DON'T LIE TO US!
TALK!!

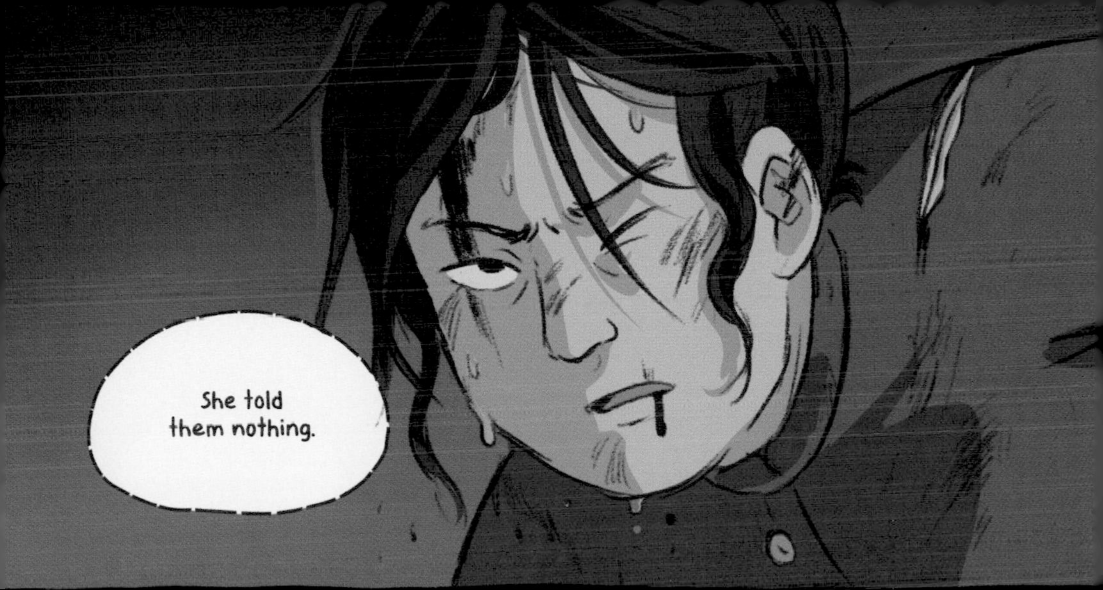
She told them nothing.

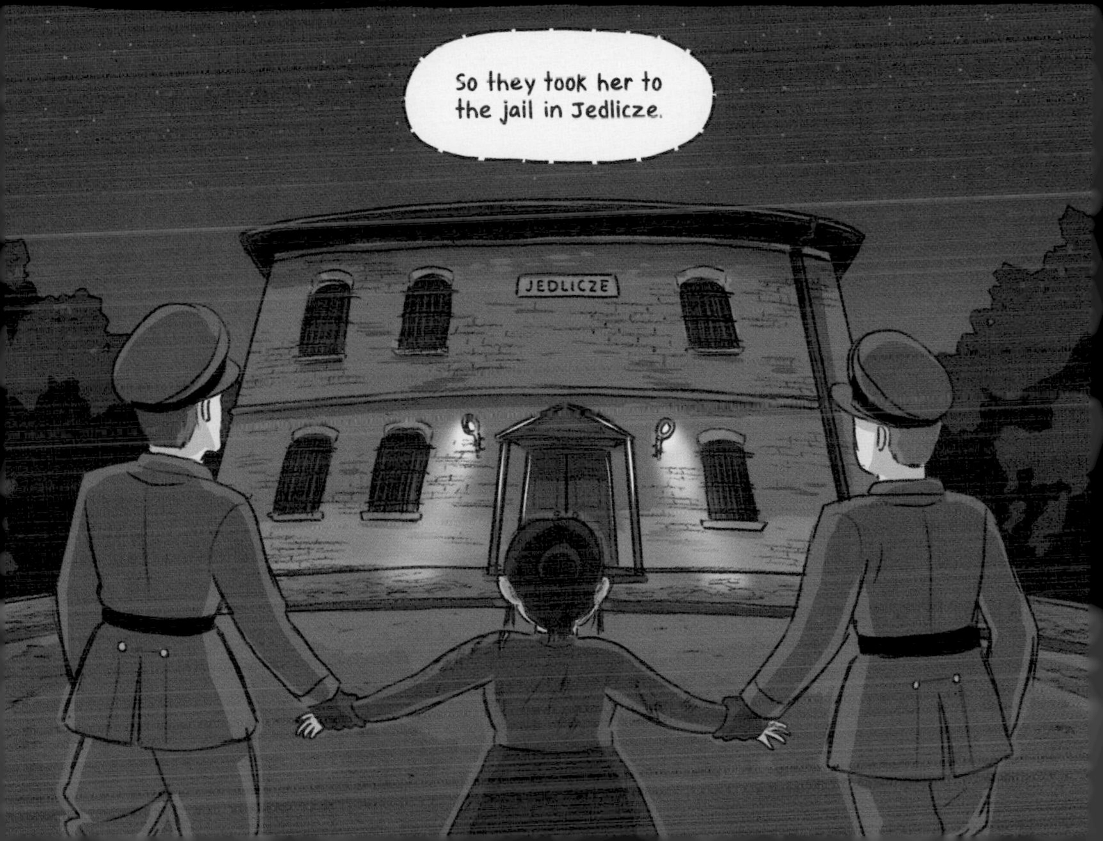
So they took her to the jail in Jedlicze.
JEDLICZE

Every morning, a German soldier comes to the Jedlicze jail to see if any Jews have been found during the night.

BANG

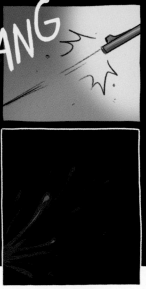

He shoots all the prisoners.

I'm so sorry, children.

Your mother is gone.

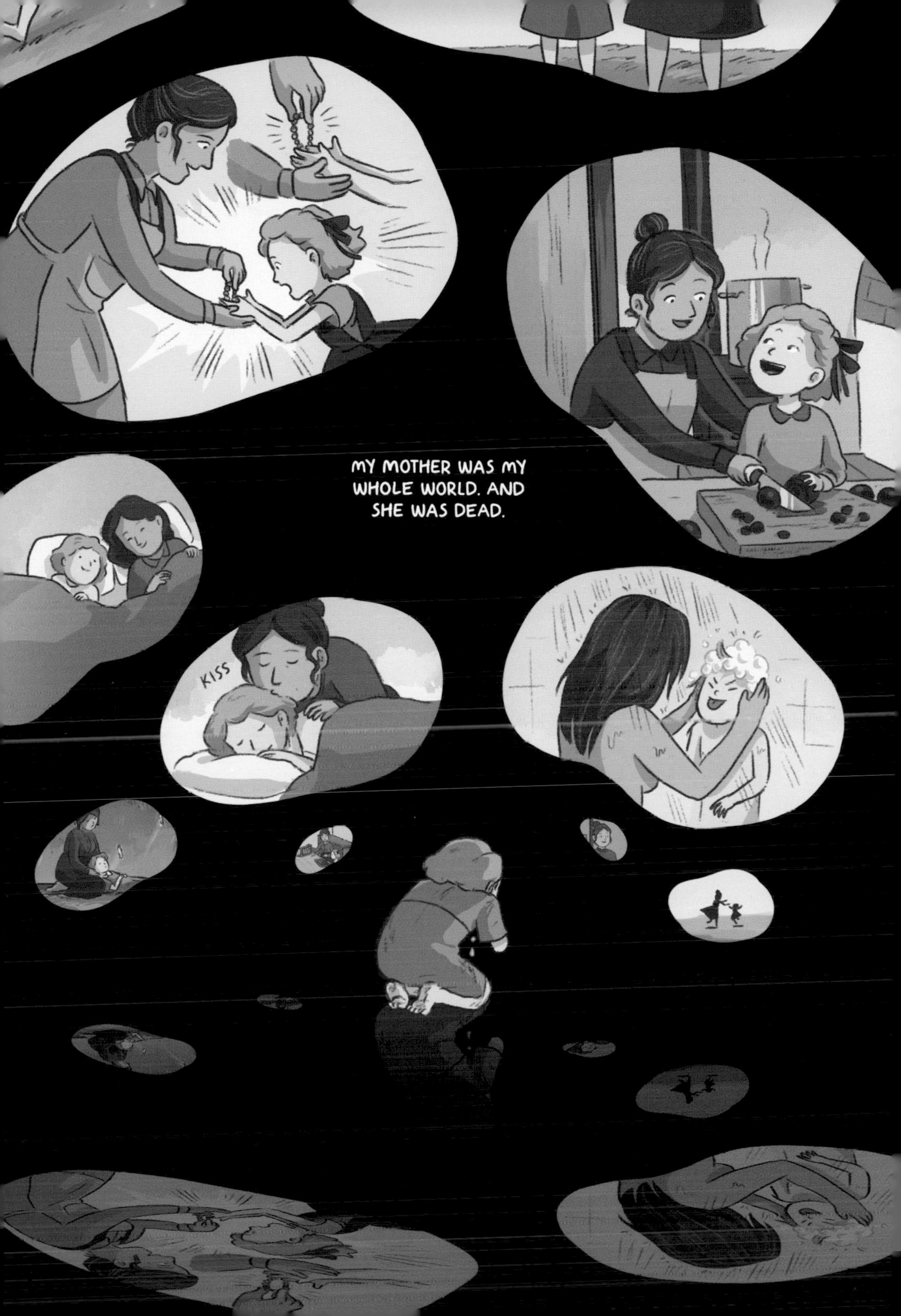
MY MOTHER WAS MY WHOLE WORLD. AND SHE WAS DEAD.
KISS

THE JOURNEY BACK TO PUDLINA'S WAS A BLUR.

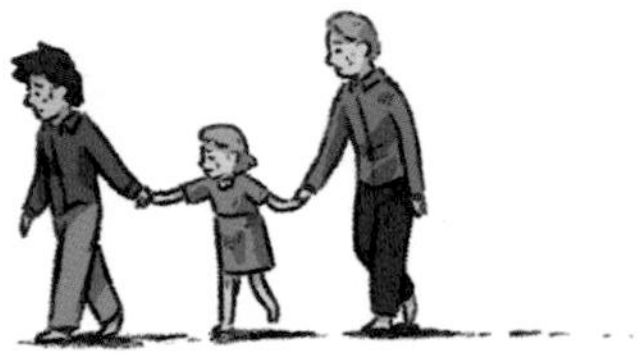

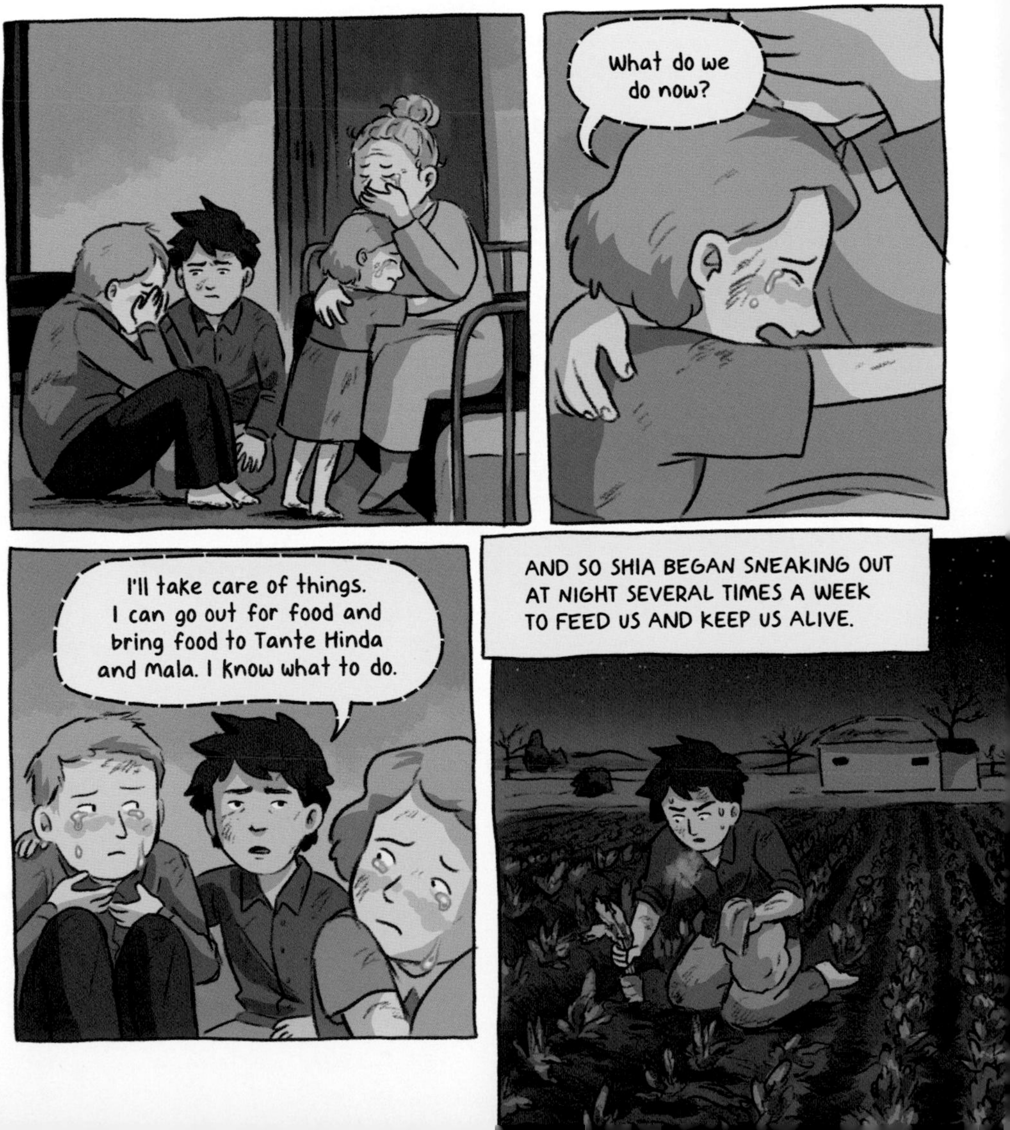
What do we do now?
I'll take care of things. I can go out for food and bring food to Tante Hinda and Mala. I know what to do.
AND SO SHIA BEGAN SNEAKING OUT AT NIGHT SEVERAL TIMES A WEEK TO FEED US AND KEEP US ALIVE.

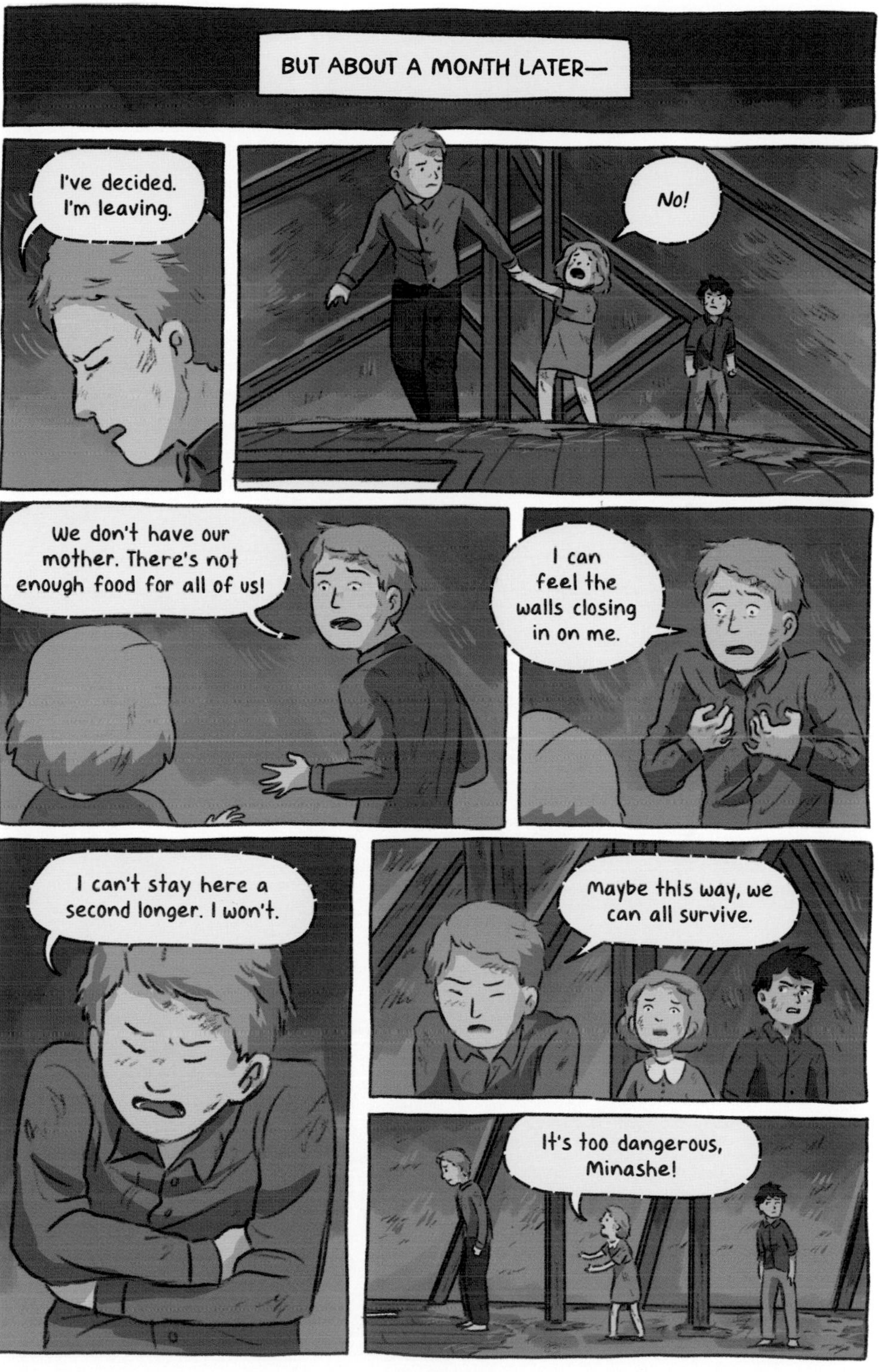
BUT ABOUT A MONTH LATER—
I've decided. I'm leaving.
No!
We don't have our mother. There's not enough food for all of us!
I can feel the walls closing in on me.
I can't stay here a second longer. I won't.
Maybe this way, we can all survive.
It's too dangerous, Minashe!

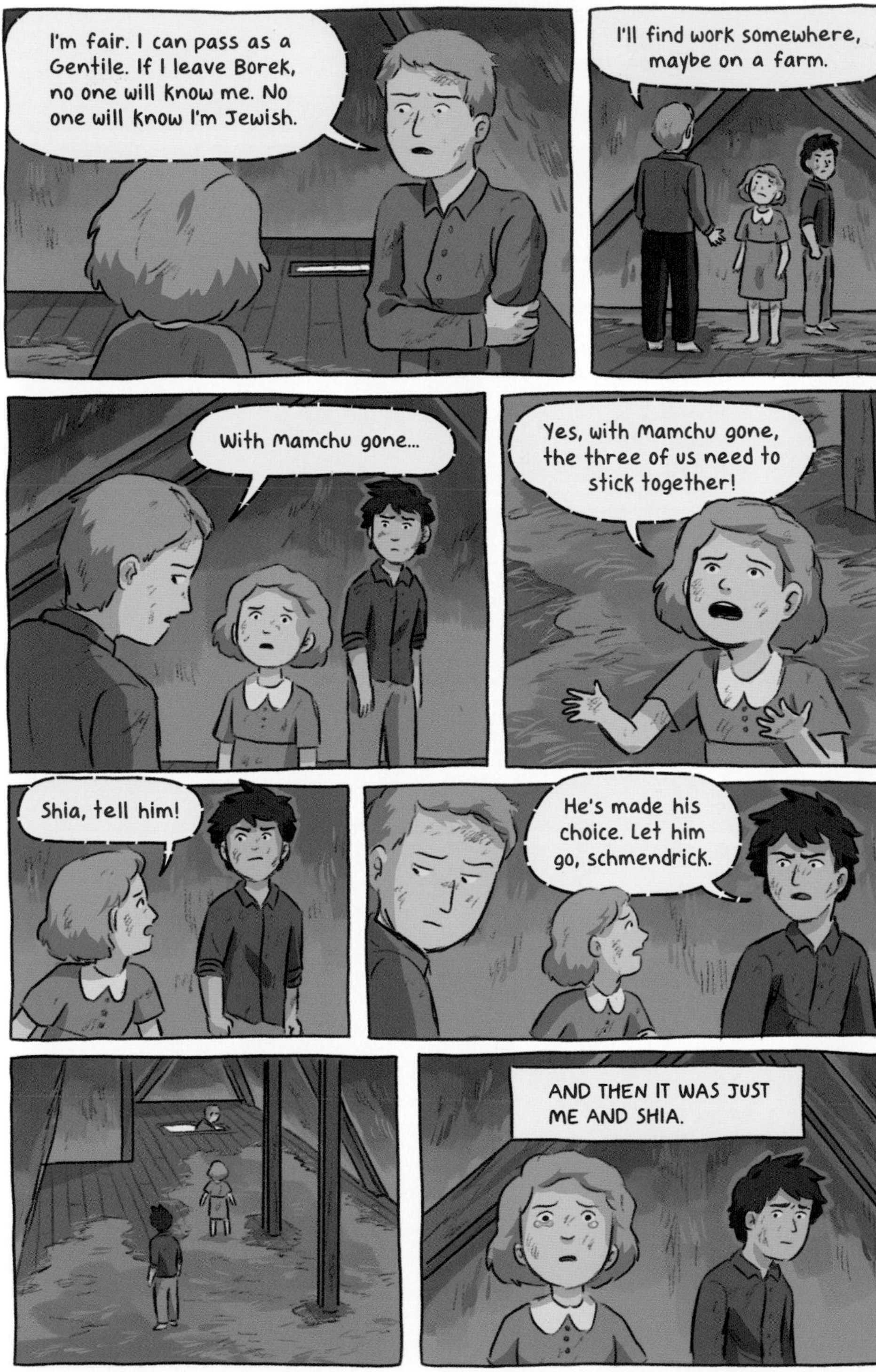
I'm fair. I can pass as a Gentile. If I leave Borek, no one will know me. No one will know I'm Jewish.
I'll find work somewhere, maybe on a farm.
With mamchu gone...
Yes, with mamchu gone, the three of us need to stick together!
Shia, tell him!
He's made his choice. Let him go, schmendrick.
AND THEN IT WAS JUST ME AND SHIA.

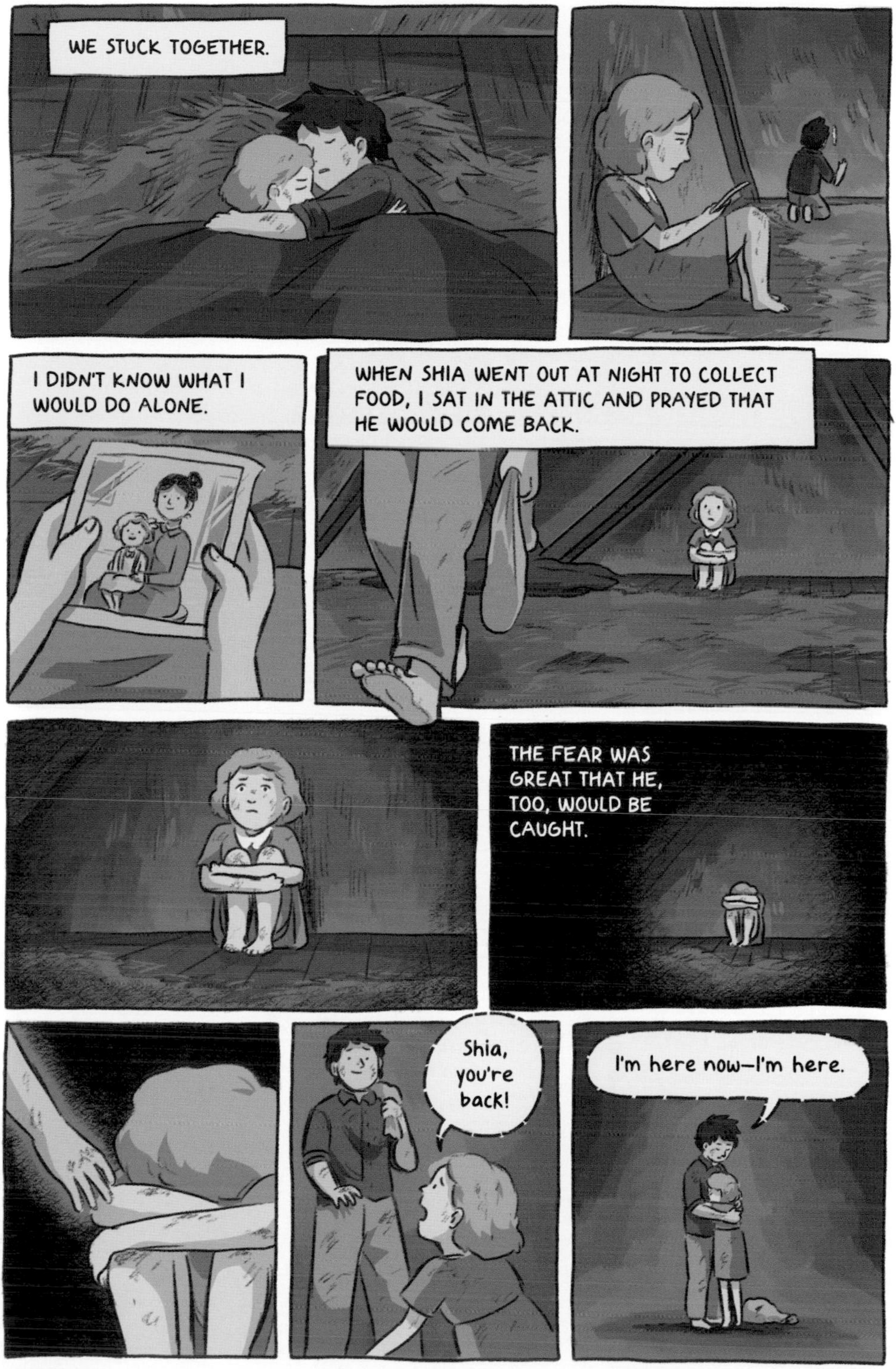
WE STUCK TOGETHER.
I DIDN'T KNOW WHAT I WOULD DO ALONE.
WHEN SHIA WENT OUT AT NIGHT TO COLLECT FOOD, I SAT IN THE ATTIC AND PRAYED THAT HE WOULD COME BACK.
THE FEAR WAS GREAT THAT HE, TOO, WOULD BE CAUGHT.
Shia, you're back!
I'm here now—I'm here.

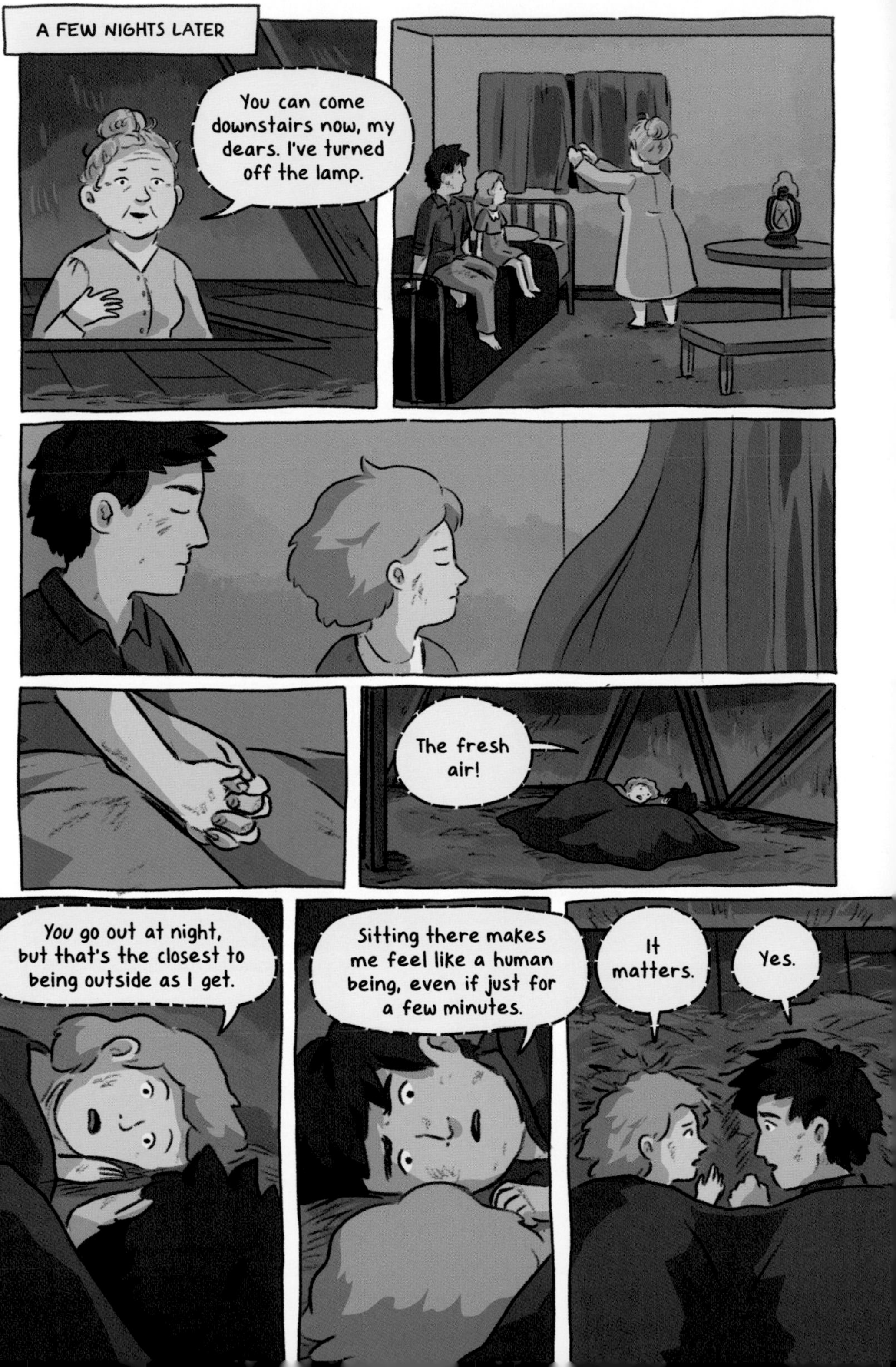
A FEW NIGHTS LATER
You can come downstairs now, my dears. I've turned off the lamp.
The fresh air!
You go out at night, but that's the closest to being outside as I get.
Sitting there makes me feel like a human being, even if just for a few minutes.
It matters.
Yes.

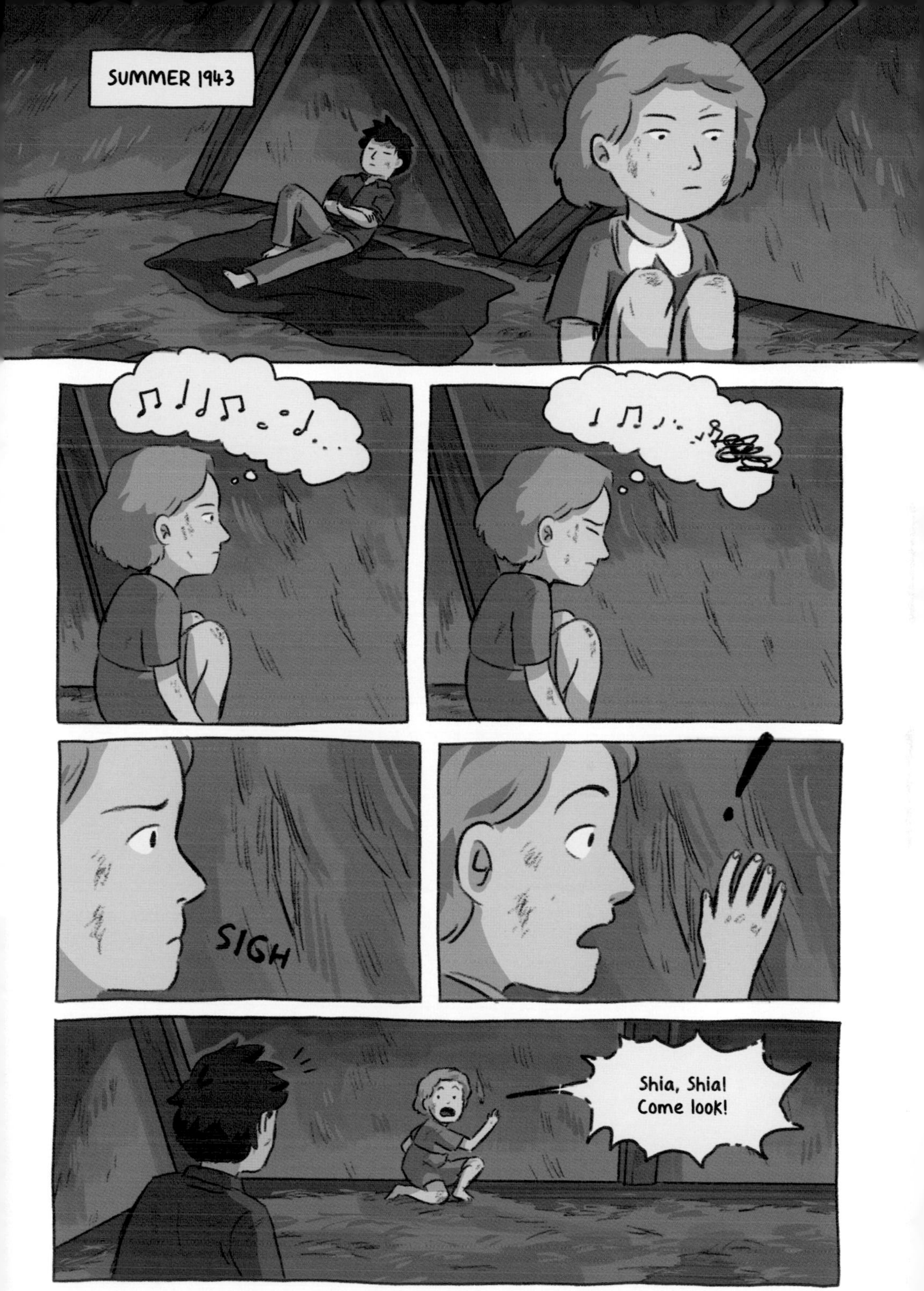
SUMMER 1943
SIGH
Shia, Shia! Come look!

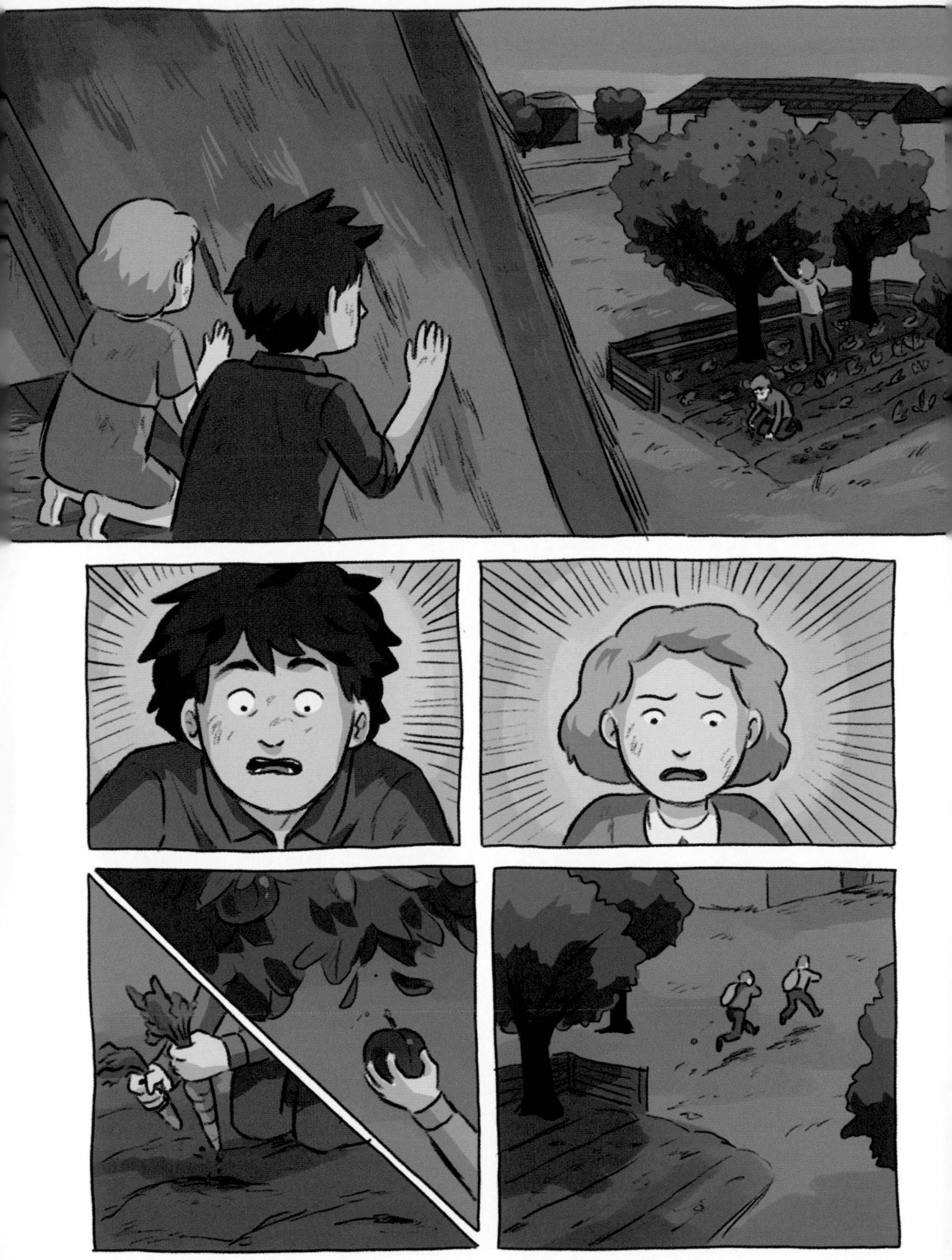

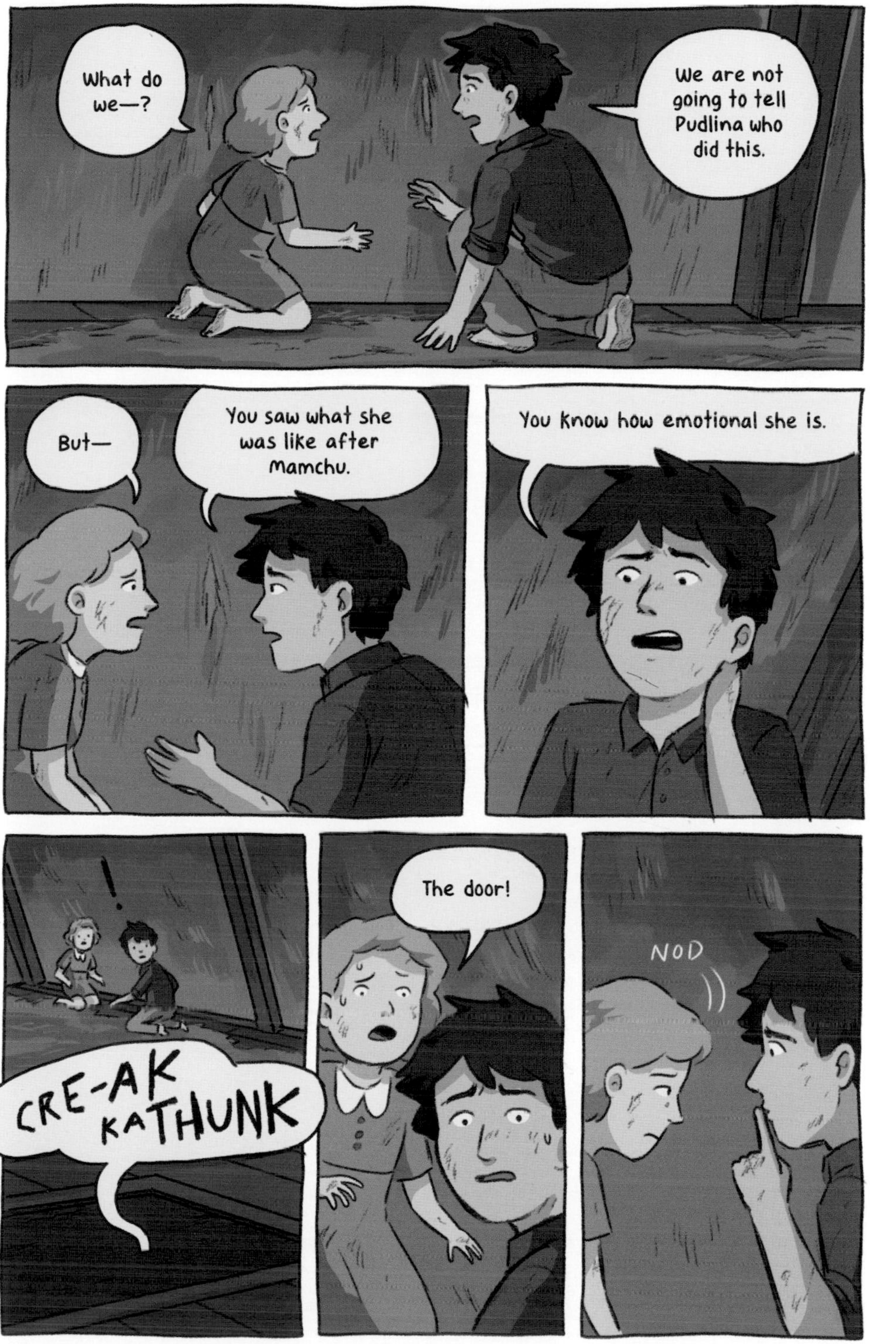
What do we—?
We are not going to tell Pudlina who did this.
But—
You saw what she was like after mamchu.
You know how emotional she is.
!
CRE-AK KATHUNK
The door!
NOD

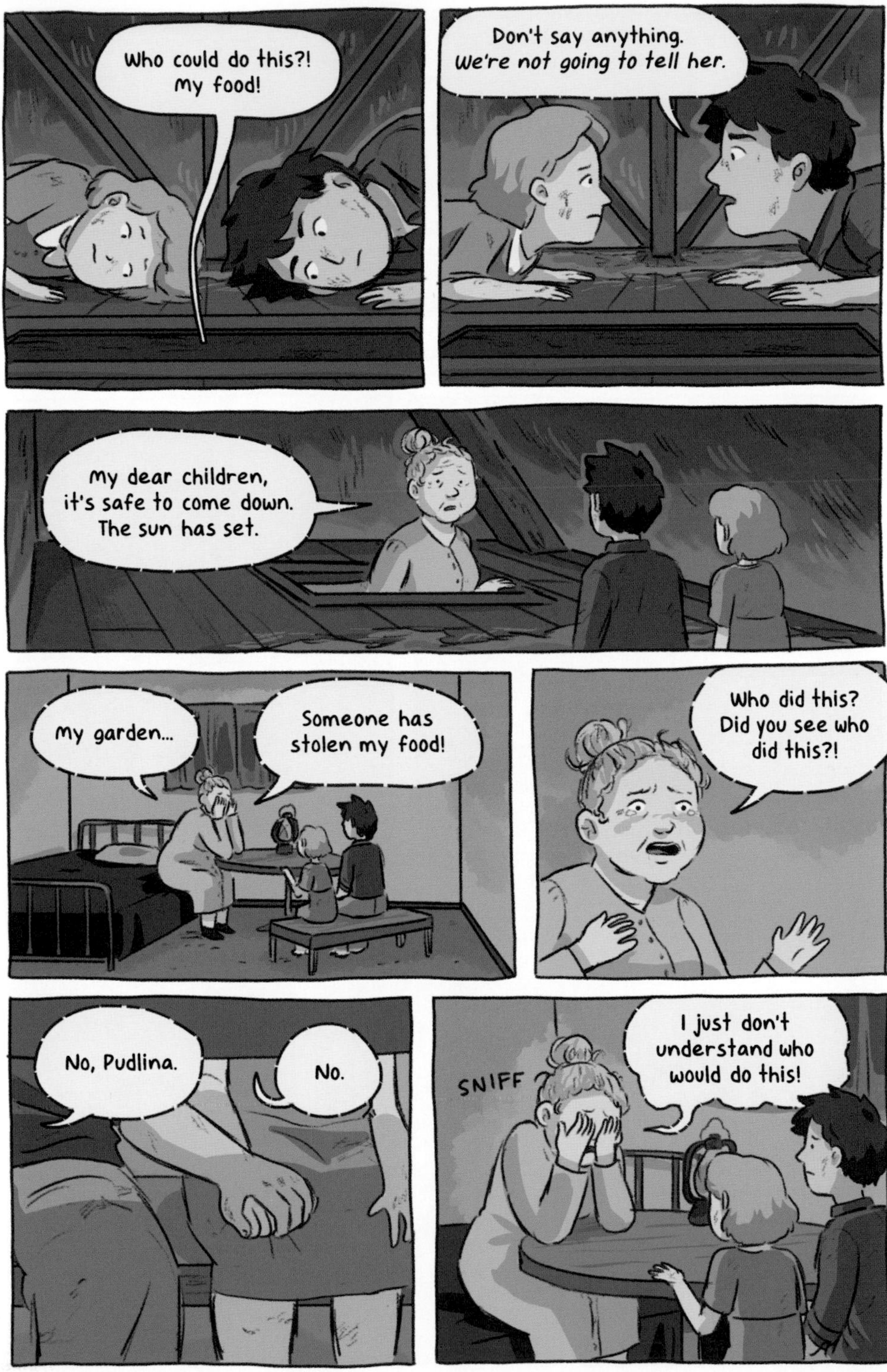
Who could do this?! My food!
Don't say anything. *We're not going to tell her.*
My dear children, it's safe to come down. The sun has set.
My garden...
Someone has stolen my food!
Who did this? Did you see who did this?!
No, Pudlina.
No.
SNIFF
I just don't understand who would do this!

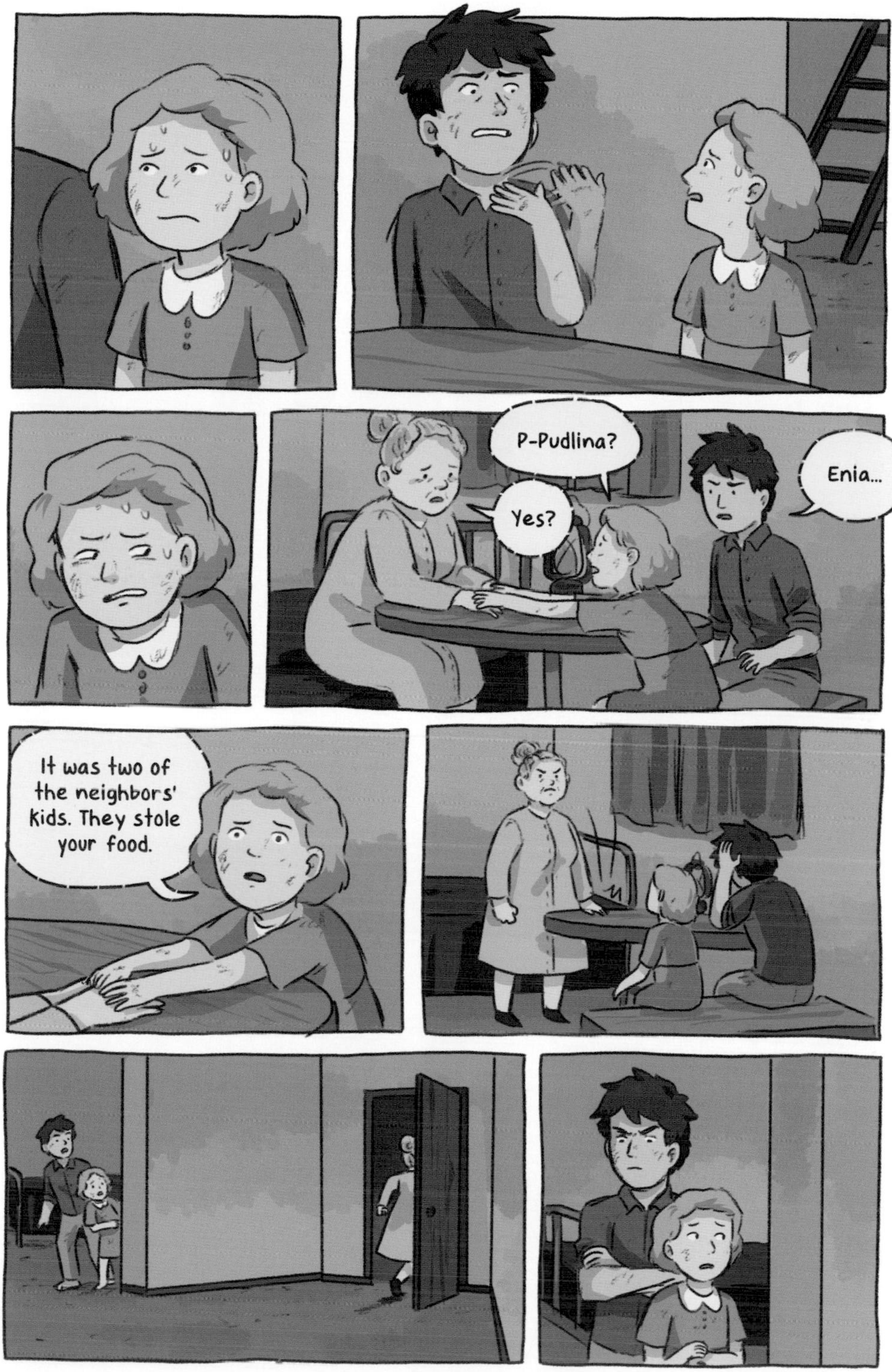
P-Pudlina?
Yes?
Enia...
It was two of the neighbors' kids. They stole your food.

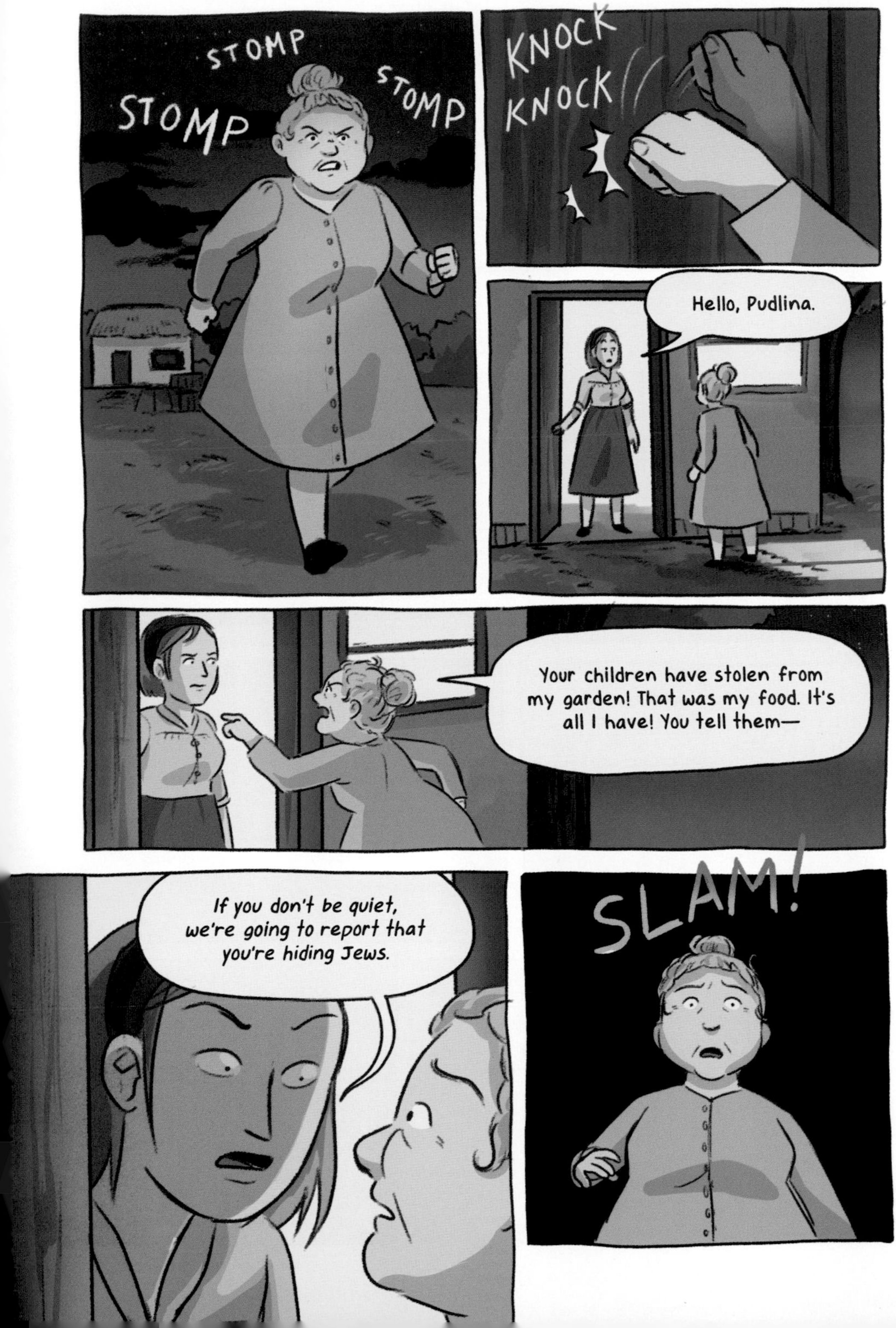
STOMP
STOMP
STOMP
KNOCK
KNOCK
Hello, Pudlina.
Your children have stolen from my garden! That was my food. It's all I have! You tell them—
If you don't be quiet, we're going to report that you're hiding Jews.
SLAM!

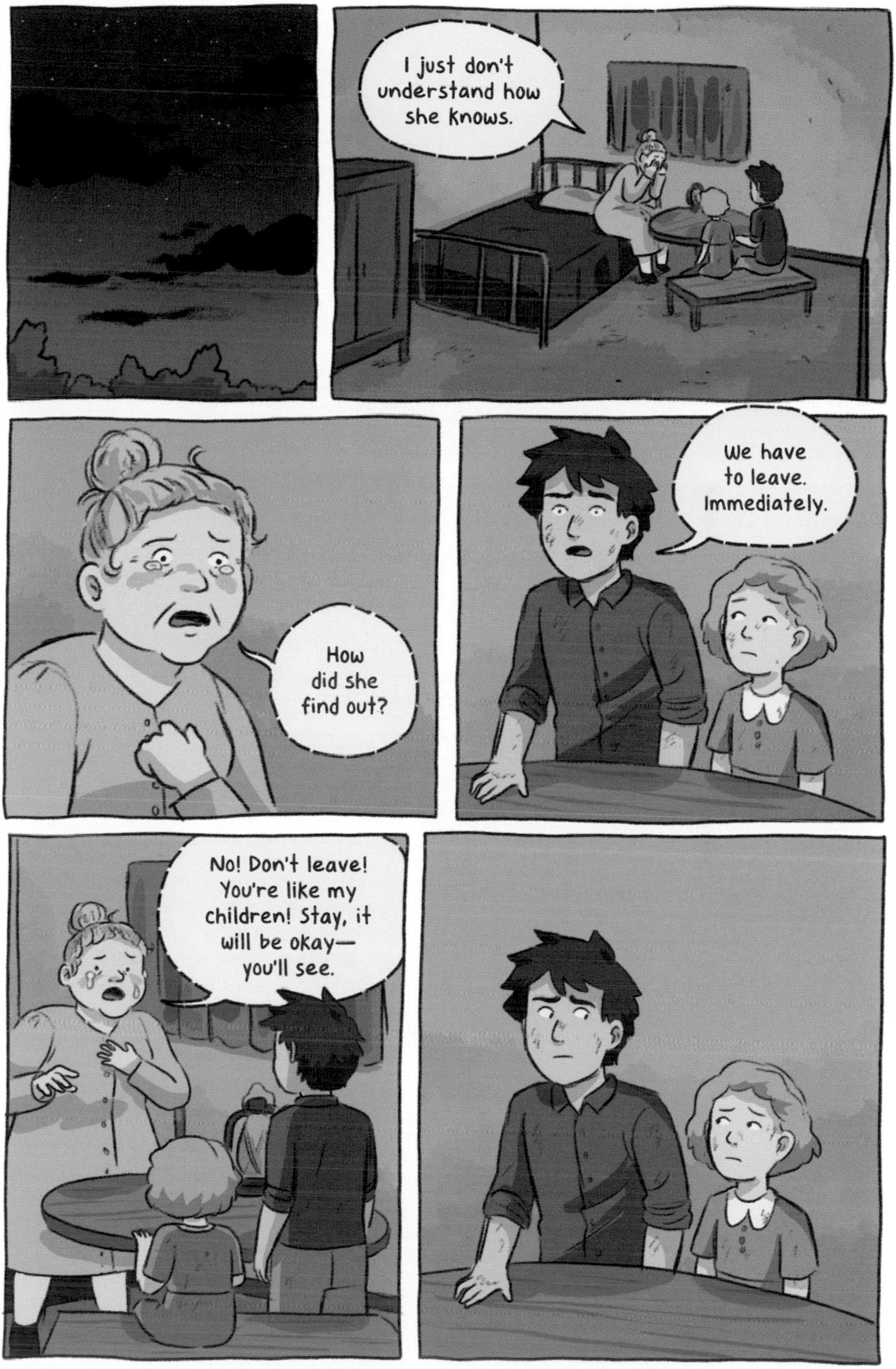
I just don't understand how she knows.
How did she find out?
We have to leave. Immediately.
No! Don't leave! You're like my children! Stay, it will be okay—you'll see.

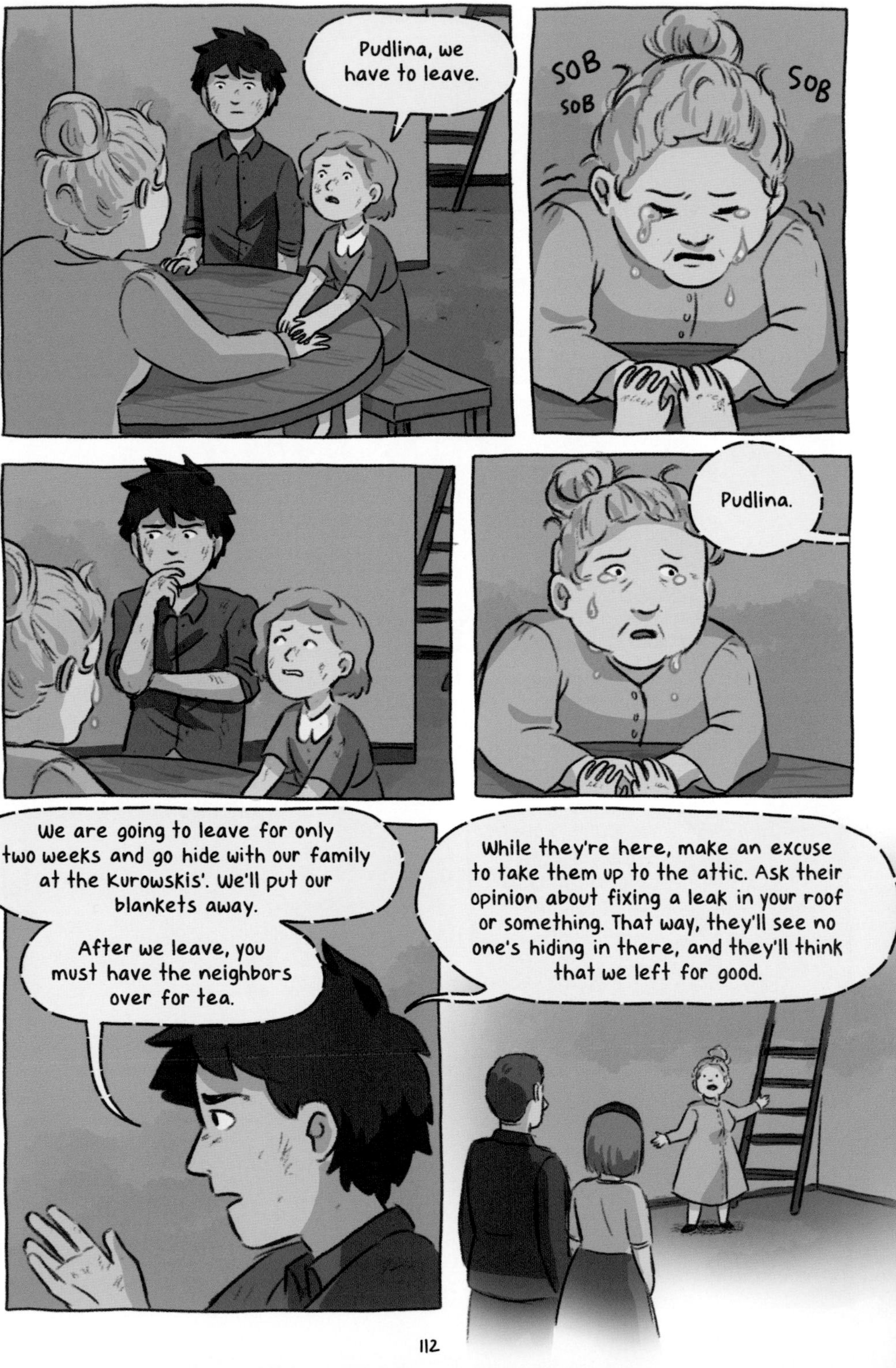
SOB
SOB
SOB
Pudlina, we have to leave.
Pudlina.
We are going to leave for only two weeks and go hide with our family at the Kurowskis'. We'll put our blankets away.
After we leave, you must have the neighbors over for tea.
While they're here, make an excuse to take them up to the attic. Ask their opinion about fixing a leak in your roof or something. That way, they'll see no one's hiding in there, and they'll think that we left for good.

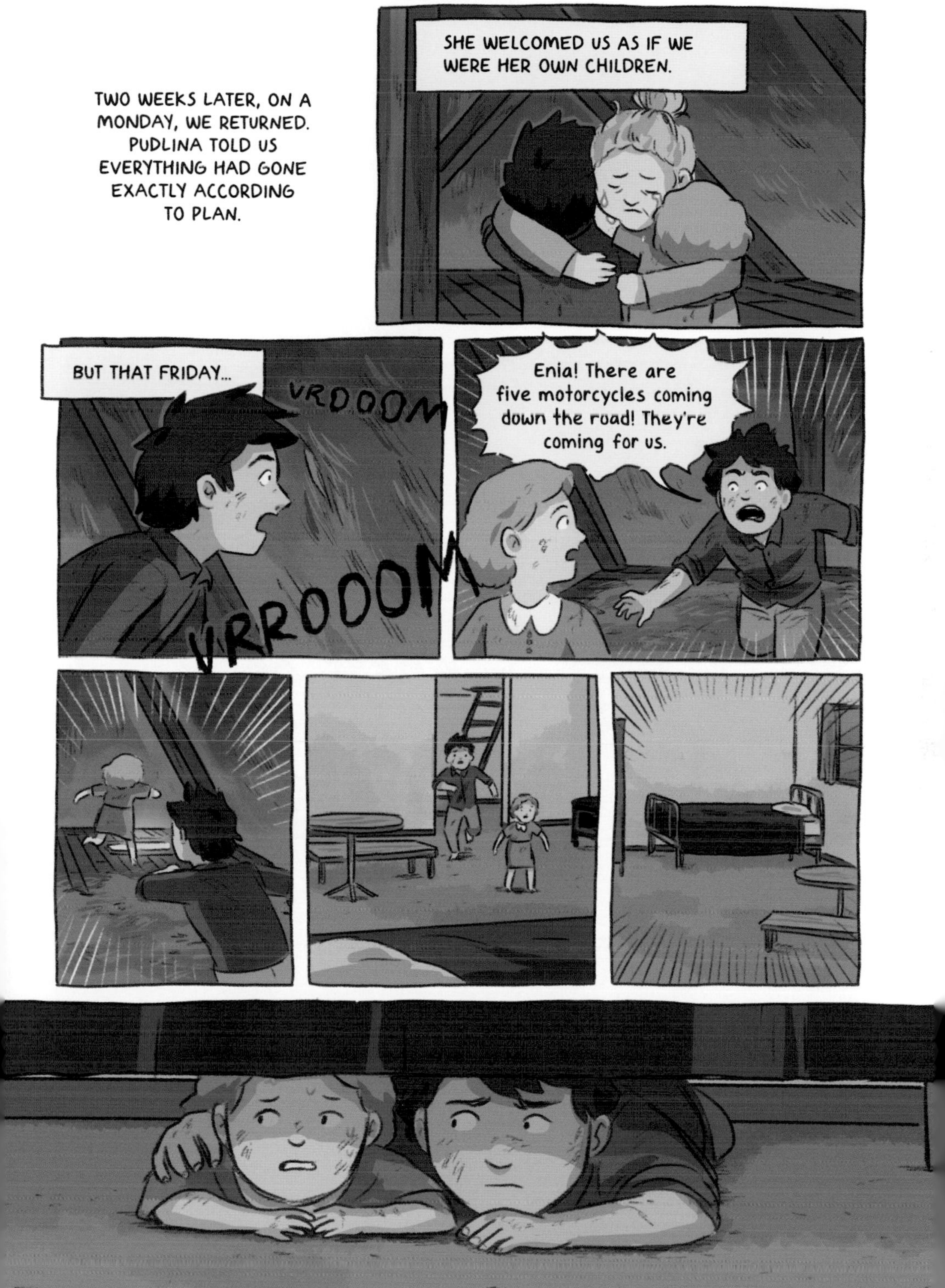
TWO WEEKS LATER, ON A MONDAY, WE RETURNED. PUDLINA TOLD US EVERYTHING HAD GONE EXACTLY ACCORDING TO PLAN.
SHE WELCOMED US AS IF WE WERE HER OWN CHILDREN.
BUT THAT FRIDAY...
VRDOOOM
VRROOOM
Enia! There are five motorcycles coming down the road! They're coming for us.

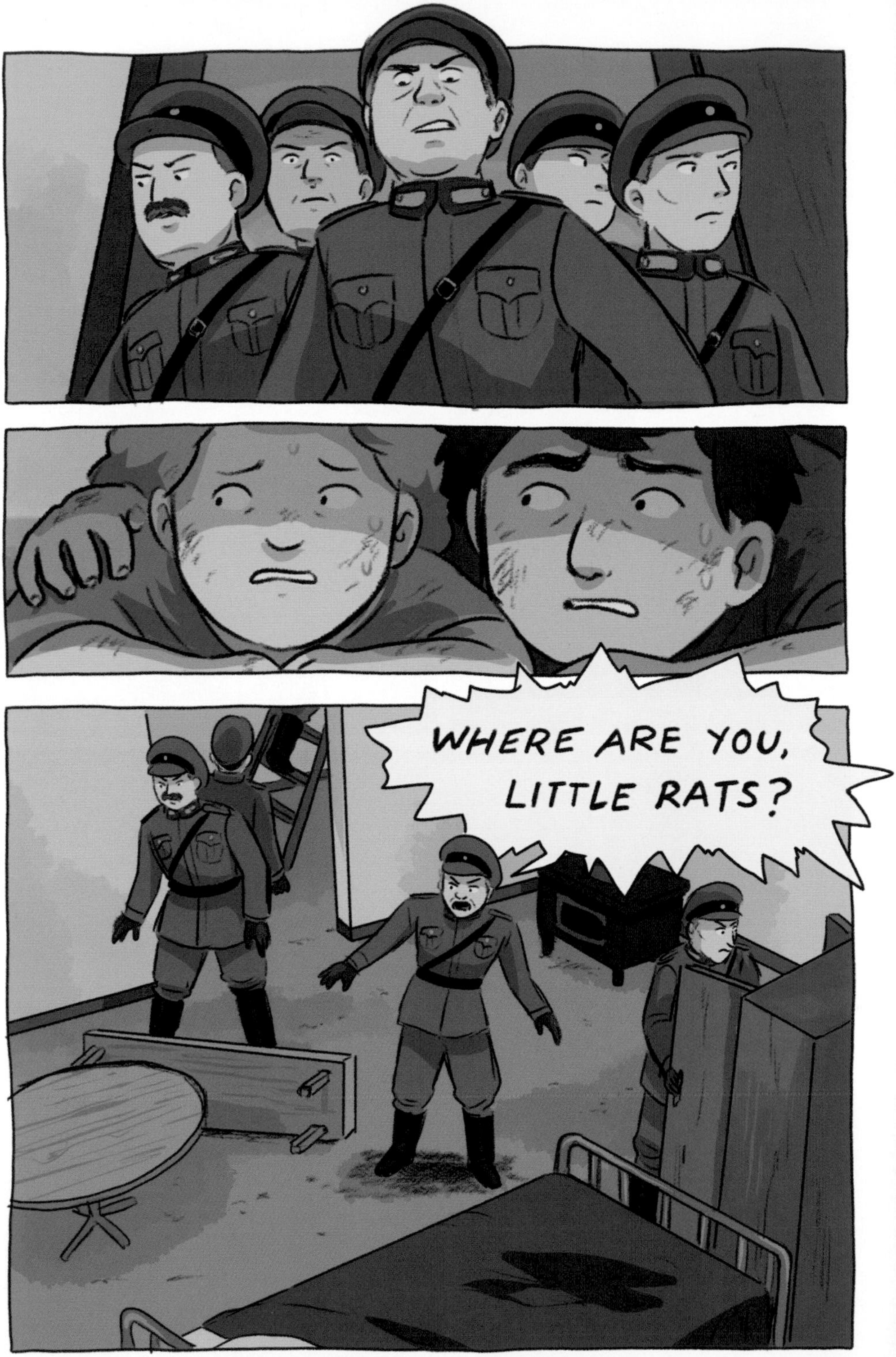
WHERE ARE YOU, LITTLE RATS?

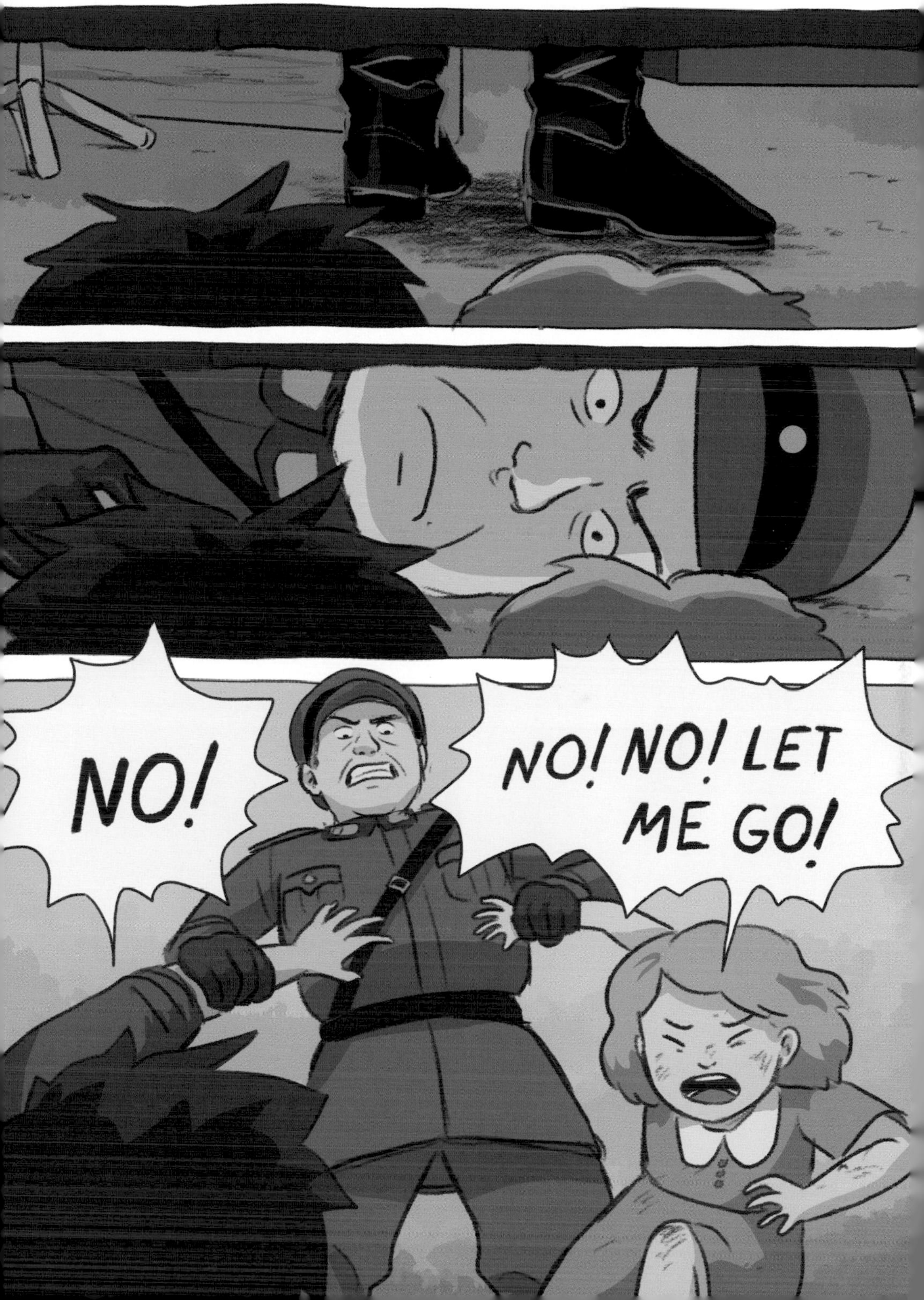
NO!
NO! NO! LET ME GO!

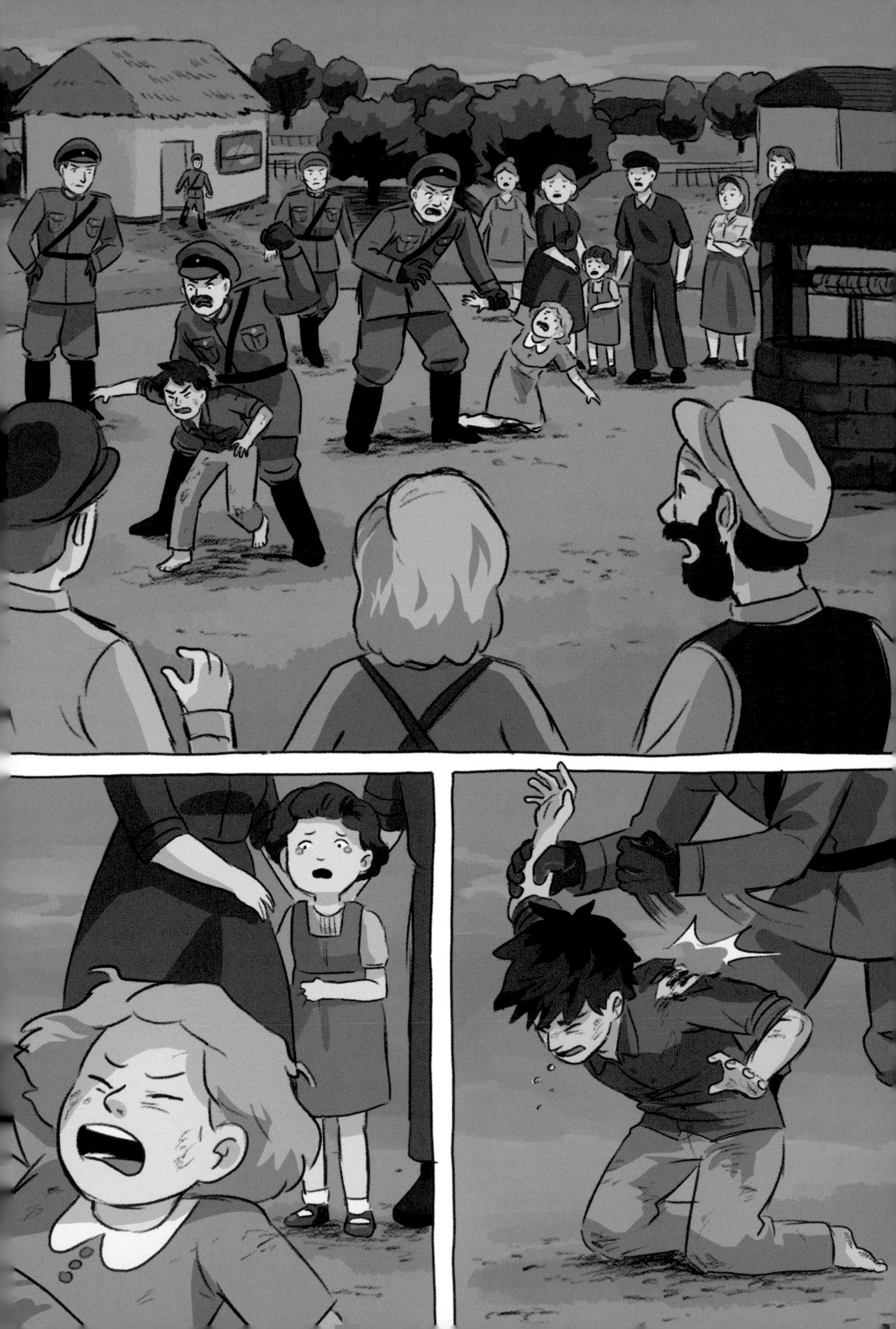

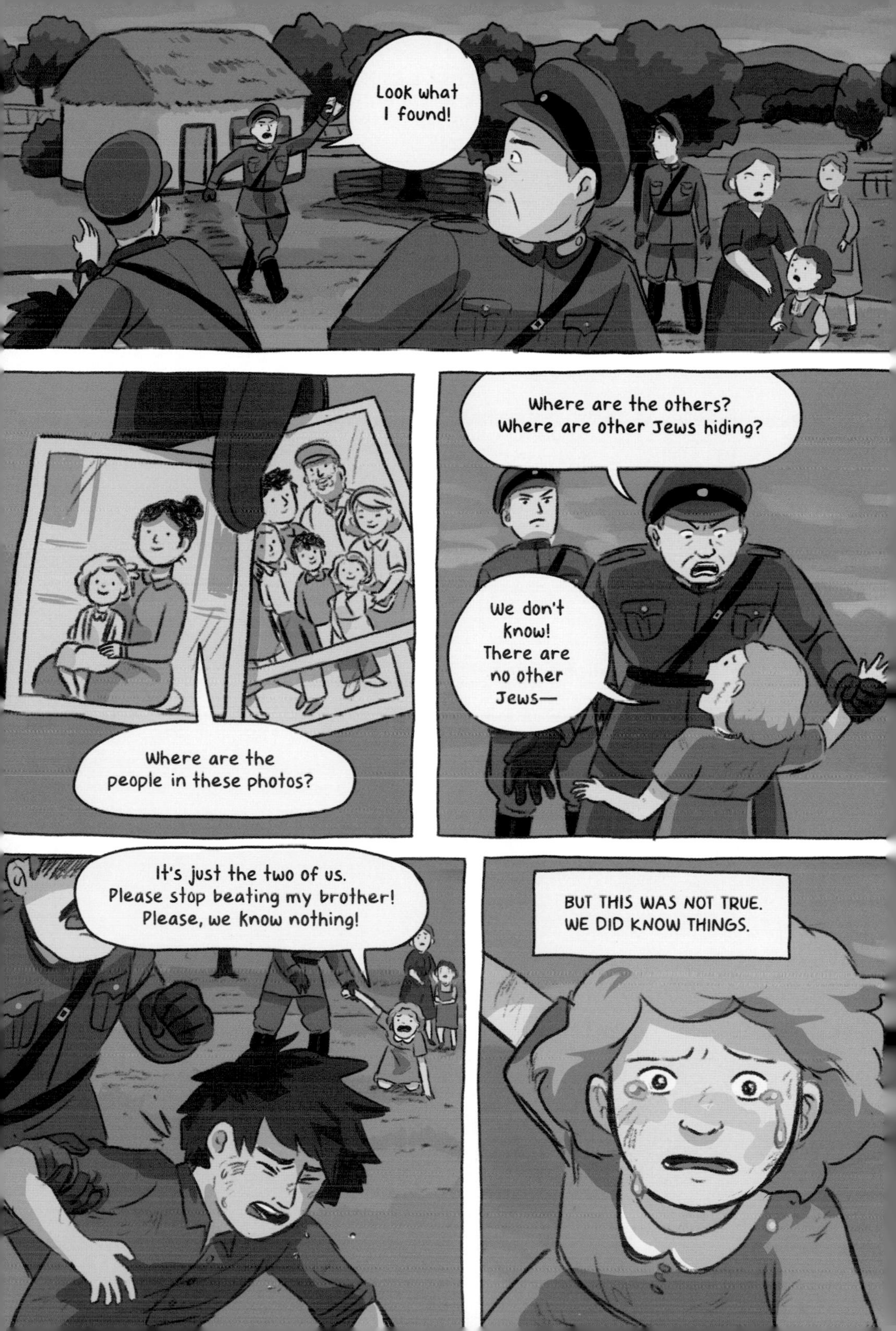
Look what I found!
Where are the people in these photos?
Where are the others? Where are other Jews hiding?
We don't know! There are no other Jews—
It's just the two of us. Please stop beating my brother! Please, we know nothing!
BUT THIS WAS NOT TRUE. WE DID KNOW THINGS.

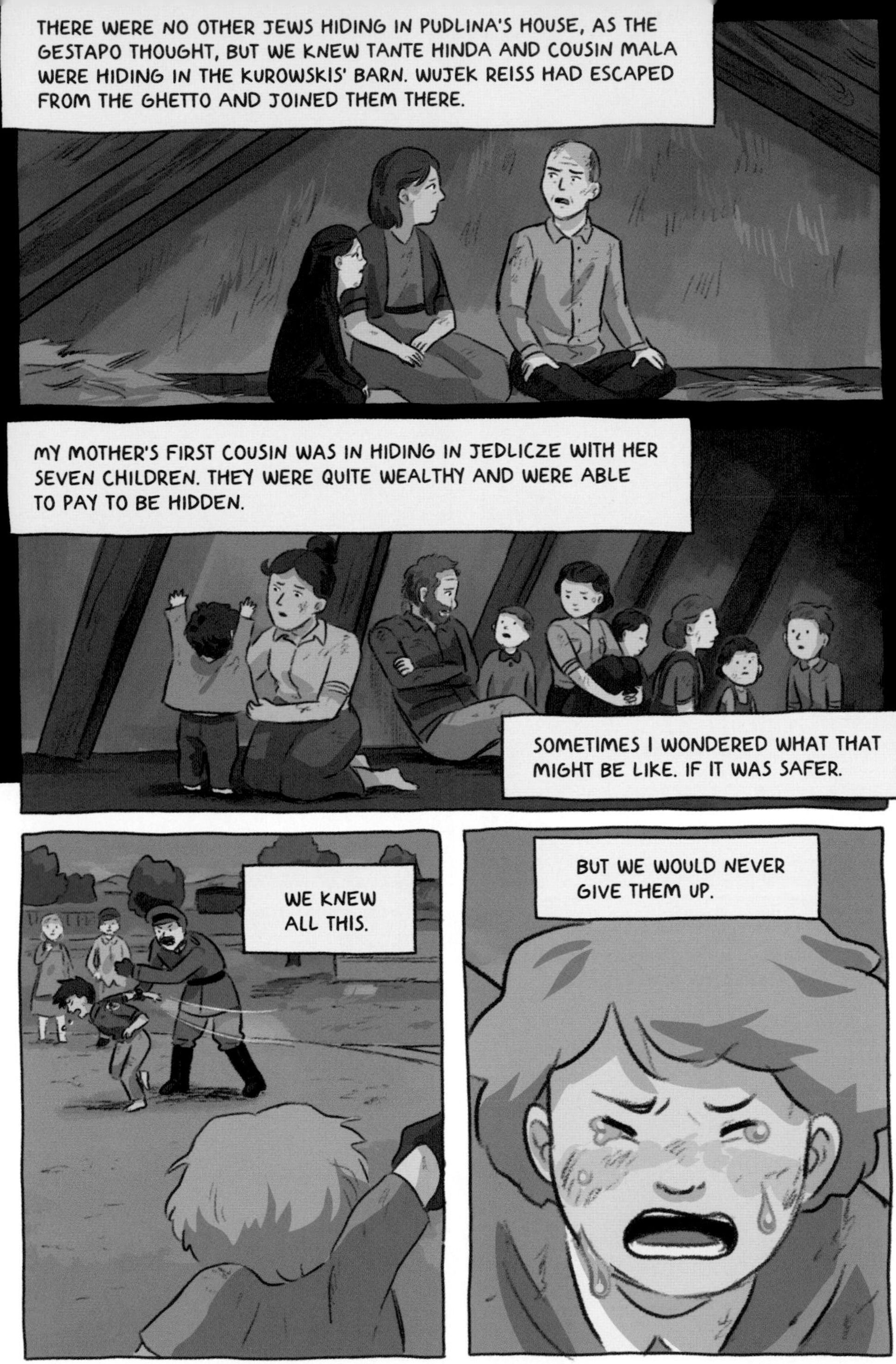
THERE WERE NO OTHER JEWS HIDING IN PUDLINA'S HOUSE, AS THE GESTAPO THOUGHT, BUT WE KNEW TANTE HINDA AND COUSIN MALA WERE HIDING IN THE KUROWSKIS' BARN. WUJEK REISS HAD ESCAPED FROM THE GHETTO AND JOINED THEM THERE.
MY MOTHER'S FIRST COUSIN WAS IN HIDING IN JEDLICZE WITH HER SEVEN CHILDREN. THEY WERE QUITE WEALTHY AND WERE ABLE TO PAY TO BE HIDDEN.
SOMETIMES I WONDERED WHAT THAT MIGHT BE LIKE. IF IT WAS SAFER.
WE KNEW ALL THIS.
BUT WE WOULD NEVER GIVE THEM UP.

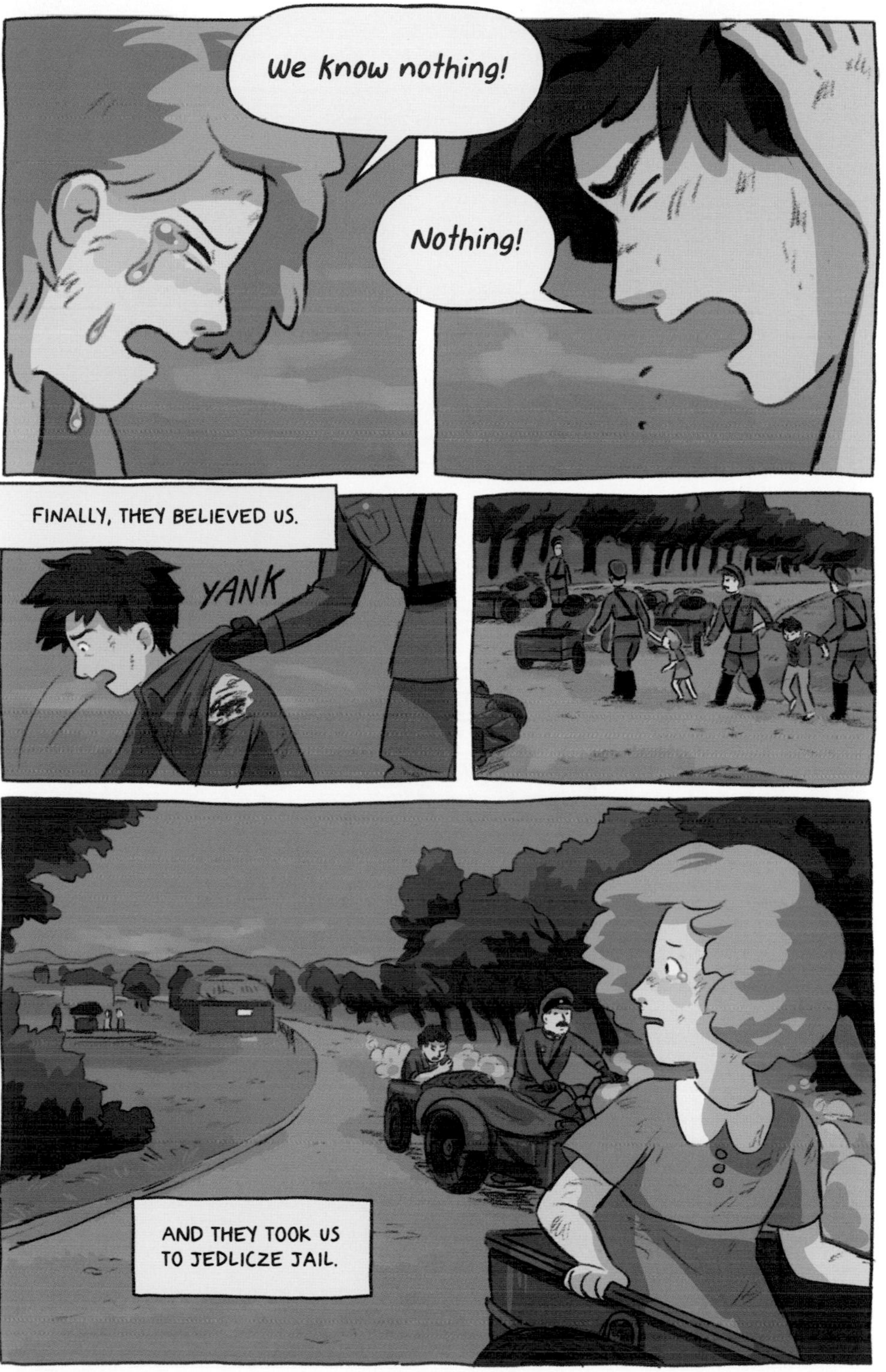

We know nothing!
Nothing!
FINALLY, THEY BELIEVED US.
YANK
AND THEY TOOK US TO JEDLICZE JAIL.

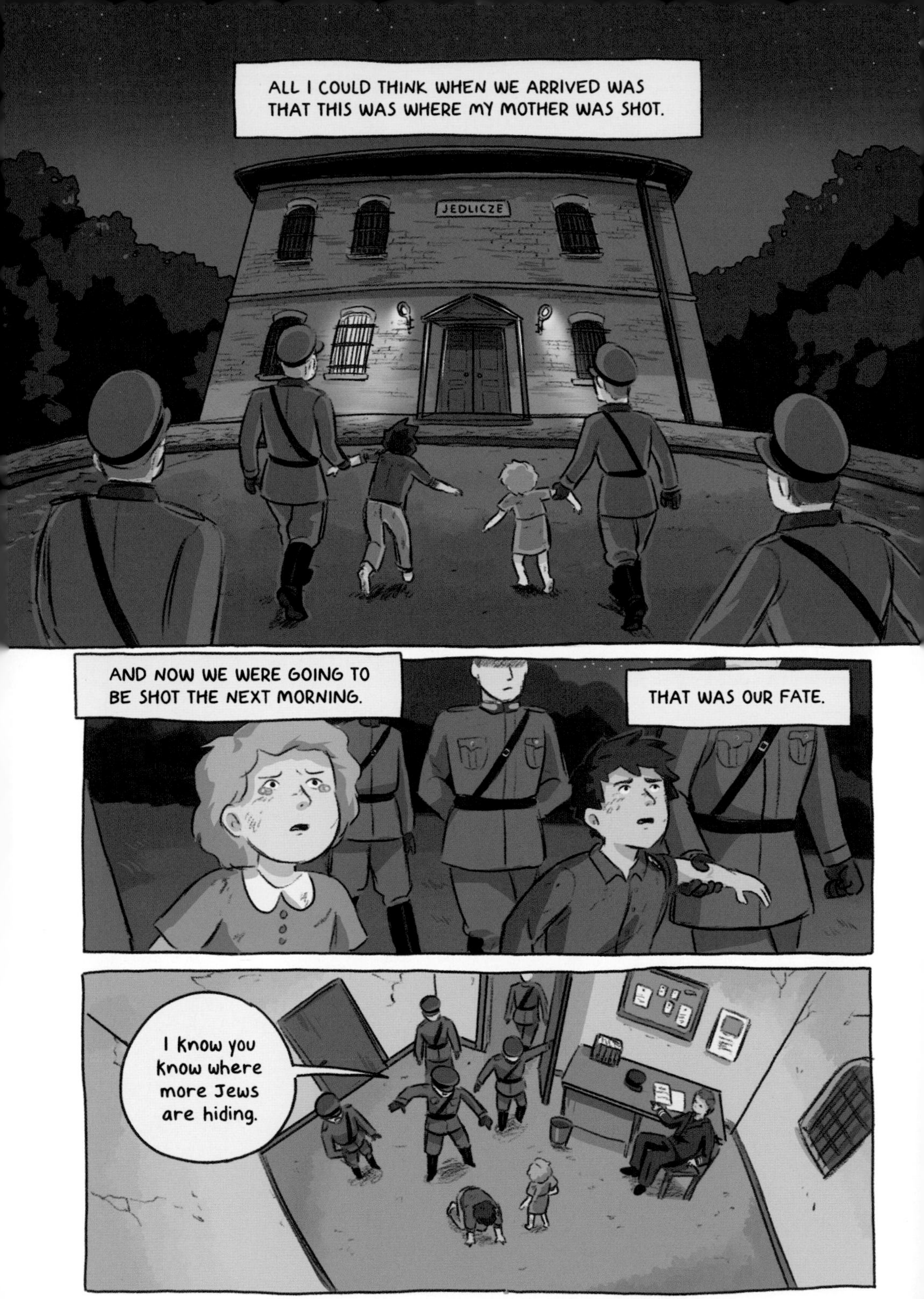
ALL I COULD THINK WHEN WE ARRIVED WAS THAT THIS WAS WHERE MY MOTHER WAS SHOT.
JEDLICZE
AND NOW WE WERE GOING TO BE SHOT THE NEXT MORNING.
THAT WAS OUR FATE.
I know you know where more Jews are hiding.

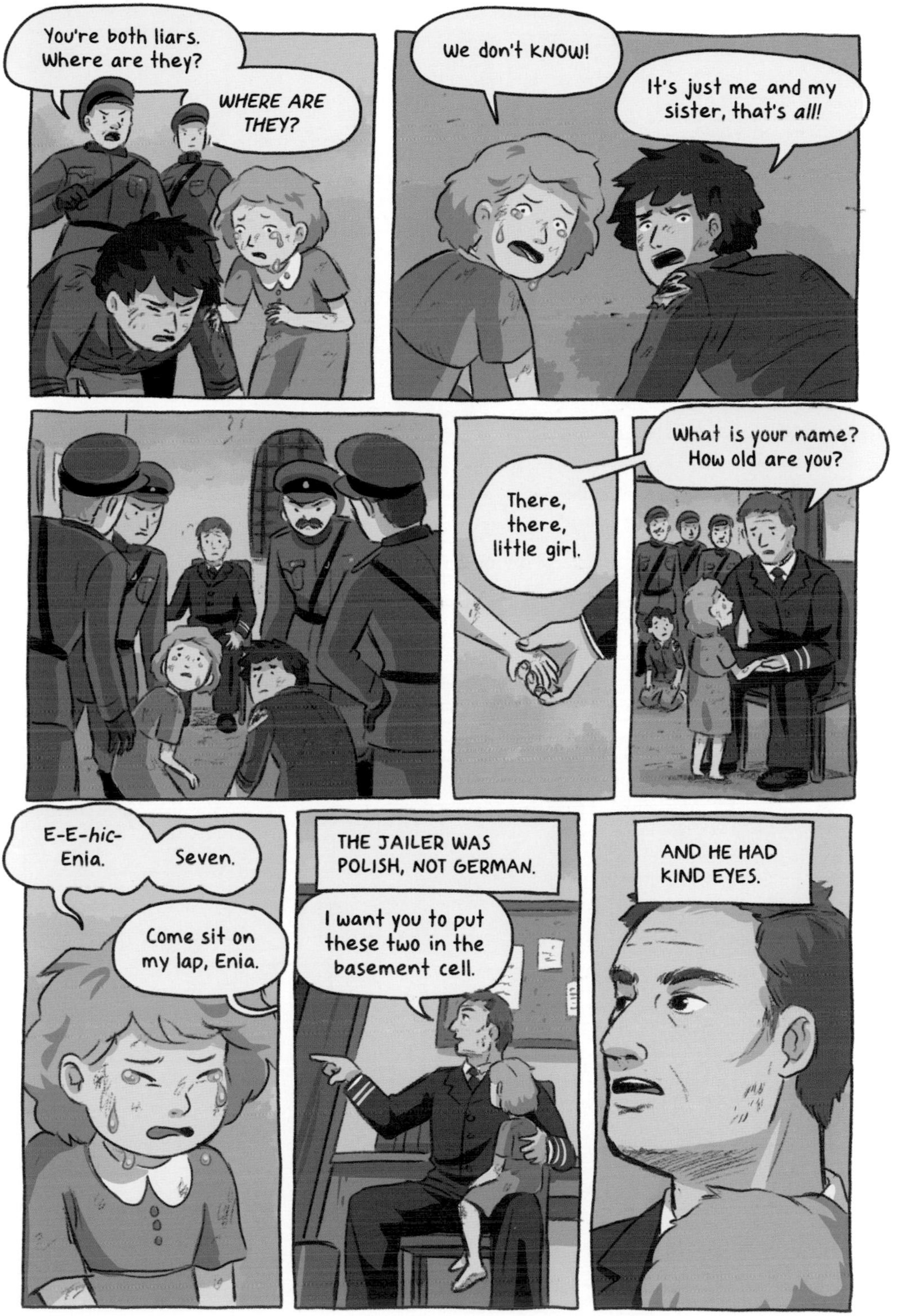
You're both liars. Where are they?
WHERE ARE THEY?
We don't KNOW!
It's just me and my sister, that's all!
What is your name? How old are you?
There, there, little girl.
E-E-hic-Enia.
Seven.
Come sit on my lap, Enia.
THE JAILER WAS POLISH, NOT GERMAN.
I want you to put these two in the basement cell.
AND HE HAD KIND EYES.

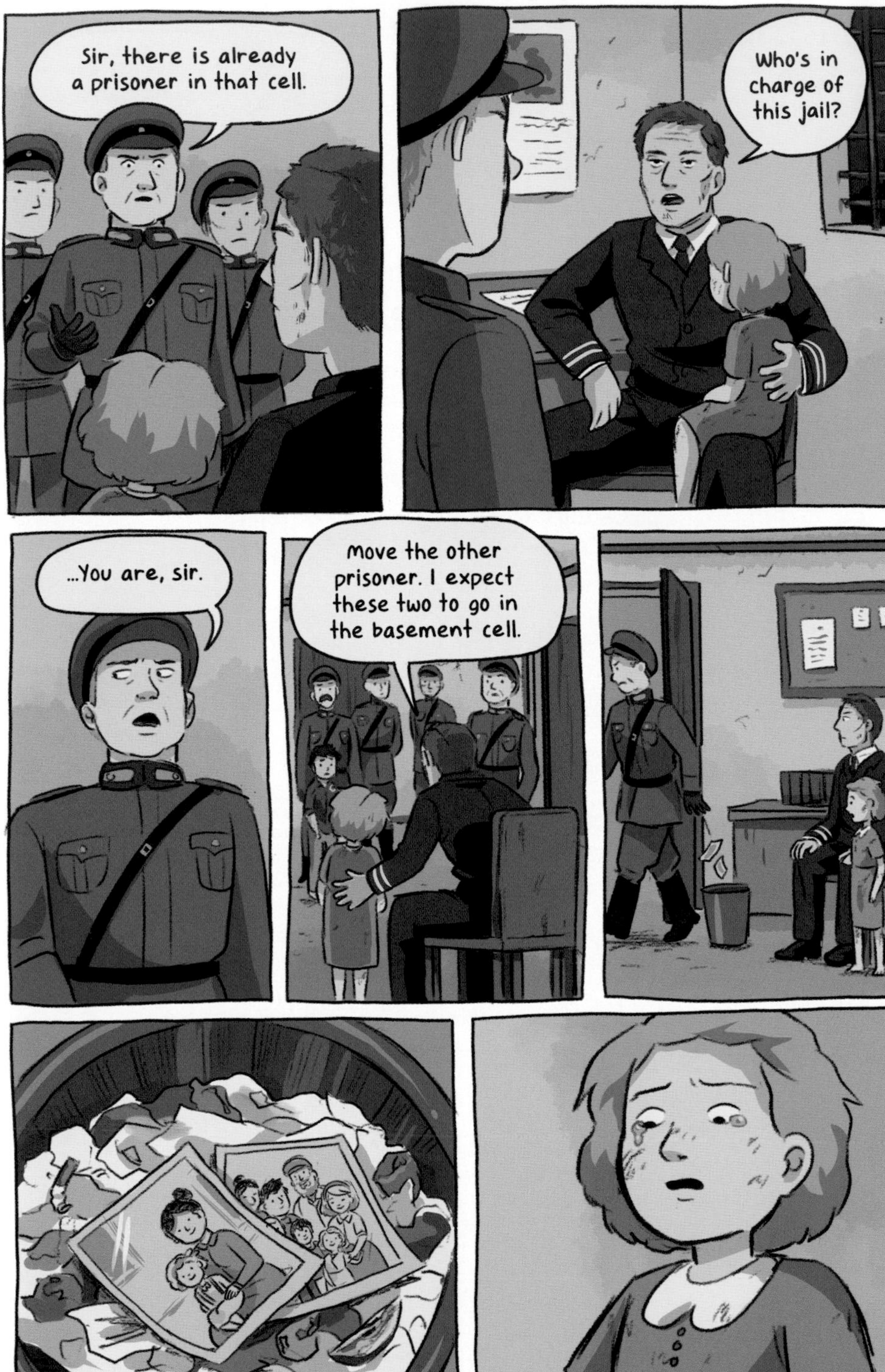
Sir, there is already a prisoner in that cell.
Who's in charge of this jail?
...You are, sir.
Move the other prisoner. I expect these two to go in the basement cell.

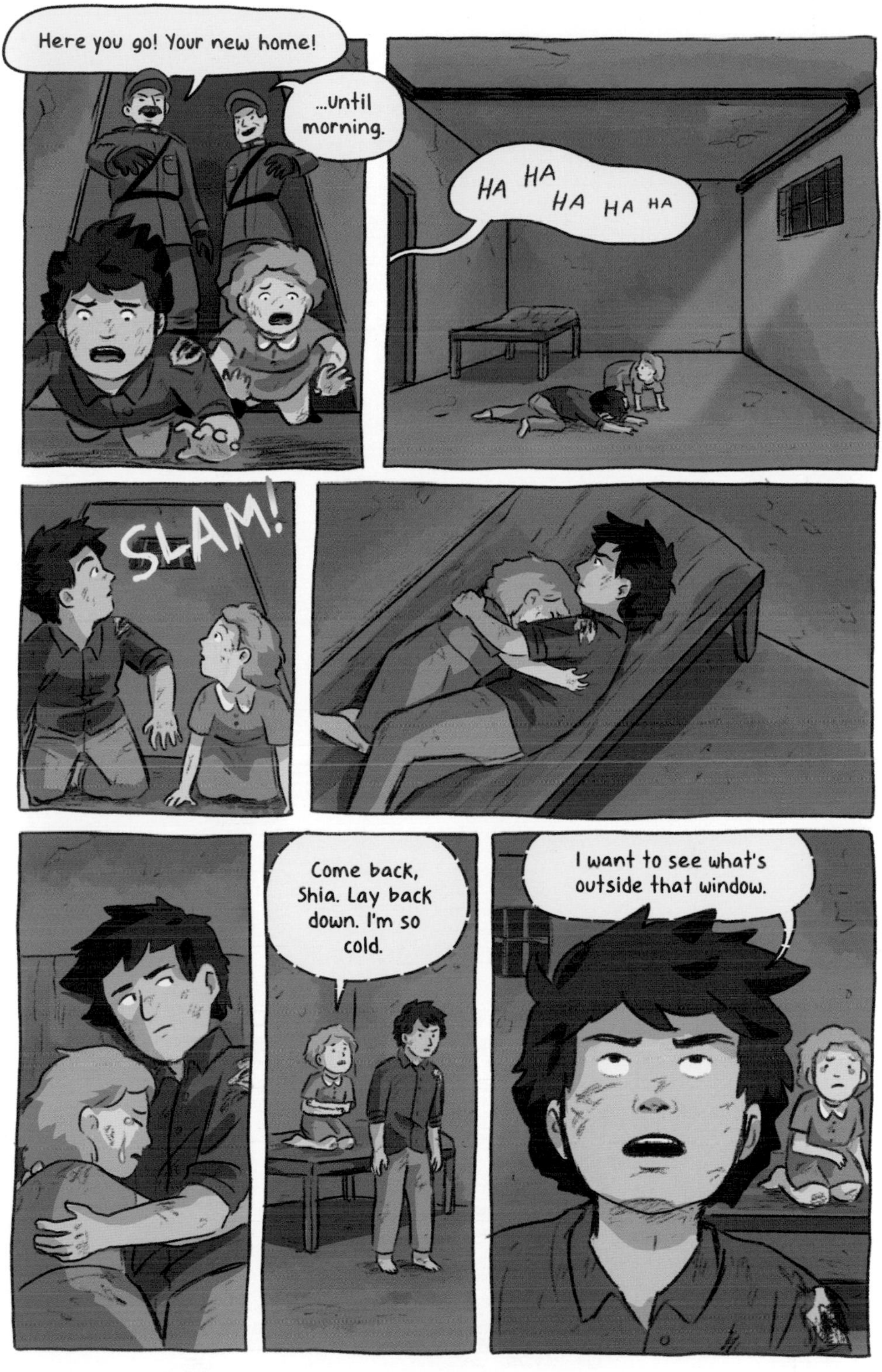
Here you go! Your new home!
...until morning.
HA HA HA HA HA
SLAM!
Come back, Shia. Lay back down. I'm so cold.
I want to see what's outside that window.

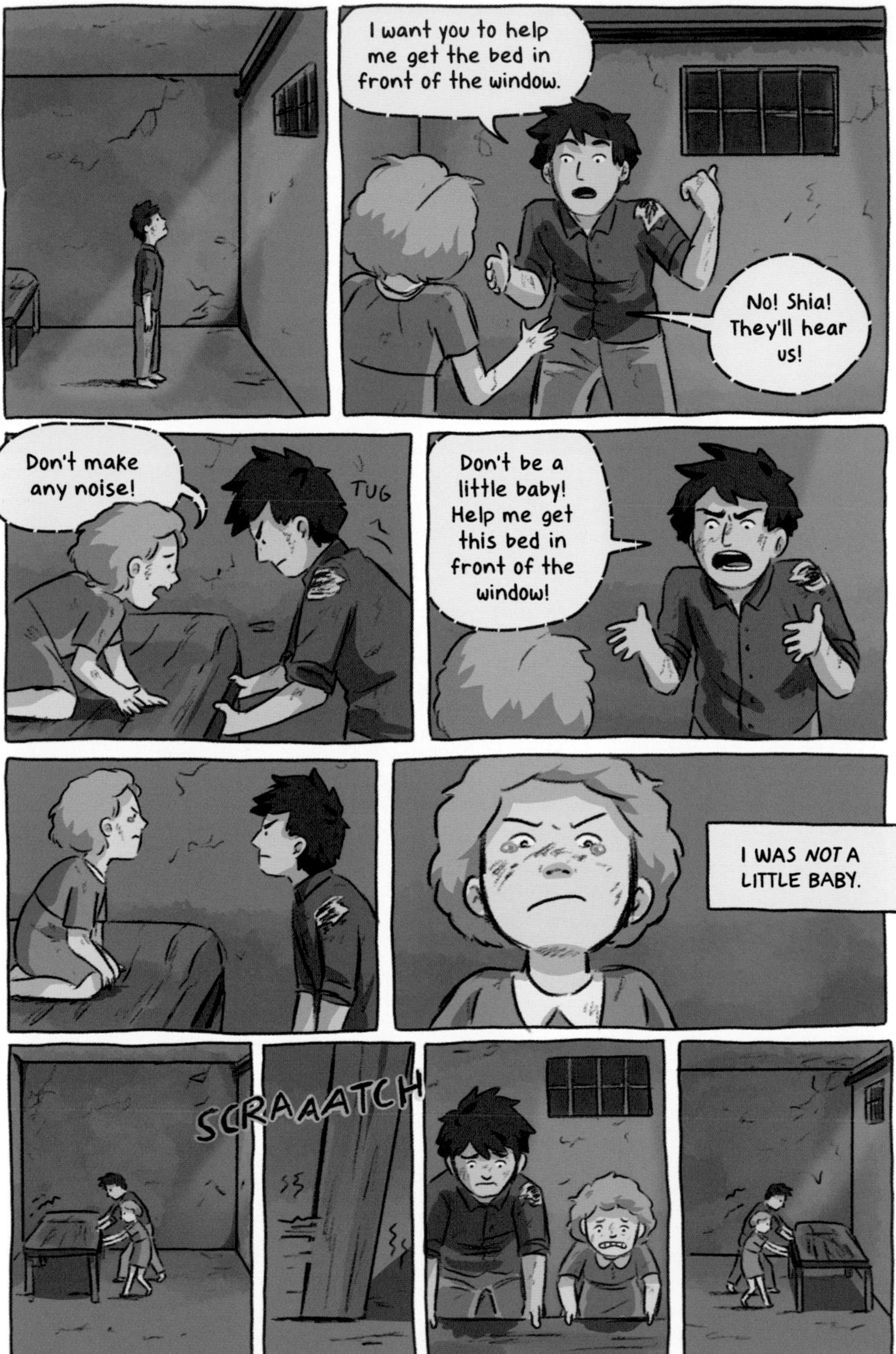
I want you to help me get the bed in front of the window.
No! Shia! They'll hear us!
Don't make any noise!
TUG
Don't be a little baby! Help me get this bed in front of the window!
I WAS *NOT* A LITTLE BABY.
SCRAAATCH

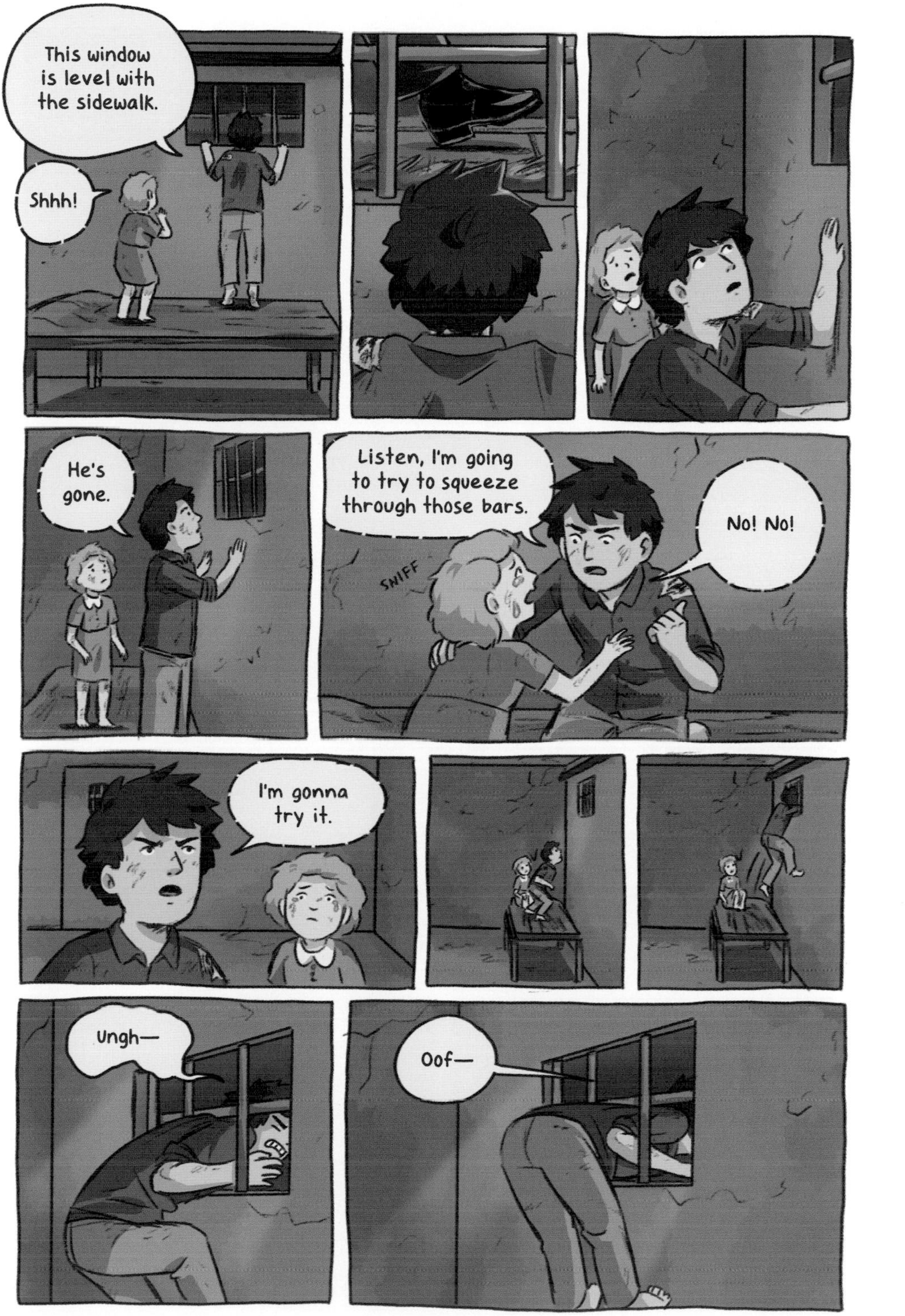
This window is level with the sidewalk.
Shhh!
He's gone.
Listen, I'm going to try to squeeze through those bars.
SNIFF
No! No!
I'm gonna try it.
Ungh—
Oof—

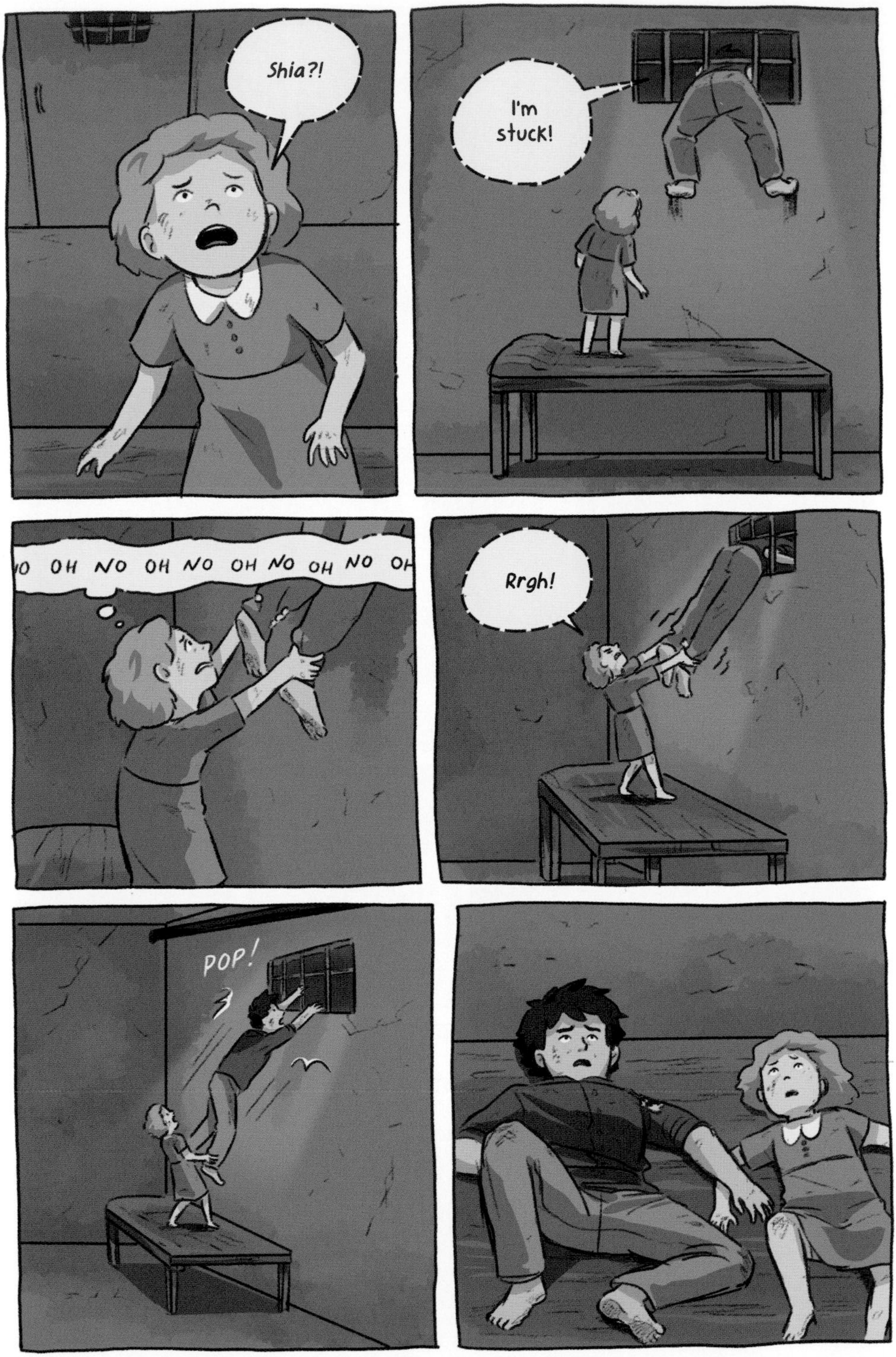

Shia?!
I'm stuck!
NO OH NO OH NO OH NO OH NO OH
Rrgh!
POP!

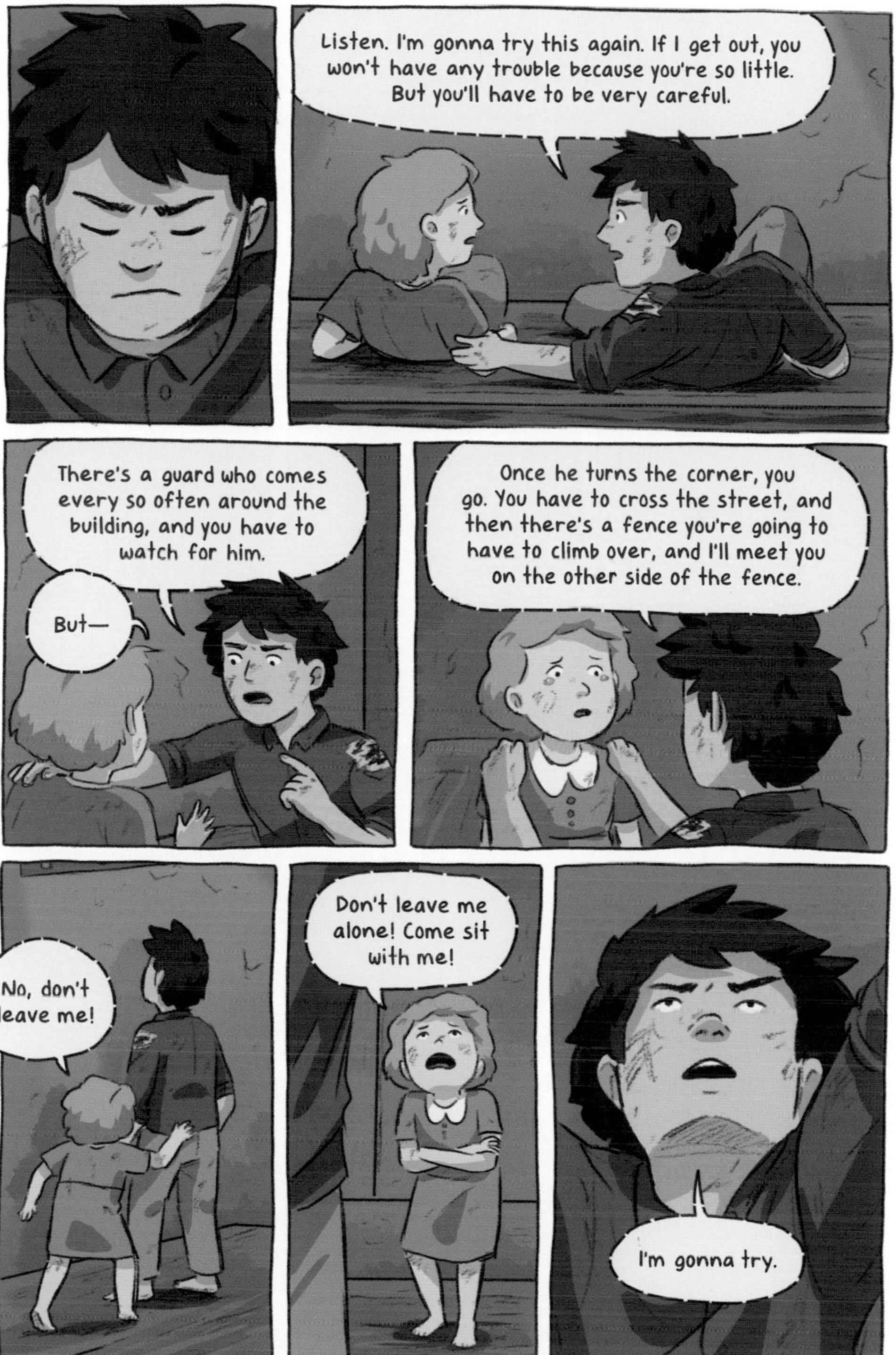
Listen. I'm gonna try this again. If I get out, you won't have any trouble because you're so little. But you'll have to be very careful.
There's a guard who comes every so often around the building, and you have to watch for him.
But—
Once he turns the corner, you go. You have to cross the street, and then there's a fence you're going to have to climb over, and I'll meet you on the other side of the fence.
No, don't leave me!
Don't leave me alone! Come sit with me!
I'm gonna try.

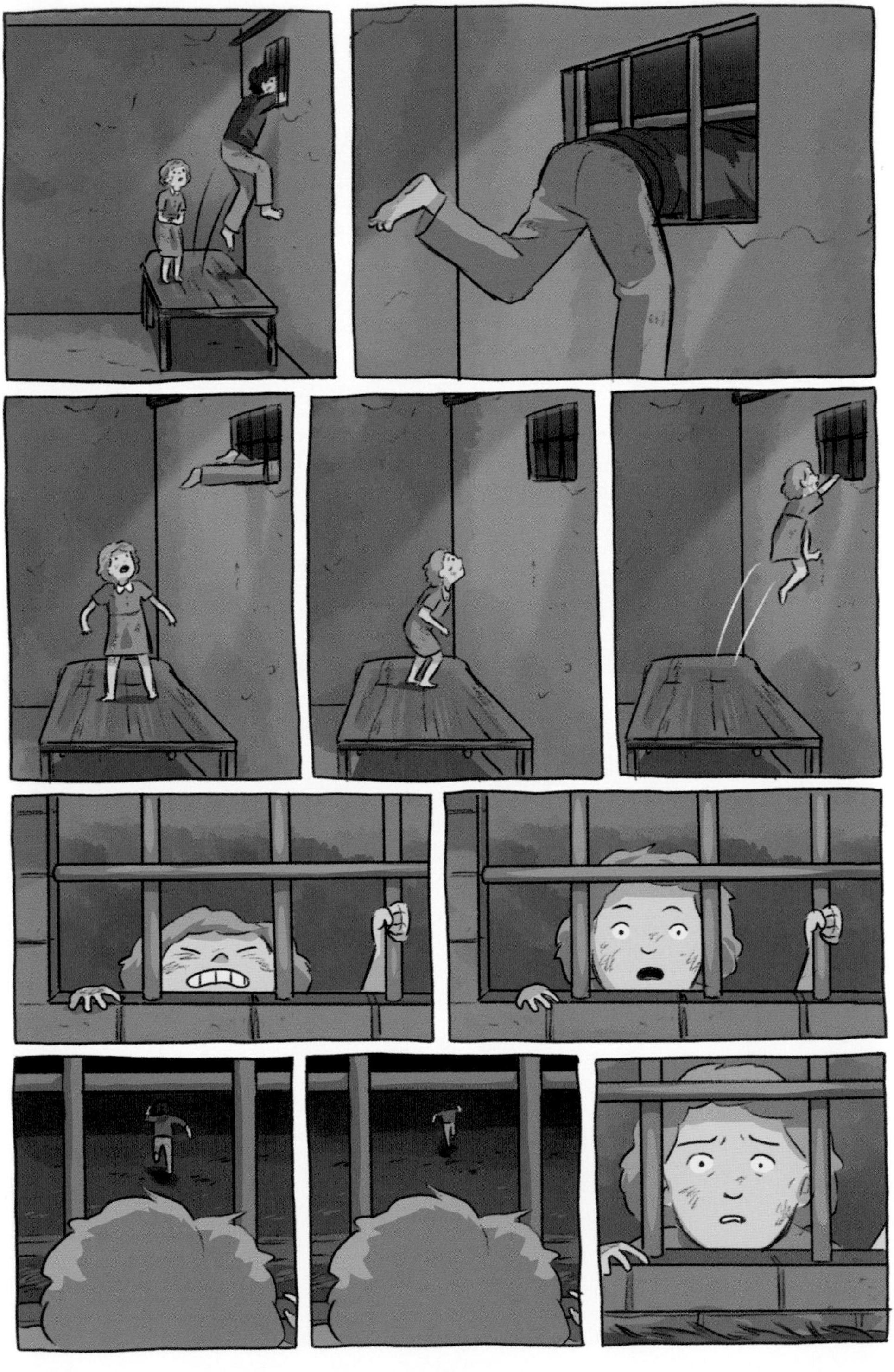

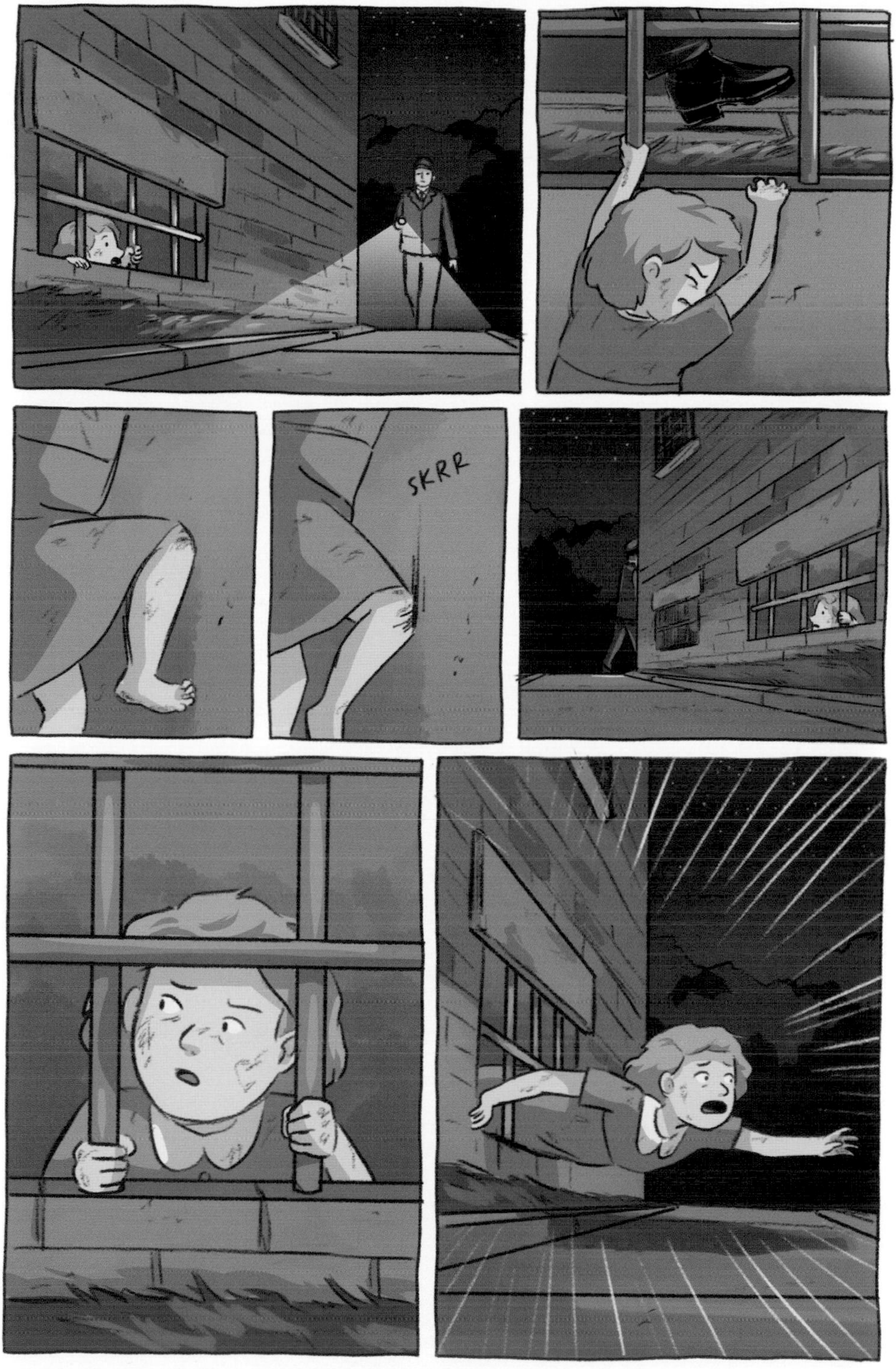
SKRR

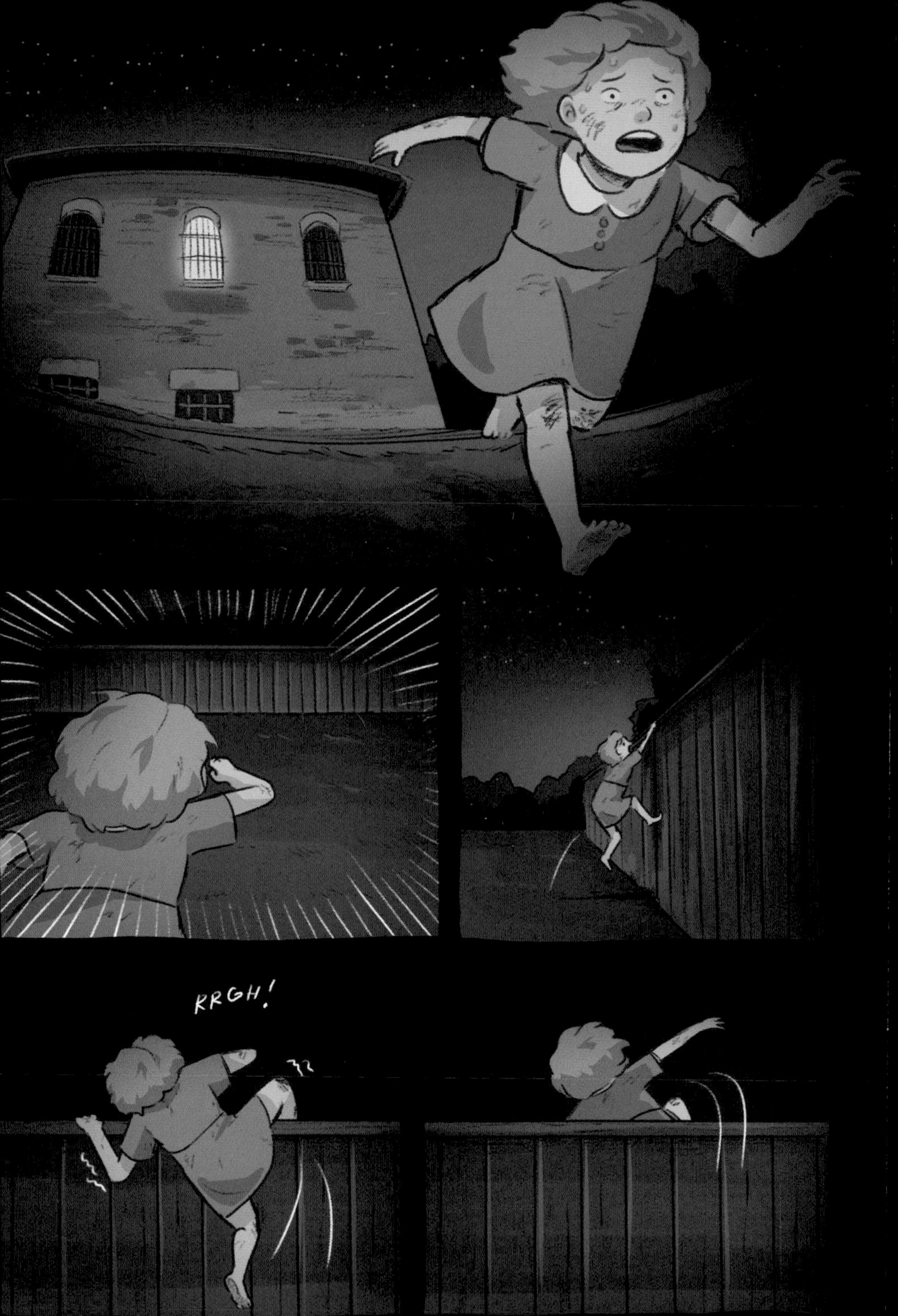
KRRGH!

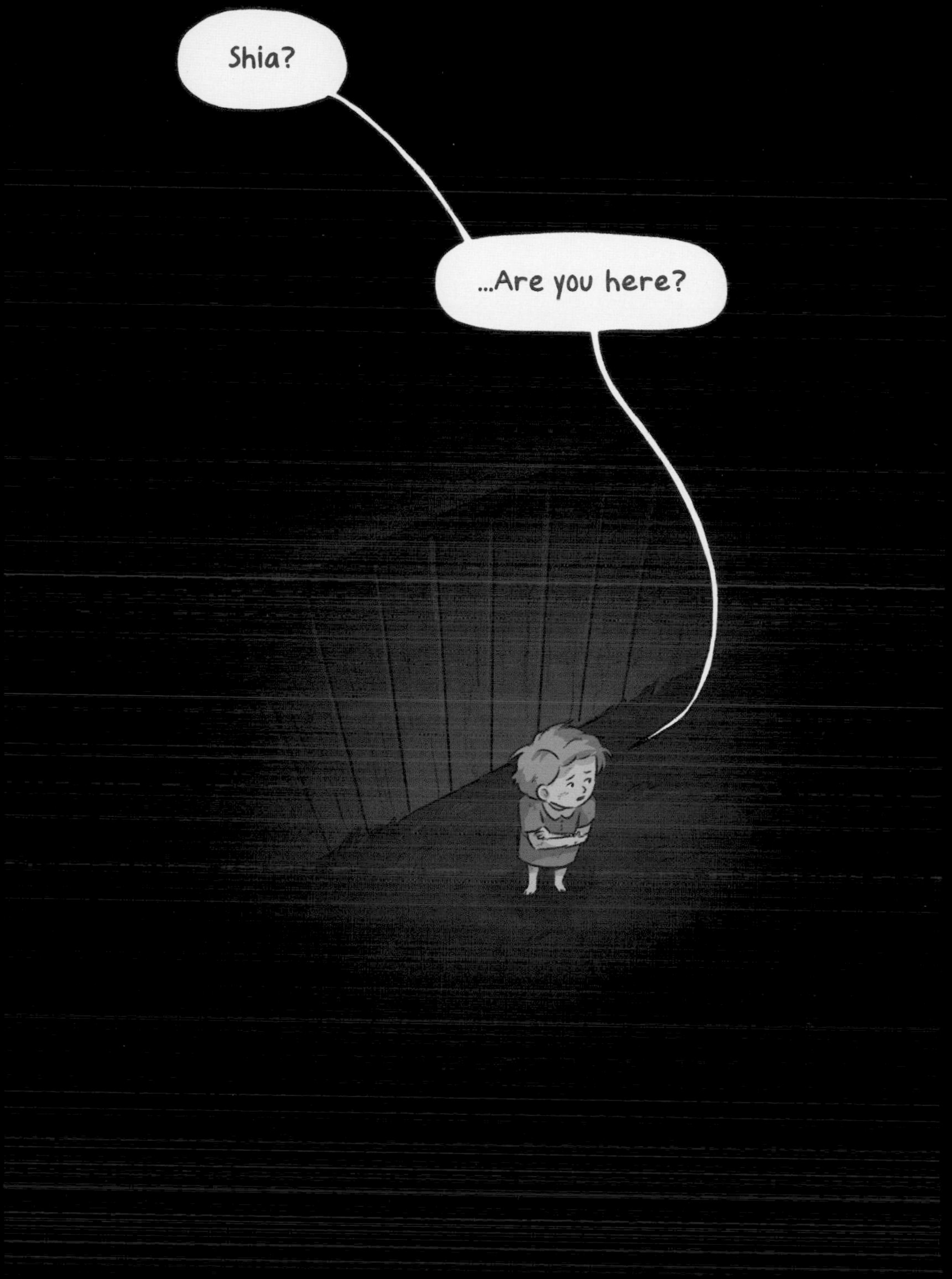
Shia?
...Are you here?

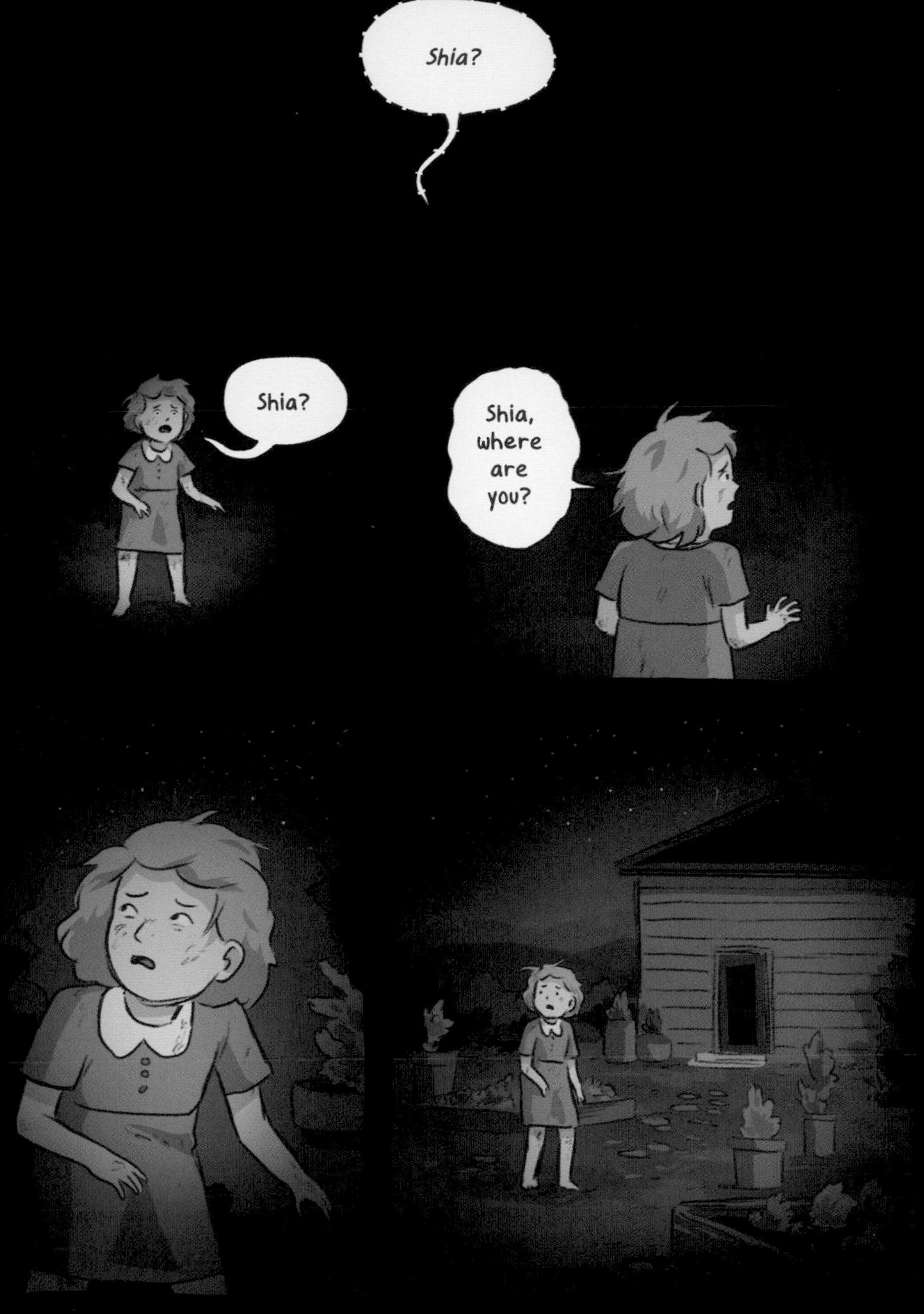
Shia?
Shia?
Shia, where are you?

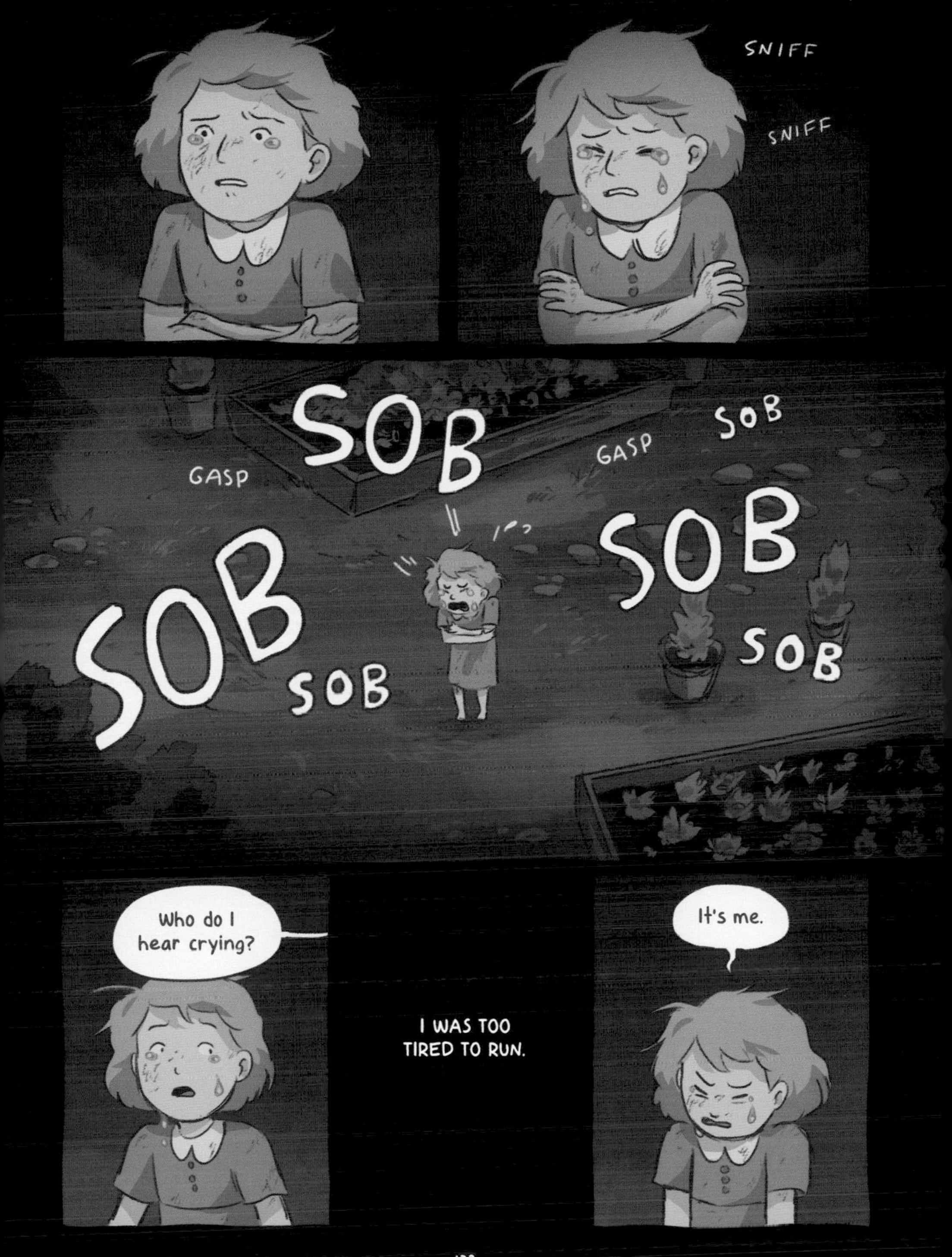
SNIFF
SNIFF
SOB
GASP
GASP
SOB
SOB
SOB
SOB
SOB
SOB
Who do I hear crying?
I WAS TOO TIRED TO RUN.
It's me.

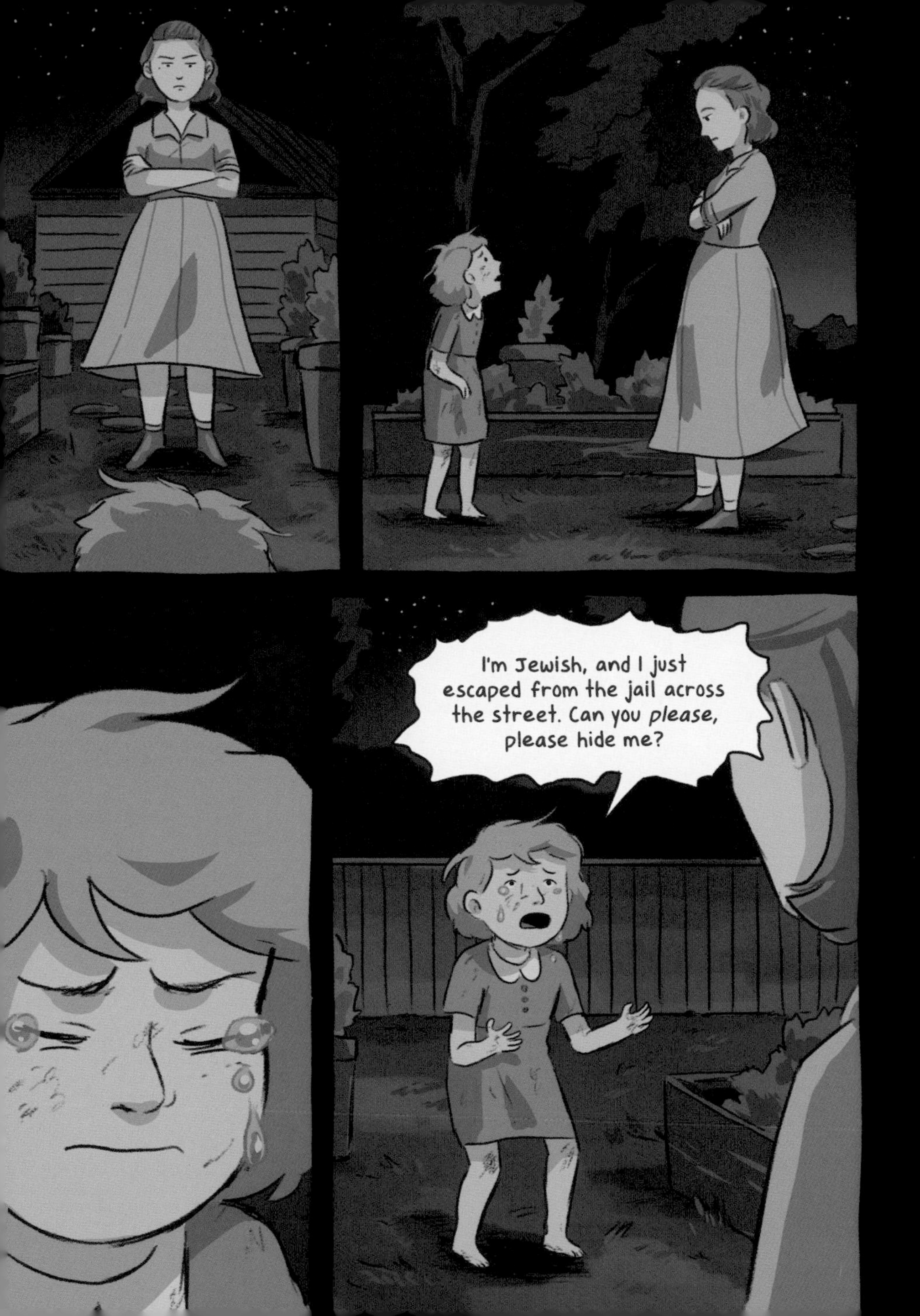
I'm Jewish, and I just escaped from the jail across the street. Can you *please*, please hide me?

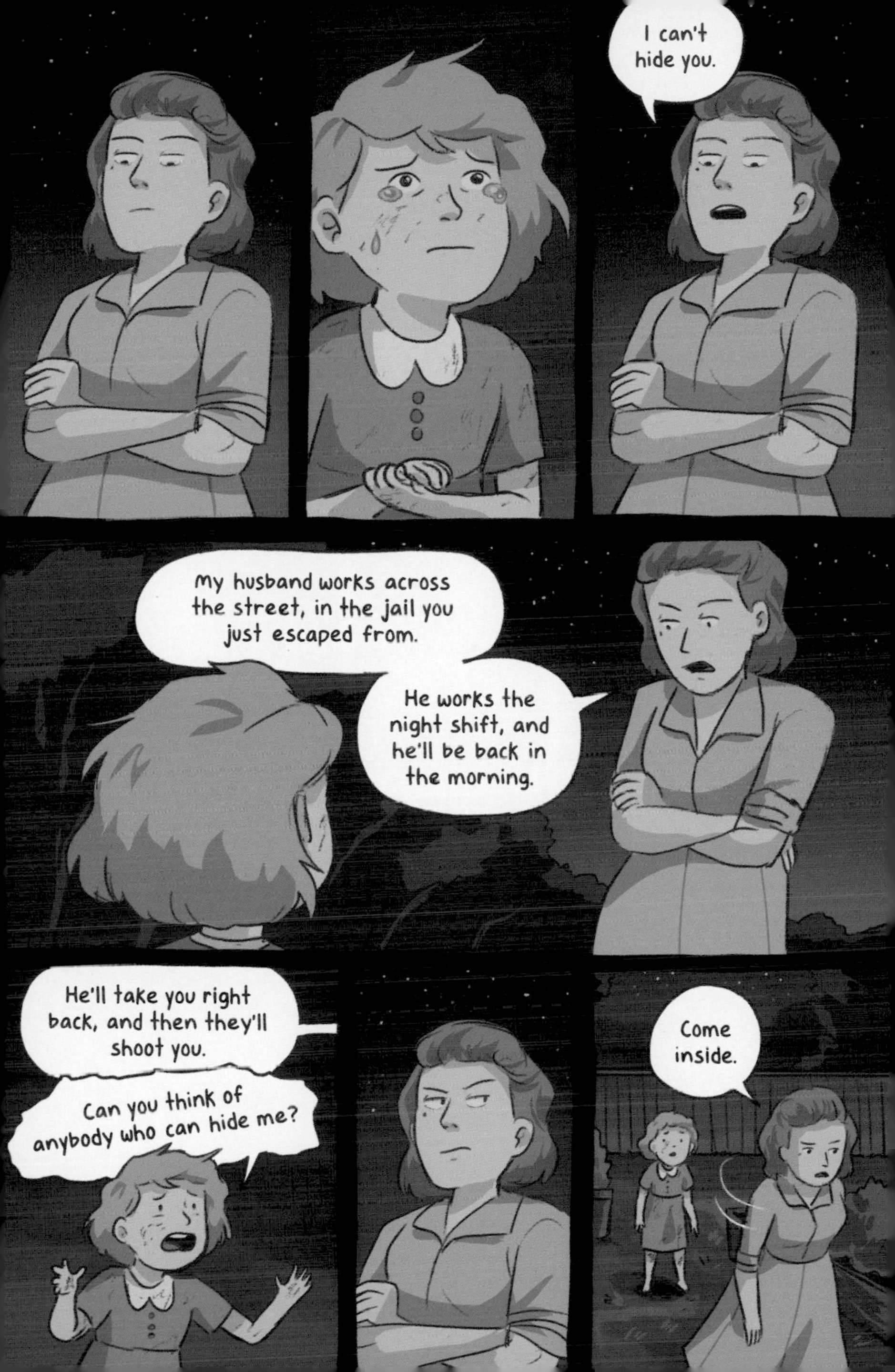
I can't hide you.
My husband works across the street, in the jail you just escaped from.
He works the night shift, and he'll be back in the morning.
He'll take you right back, and then they'll shoot you.
Can you think of anybody who can hide me?
Come inside.

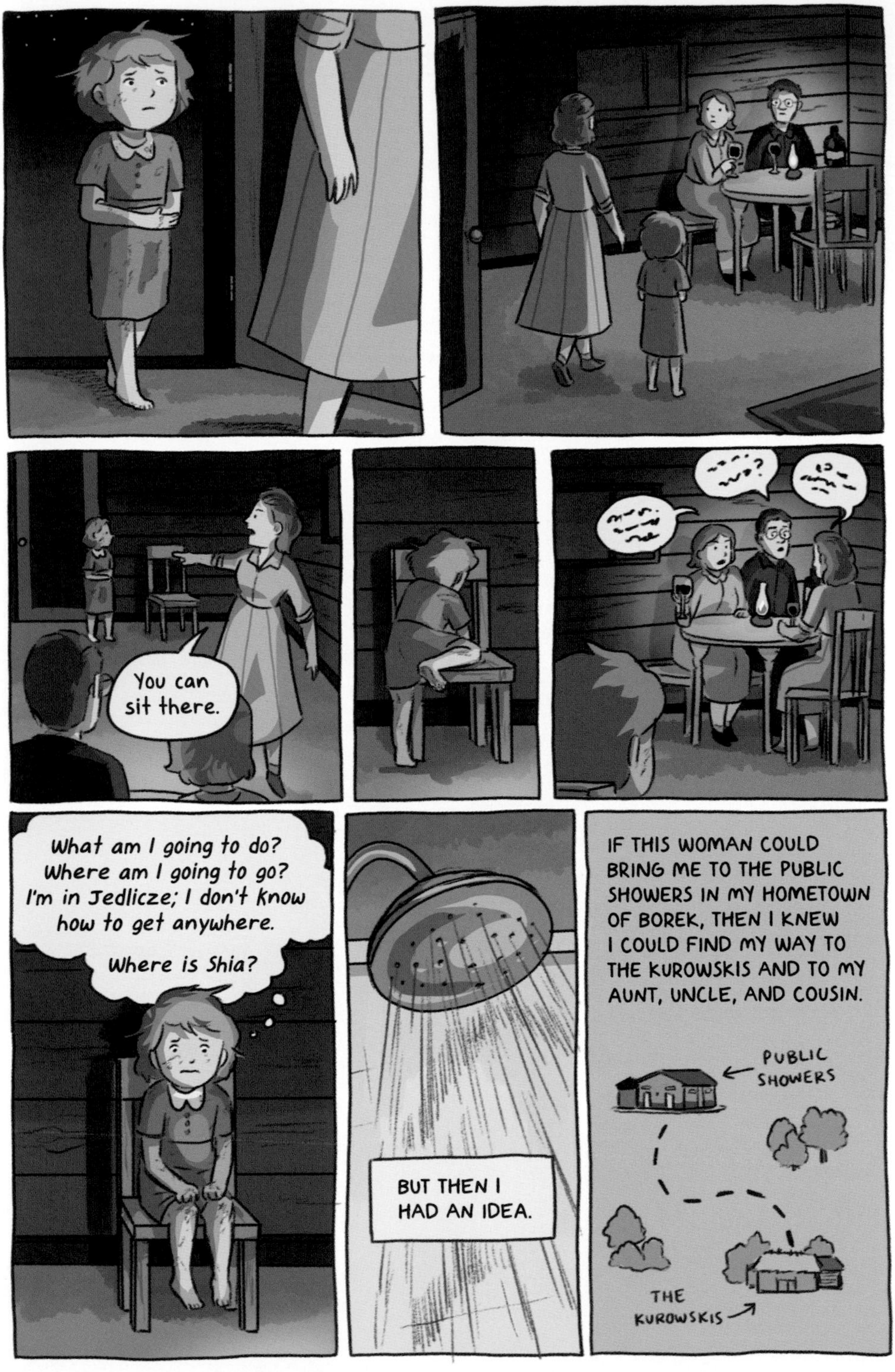
You can sit there.
What am I going to do? Where am I going to go? I'm in Jedlicze; I don't know how to get anywhere.
Where is Shia?
BUT THEN I HAD AN IDEA.
IF THIS WOMAN COULD BRING ME TO THE PUBLIC SHOWERS IN MY HOMETOWN OF BOREK, THEN I KNEW I COULD FIND MY WAY TO THE KUROWSKIS AND TO MY AUNT, UNCLE, AND COUSIN.
PUBLIC SHOWERS
THE KUROWSKIS

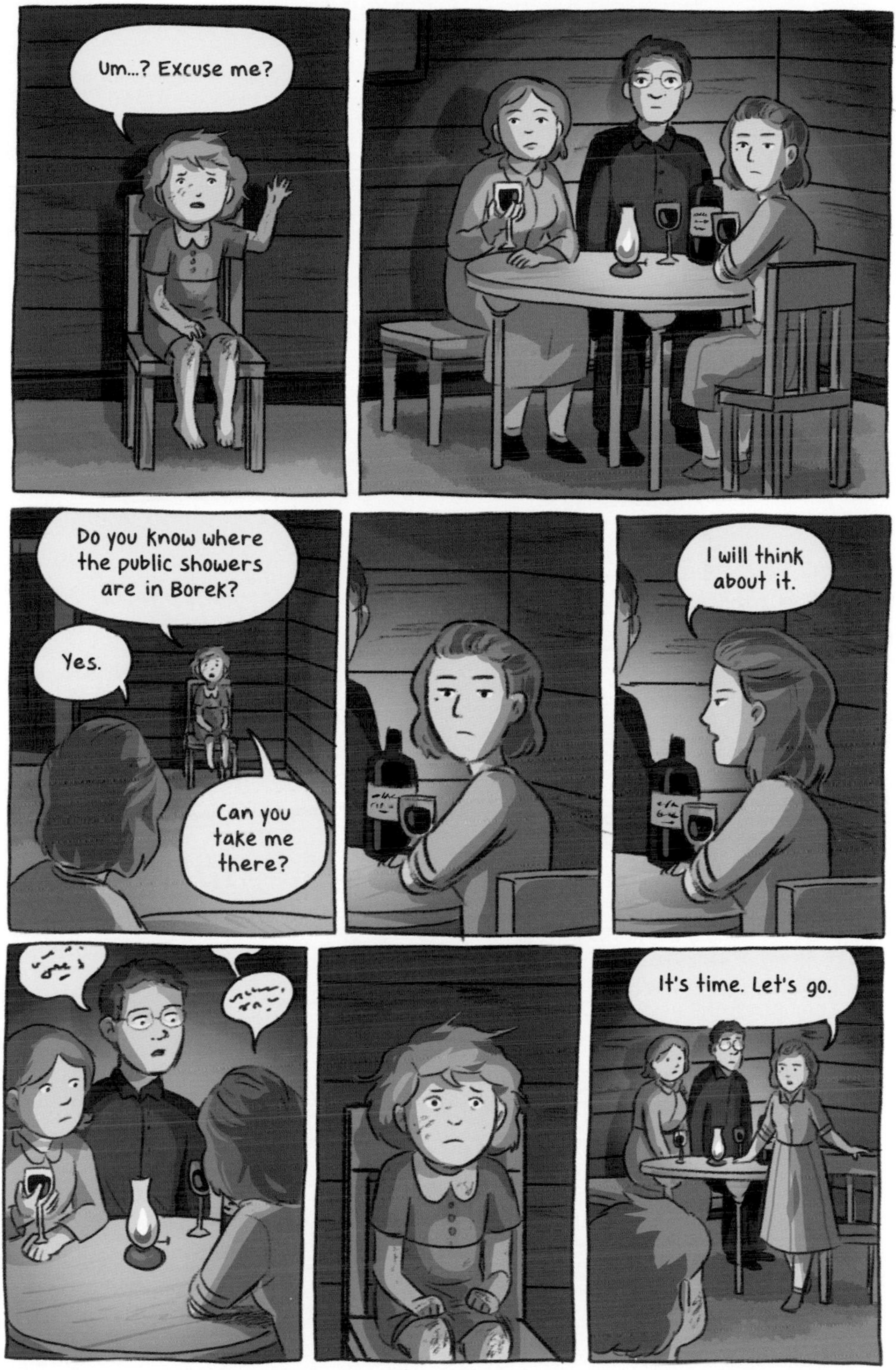
Um...? Excuse me?
Do you know where the public showers are in Borek?
Yes.
Can you take me there?
I will think about it.
It's time. Let's go.

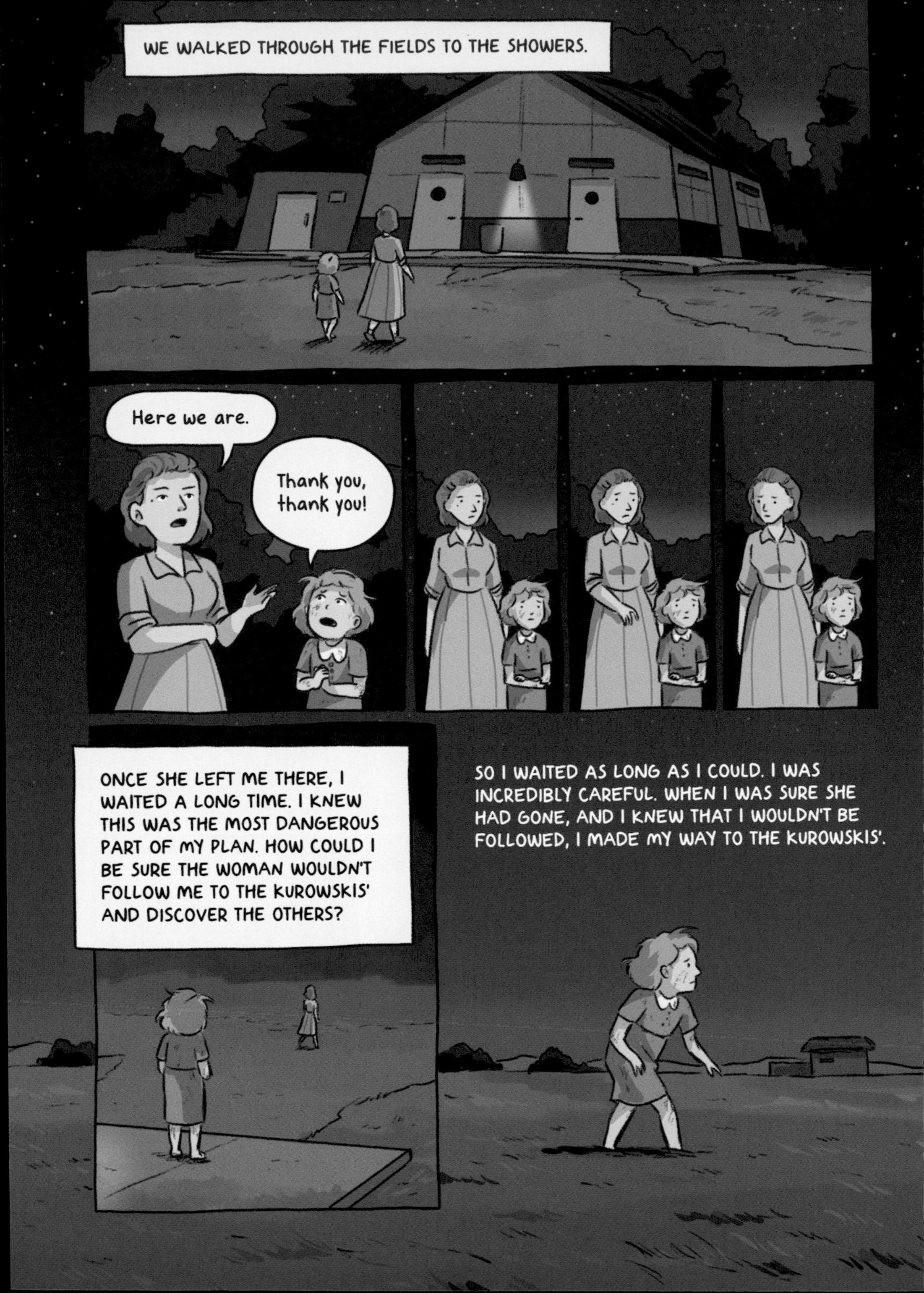
WE WALKED THROUGH THE FIELDS TO THE SHOWERS.
Here we are.
Thank you, thank you!
ONCE SHE LEFT ME THERE, I WAITED A LONG TIME. I KNEW THIS WAS THE MOST DANGEROUS PART OF MY PLAN. HOW COULD I BE SURE THE WOMAN WOULDN'T FOLLOW ME TO THE KUROWSKIS' AND DISCOVER THE OTHERS?
SO I WAITED AS LONG AS I COULD. I WAS INCREDIBLY CAREFUL. WHEN I WAS SURE SHE HAD GONE, AND I KNEW THAT I WOULDN'T BE FOLLOWED, I MADE MY WAY TO THE KUROWSKIS'.

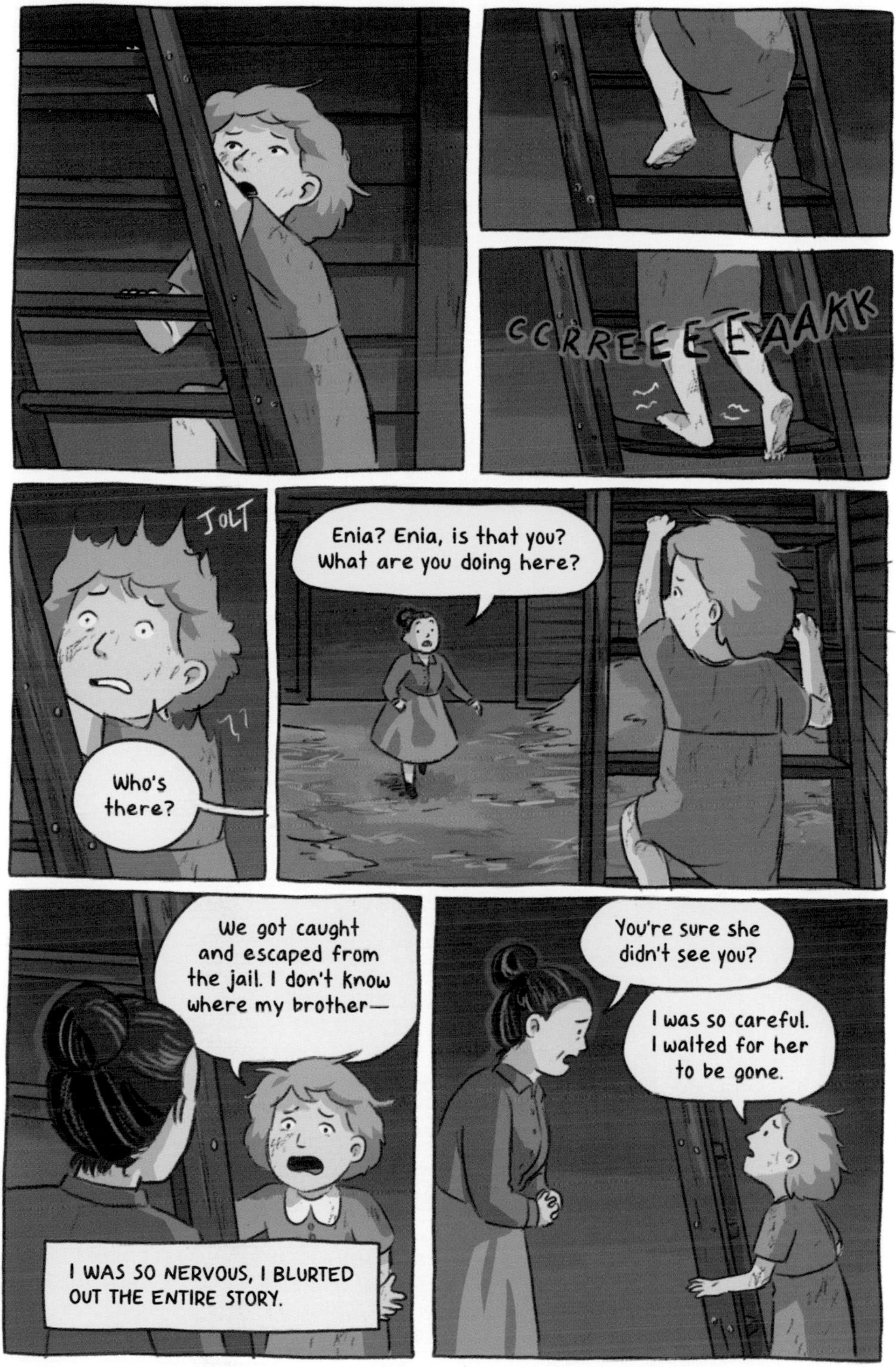
CCRREEEEAAKK
JOLT
Who's there?
Enia? Enia, is that you? What are you doing here?
We got caught and escaped from the jail. I don't know where my brother—
I WAS SO NERVOUS, I BLURTED OUT THE ENTIRE STORY.
You're sure she didn't see you?
I was so careful. I waited for her to be gone.

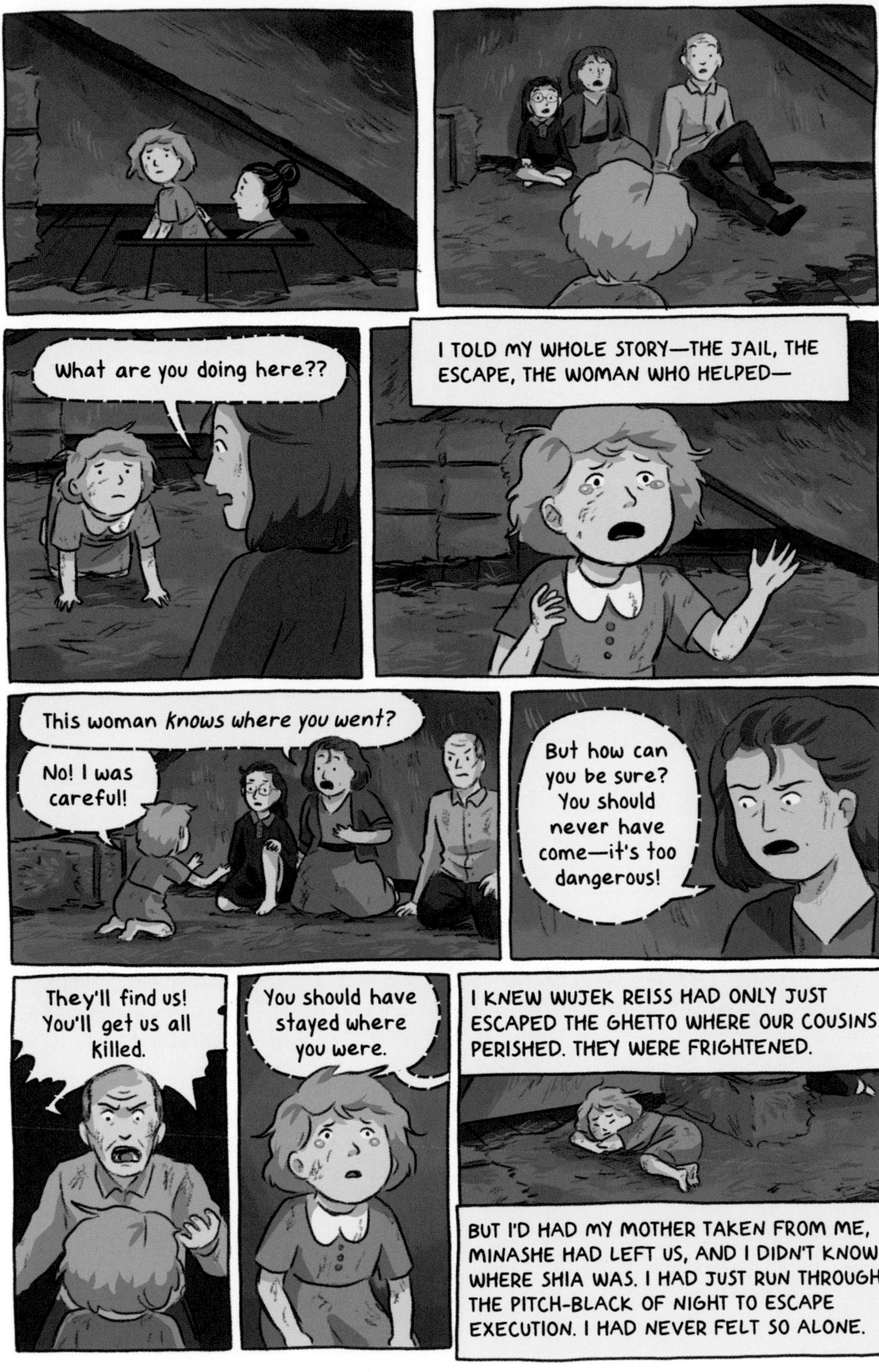
What are you doing here??
I TOLD MY WHOLE STORY—THE JAIL, THE ESCAPE, THE WOMAN WHO HELPED—
This woman knows where you went?
No! I was careful!
But how can you be sure? You should never have come—it's too dangerous!
They'll find us! You'll get us all killed.
You should have stayed where you were.
I KNEW WUJEK REISS HAD ONLY JUST ESCAPED THE GHETTO WHERE OUR COUSINS PERISHED. THEY WERE FRIGHTENED.
BUT I'D HAD MY MOTHER TAKEN FROM ME, MINASHE HAD LEFT US, AND I DIDN'T KNOW WHERE SHIA WAS. I HAD JUST RUN THROUGH THE PITCH-BLACK OF NIGHT TO ESCAPE EXECUTION. I HAD NEVER FELT SO ALONE.

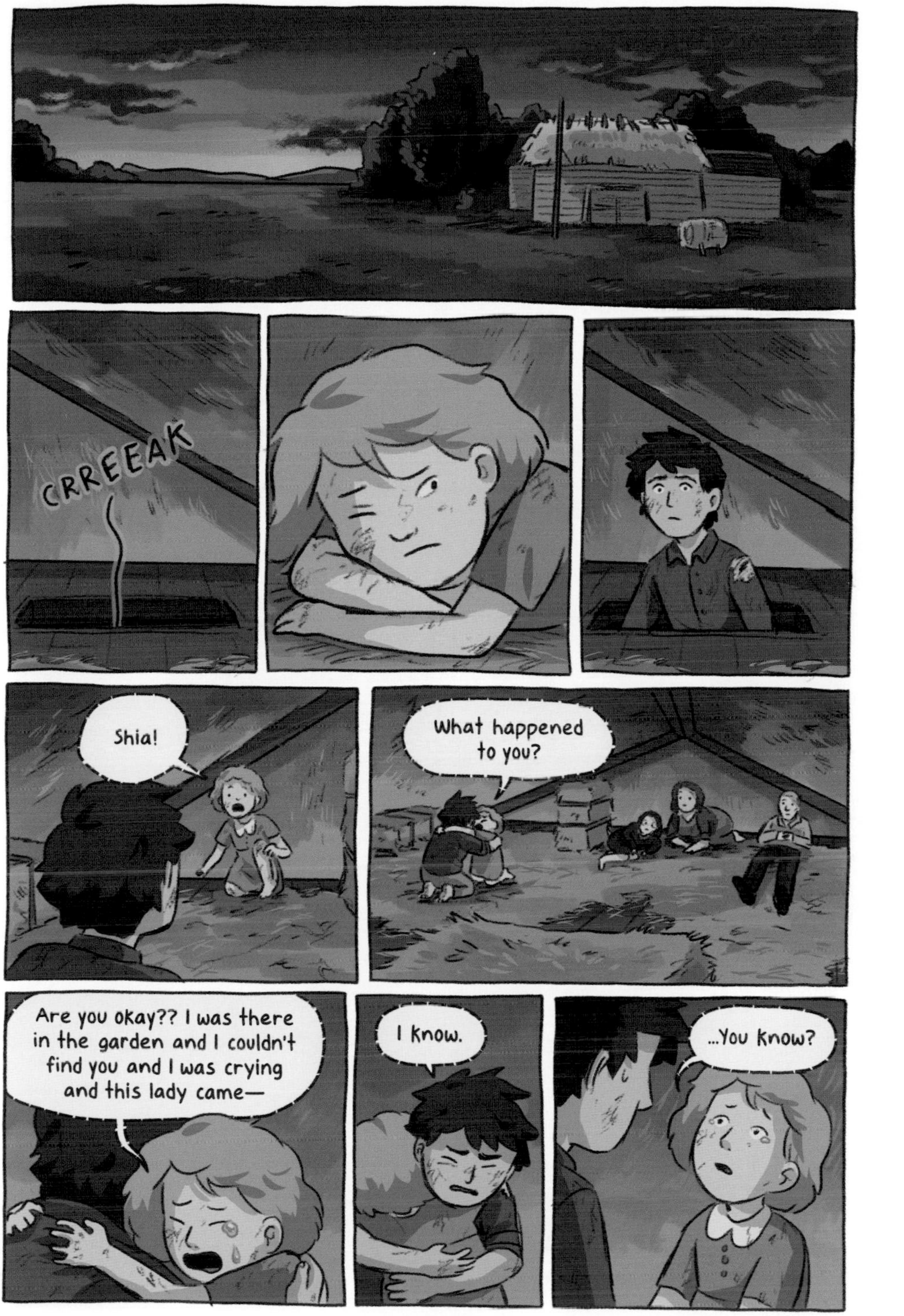
CRREEAK
Shia!
What happened to you?
Are you okay?? I was there in the garden and I couldn't find you and I was crying and this lady came—
I know.
...You know?

I heard you crying, and I ran. I thought you'd give us both away.

I LATER LEARNED HE HADN'T WAITED FOR ME AT ALL.

CRUNCH!

AS SOON AS HE'D HIT THE OTHER SIDE OF THE FENCE, HE HAD PANICKED AND KEPT GOING.

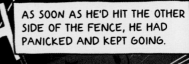

HE COULDN'T THINK ABOUT ME.

THAT WAS HARD TO HEAR.

BUT I REALIZED I SURVIVED SO LONG BECAUSE OF HIM.

SO I FORGAVE HIM.

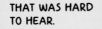

EVENTUALLY, WE SETTLED INTO A ROUTINE.

WE HAD TO. WE HAD NOWHERE ELSE TO GO. MY BROTHER AND I HAD A SPACE ON ONE SIDE OF THE ATTIC. BEHIND A ROW OF HAY BALES WERE MY AUNT, UNCLE, AND COUSIN.

SHIA AND I SLEPT HERE

WUJEK REISS, TANTE HINDA, AND MALA SLEPT HERE

LADDER TO FIRST FLOOR OF BARN

WASTE PAIL

MY AUNT WAS STILL VERY SICK WITH CANCER.

MY BROTHER WENT OUT TWO TO THREE NIGHTS A WEEK TO FIND US FOOD.

MALA, SHIA, AND I LOOKED OUT OF PEEPHOLES, TRYING TO SEE THE WORLD OUTSIDE.

I WONDERED ABOUT PUDLINA.

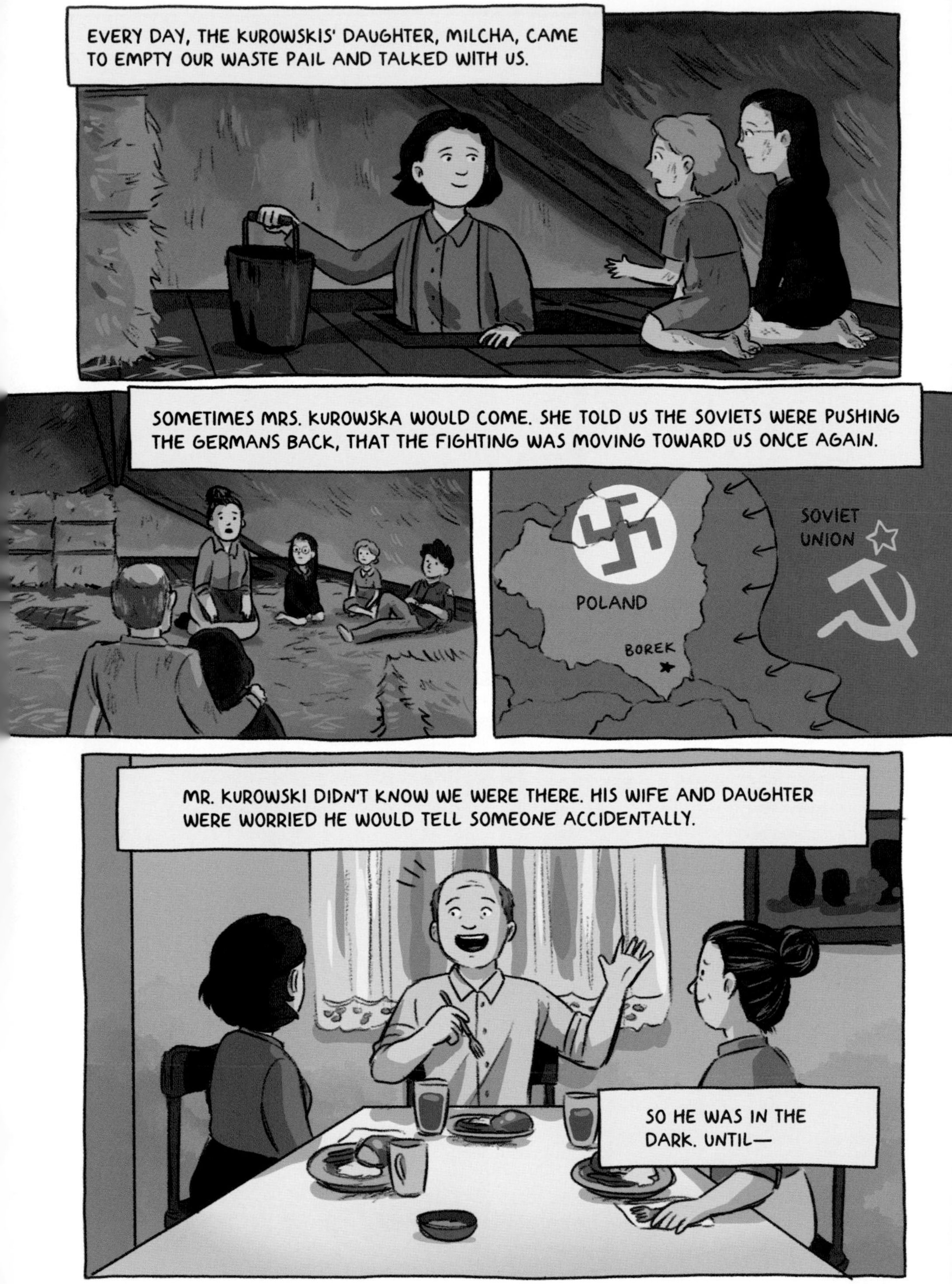
EVERY DAY, THE KUROWSKIS' DAUGHTER, MILCHA, CAME TO EMPTY OUR WASTE PAIL AND TALKED WITH US.
SOMETIMES MRS. KUROWSKA WOULD COME. SHE TOLD US THE SOVIETS WERE PUSHING THE GERMANS BACK, THAT THE FIGHTING WAS MOVING TOWARD US ONCE AGAIN.
SOVIET UNION
POLAND
BOREK
MR. KUROWSKI DIDN'T KNOW WE WERE THERE. HIS WIFE AND DAUGHTER WERE WORRIED HE WOULD TELL SOMEONE ACCIDENTALLY.
SO HE WAS IN THE DARK. UNTIL—

FALL 1943

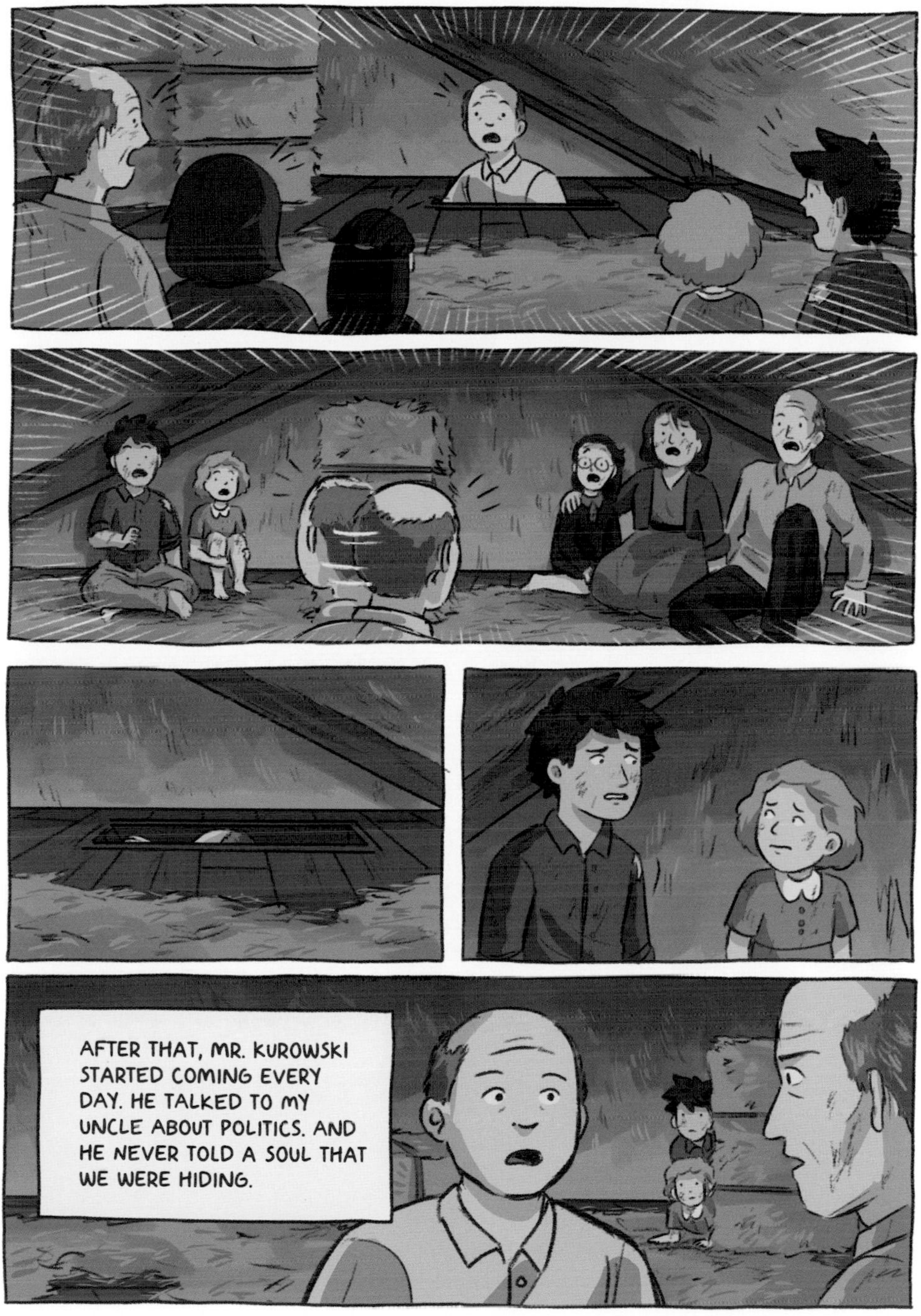
AFTER THAT, MR. KUROWSKI STARTED COMING EVERY DAY. HE TALKED TO MY UNCLE ABOUT POLITICS. AND HE NEVER TOLD A SOUL THAT WE WERE HIDING.

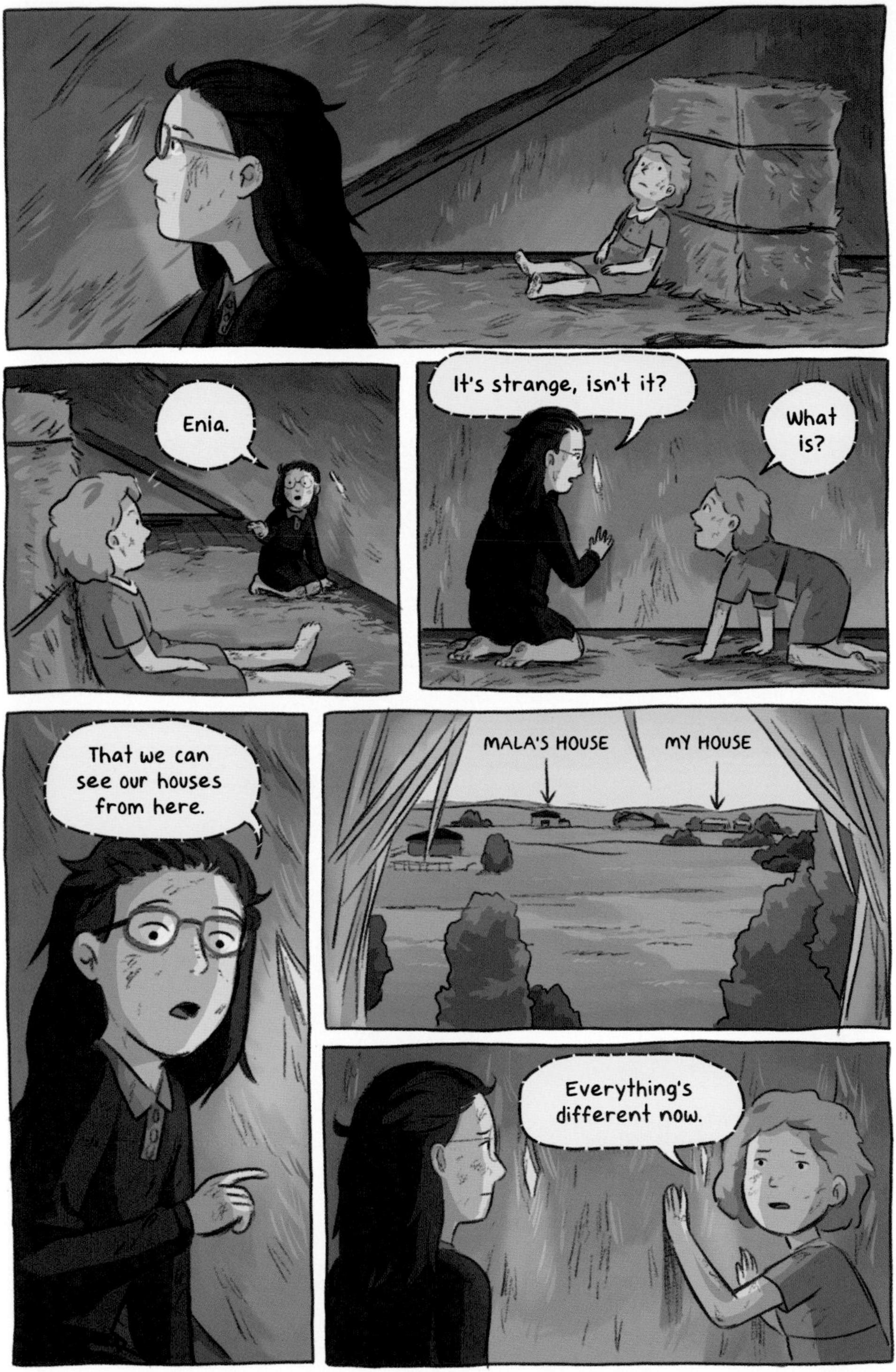

Enia.
It's strange, isn't it?
What is?
That we can see our houses from here.
MALA'S HOUSE
MY HOUSE
Everything's different now.

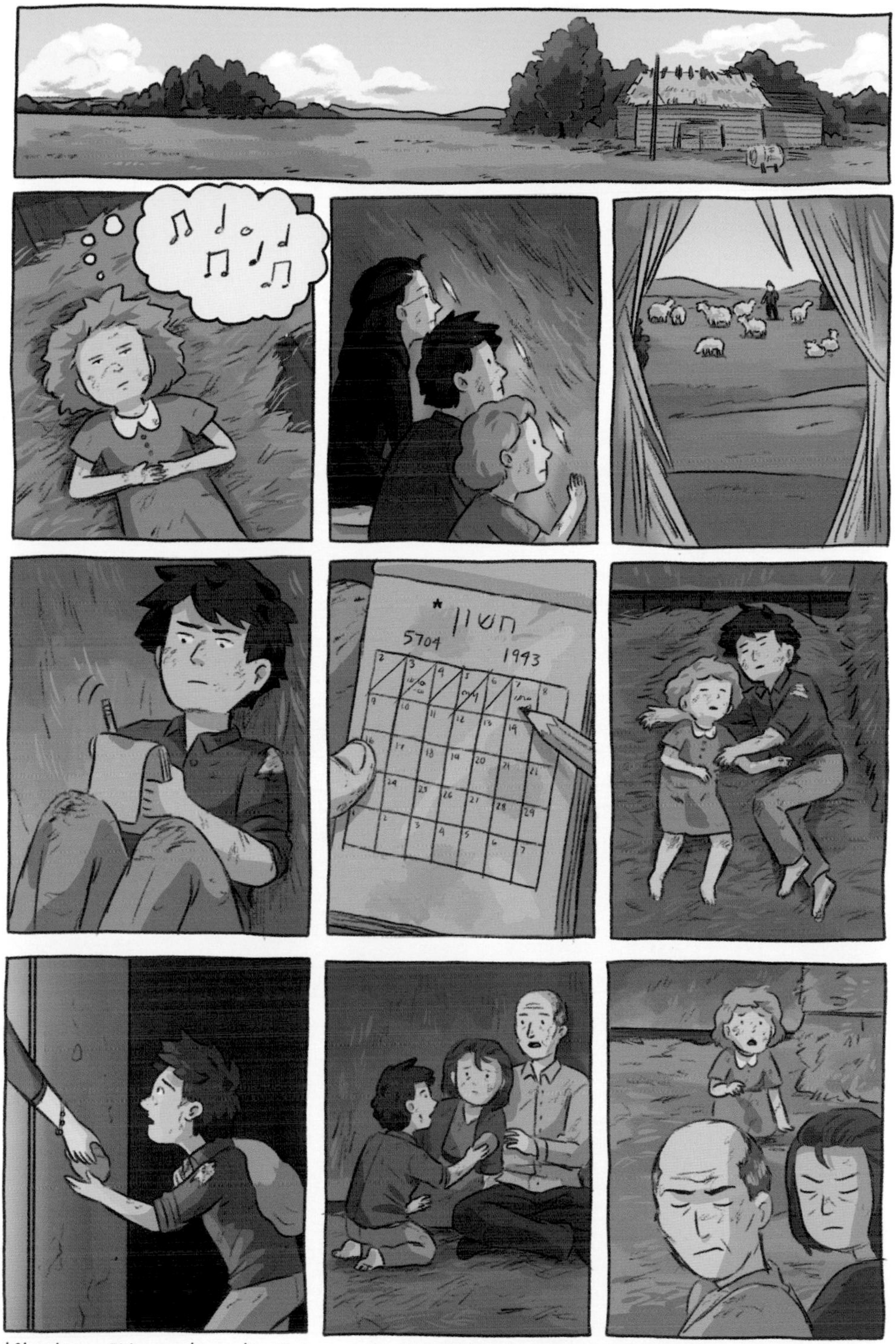
*חשון
5704
1943

*Cheshvan. This month on the Hebrew calendar falls between October and November on the Gregorian calendar.

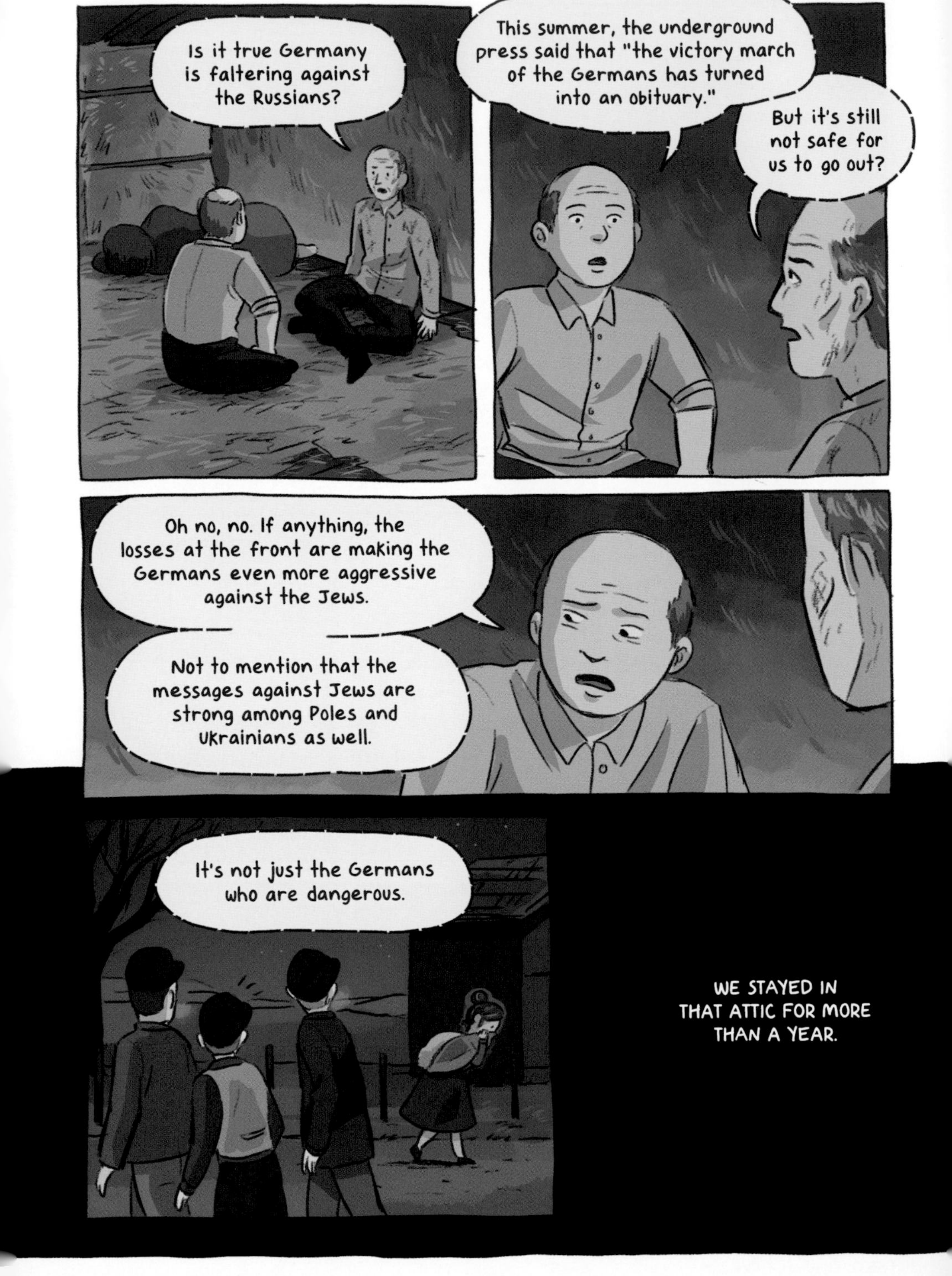
Is it true Germany is faltering against the Russians?
This summer, the underground press said that "the victory march of the Germans has turned into an obituary."
But it's still not safe for us to go out?
Oh no, no. If anything, the losses at the front are making the Germans even more aggressive against the Jews.
Not to mention that the messages against Jews are strong among Poles and Ukrainians as well.
It's not just the Germans who are dangerous.
WE STAYED IN THAT ATTIC FOR MORE THAN A YEAR.

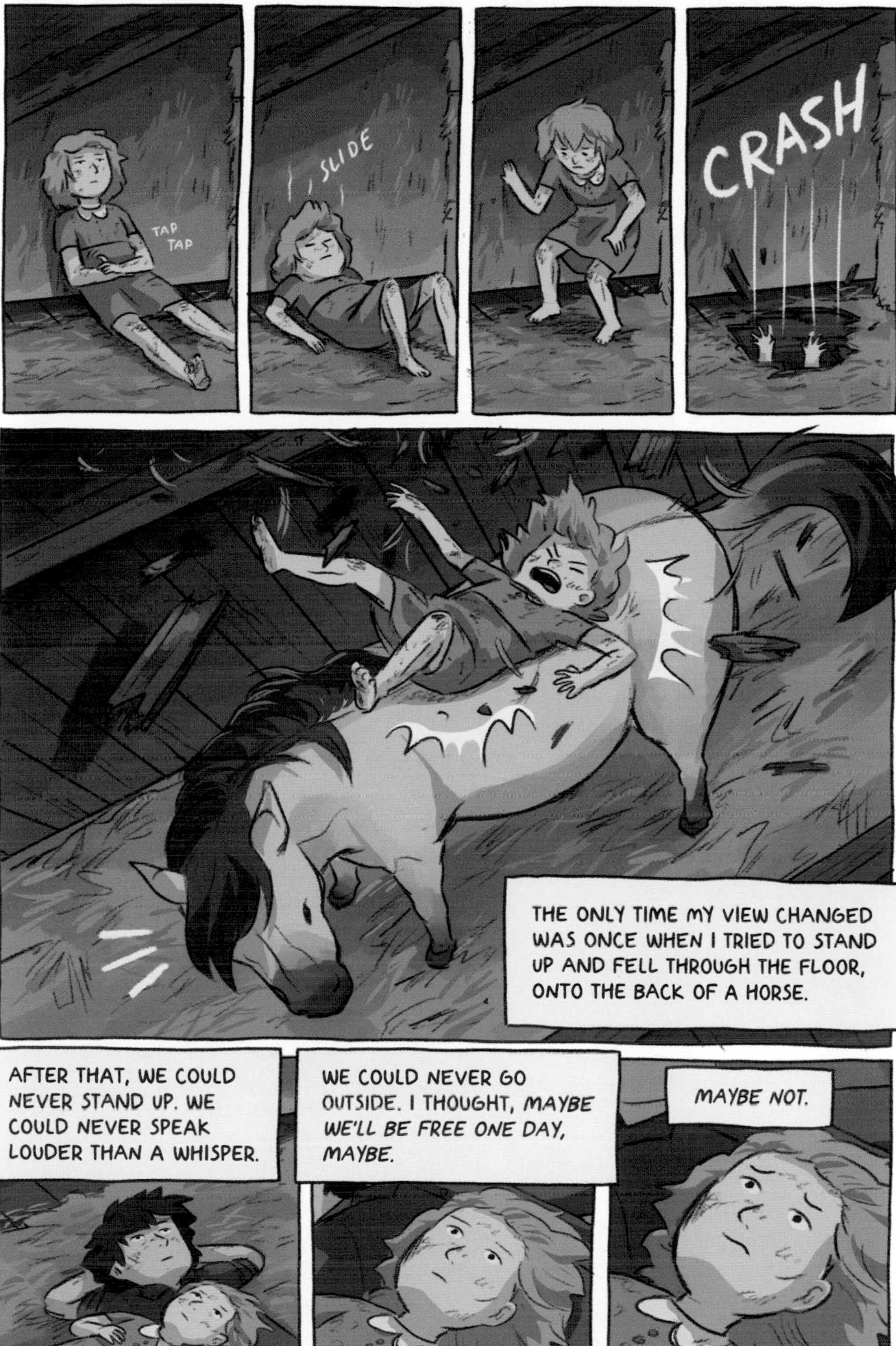

TAP TAP
SLIDE
CRASH
THE ONLY TIME MY VIEW CHANGED WAS ONCE WHEN I TRIED TO STAND UP AND FELL THROUGH THE FLOOR, ONTO THE BACK OF A HORSE.
AFTER THAT, WE COULD NEVER STAND UP. WE COULD NEVER SPEAK LOUDER THAN A WHISPER.
WE COULD NEVER GO OUTSIDE. I THOUGHT, *MAYBE WE'LL BE FREE ONE DAY, MAYBE.*
MAYBE NOT.

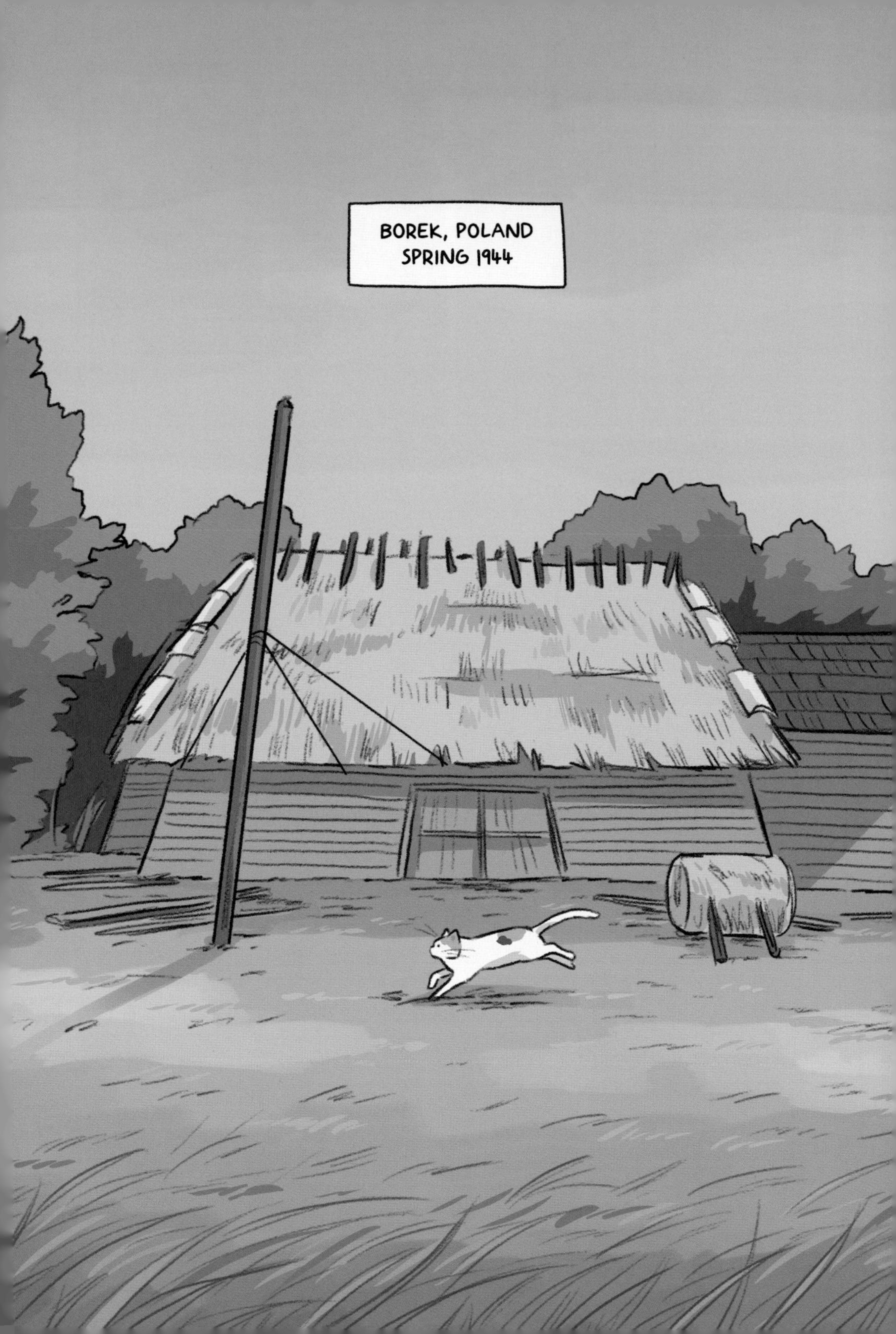
BOREK, POLAND
SPRING 1944

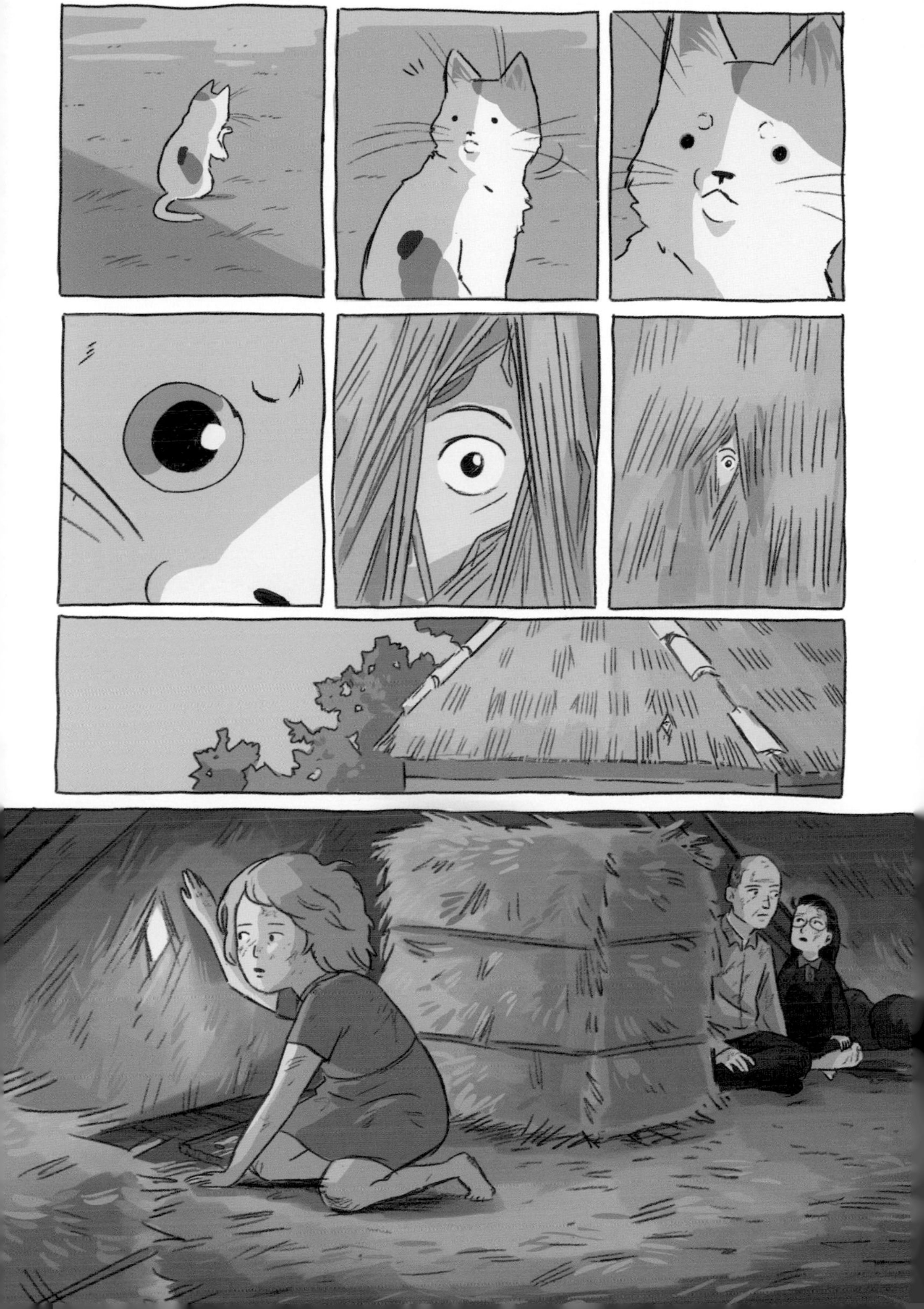

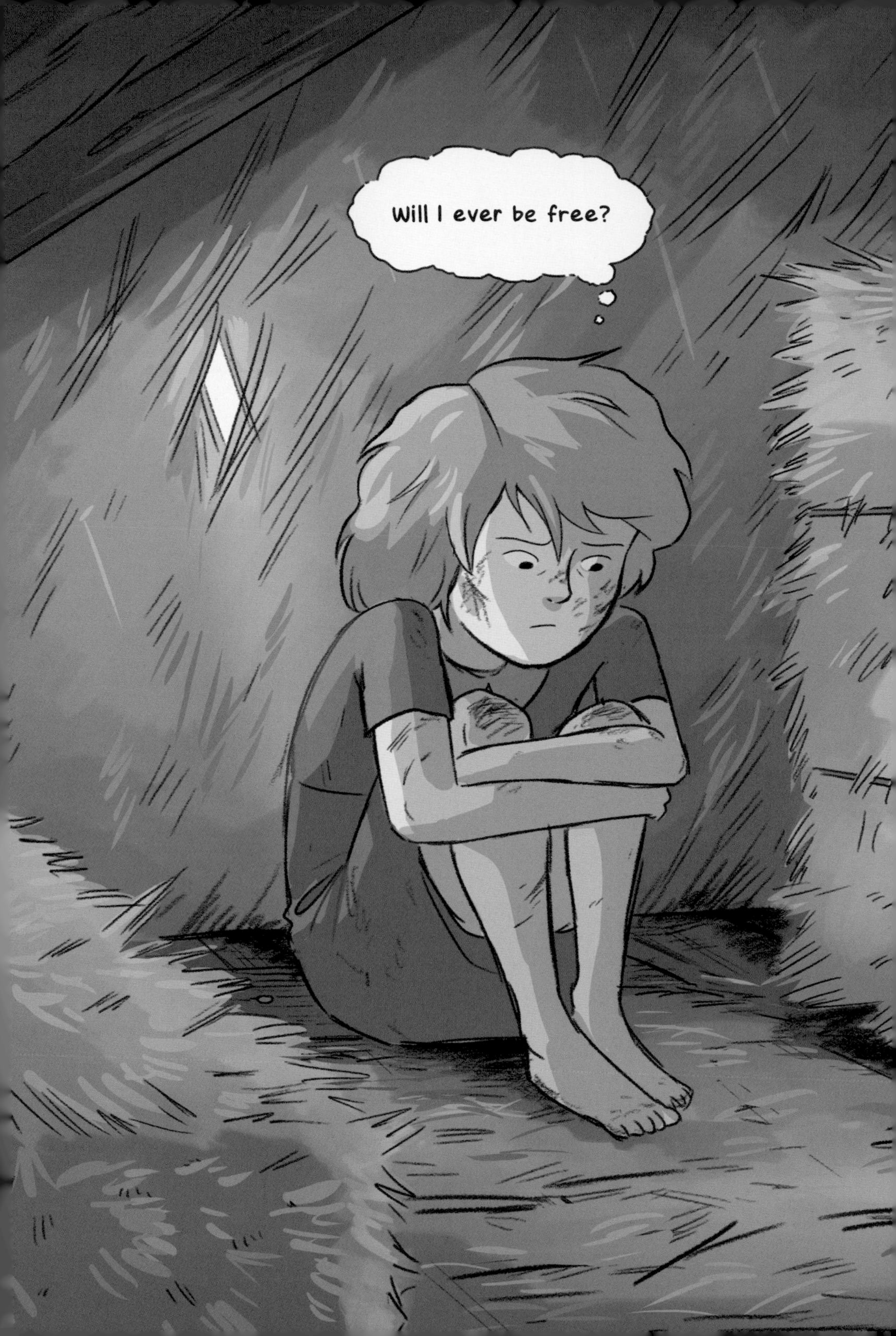
Will I ever be free?

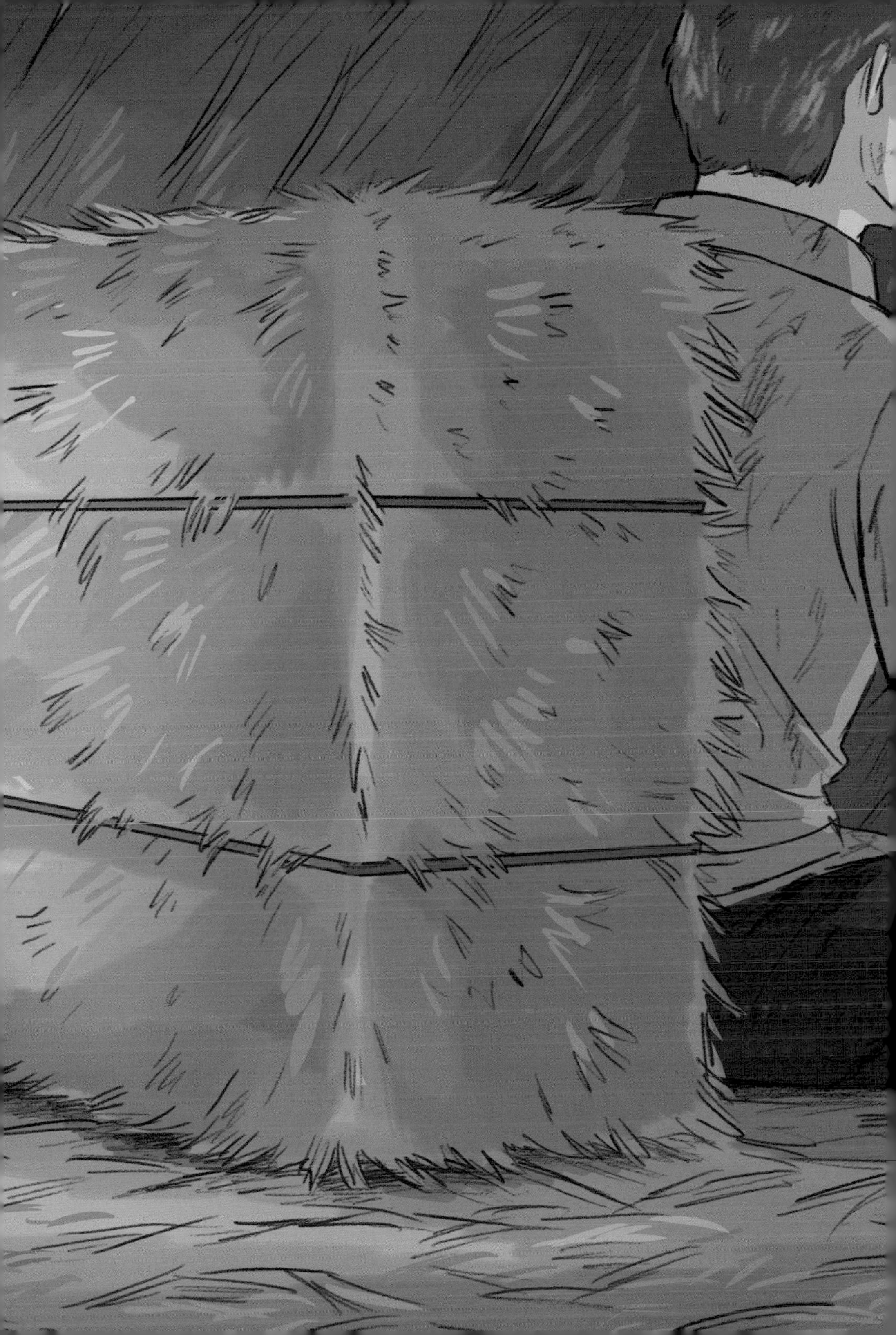

PART 3:

LIBERATION
1944–1947

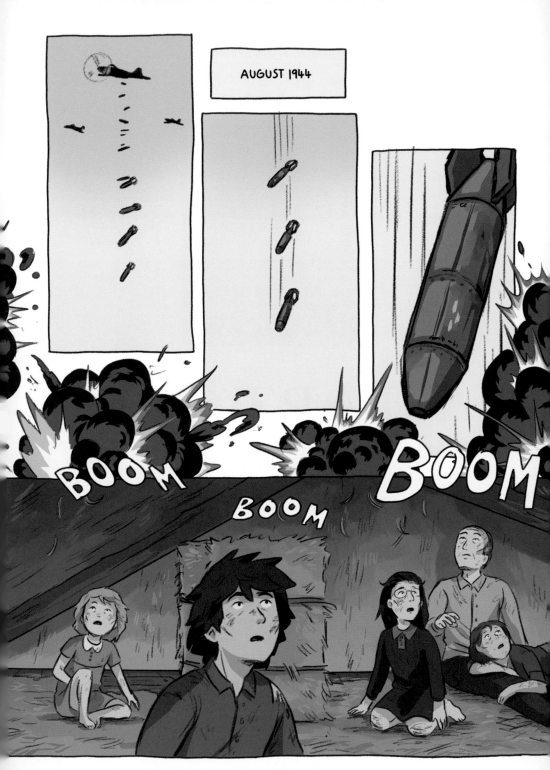

AUGUST 1944

BOOM BOOM BOOM

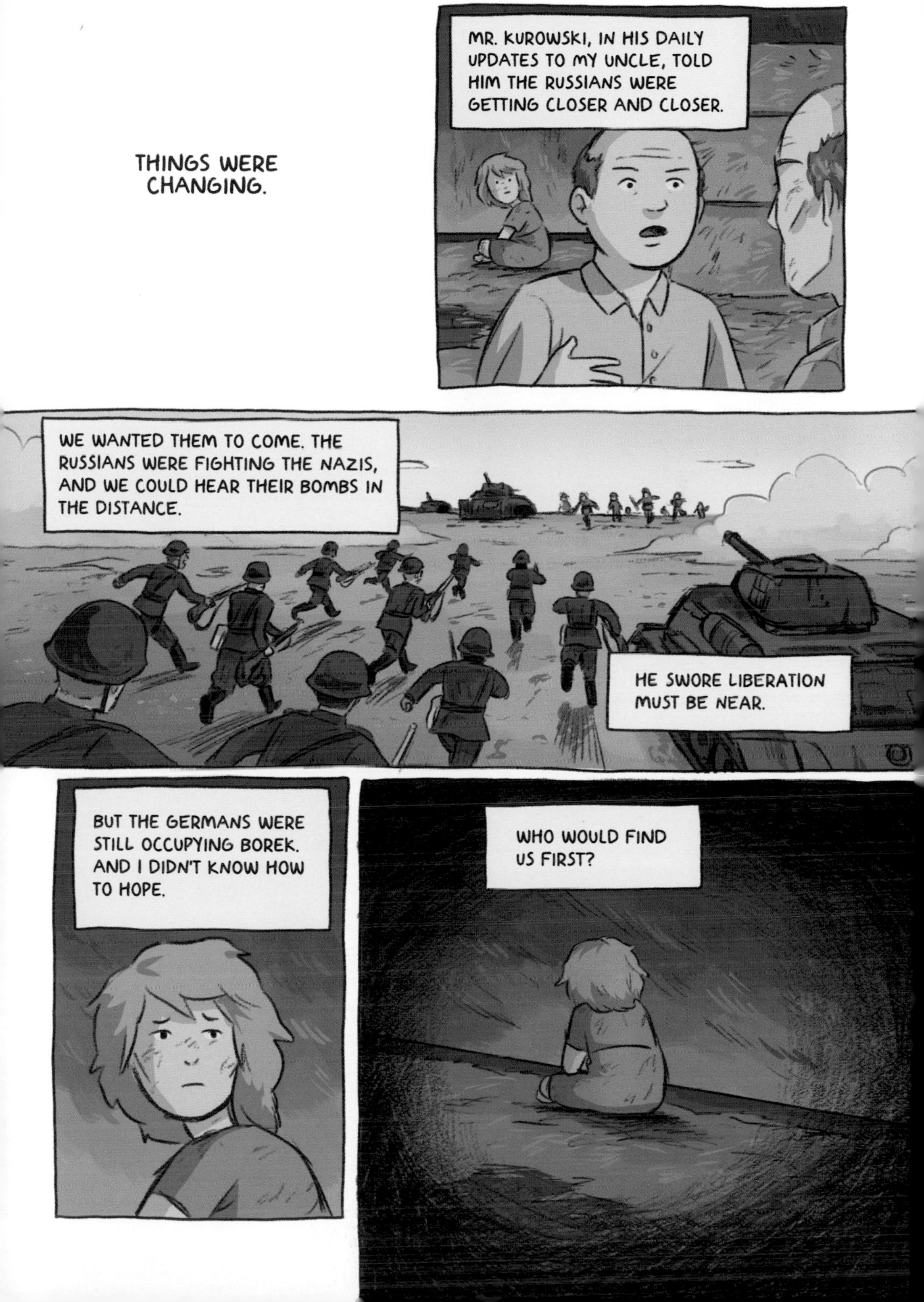
THINGS WERE CHANGING.
MR. KUROWSKI, IN HIS DAILY UPDATES TO MY UNCLE, TOLD HIM THE RUSSIANS WERE GETTING CLOSER AND CLOSER.
WE WANTED THEM TO COME. THE RUSSIANS WERE FIGHTING THE NAZIS, AND WE COULD HEAR THEIR BOMBS IN THE DISTANCE.
HE SWORE LIBERATION MUST BE NEAR.
BUT THE GERMANS WERE STILL OCCUPYING BOREK. AND I DIDN'T KNOW HOW TO HOPE.
WHO WOULD FIND US FIRST?

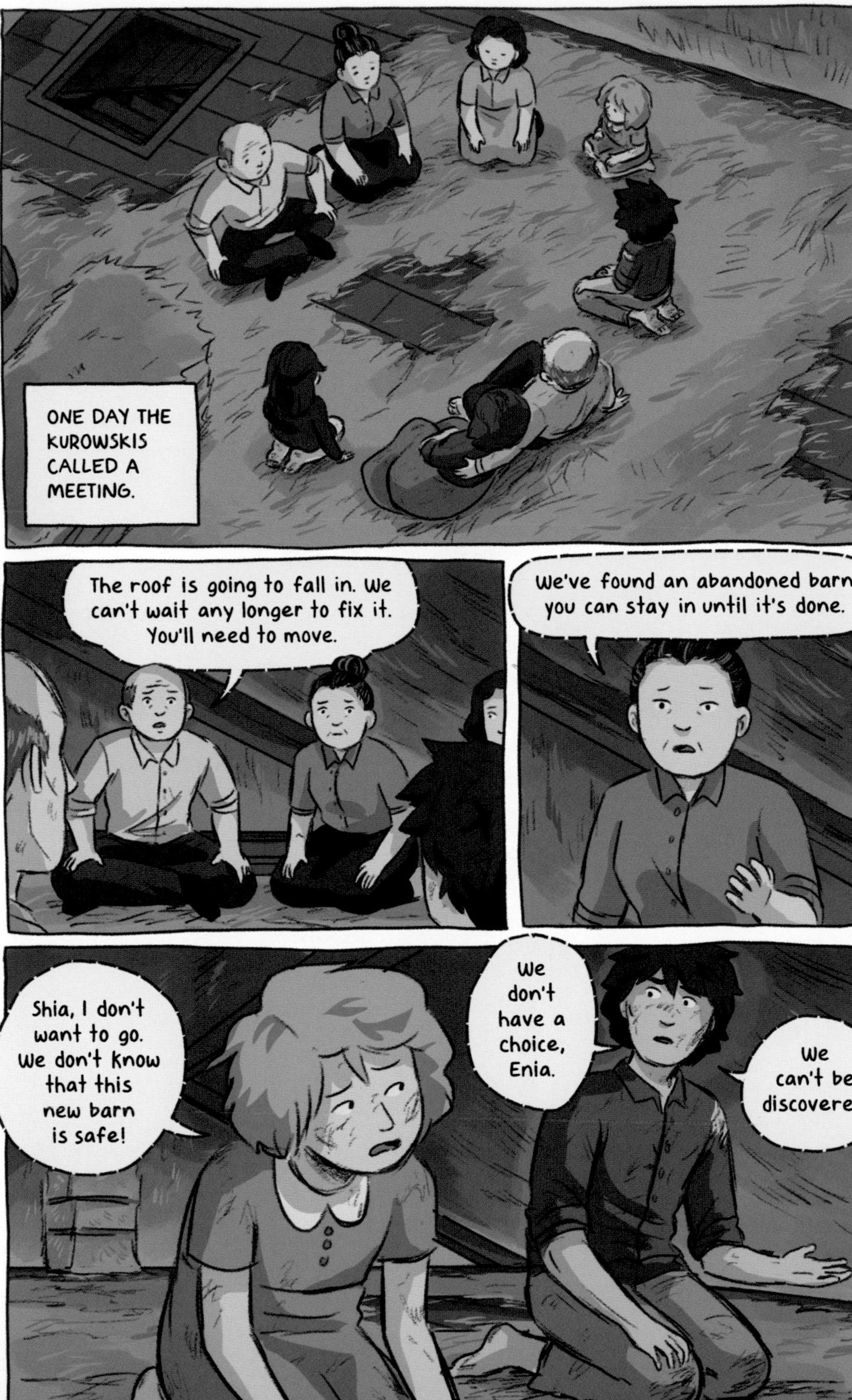
ONE DAY THE KUROWSKIS CALLED A MEETING.
The roof is going to fall in. We can't wait any longer to fix it. You'll need to move.
We've found an abandoned barn you can stay in until it's done.
Shia, I don't want to go. We don't know that this new barn is safe!
We don't have a choice, Enia.
We can't be discovered.

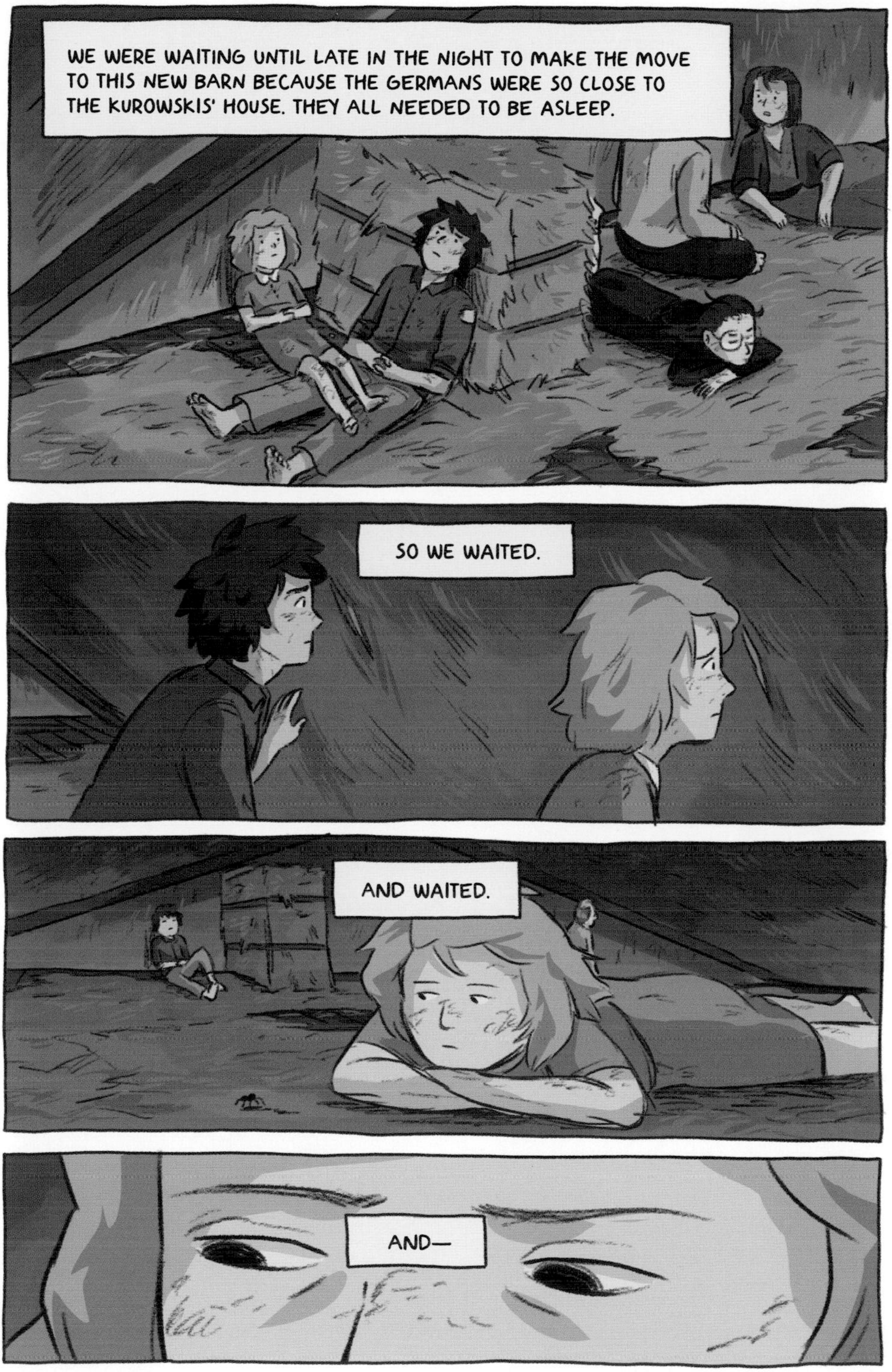
WE WERE WAITING UNTIL LATE IN THE NIGHT TO MAKE THE MOVE TO THIS NEW BARN BECAUSE THE GERMANS WERE SO CLOSE TO THE KUROWSKIS' HOUSE. THEY ALL NEEDED TO BE ASLEEP.
SO WE WAITED.
AND WAITED.
AND—

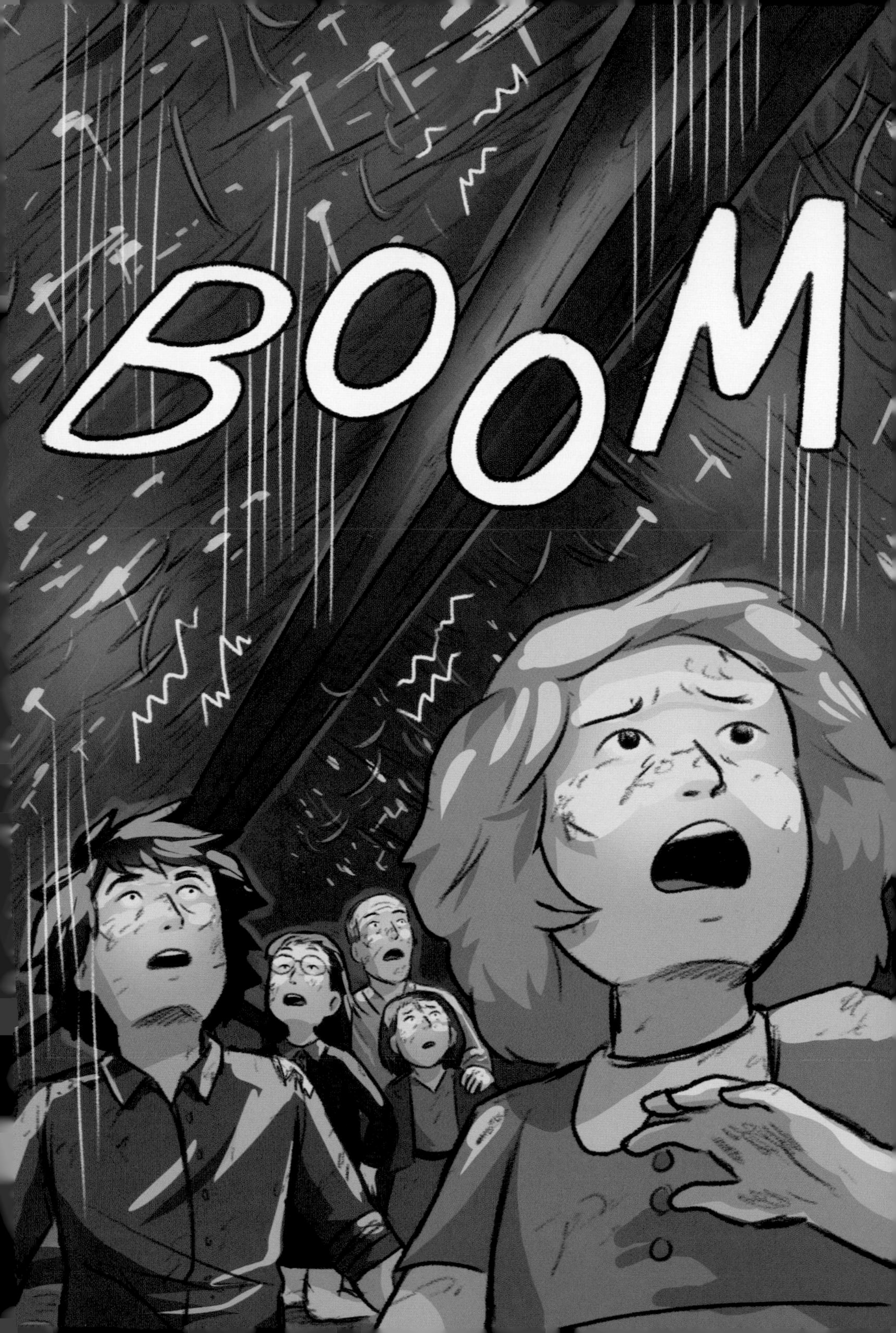
BOOM

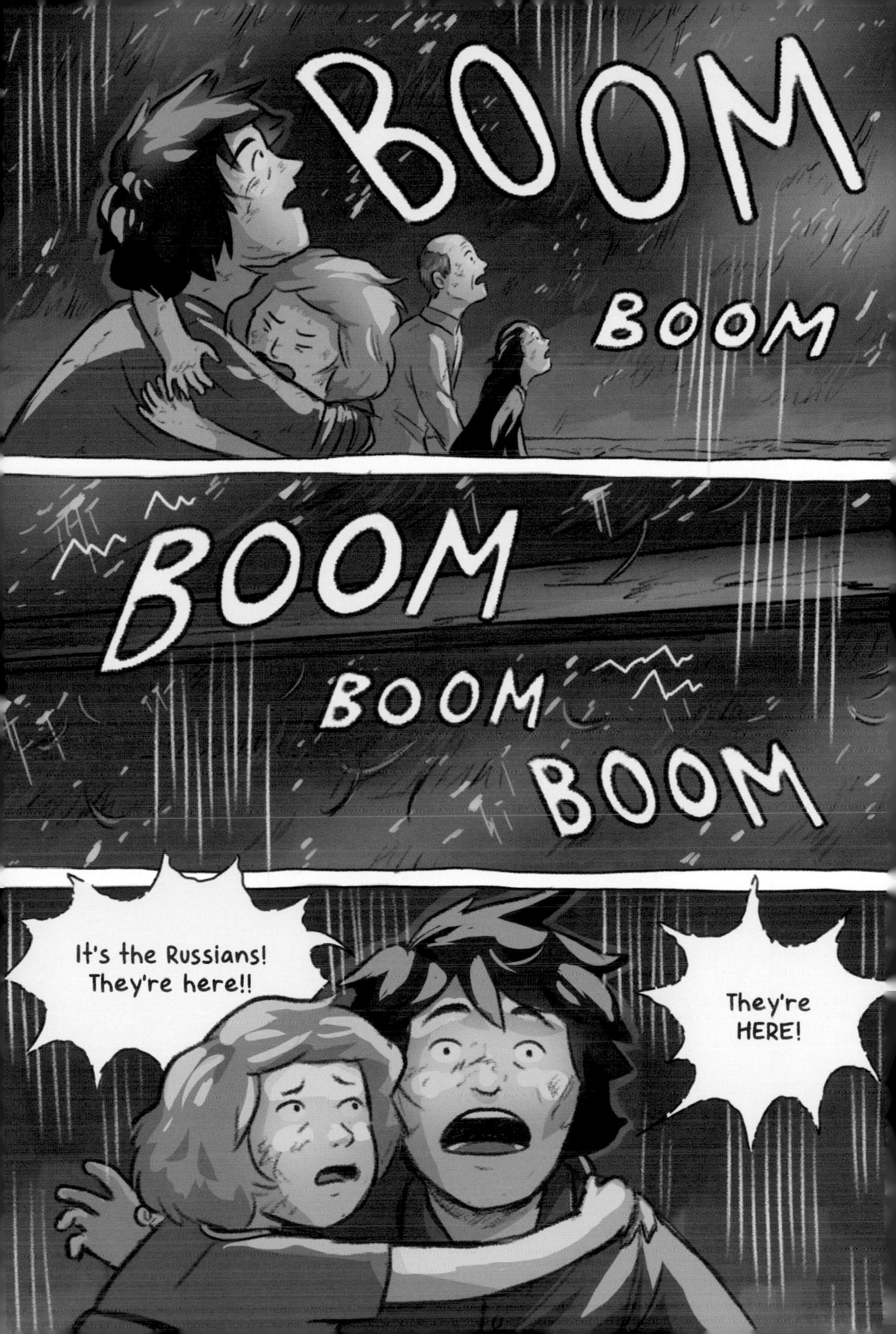
BOOM
BOOM
BOOM
BOOM
BOOM
It's the Russians! They're here!!
They're HERE!

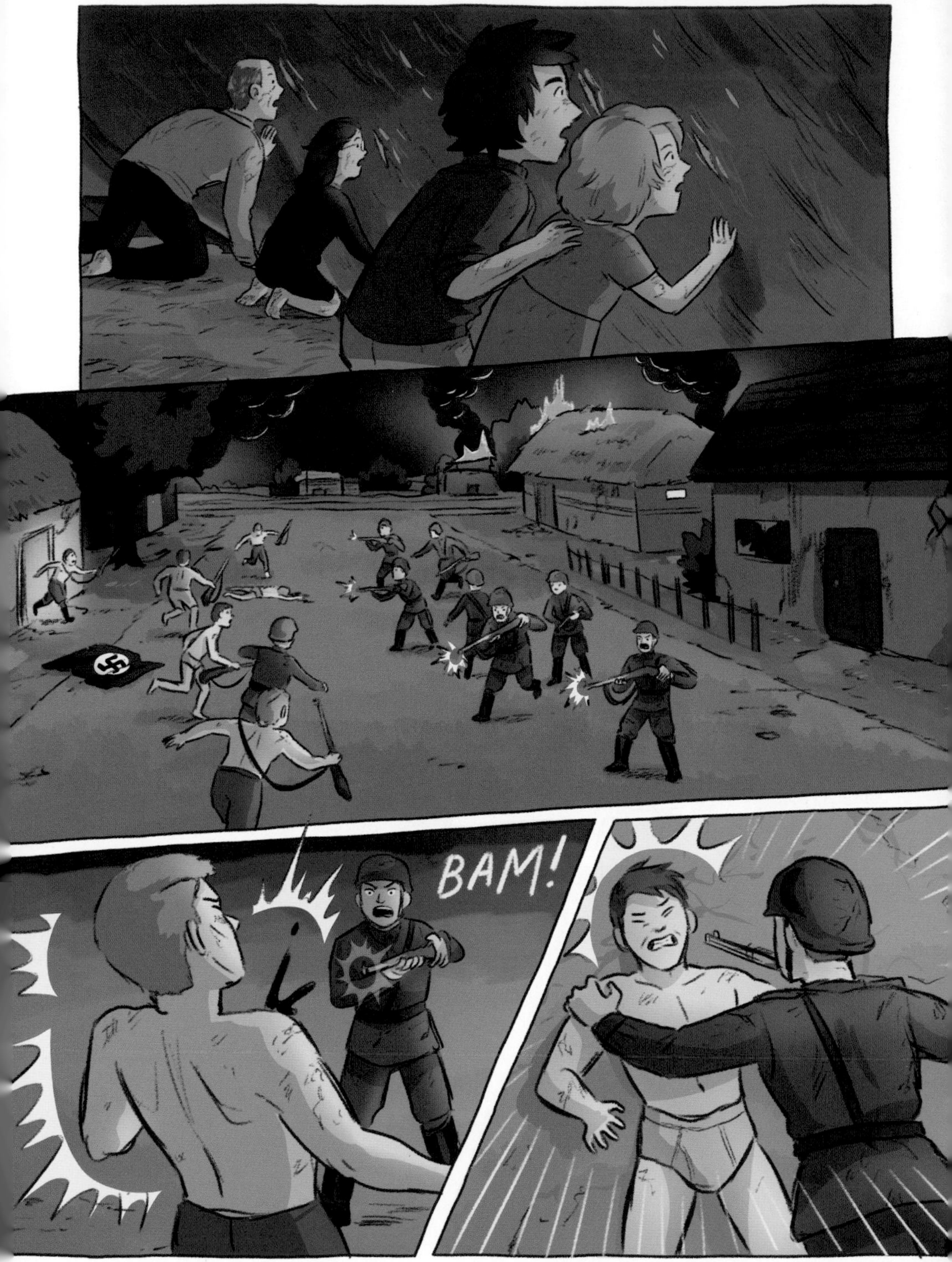
BAM!

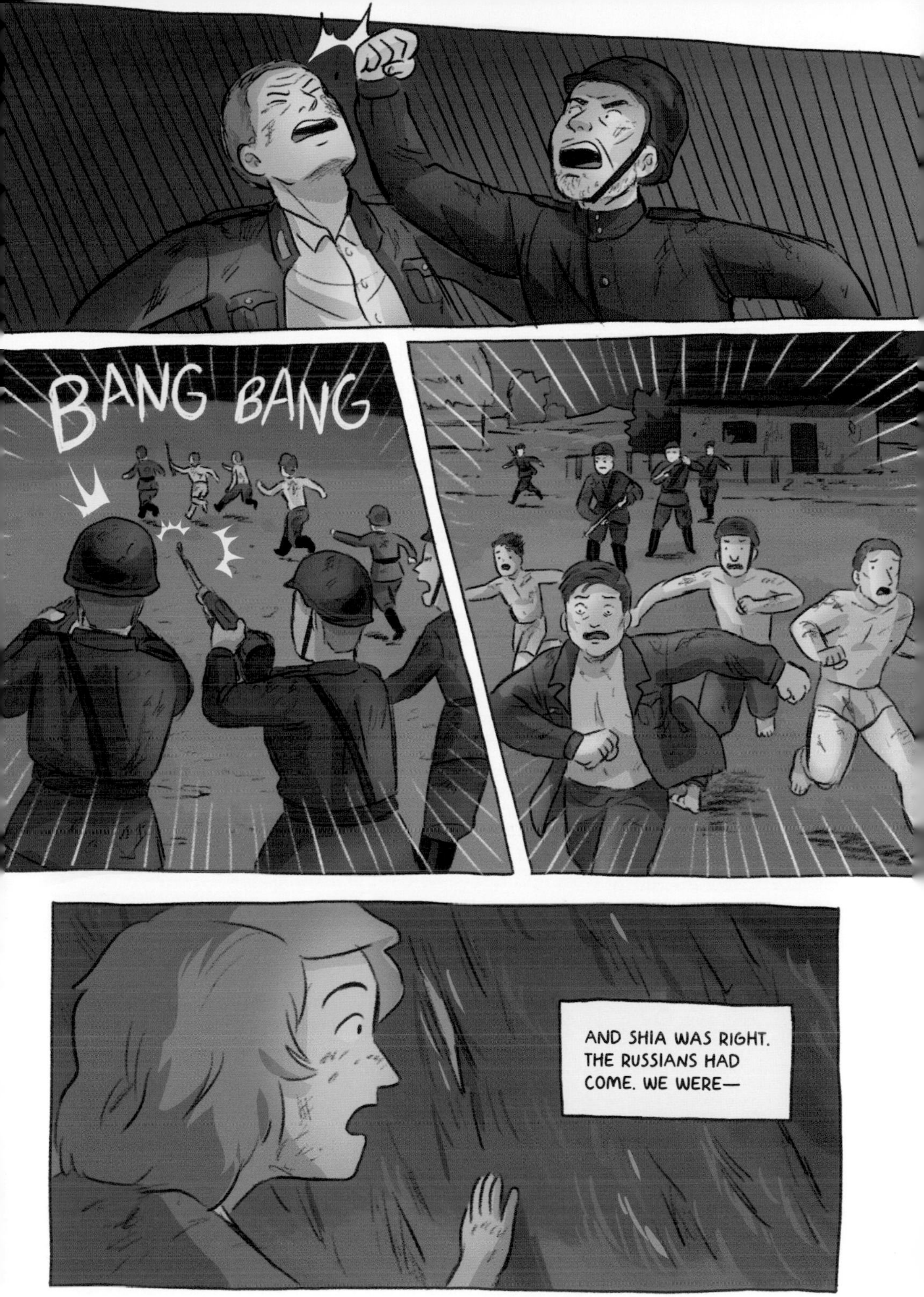
BANG BANG
AND SHIA WAS RIGHT. THE RUSSIANS HAD COME. WE WERE—

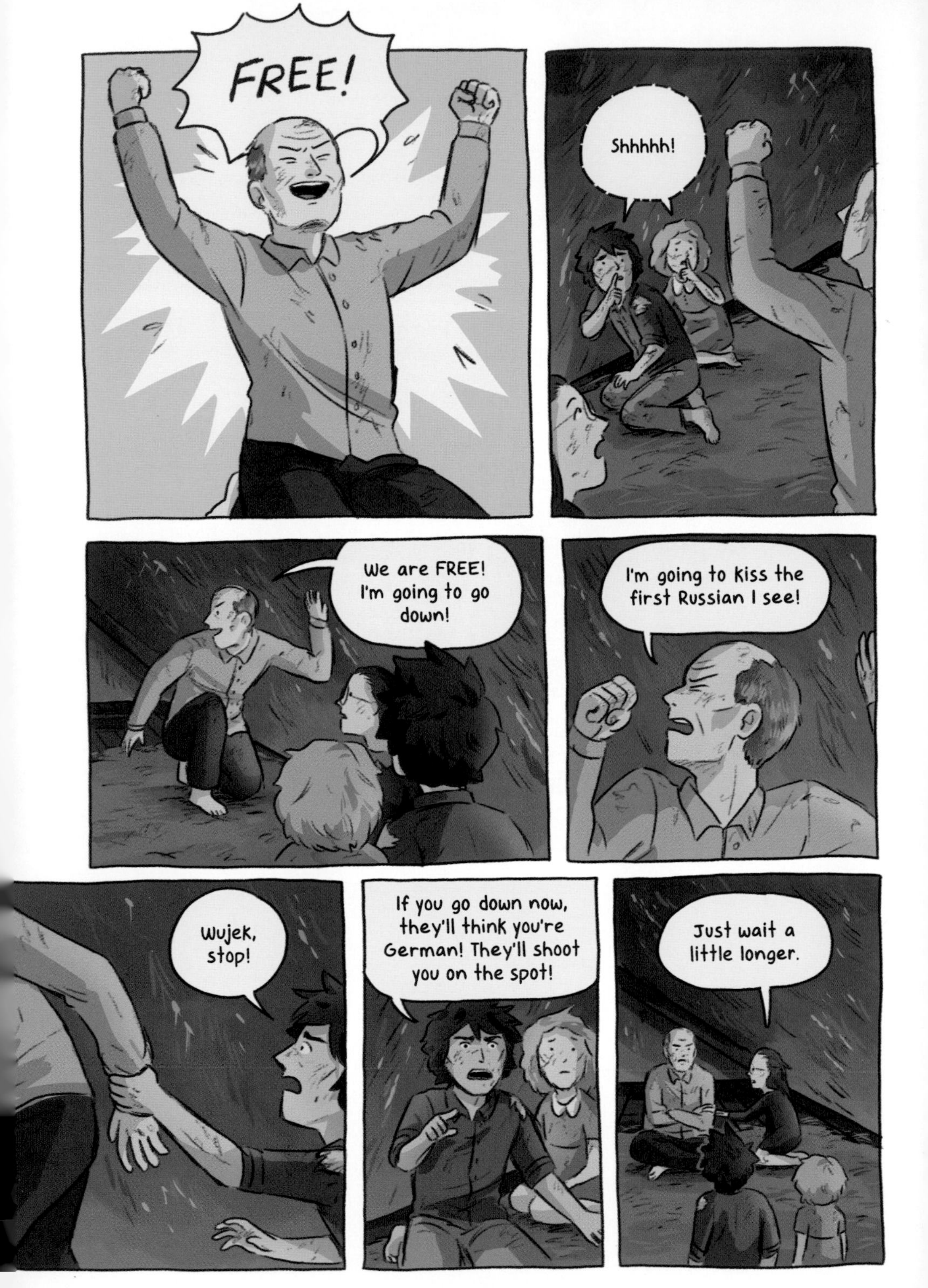
FREE!
Shhhhh!
We are FREE! I'm going to go down!
I'm going to kiss the first Russian I see!
Wujek, stop!
If you go down now, they'll think you're German! They'll shoot you on the spot!
Just wait a little longer.

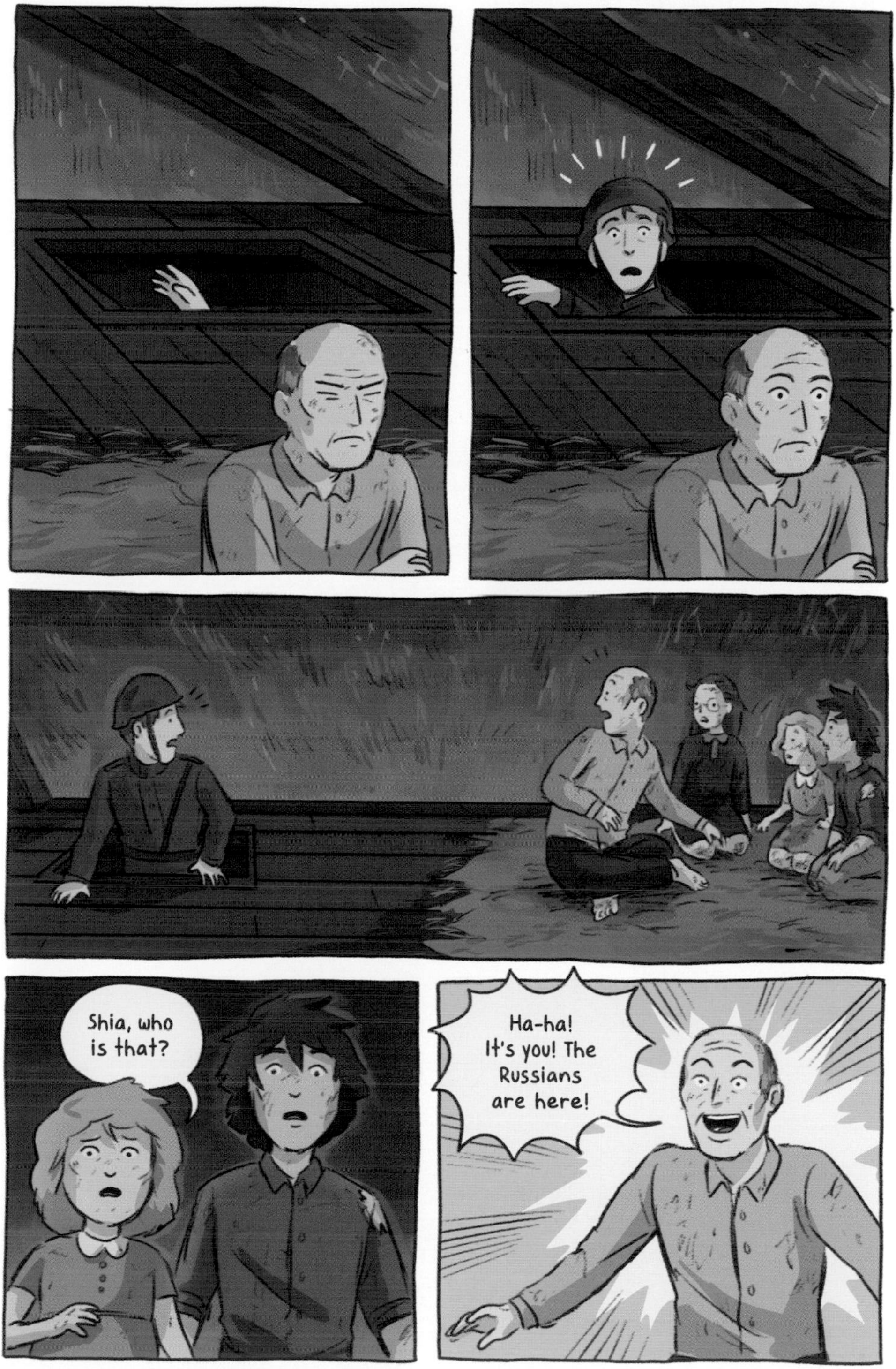
Shia, who is that?
Ha-ha! It's you! The Russians are here!

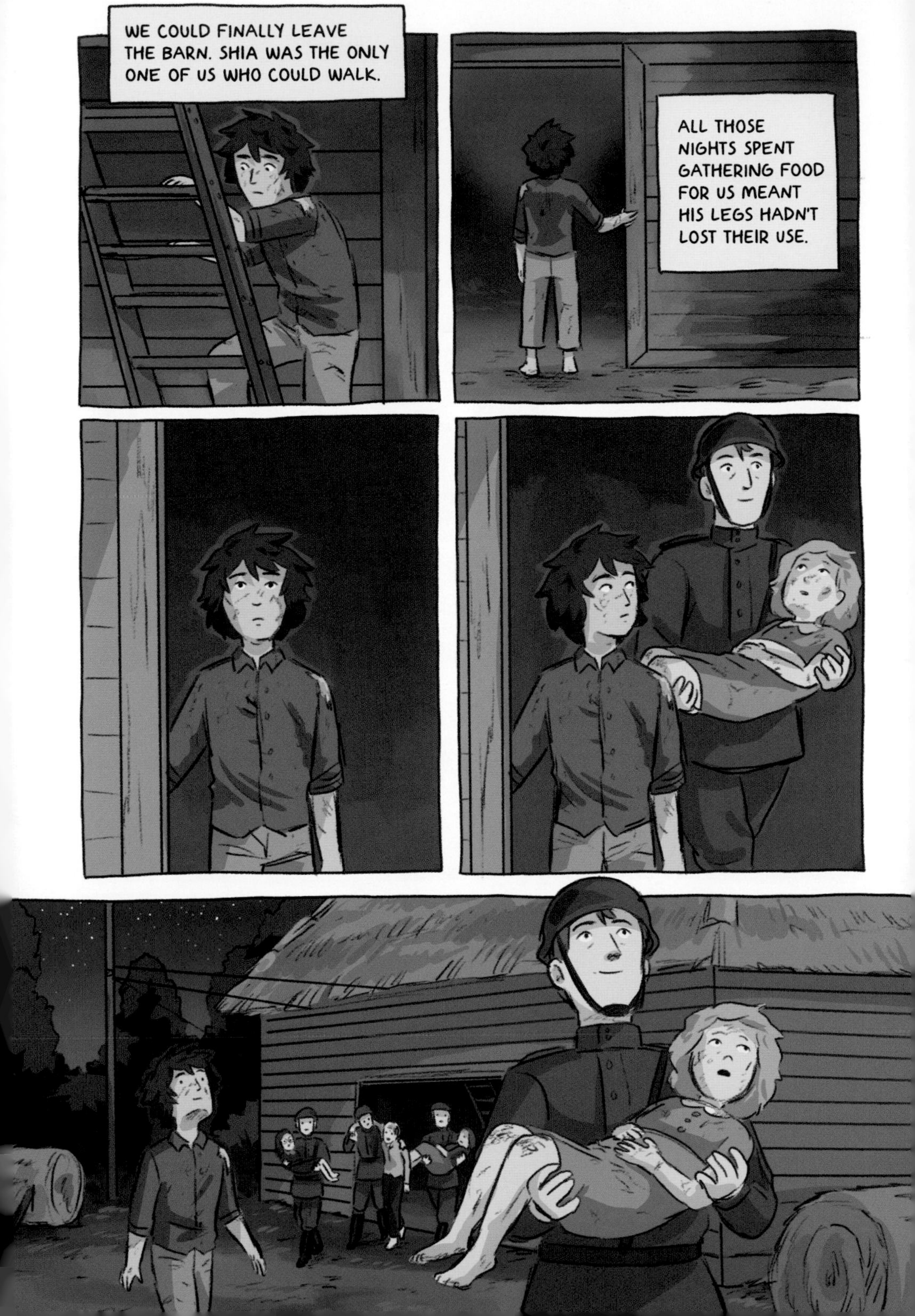
WE COULD FINALLY LEAVE THE BARN. SHIA WAS THE ONLY ONE OF US WHO COULD WALK.
ALL THOSE NIGHTS SPENT GATHERING FOOD FOR US MEANT HIS LEGS HADN'T LOST THEIR USE.

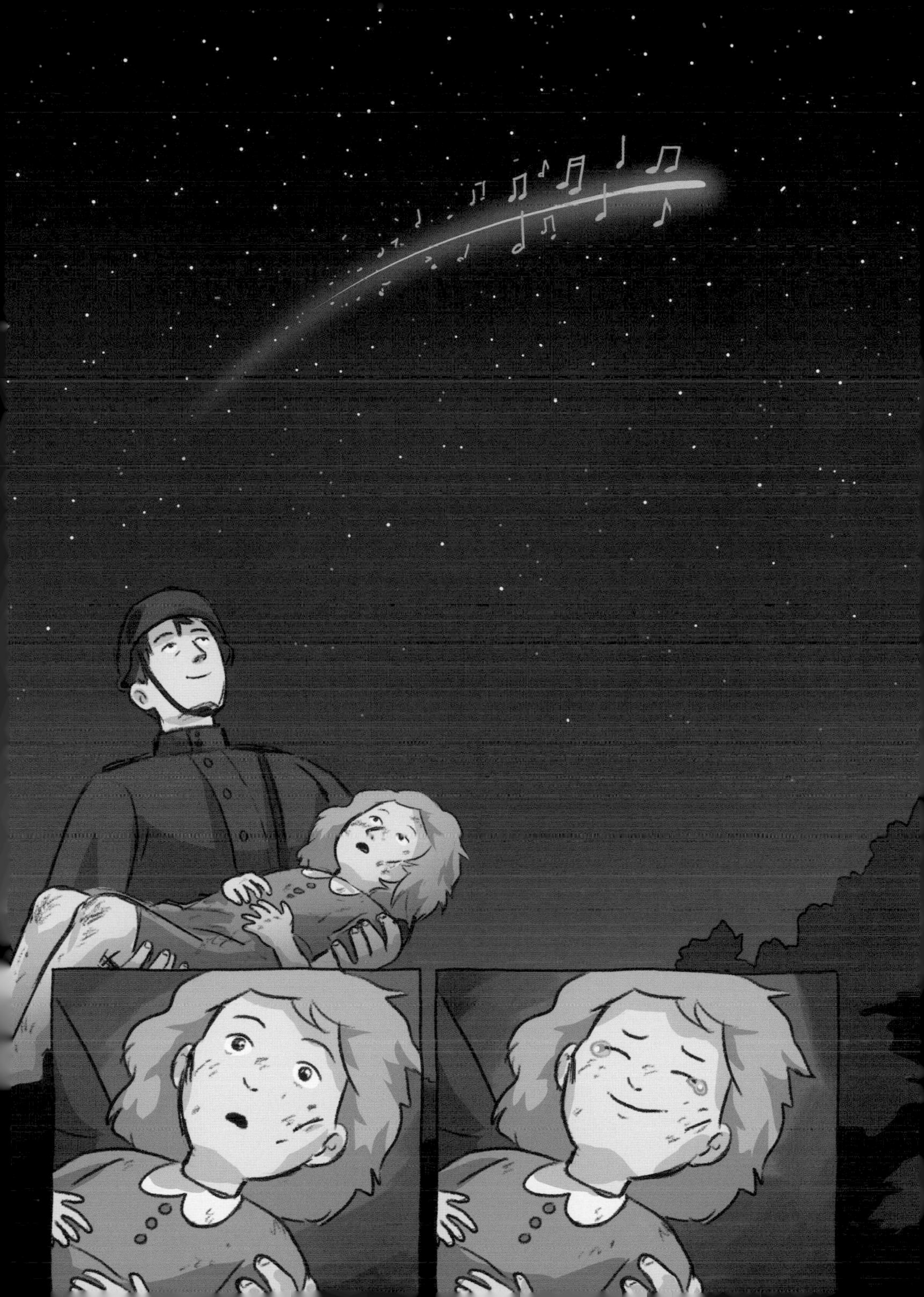

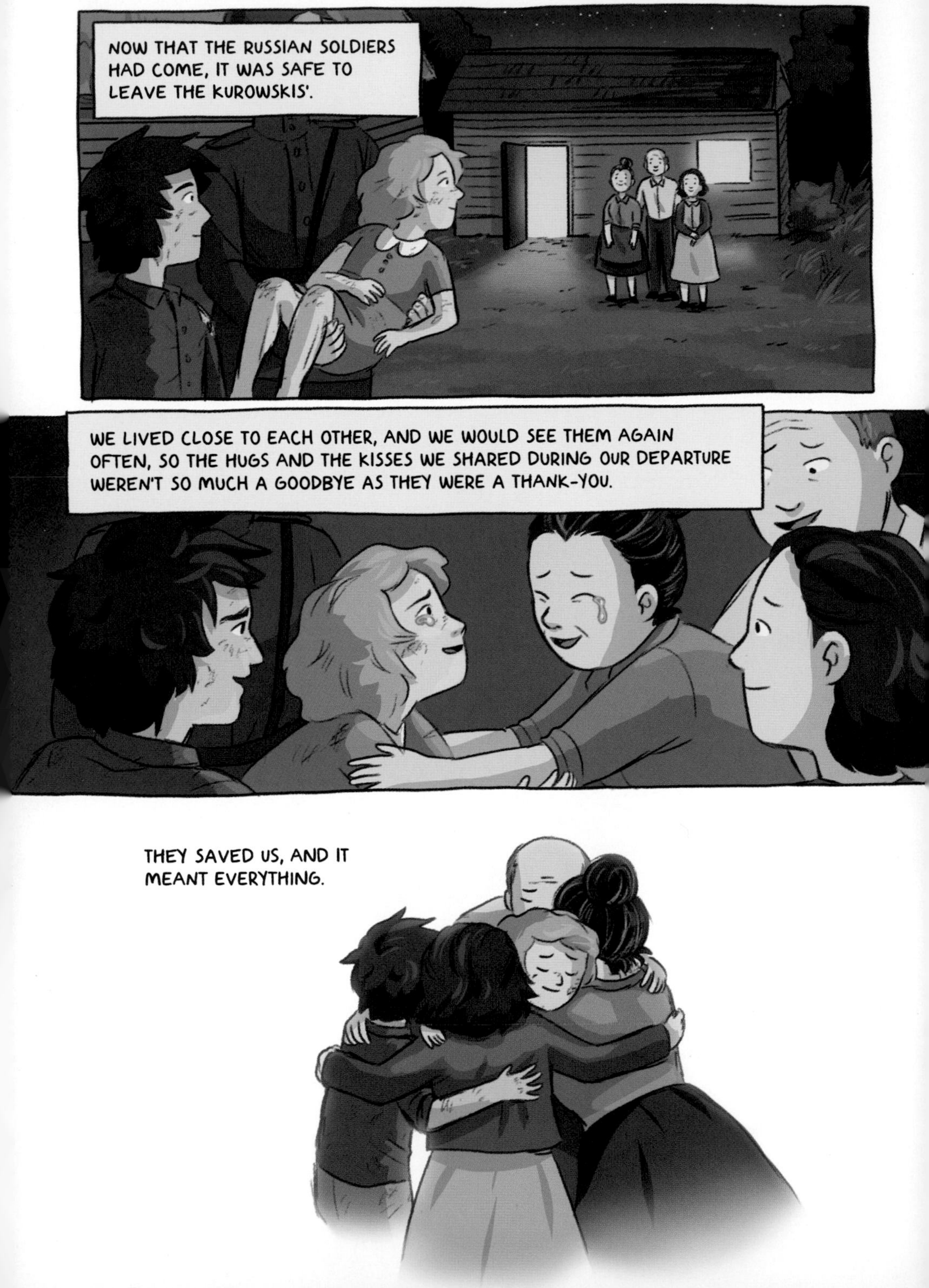
NOW THAT THE RUSSIAN SOLDIERS HAD COME, IT WAS SAFE TO LEAVE THE KUROWSKIS'.
WE LIVED CLOSE TO EACH OTHER, AND WE WOULD SEE THEM AGAIN OFTEN, SO THE HUGS AND THE KISSES WE SHARED DURING OUR DEPARTURE WEREN'T SO MUCH A GOODBYE AS THEY WERE A THANK-YOU.
THEY SAVED US, AND IT MEANT EVERYTHING.

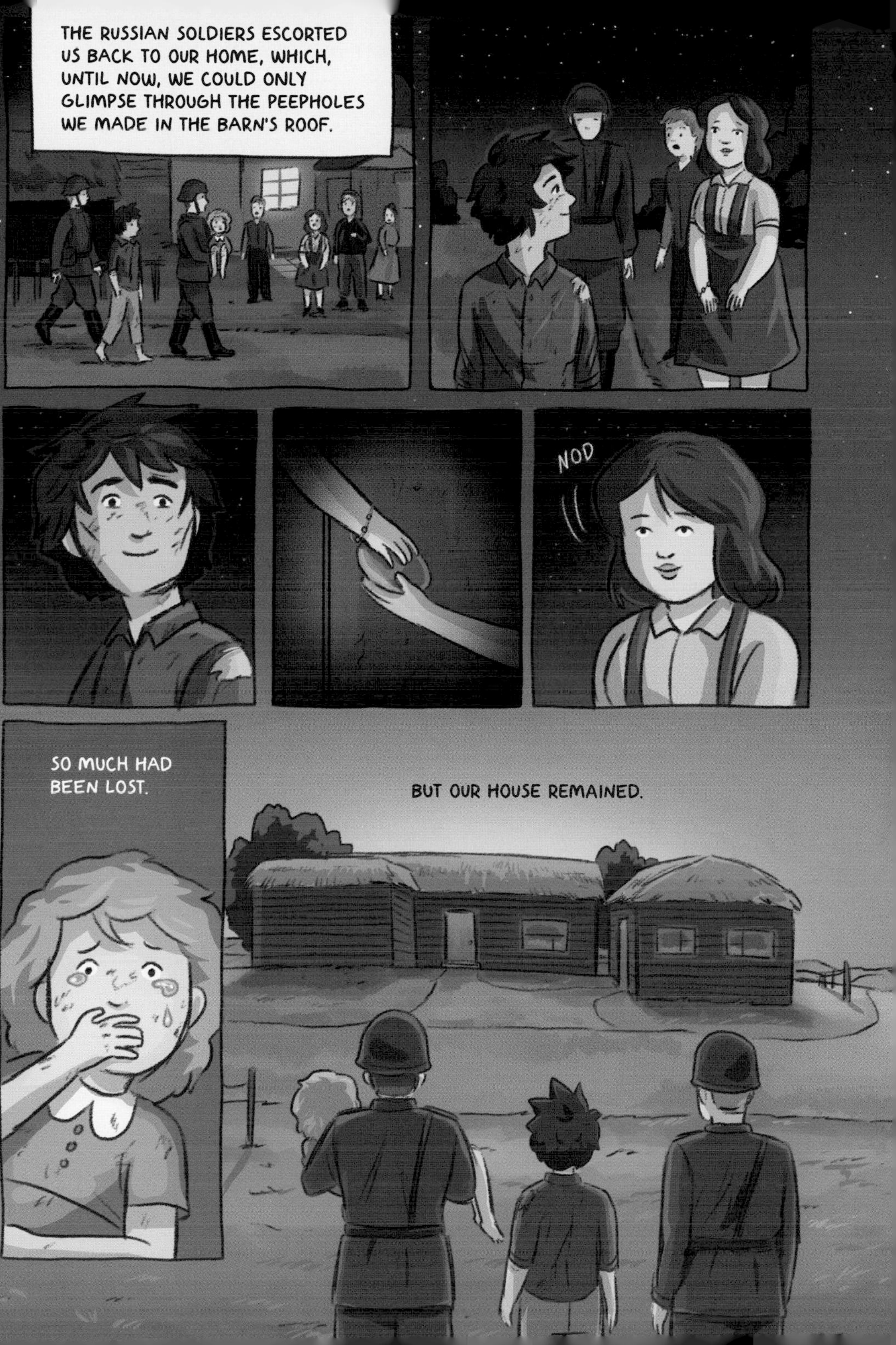
THE RUSSIAN SOLDIERS ESCORTED US BACK TO OUR HOME, WHICH, UNTIL NOW, WE COULD ONLY GLIMPSE THROUGH THE PEEPHOLES WE MADE IN THE BARN'S ROOF.
NOD
SO MUCH HAD BEEN LOST.
BUT OUR HOUSE REMAINED.

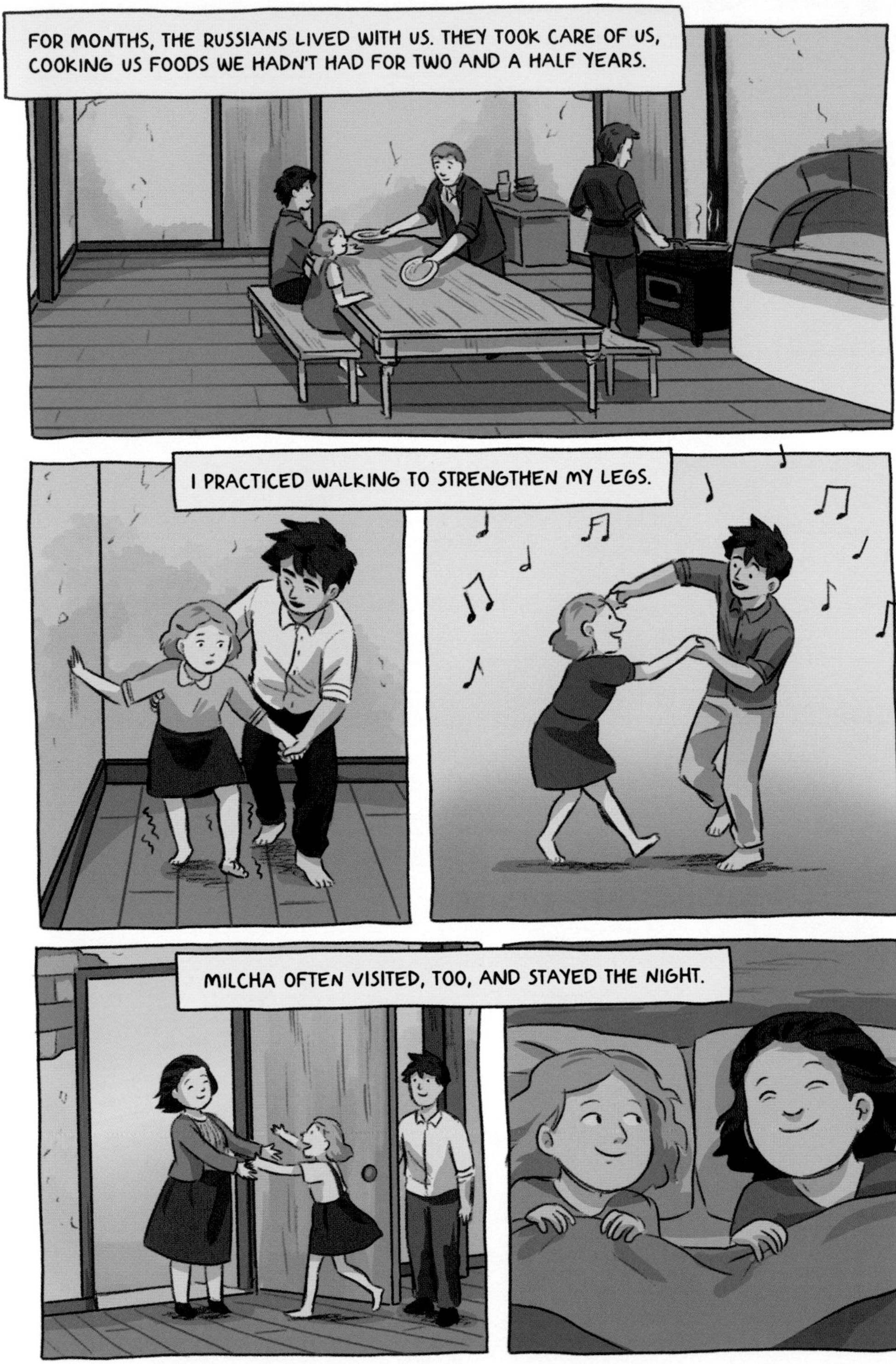
FOR MONTHS, THE RUSSIANS LIVED WITH US. THEY TOOK CARE OF US, COOKING US FOODS WE HADN'T HAD FOR TWO AND A HALF YEARS.
I PRACTICED WALKING TO STRENGTHEN MY LEGS.
MILCHA OFTEN VISITED, TOO, AND STAYED THE NIGHT.

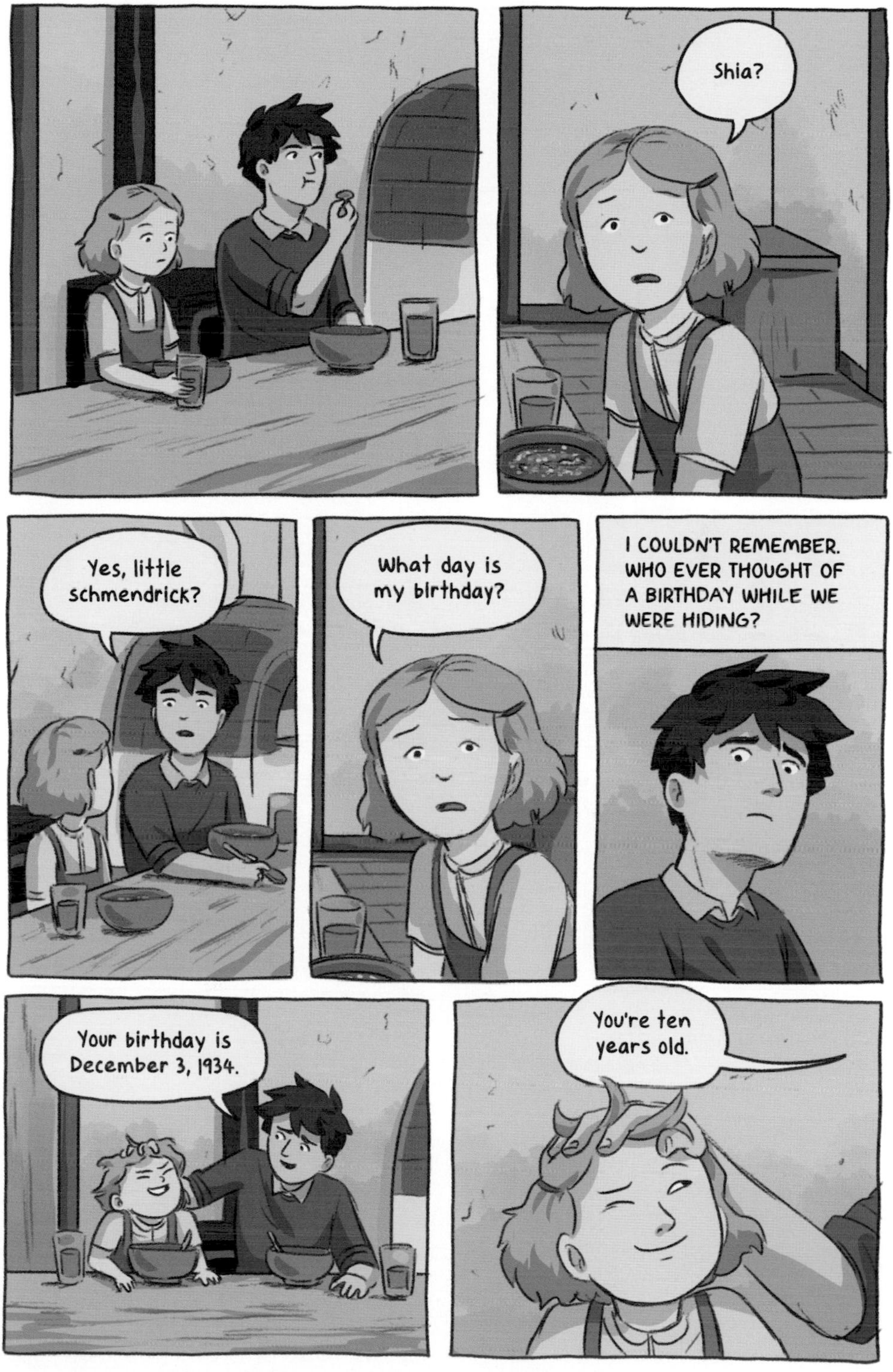
Shia?
Yes, little schmendrick?
What day is my birthday?
I COULDN'T REMEMBER. WHO EVER THOUGHT OF A BIRTHDAY WHILE WE WERE HIDING?
Your birthday is December 3, 1934.
You're ten years old.

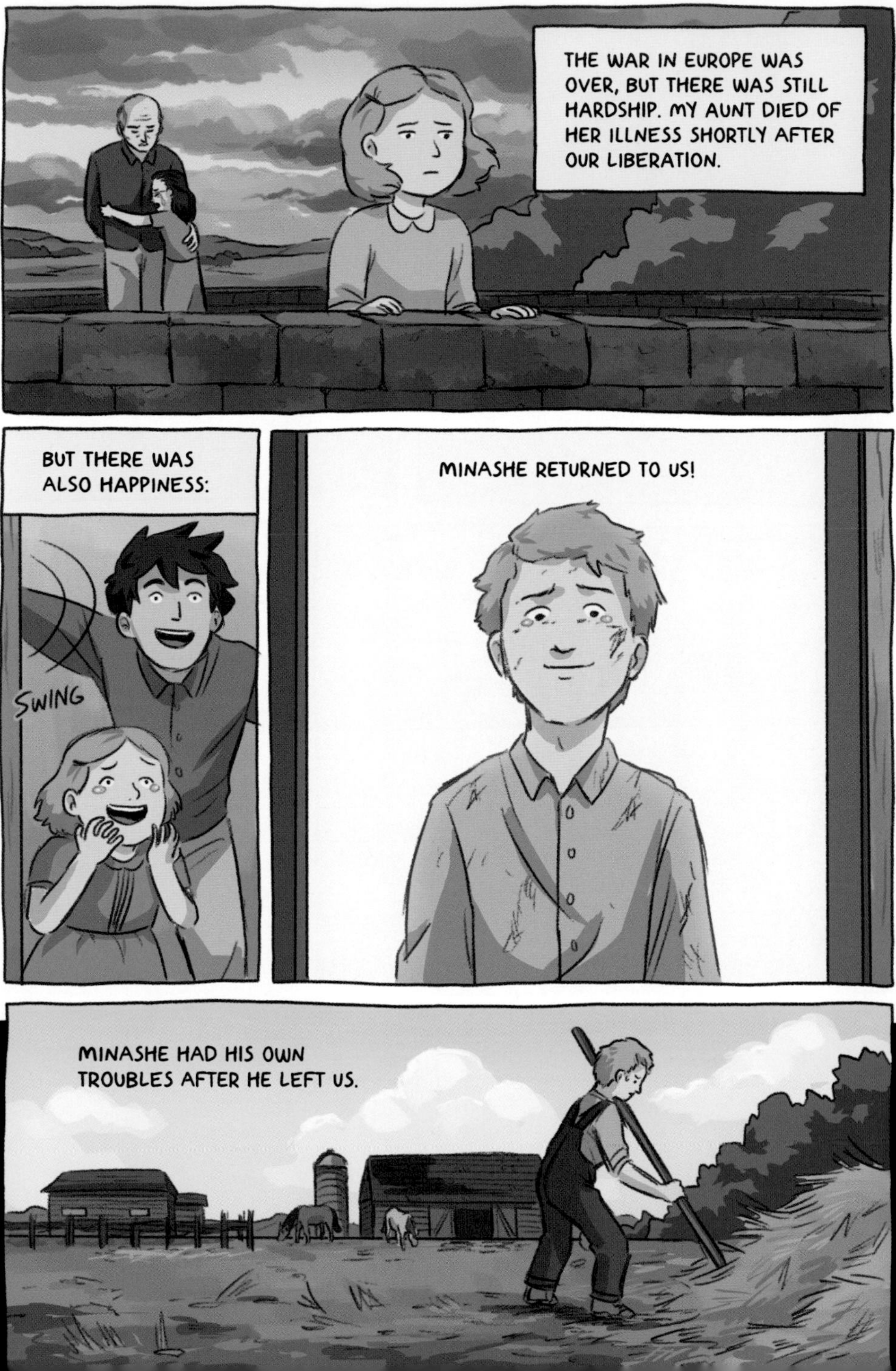
THE WAR IN EUROPE WAS OVER, BUT THERE WAS STILL HARDSHIP. MY AUNT DIED OF HER ILLNESS SHORTLY AFTER OUR LIBERATION.
BUT THERE WAS ALSO HAPPINESS:
SWING
MINASHE RETURNED TO US!
MINASHE HAD HIS OWN TROUBLES AFTER HE LEFT US.

THE KUROWSKI FAMILY TOOK US IN AND KEPT US
SAFE. BESIDES MILCHA, THEY HAD TWO OTHER
CHILDREN, GROWN SONS WHO WERE MARRIED
WITH HOMES OF THEIR OWN. EVEN THEY DID
NOT KNOW WE HAD HIDDEN IN THEIR PARENTS'
BARN UNTIL AFTER THE RUSSIANS CAME.

THE TWO SONS

BUT THEY ALSO HAD A RELATIVE WHO
GREW UP IN THE VILLAGE WHERE MINASHE
WAS HIDING IN PLAIN SIGHT.

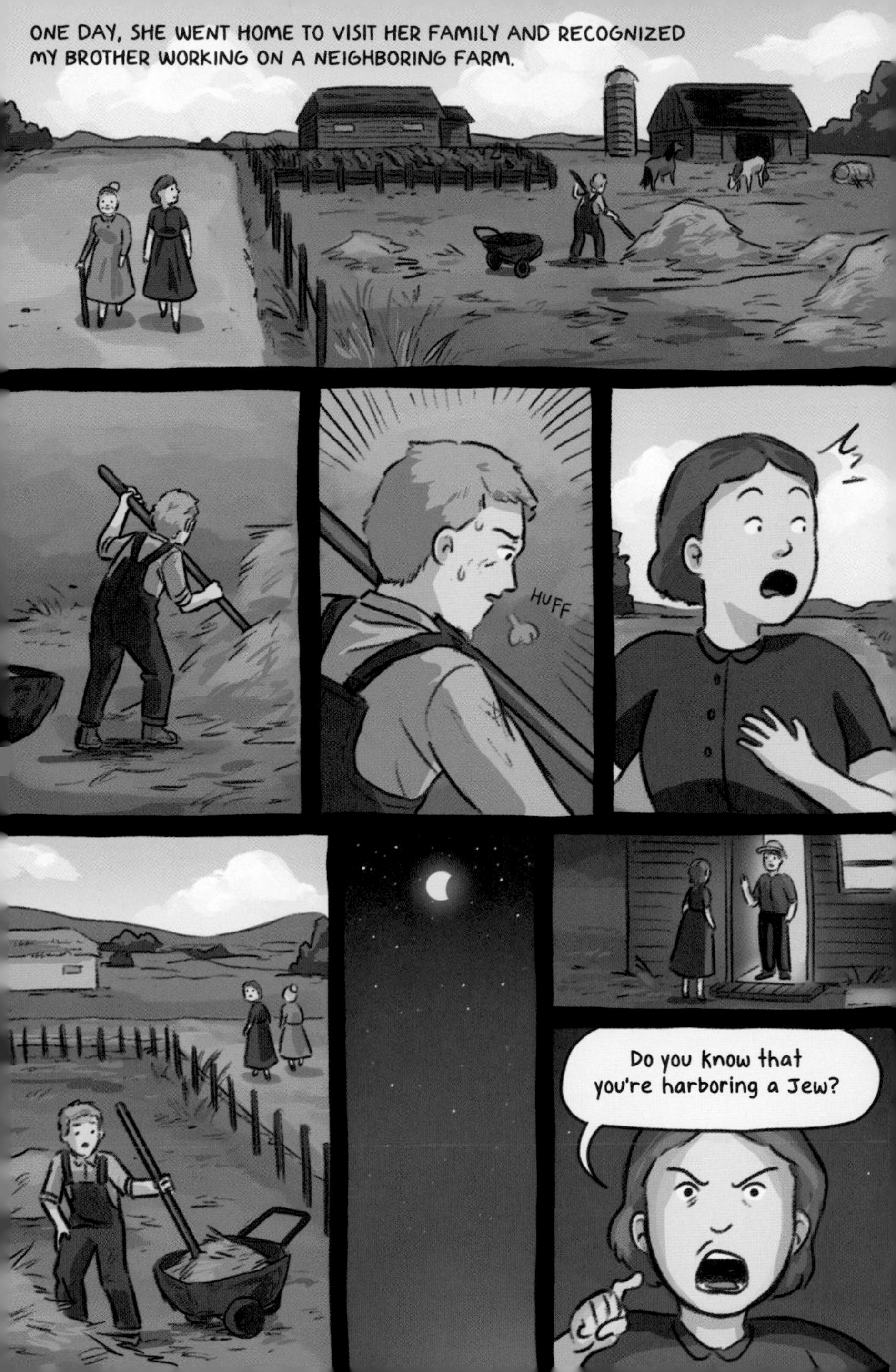

ONE DAY, SHE WENT HOME TO VISIT HER FAMILY AND RECOGNIZED MY BROTHER WORKING ON A NEIGHBORING FARM.
HUFF
Do you know that you're harboring a Jew?

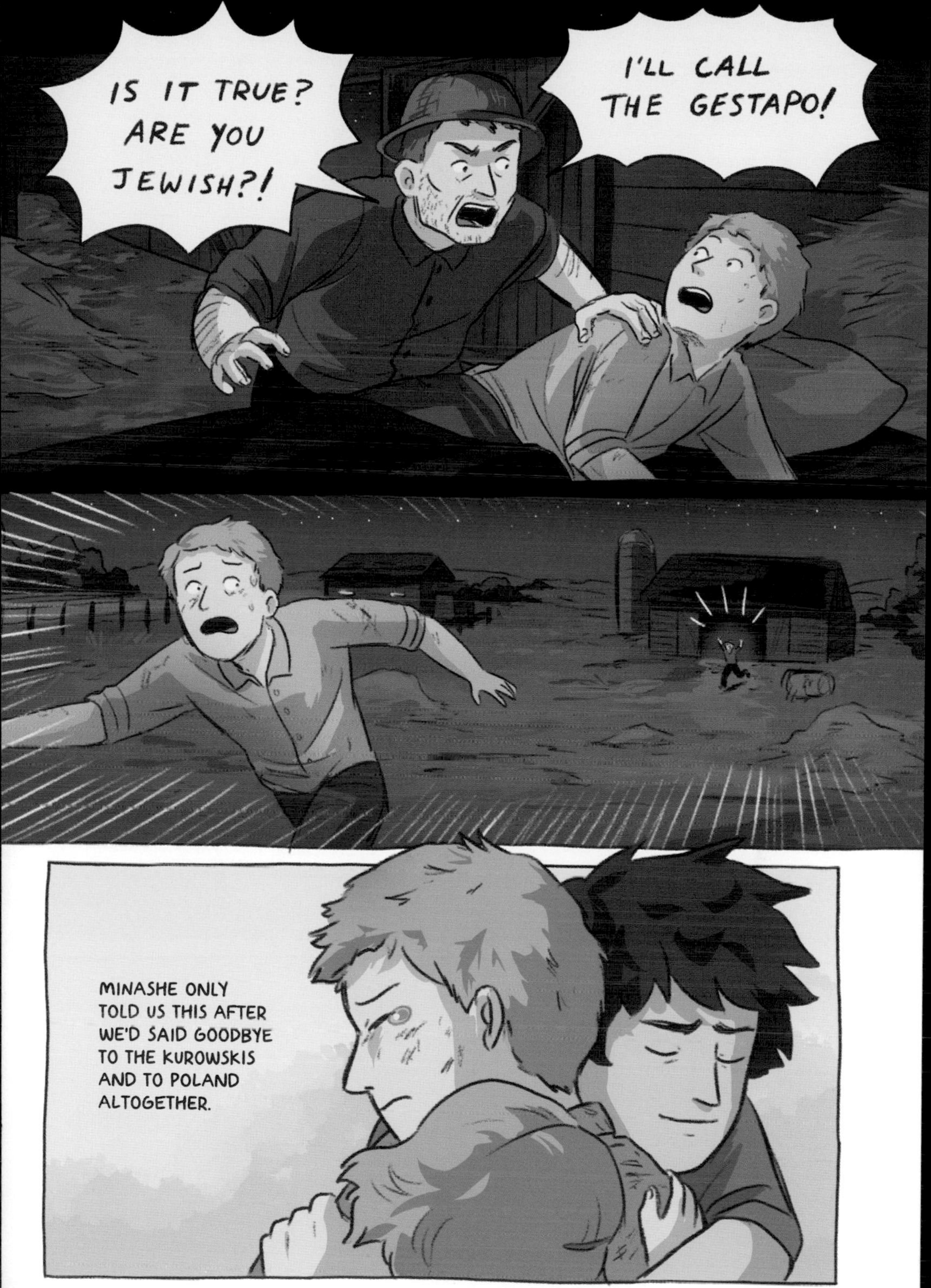
IS IT TRUE? ARE YOU JEWISH?!
I'LL CALL THE GESTAPO!
MINASHE ONLY TOLD US THIS AFTER WE'D SAID GOODBYE TO THE KUROWSKIS AND TO POLAND ALTOGETHER.

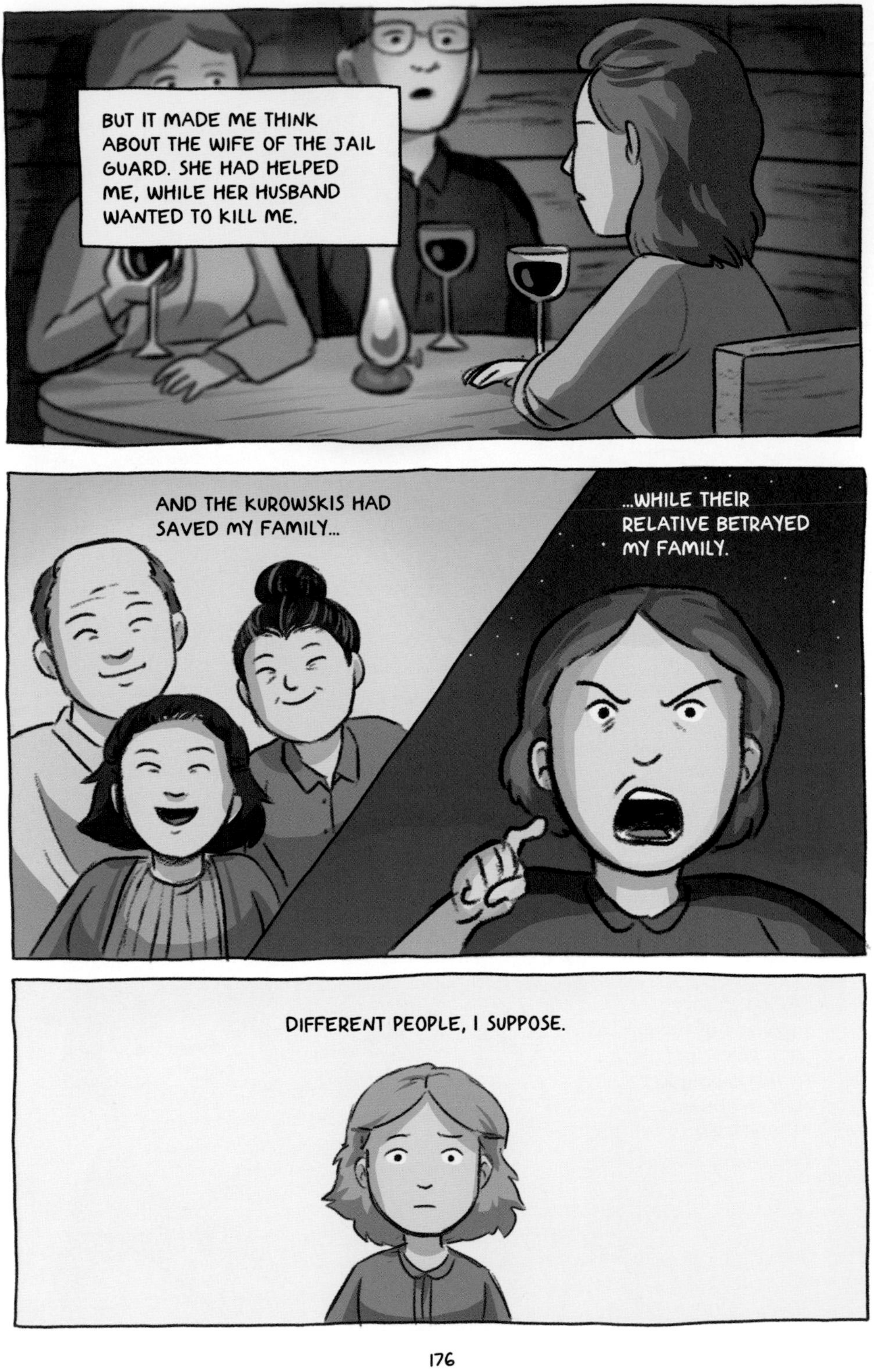
BUT IT MADE ME THINK ABOUT THE WIFE OF THE JAIL GUARD. SHE HAD HELPED ME, WHILE HER HUSBAND WANTED TO KILL ME.
AND THE KUROWSKIS HAD SAVED MY FAMILY...
...WHILE THEIR RELATIVE BETRAYED MY FAMILY.
DIFFERENT PEOPLE, I SUPPOSE.

EVENTUALLY, HOWEVER, THE RUSSIANS HAD TO LEAVE BOREK AND THINGS IMMEDIATELY GOT BAD.

POLISH YOUTHS WOULD COME AND PULL JEWS OUT OF THEIR HOMES AND SHOOT THEM.

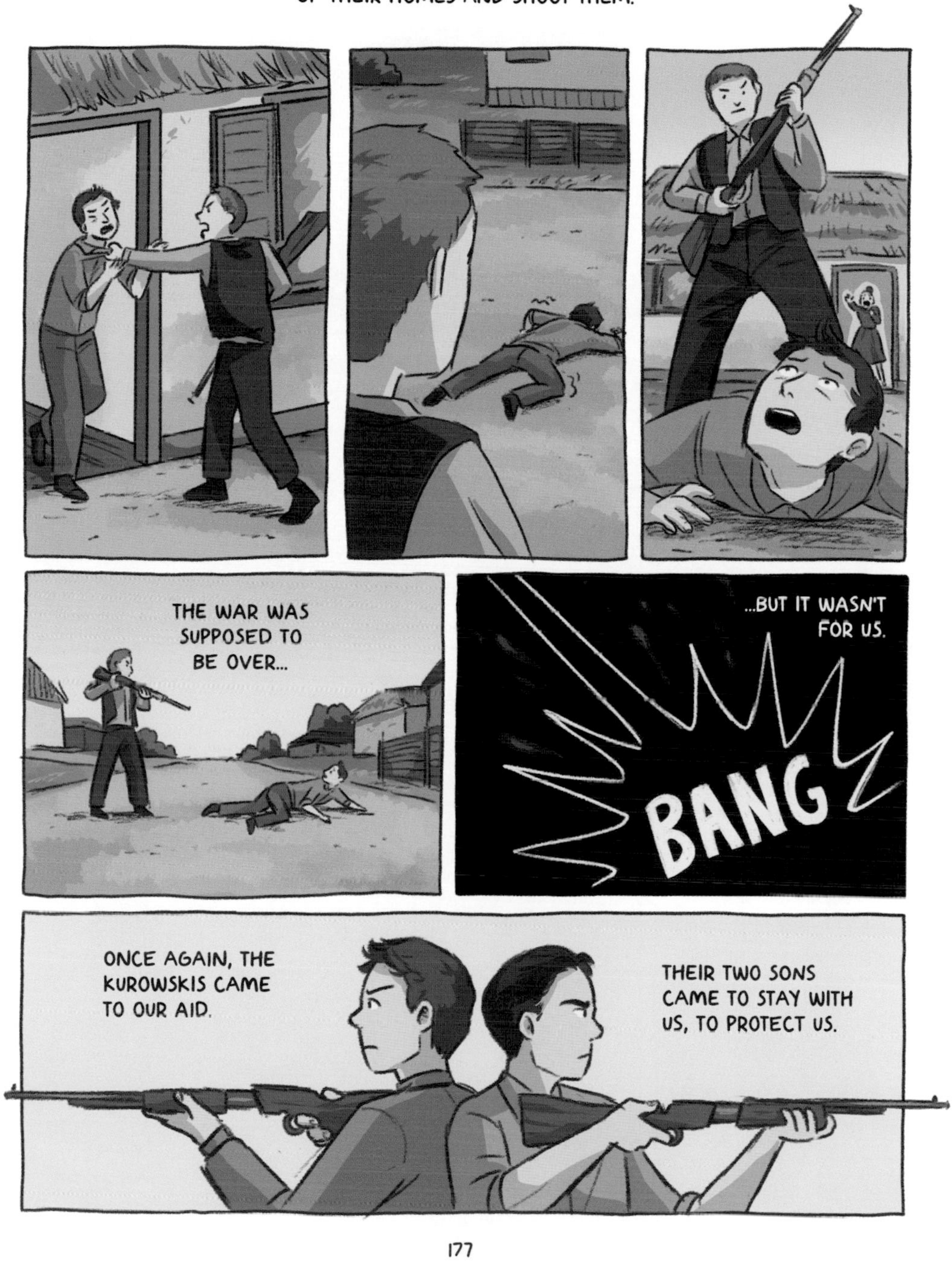
THE WAR WAS SUPPOSED TO BE OVER...
BANG
...BUT IT WASN'T FOR US.
ONCE AGAIN, THE KUROWSKIS CAME TO OUR AID.
THEIR TWO SONS CAME TO STAY WITH US, TO PROTECT US.

Jews, come out of the house!

HA HA HA HA

HA HA HA

Get out of here!

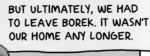

BUT ULTIMATELY, WE HAD TO LEAVE BOREK. IT WASN'T OUR HOME ANY LONGER.

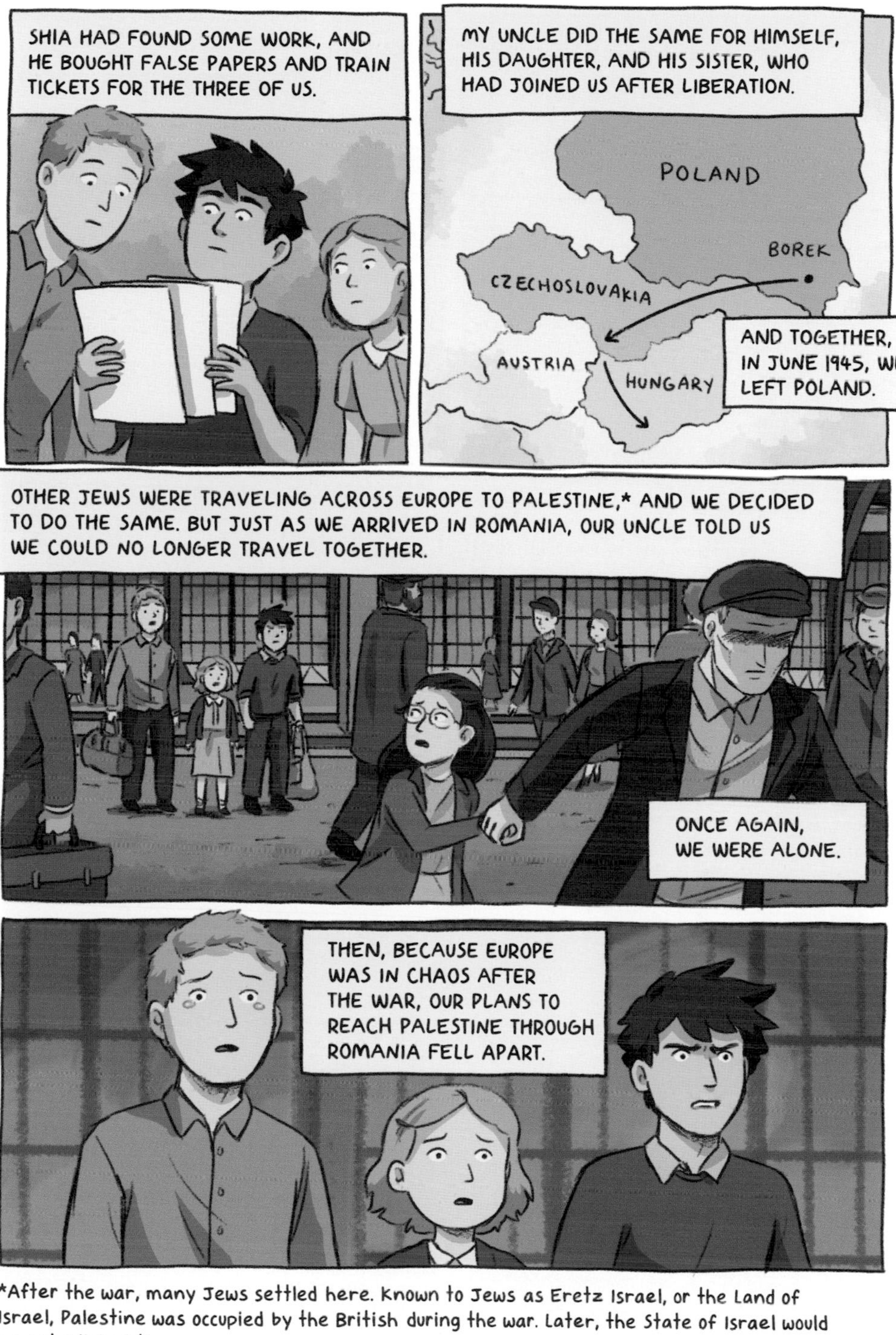
SHIA HAD FOUND SOME WORK, AND HE BOUGHT FALSE PAPERS AND TRAIN TICKETS FOR THE THREE OF US.
MY UNCLE DID THE SAME FOR HIMSELF, HIS DAUGHTER, AND HIS SISTER, WHO HAD JOINED US AFTER LIBERATION.
POLAND
BOREK
CZECHOSLOVAKIA
AUSTRIA
HUNGARY
AND TOGETHER, IN JUNE 1945, WE LEFT POLAND.
OTHER JEWS WERE TRAVELING ACROSS EUROPE TO PALESTINE,* AND WE DECIDED TO DO THE SAME. BUT JUST AS WE ARRIVED IN ROMANIA, OUR UNCLE TOLD US WE COULD NO LONGER TRAVEL TOGETHER.
ONCE AGAIN, WE WERE ALONE.
THEN, BECAUSE EUROPE WAS IN CHAOS AFTER THE WAR, OUR PLANS TO REACH PALESTINE THROUGH ROMANIA FELL APART.

*After the war, many Jews settled here. Known to Jews as Eretz Israel, or the Land of Israel, Palestine was occupied by the British during the war. Later, the State of Israel would be established there.

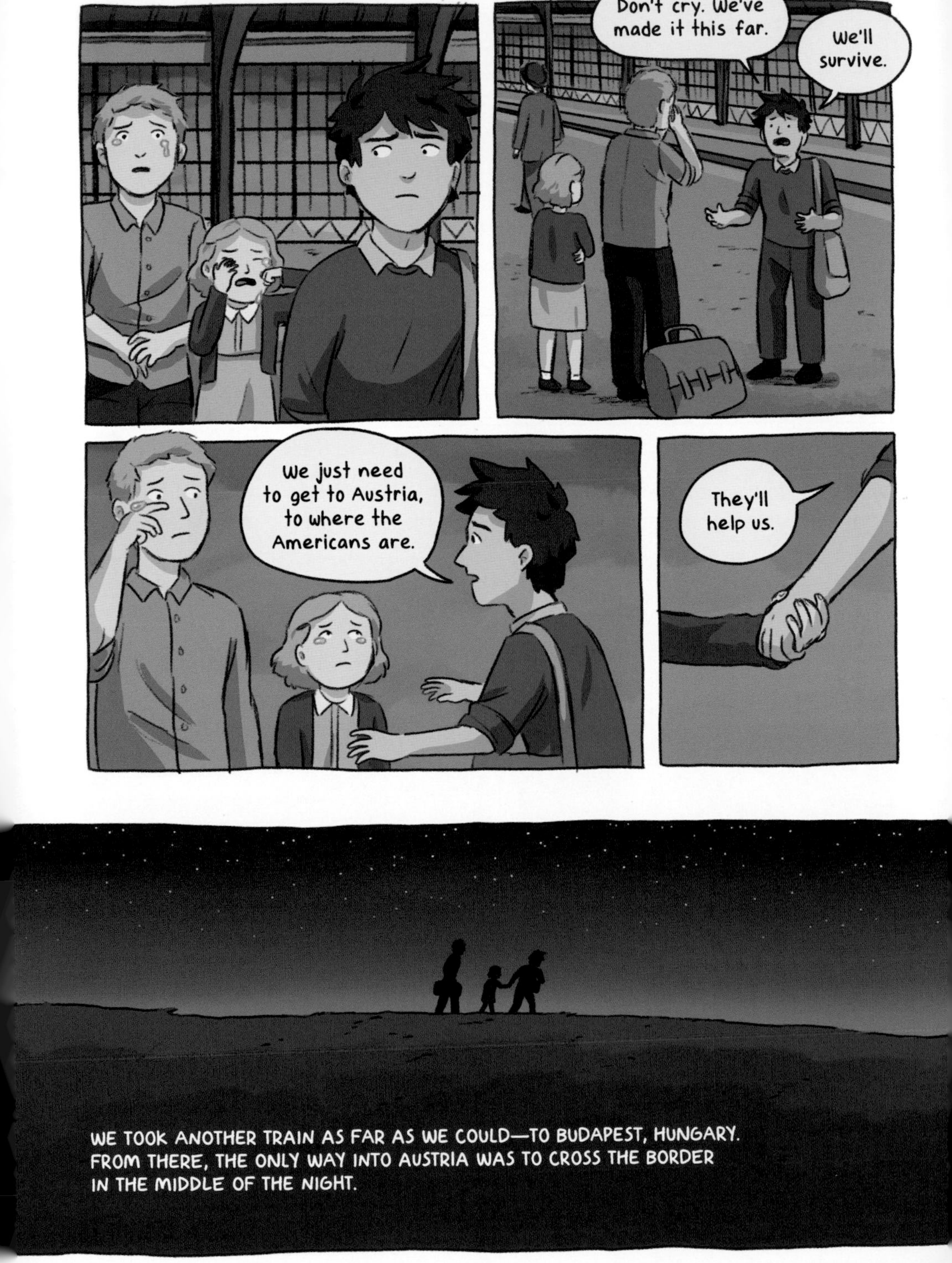
Don't cry. We've made it this far.
We'll survive.
We just need to get to Austria, to where the Americans are.
They'll help us.
WE TOOK ANOTHER TRAIN AS FAR AS WE COULD—TO BUDAPEST, HUNGARY. FROM THERE, THE ONLY WAY INTO AUSTRIA WAS TO CROSS THE BORDER IN THE MIDDLE OF THE NIGHT.

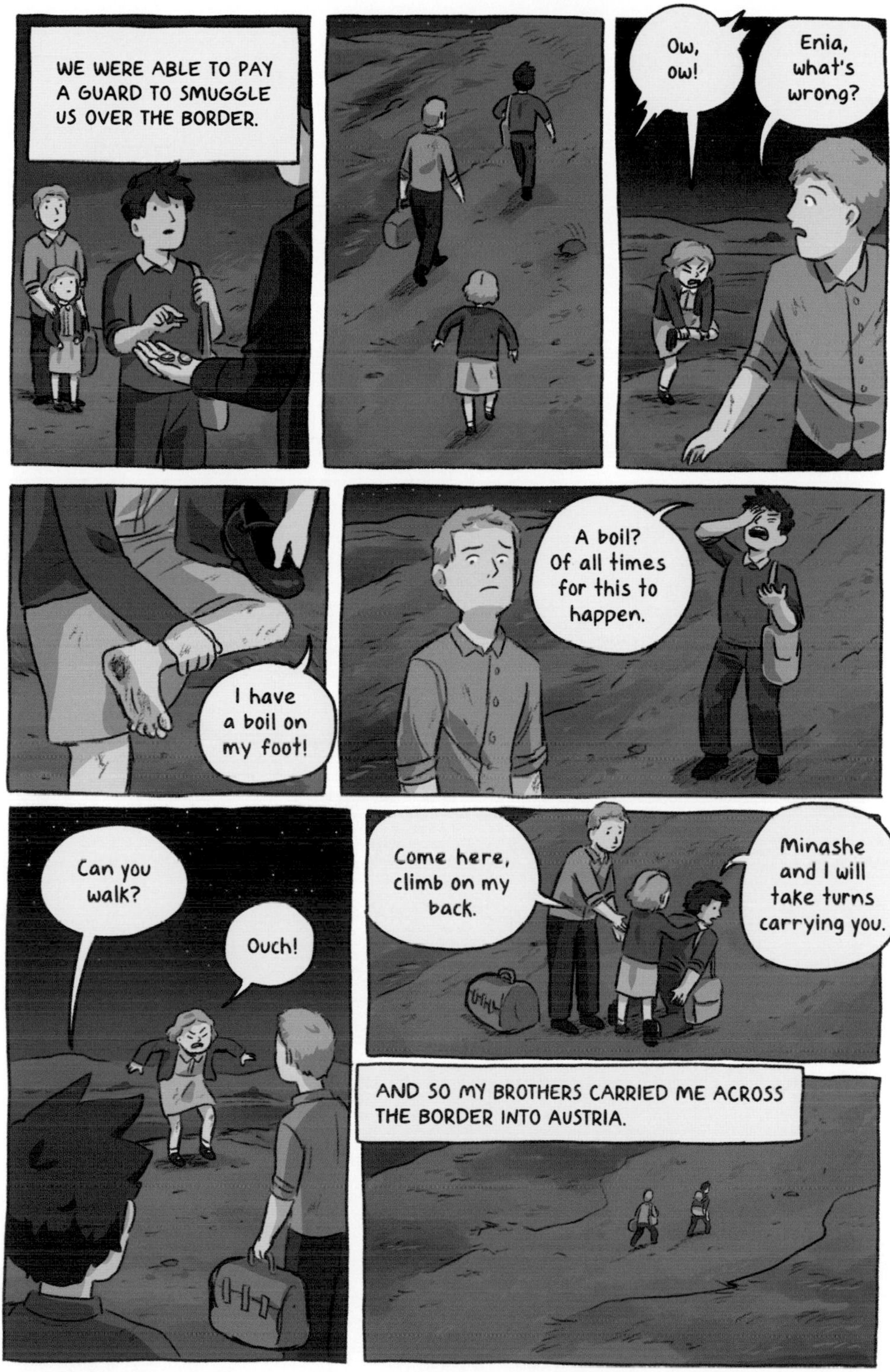
WE WERE ABLE TO PAY A GUARD TO SMUGGLE US OVER THE BORDER.
Ow, ow!
Enia, what's wrong?
I have a boil on my foot!
A boil? Of all times for this to happen.
Can you walk?
Ouch!
Come here, climb on my back.
Minashe and I will take turns carrying you.
AND SO MY BROTHERS CARRIED ME ACROSS THE BORDER INTO AUSTRIA.

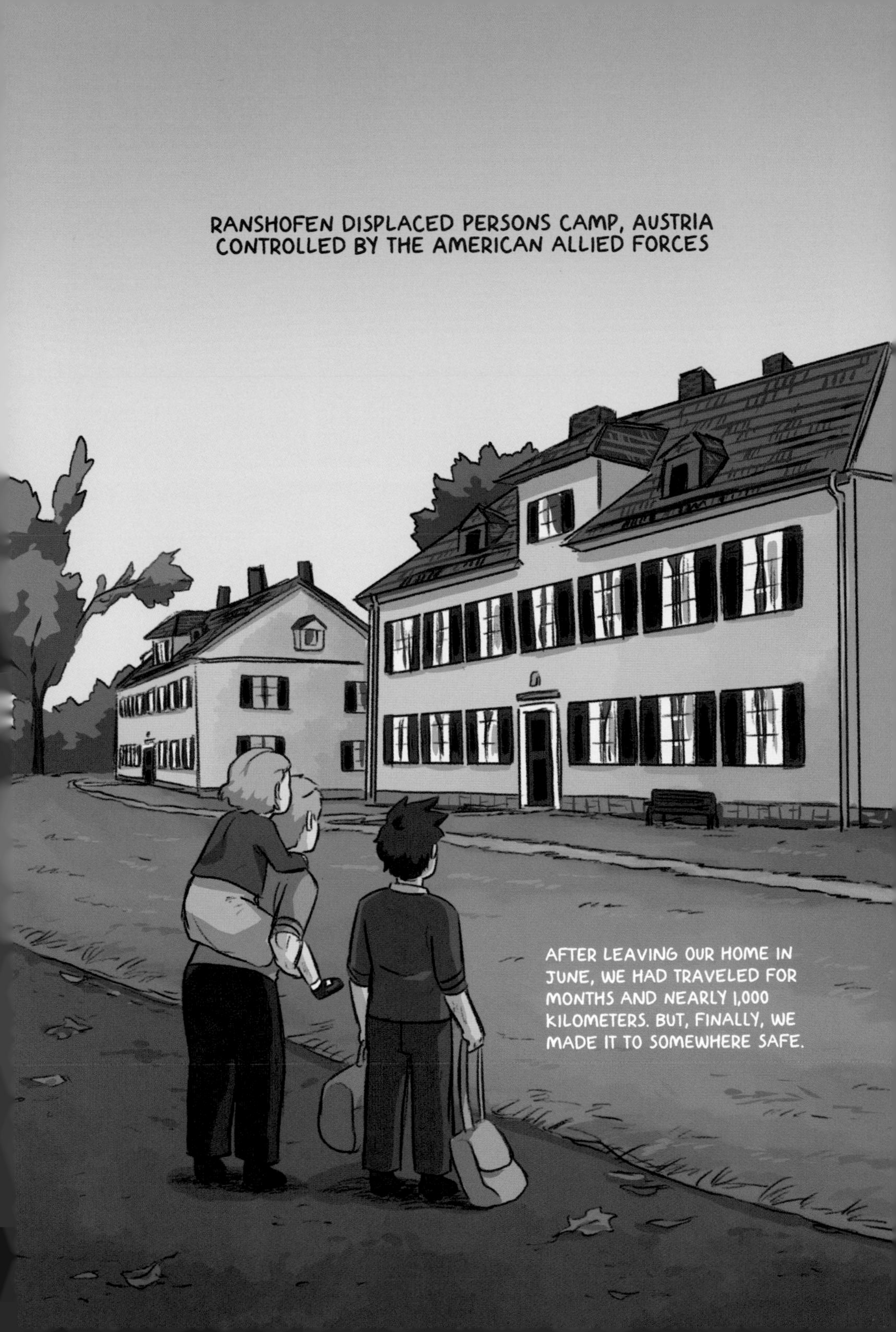
RANSHOFEN DISPLACED PERSONS CAMP, AUSTRIA
CONTROLLED BY THE AMERICAN ALLIED FORCES
AFTER LEAVING OUR HOME IN JUNE, WE HAD TRAVELED FOR MONTHS AND NEARLY 1,000 KILOMETERS. BUT, FINALLY, WE MADE IT TO SOMEWHERE SAFE.

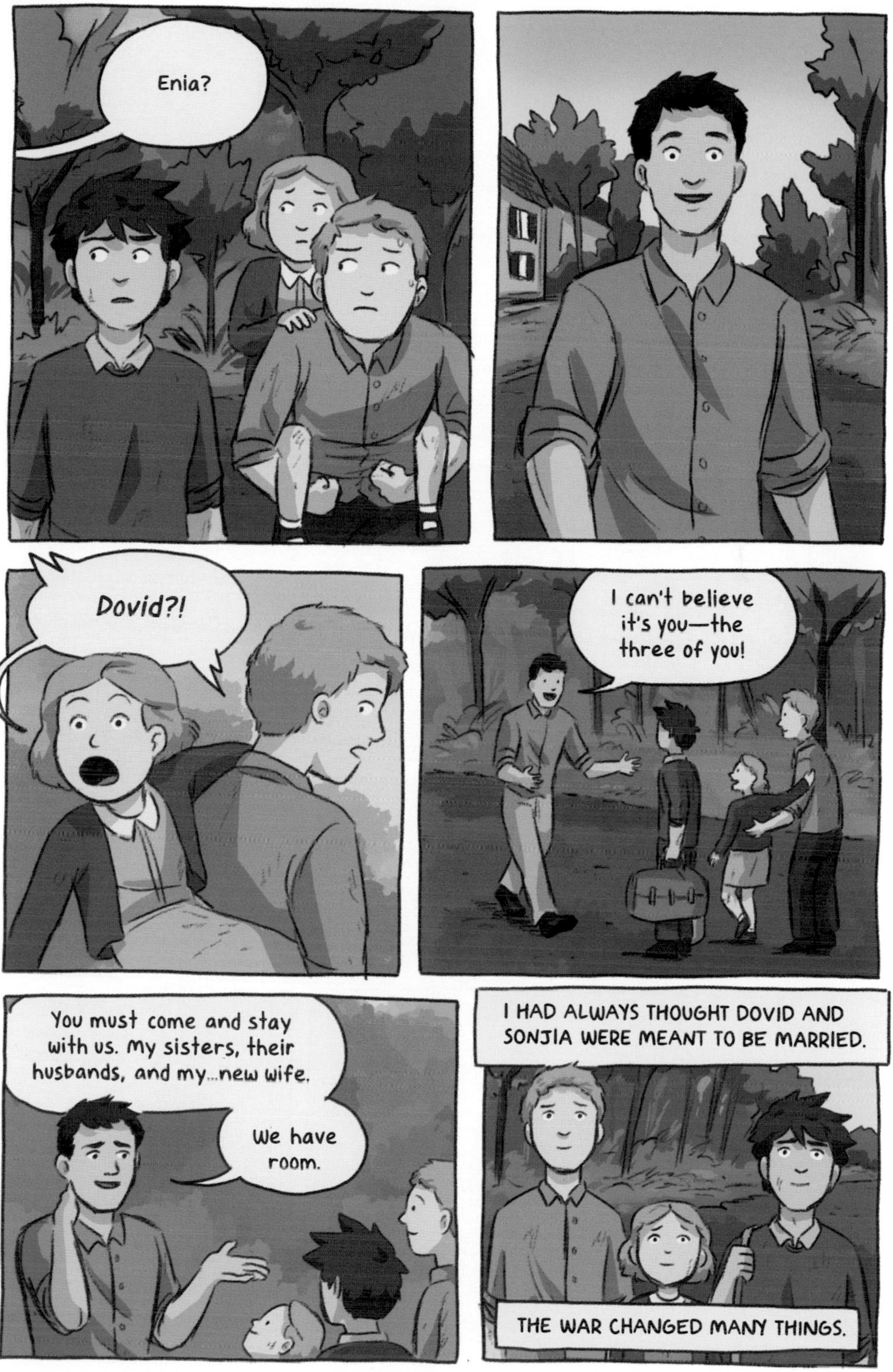
Enia?
Dovid?!
I can't believe it's you—the three of you!
You must come and stay with us. My sisters, their husbands, and my...new wife.
We have room.
I HAD ALWAYS THOUGHT DOVID AND SONJIA WERE MEANT TO BE MARRIED.
THE WAR CHANGED MANY THINGS.

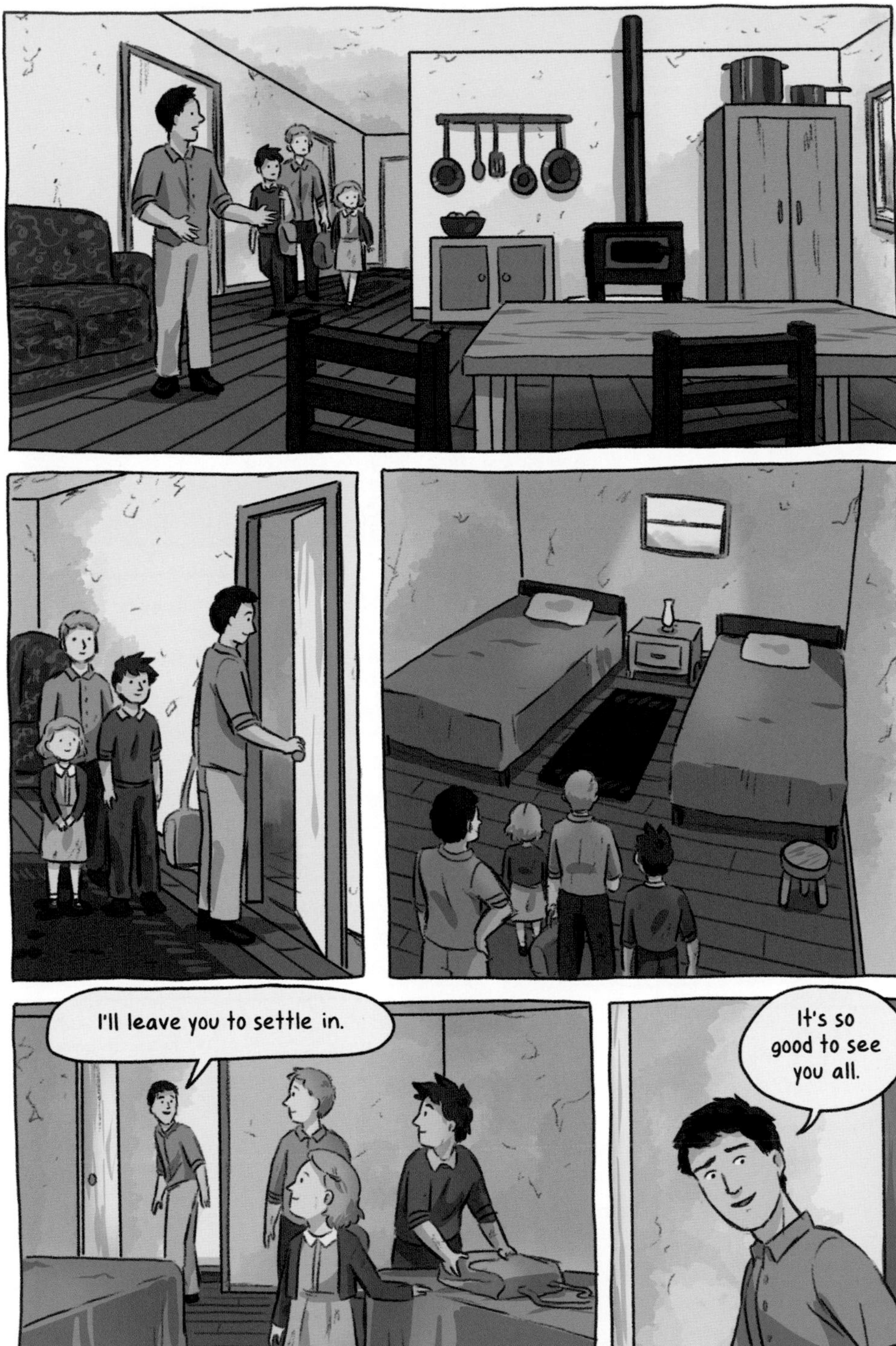
I'll leave you to settle in.
It's so good to see you all.

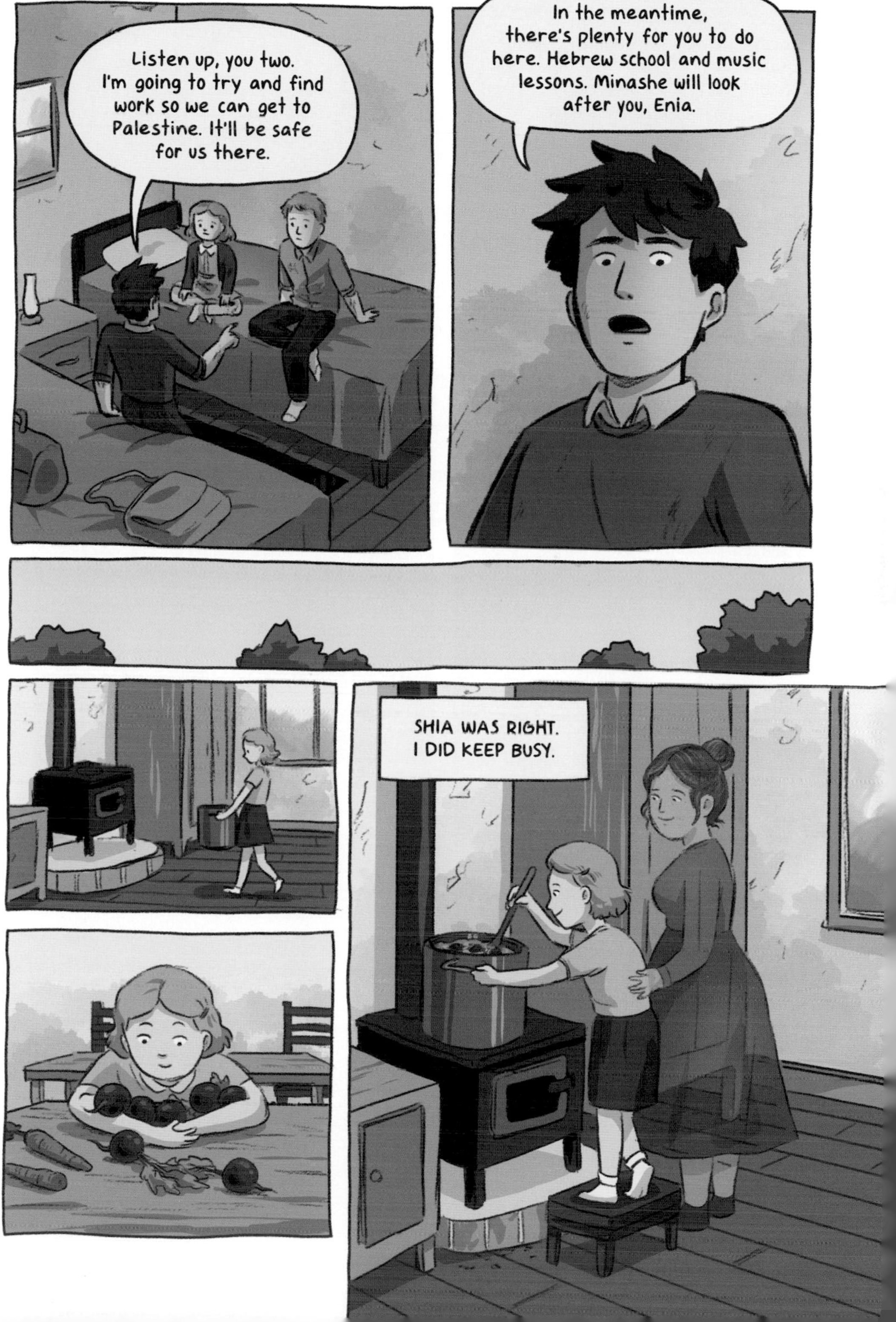
Listen up, you two. I'm going to try and find work so we can get to Palestine. It'll be safe for us there.
In the meantime, there's plenty for you to do here. Hebrew school and music lessons. Minashe will look after you, Enia.
SHIA WAS RIGHT. I DID KEEP BUSY.

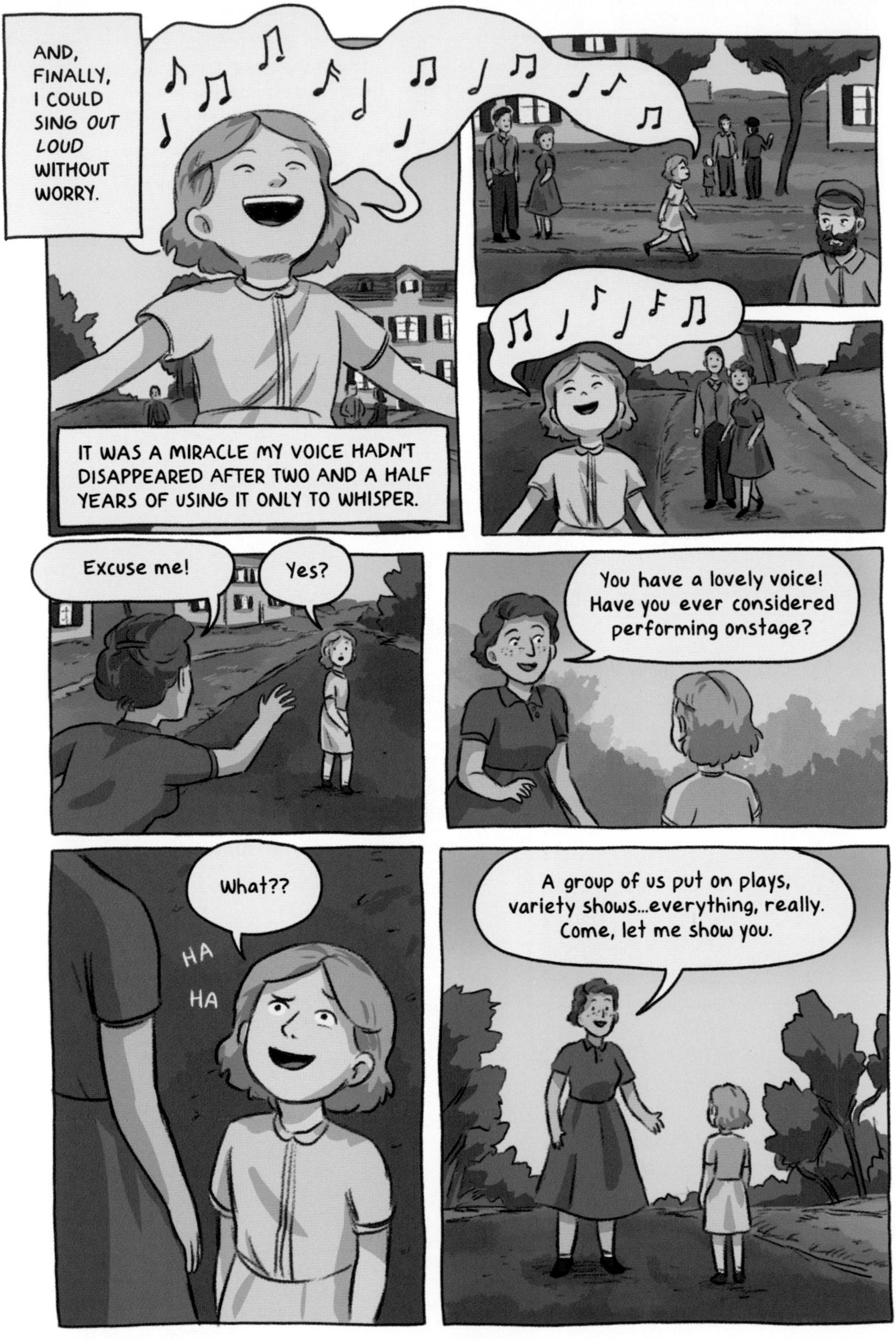
AND, FINALLY, I COULD SING *OUT LOUD* WITHOUT WORRY.
IT WAS A MIRACLE MY VOICE HADN'T DISAPPEARED AFTER TWO AND A HALF YEARS OF USING IT ONLY TO WHISPER.
Excuse me!
Yes?
You have a lovely voice! Have you ever considered performing onstage?
What??
HA
HA
A group of us put on plays, variety shows...everything, really. Come, let me show you.

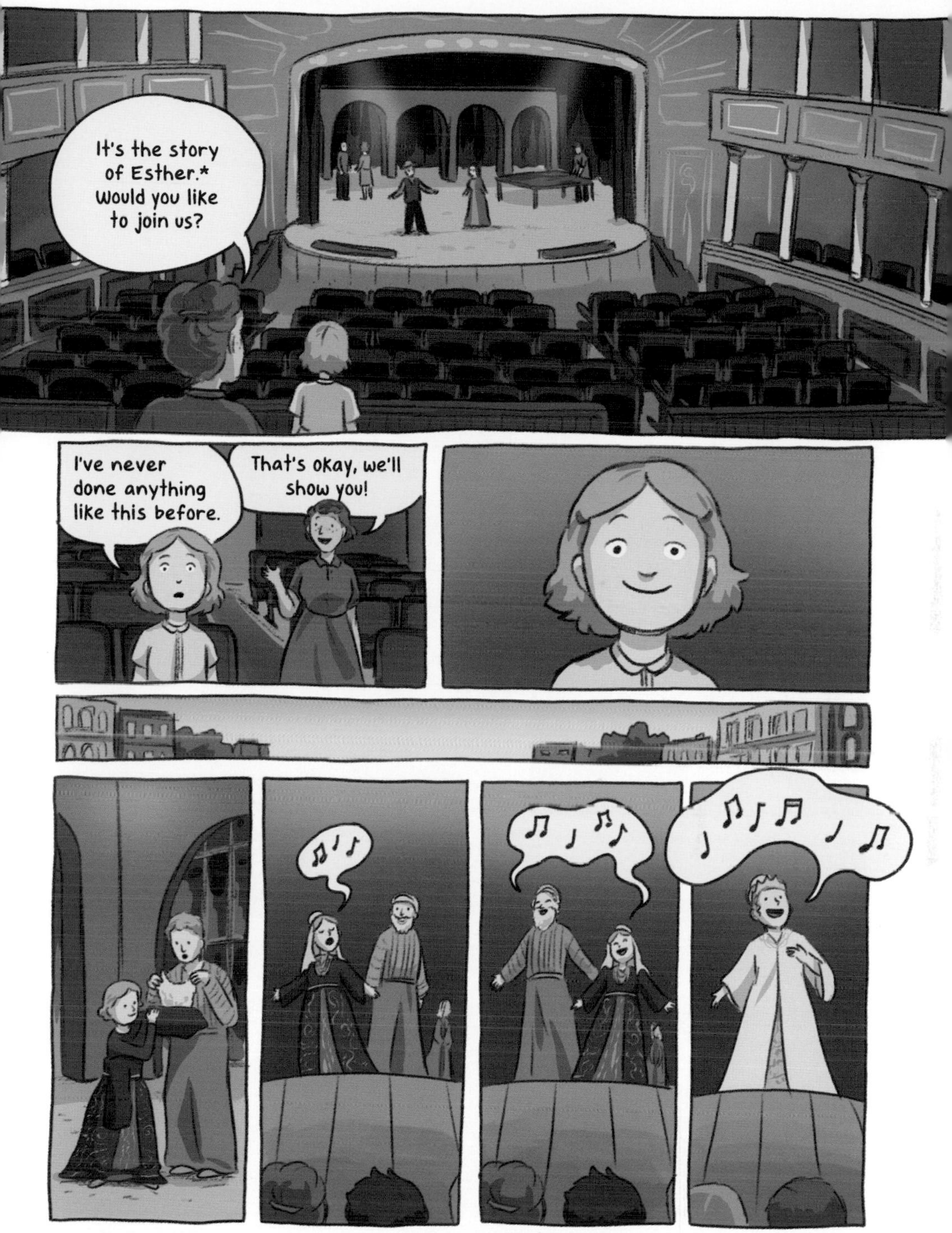
It's the story of Esther.* Would you like to join us?
I've never done anything like this before.
That's okay, we'll show you!

*The story of Queen Esther was from the Tanakh (the Jewish scriptures that include the Torah), which I was learning more about in Hebrew School.

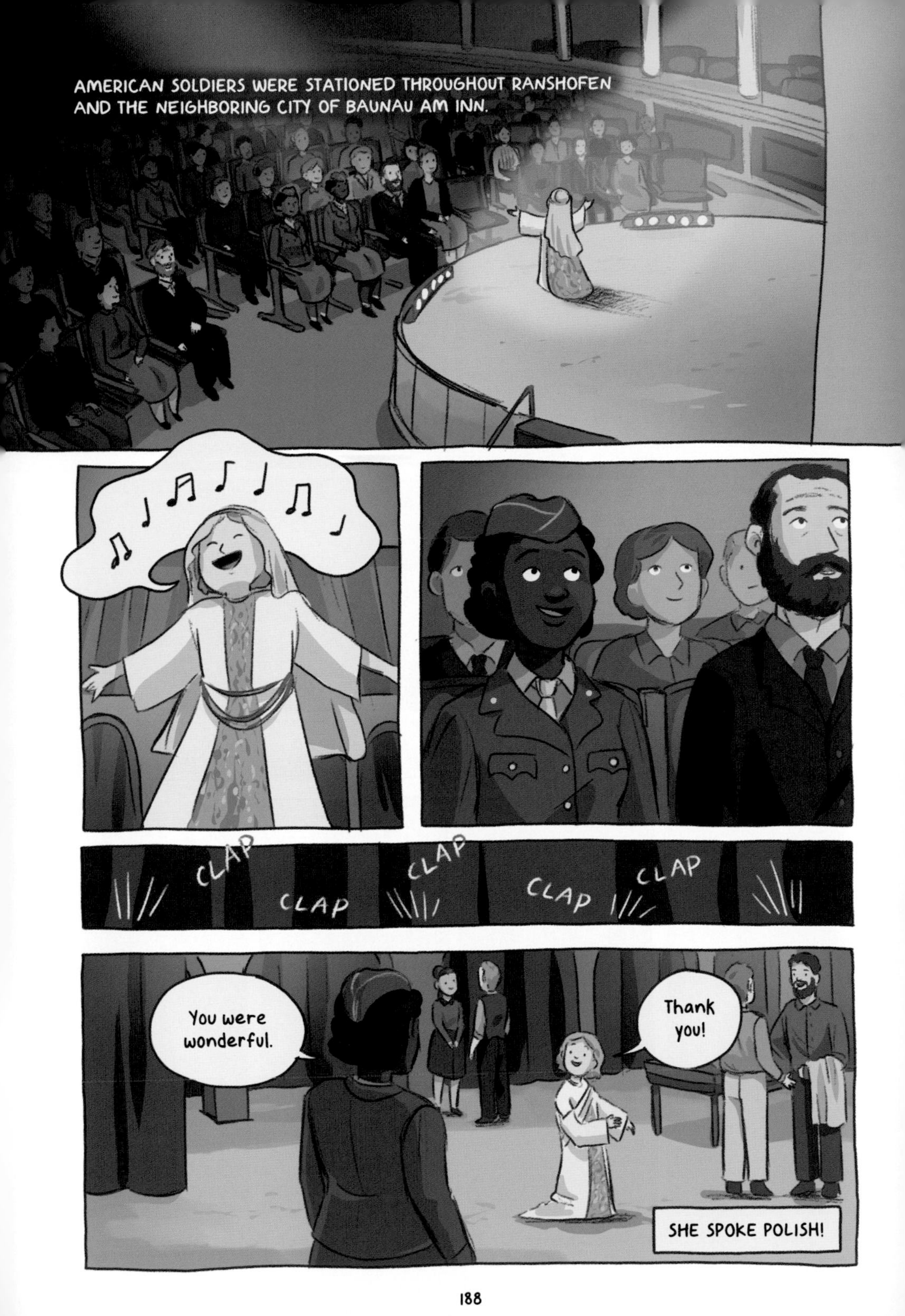

AMERICAN SOLDIERS WERE STATIONED THROUGHOUT RANSHOFEN AND THE NEIGHBORING CITY OF BAUNAU AM INN.
CLAP
CLAP
CLAP
CLAP
CLAP
You were wonderful.
Thank you!
SHE SPOKE POLISH!

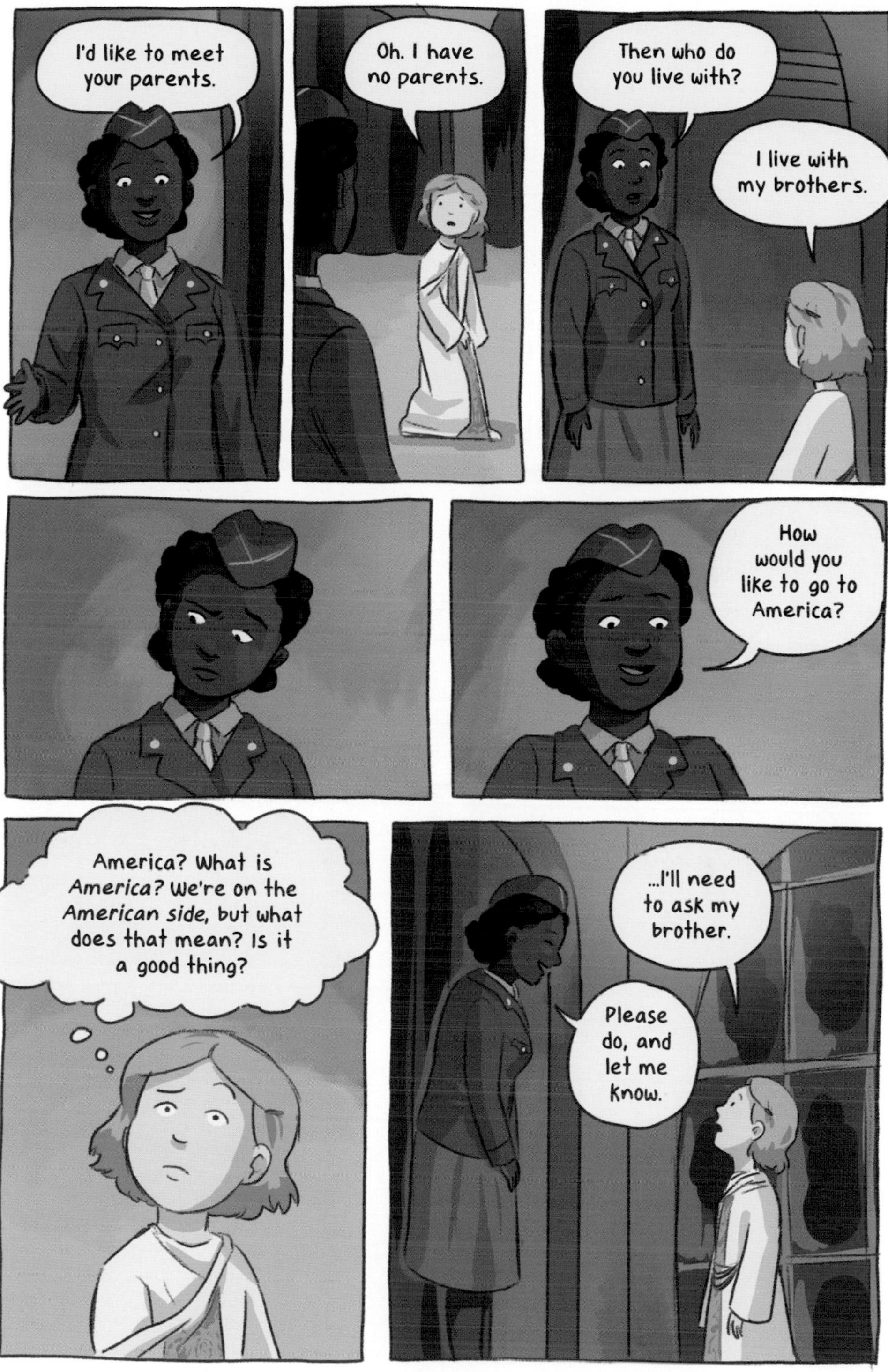
I'd like to meet your parents.
Oh. I have no parents.
Then who do you live with?
I live with my brothers.
How would you like to go to America?
America? What is America? We're on the American side, but what does that mean? Is it a good thing?
...I'll need to ask my brother.
Please do, and let me know.

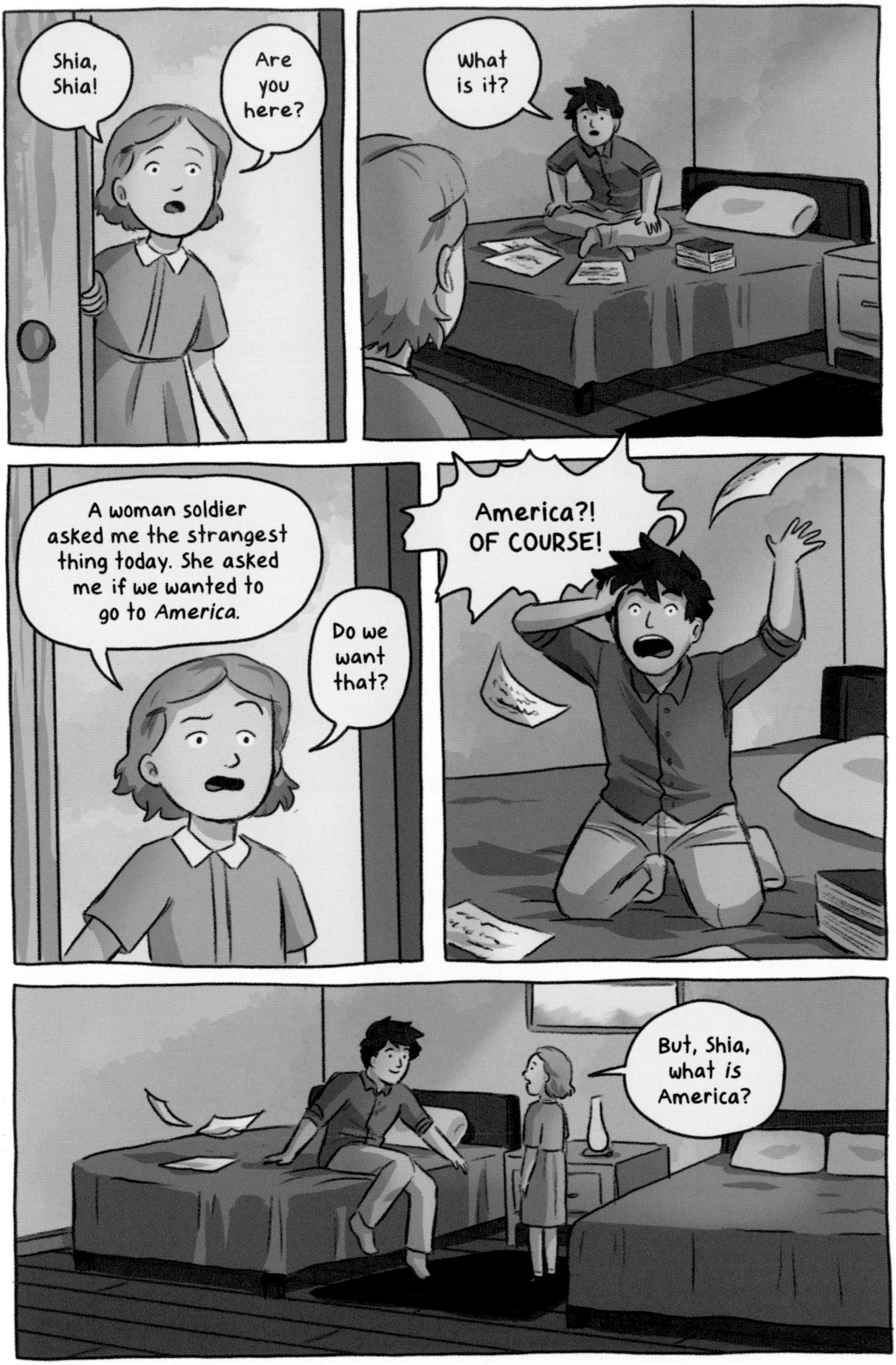
Shia,
Shia!
Are
you
here?
What
is it?
A woman soldier
asked me the strangest
thing today. She asked
me if we wanted to
go to *America*.
Do we
want
that?
America?!
OF COURSE!
But, Shia,
what *is*
America?

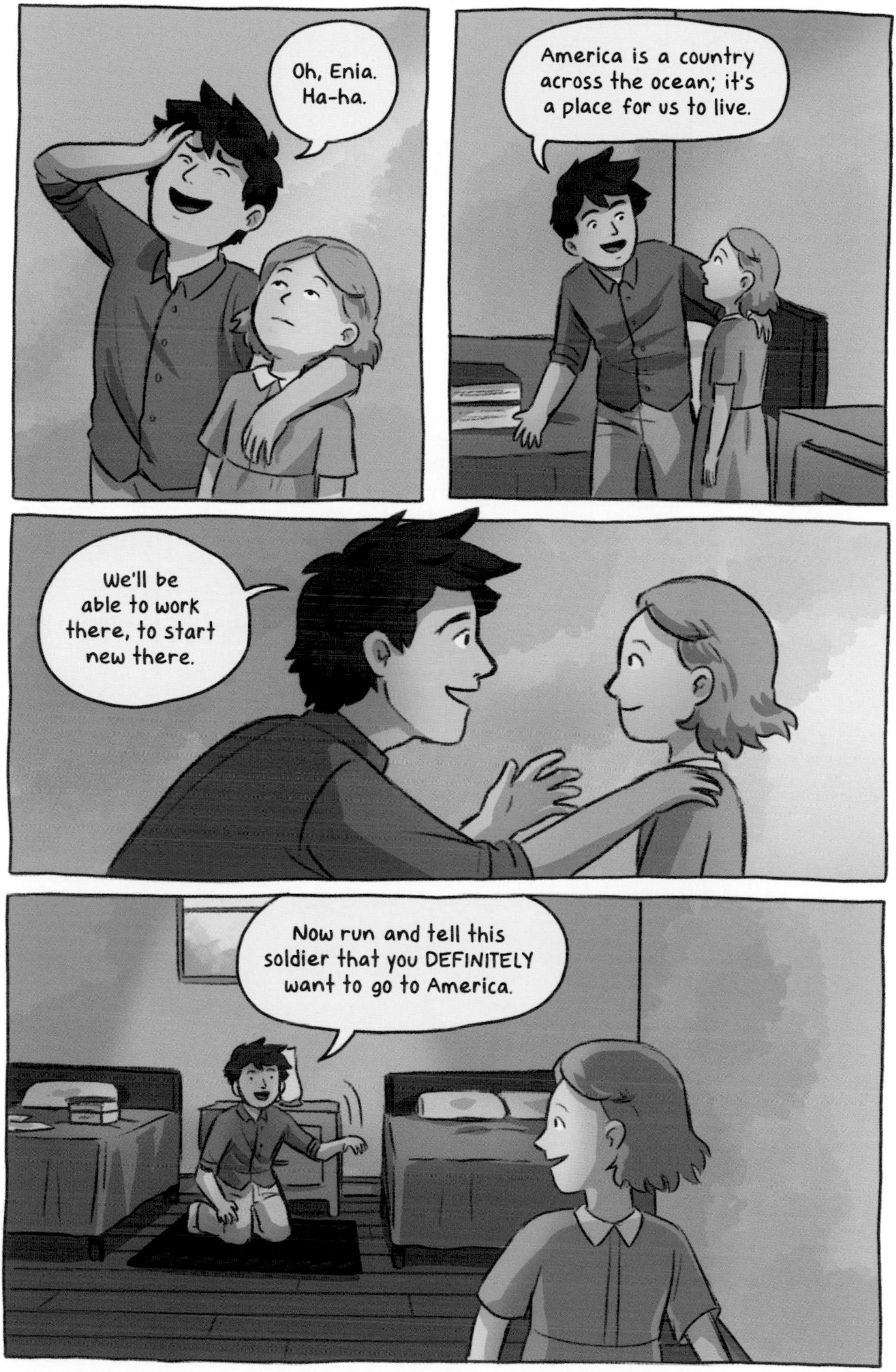
Oh, Enia. Ha-ha.
America is a country across the ocean; it's a place for us to live.
We'll be able to work there, to start new there.
Now run and tell this soldier that you DEFINITELY want to go to America.

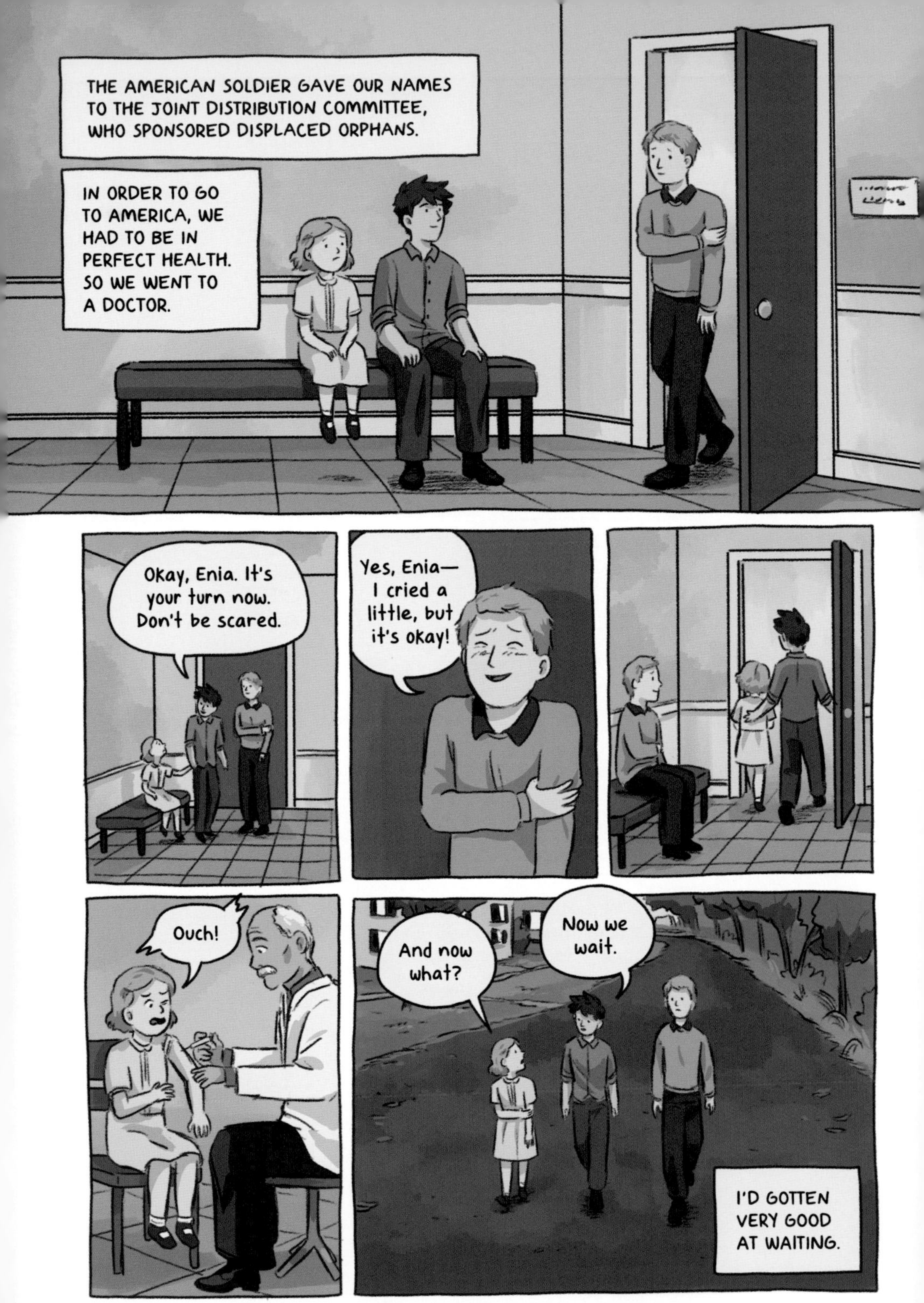
THE AMERICAN SOLDIER GAVE OUR NAMES TO THE JOINT DISTRIBUTION COMMITTEE, WHO SPONSORED DISPLACED ORPHANS.
IN ORDER TO GO TO AMERICA, WE HAD TO BE IN PERFECT HEALTH. SO WE WENT TO A DOCTOR.
Okay, Enia. It's your turn now. Don't be scared.
Yes, Enia— I cried a little, but it's okay!
Ouch!
And now what?
Now we wait.
I'D GOTTEN VERY GOOD AT WAITING.

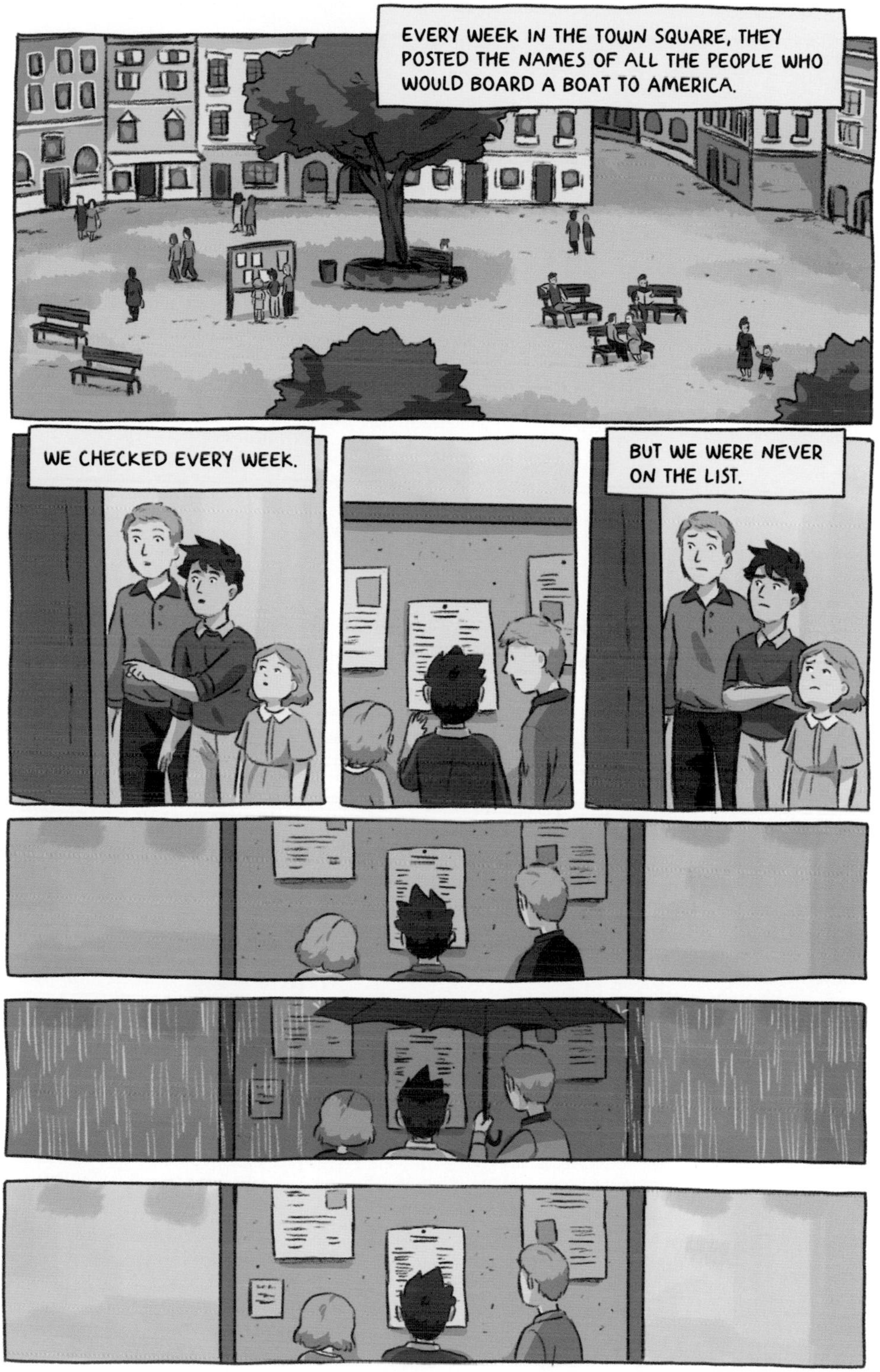
EVERY WEEK IN THE TOWN SQUARE, THEY POSTED THE NAMES OF ALL THE PEOPLE WHO WOULD BOARD A BOAT TO AMERICA.
WE CHECKED EVERY WEEK.
BUT WE WERE NEVER ON THE LIST.

Feld, Shia

There it is! There's my name! It's happening!

We're going to America!

Feder, Sh...
Feinstein, Menad...
Feld, Shia
Feld, Minashe
Feldsher, Zofia
Feldsh...aria
Fishe...
Glazer,...nał
Gross, Fenks

Wait. Where's Enia?

I'm right here.

No, where's your name on the list? It's not here!

Let me see.

I COULDN'T READ.

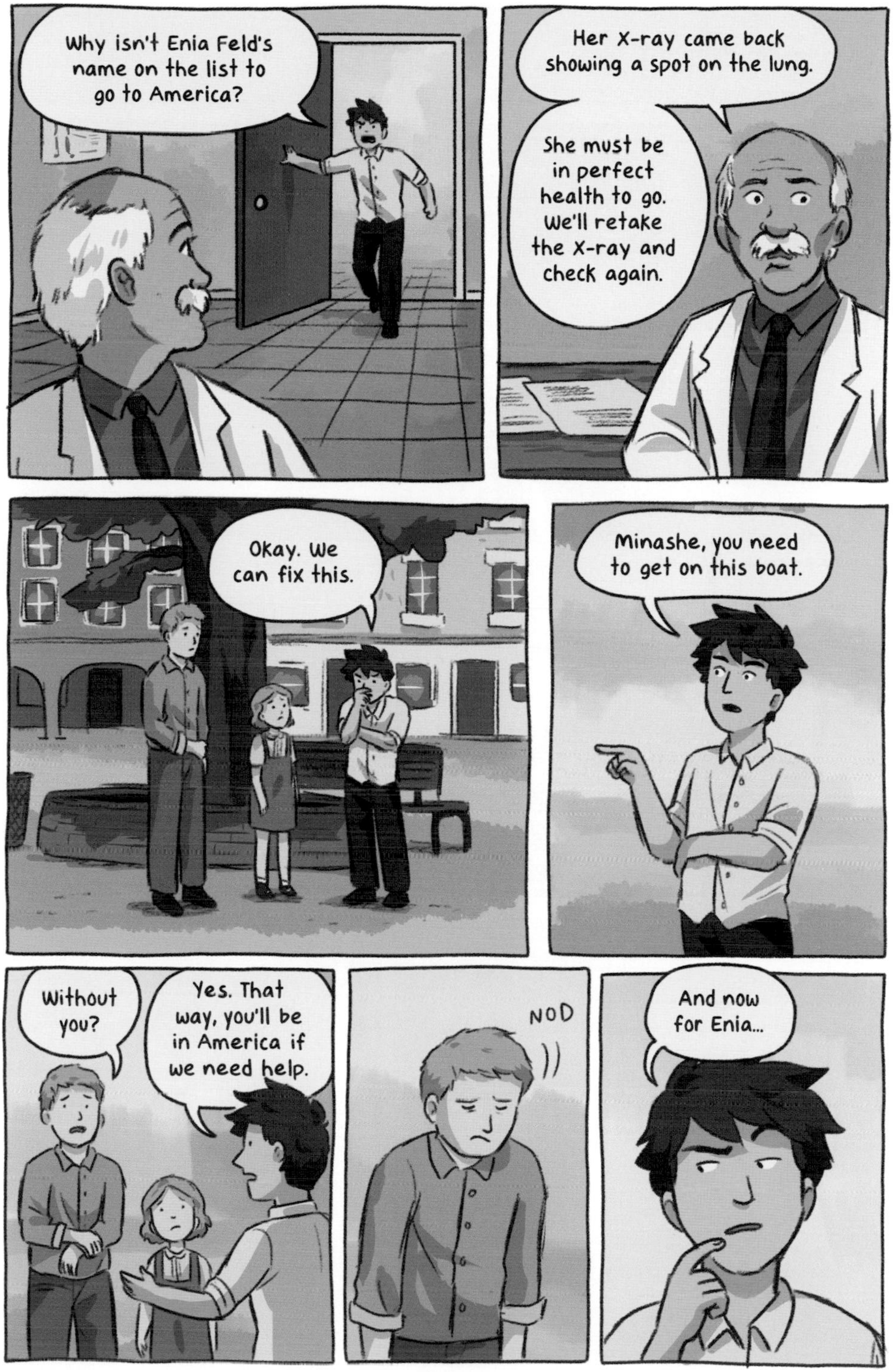
Why isn't Enia Feld's name on the list to go to America?
Her X-ray came back showing a spot on the lung.
She must be in perfect health to go. We'll retake the X-ray and check again.
Okay. We can fix this.
Minashe, you need to get on this boat.
Without you?
Yes. That way, you'll be in America if we need help.
NOD
And now for Enia...

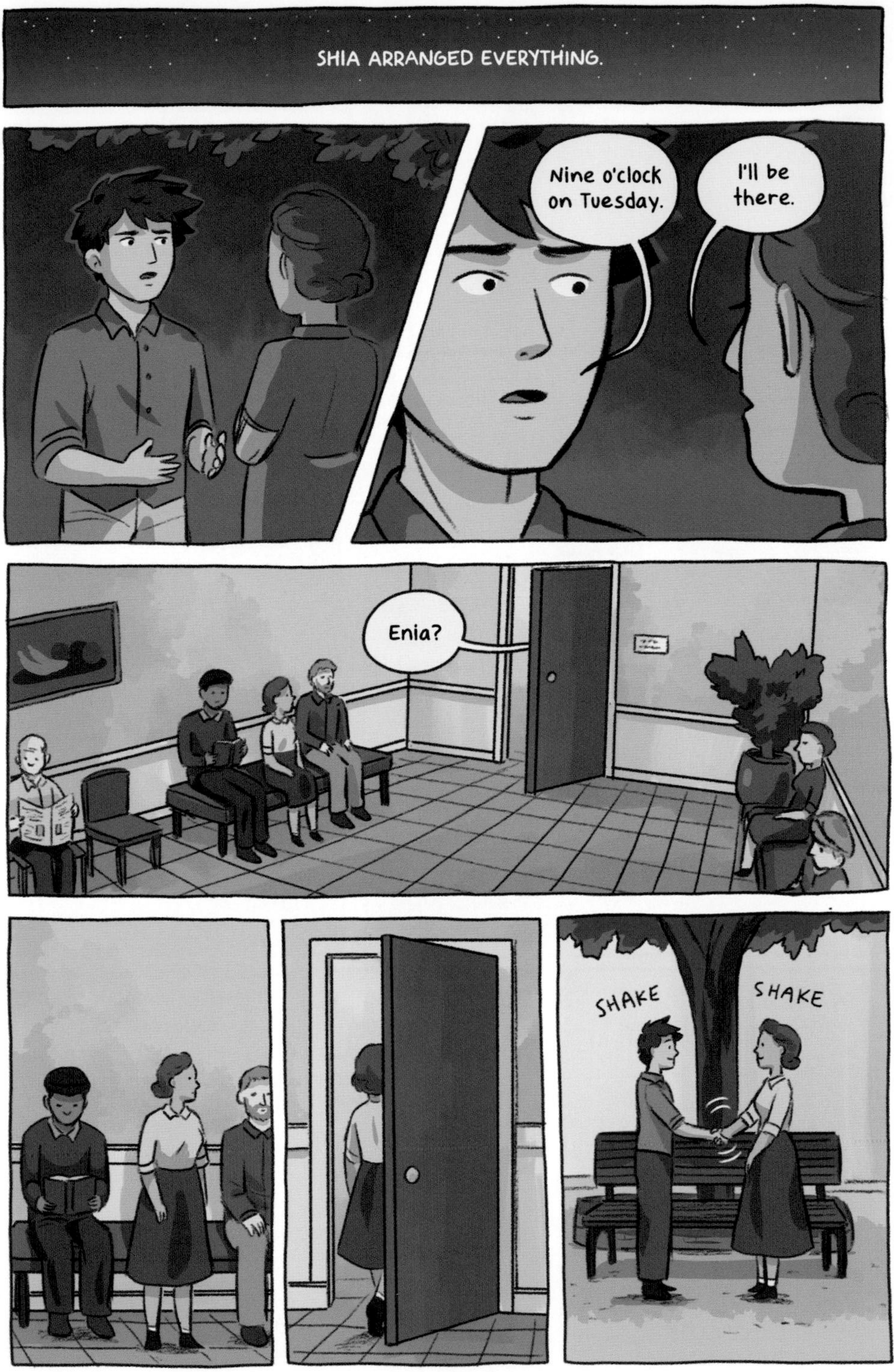
SHIA ARRANGED EVERYTHING.
Nine o'clock on Tuesday.
I'll be there.
Enia?
SHAKE
SHAKE

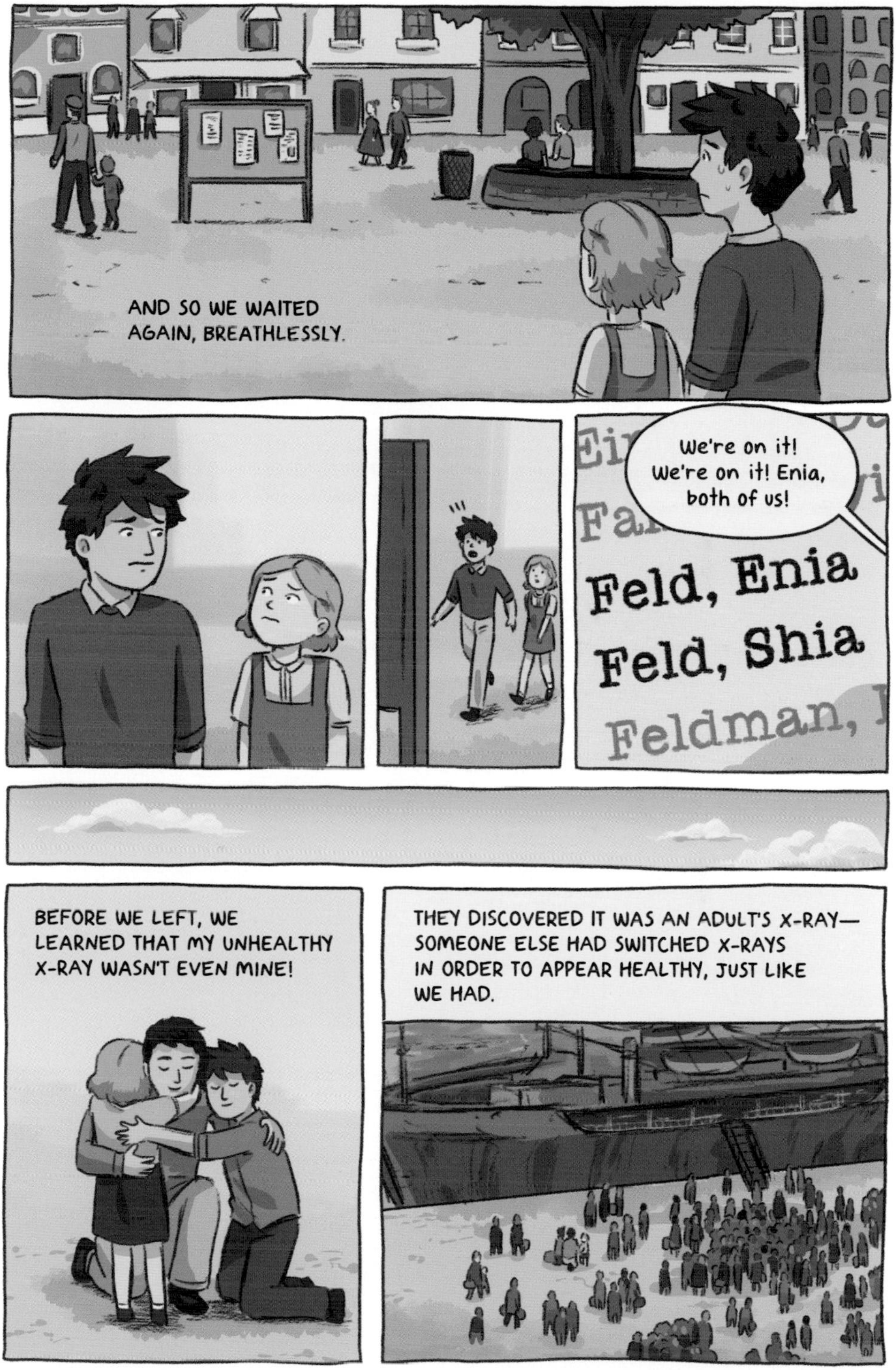
AND SO WE WAITED AGAIN, BREATHLESSLY.
We're on it! We're on it! Enia, both of us!
Feld, Enia
Feld, Shia
Feldman,
BEFORE WE LEFT, WE LEARNED THAT MY UNHEALTHY X-RAY WASN'T EVEN MINE!
THEY DISCOVERED IT WAS AN ADULT'S X-RAY—SOMEONE ELSE HAD SWITCHED X-RAYS IN ORDER TO APPEAR HEALTHY, JUST LIKE WE HAD.

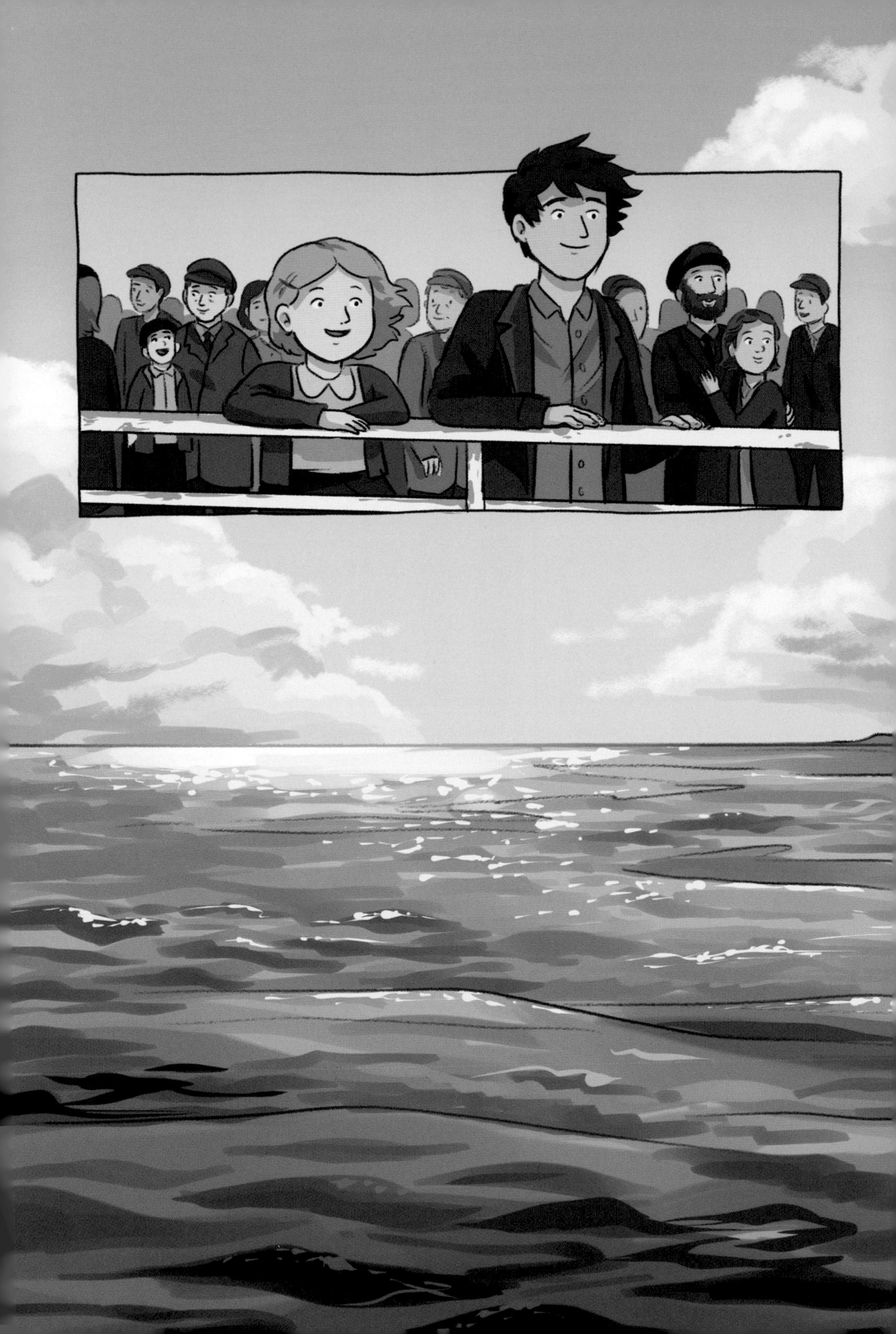

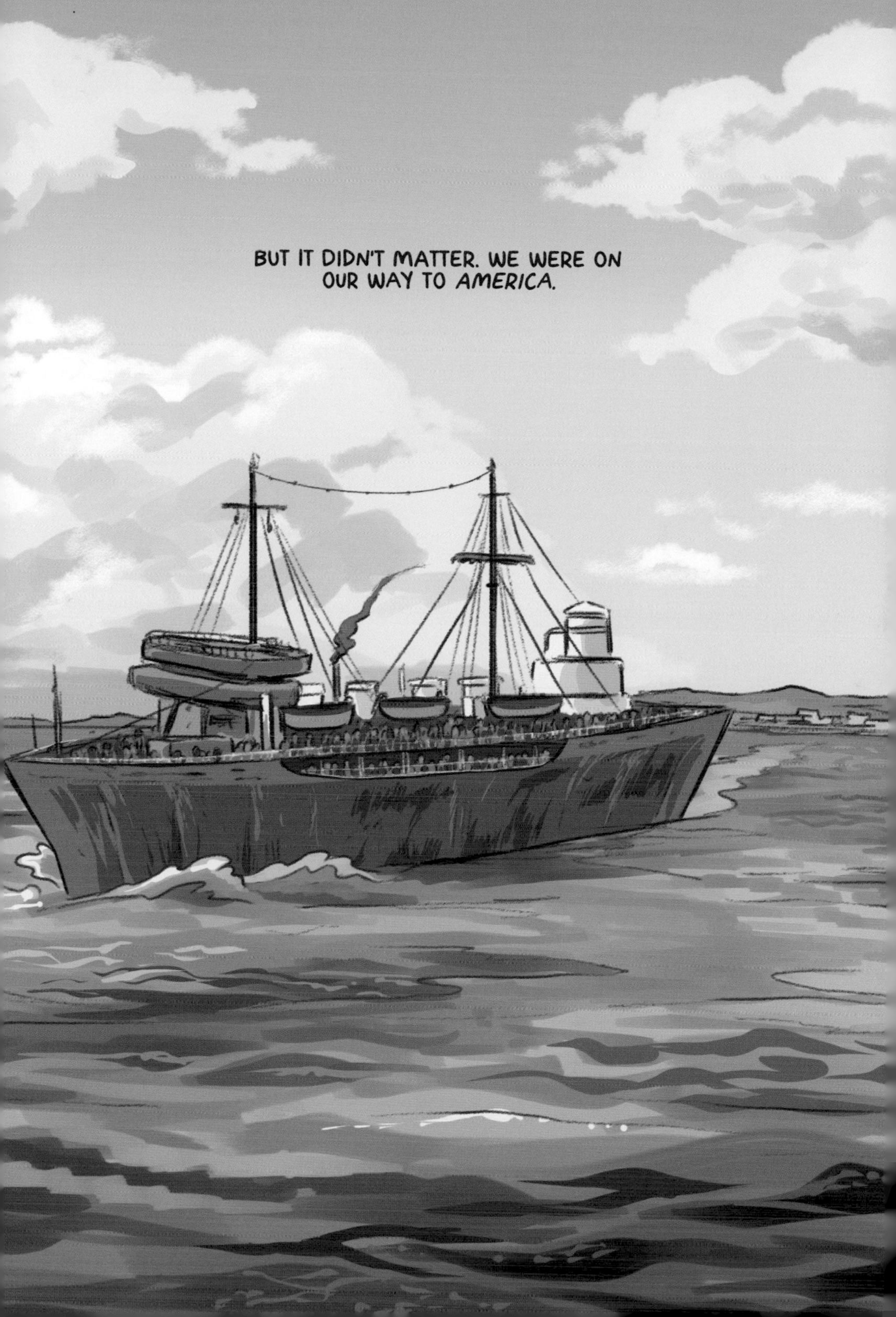
BUT IT DIDN'T MATTER. WE WERE ON OUR WAY TO *AMERICA*.

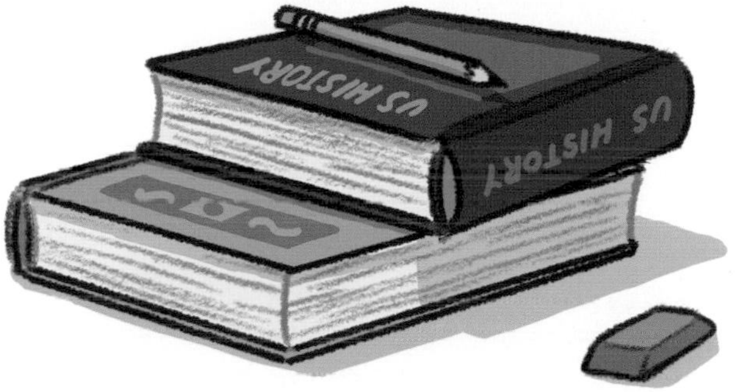
US HISTORY
US HISTORY

PART 4:

A NEW BEGINNING

1947–1951

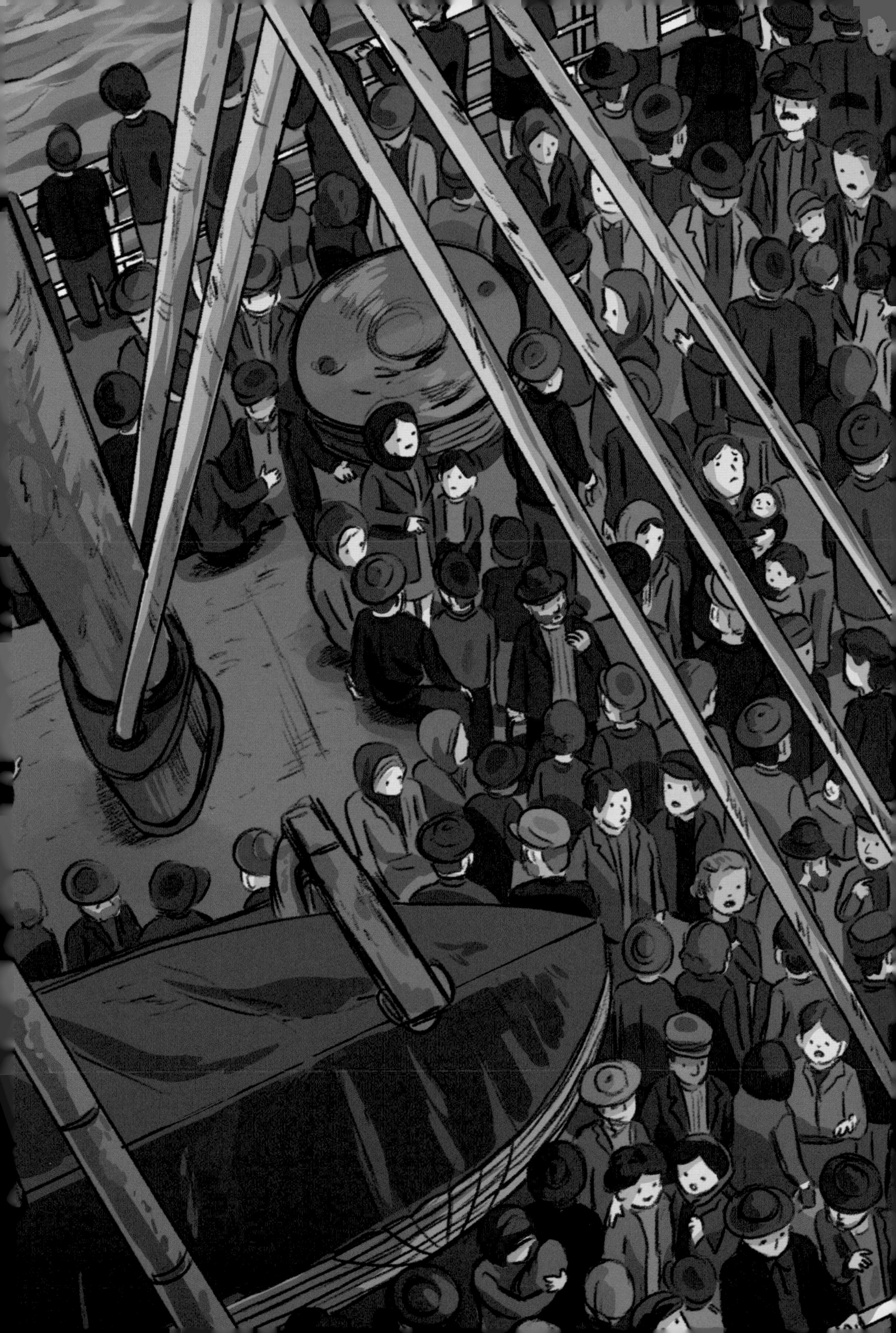

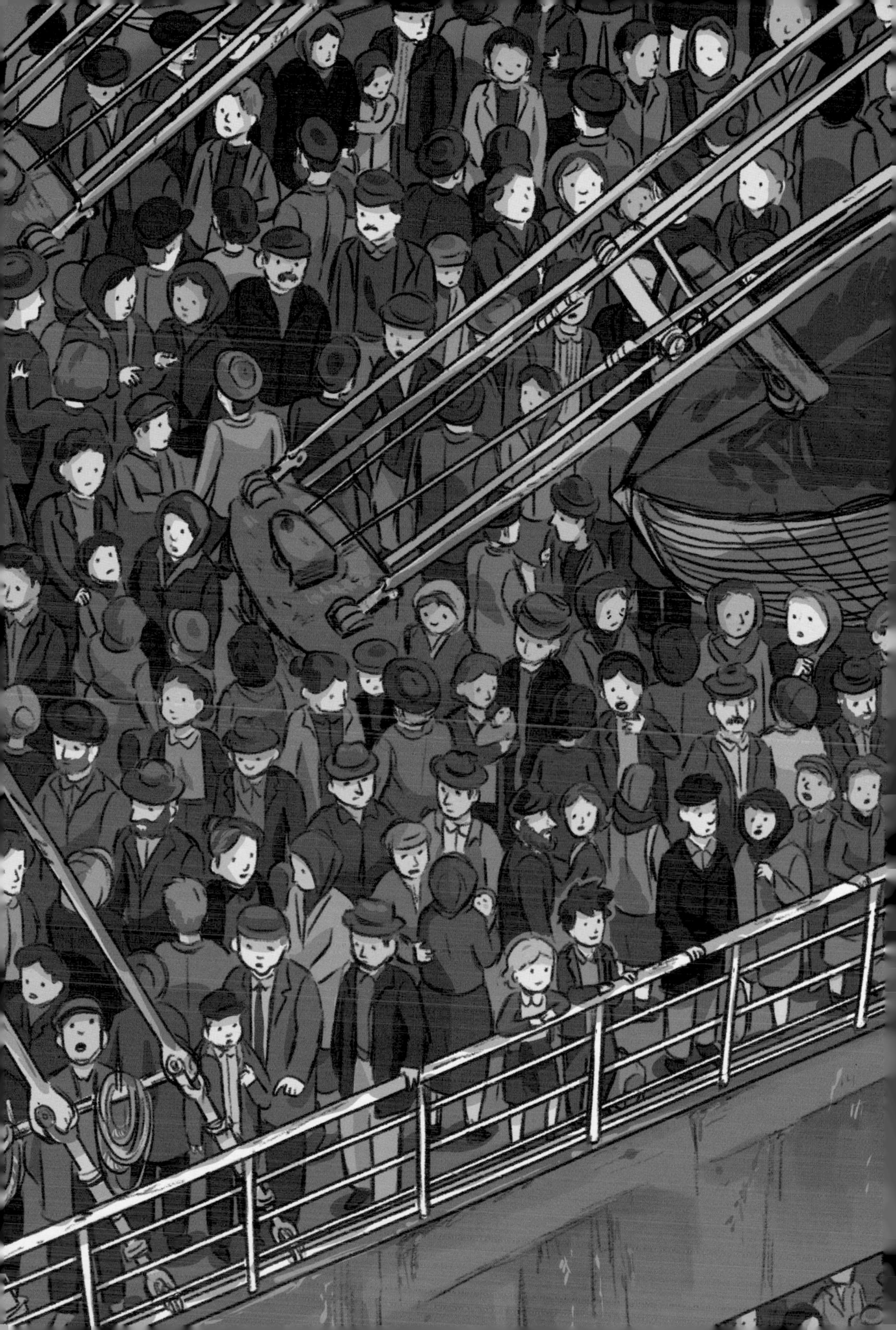

WE WERE SO EXCITED!

BUT, OH, THE TRIP WAS AWFUL. WE BROKE DOWN IN THE ENGLISH CHANNEL AND HAD TO WAIT FOR A NEW SHIP TO COME FROM THE UNITED STATES TO RESCUE US.

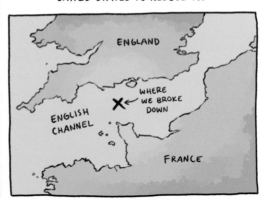

ENGLAND

WHERE WE BROKE DOWN

ENGLISH CHANNEL

FRANCE

OUR NEW SHIP WAS THE *MARINE MARLIN*.

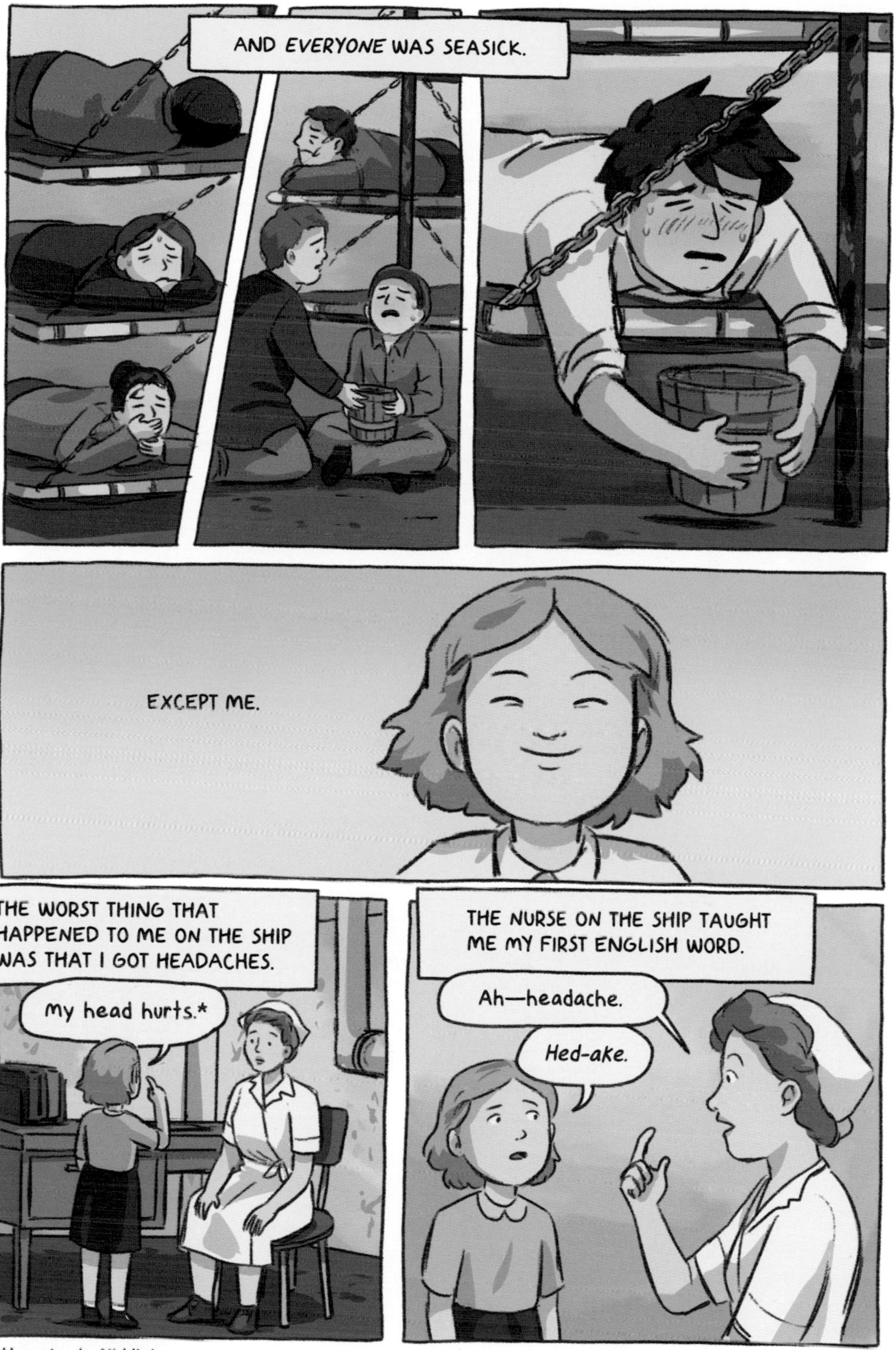
AND EVERYONE WAS SEASICK.
EXCEPT ME.
THE WORST THING THAT HAPPENED TO ME ON THE SHIP WAS THAT I GOT HEADACHES.
my head hurts.*
THE NURSE ON THE SHIP TAUGHT ME MY FIRST ENGLISH WORD.
Ah—headache.
Hed-ake.

*I spoke in Yiddish.

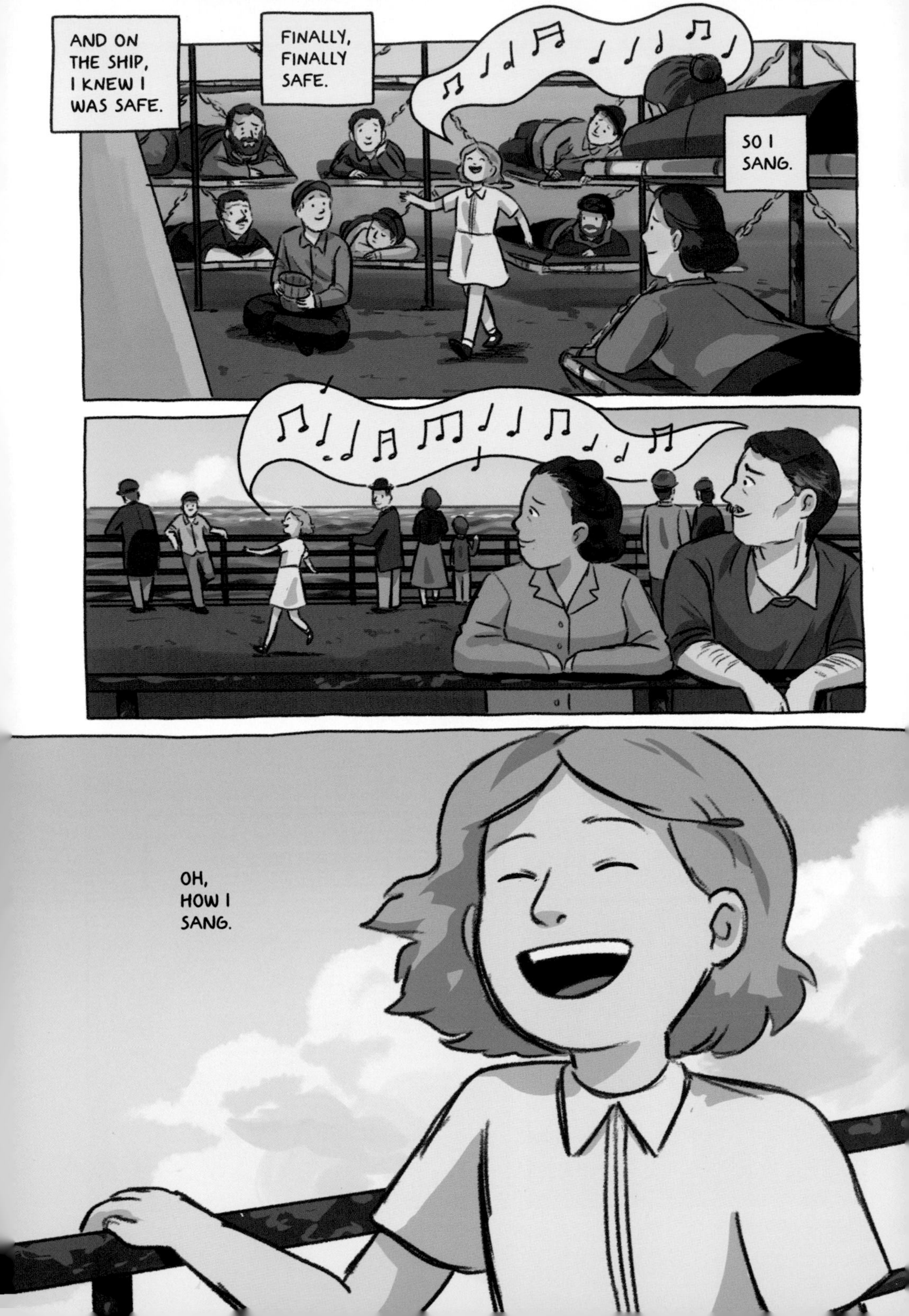
AND ON THE SHIP, I KNEW I WAS SAFE.
FINALLY, FINALLY SAFE.
SO I SANG.
OH, HOW I SANG.

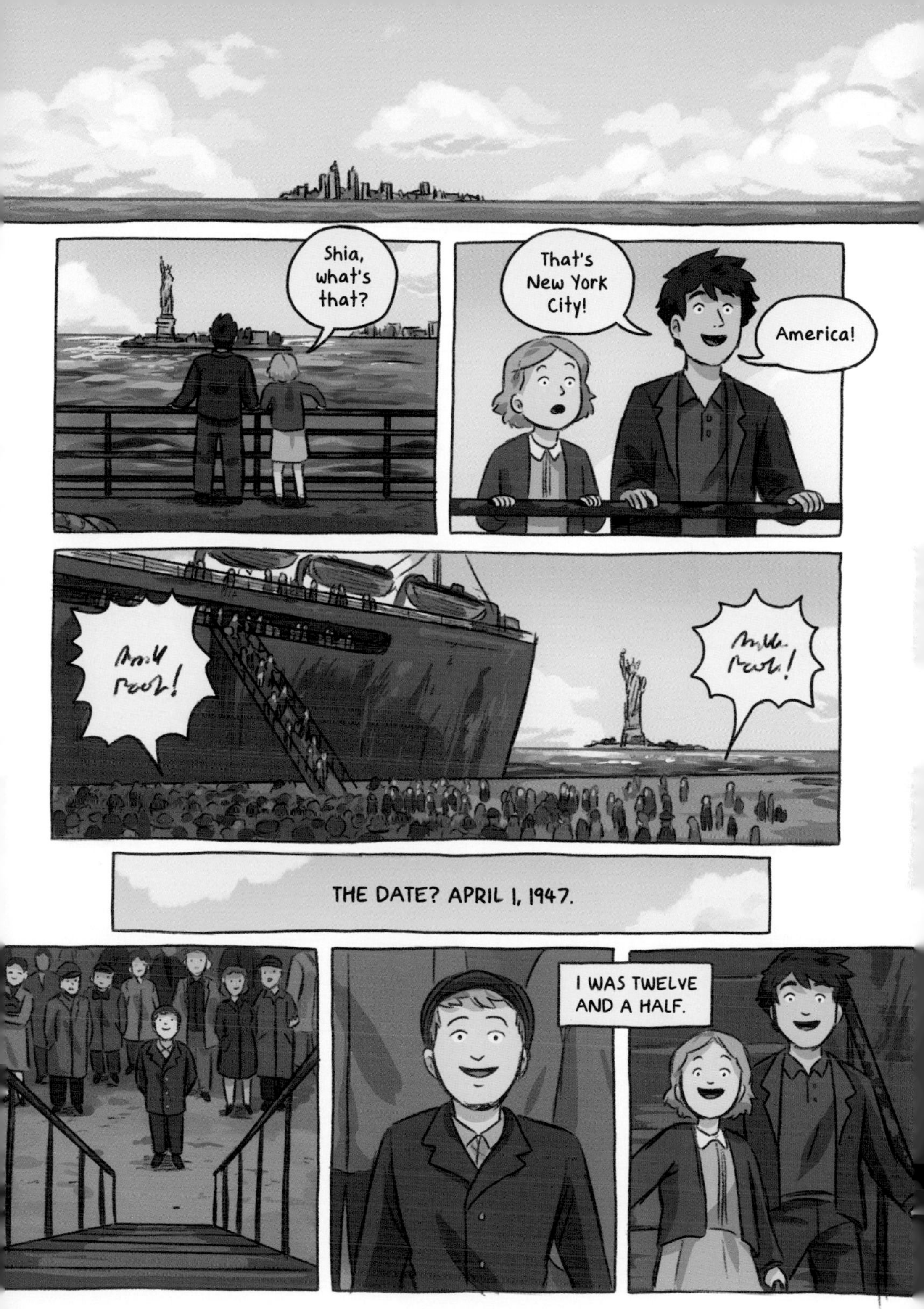
Shia, what's that?
That's New York City!
America!
THE DATE? APRIL 1, 1947.
I WAS TWELVE AND A HALF.

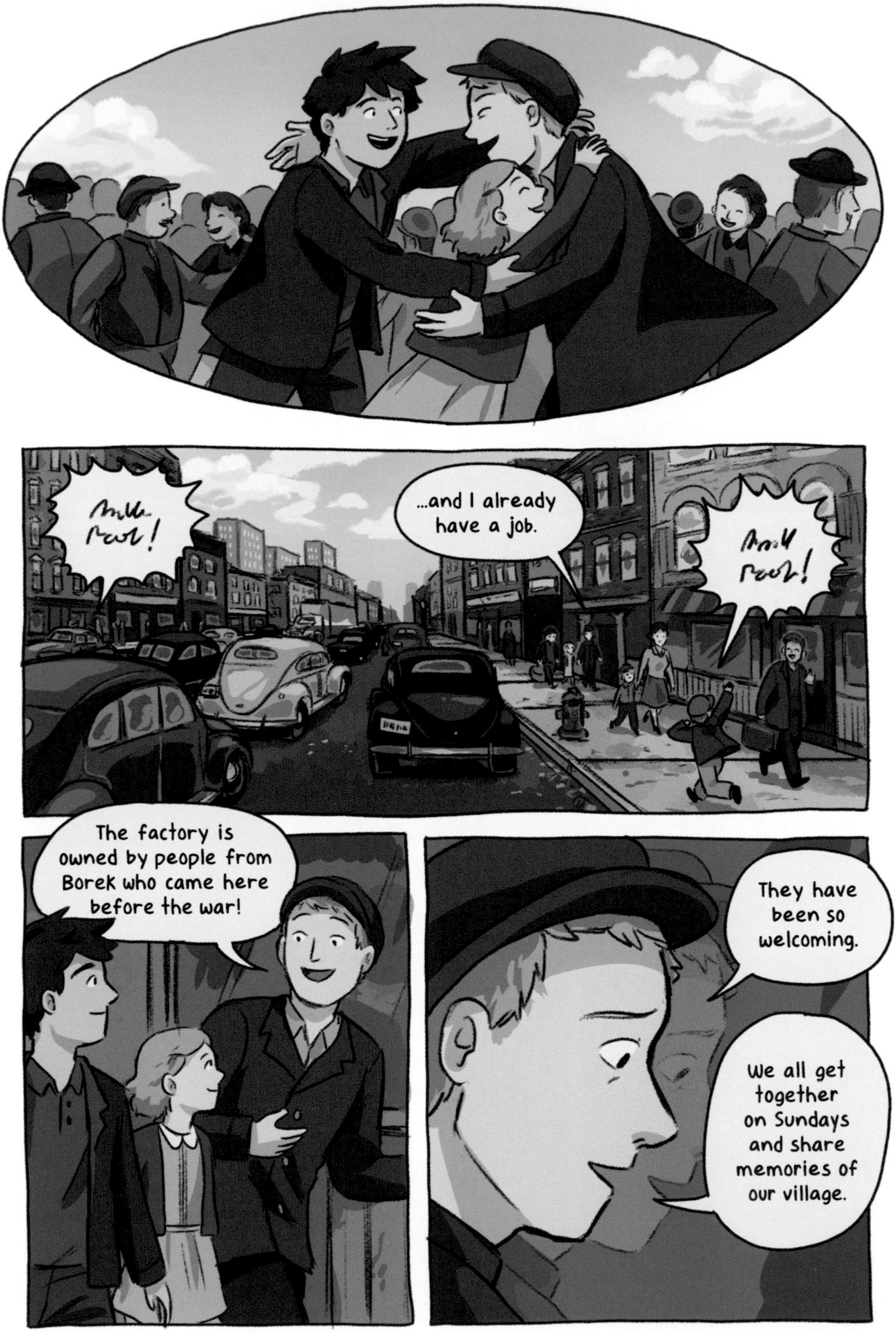
...and I already have a job.
The factory is owned by people from Borek who came here before the war!
They have been so welcoming.
We all get together on Sundays and share memories of our village.

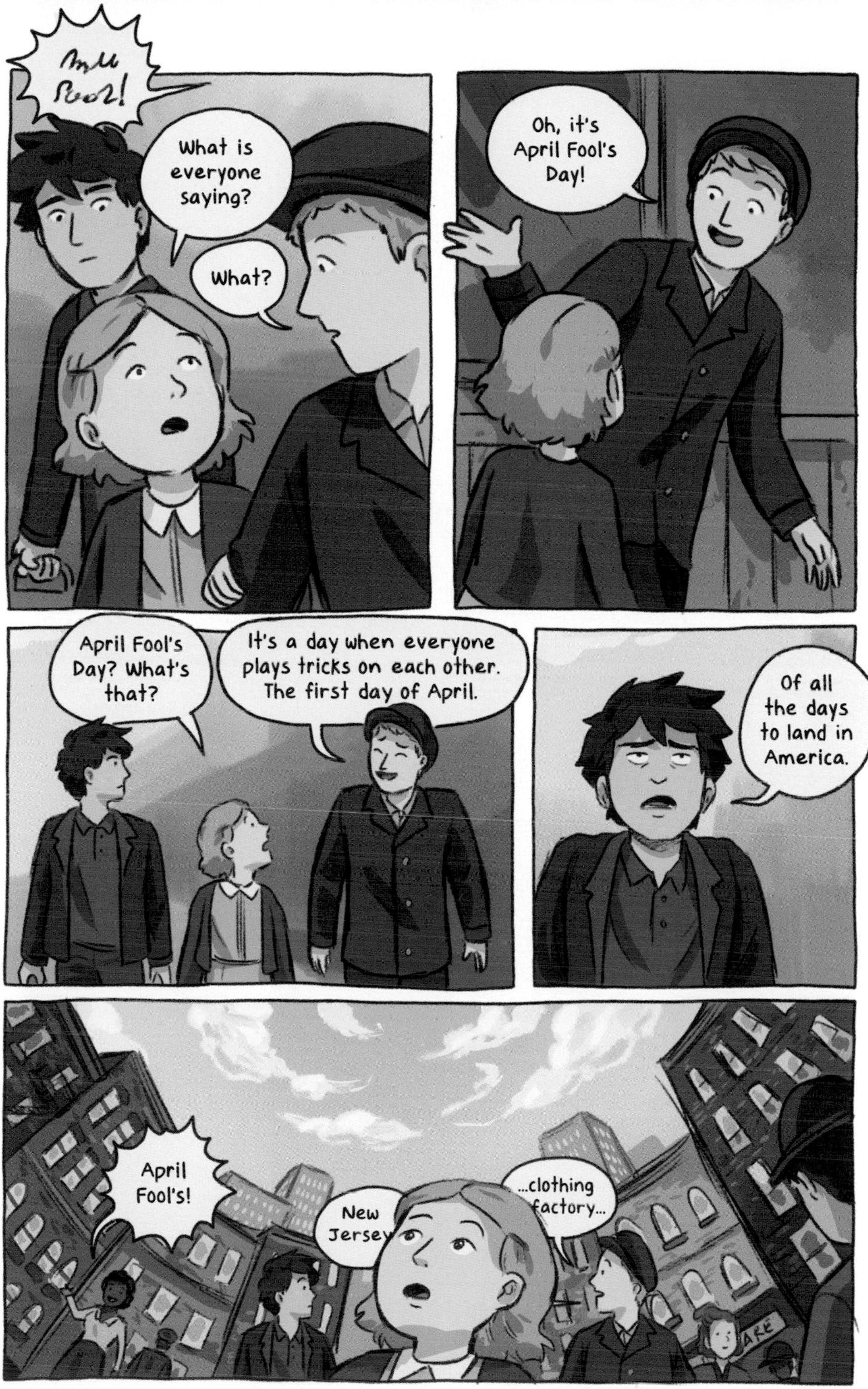

What is everyone saying?
What?
Oh, it's April Fool's Day!
April Fool's Day? What's that?
It's a day when everyone plays tricks on each other. The first day of April.
Of all the days to land in America.
April Fool's!
New Jersey
...clothing factory...

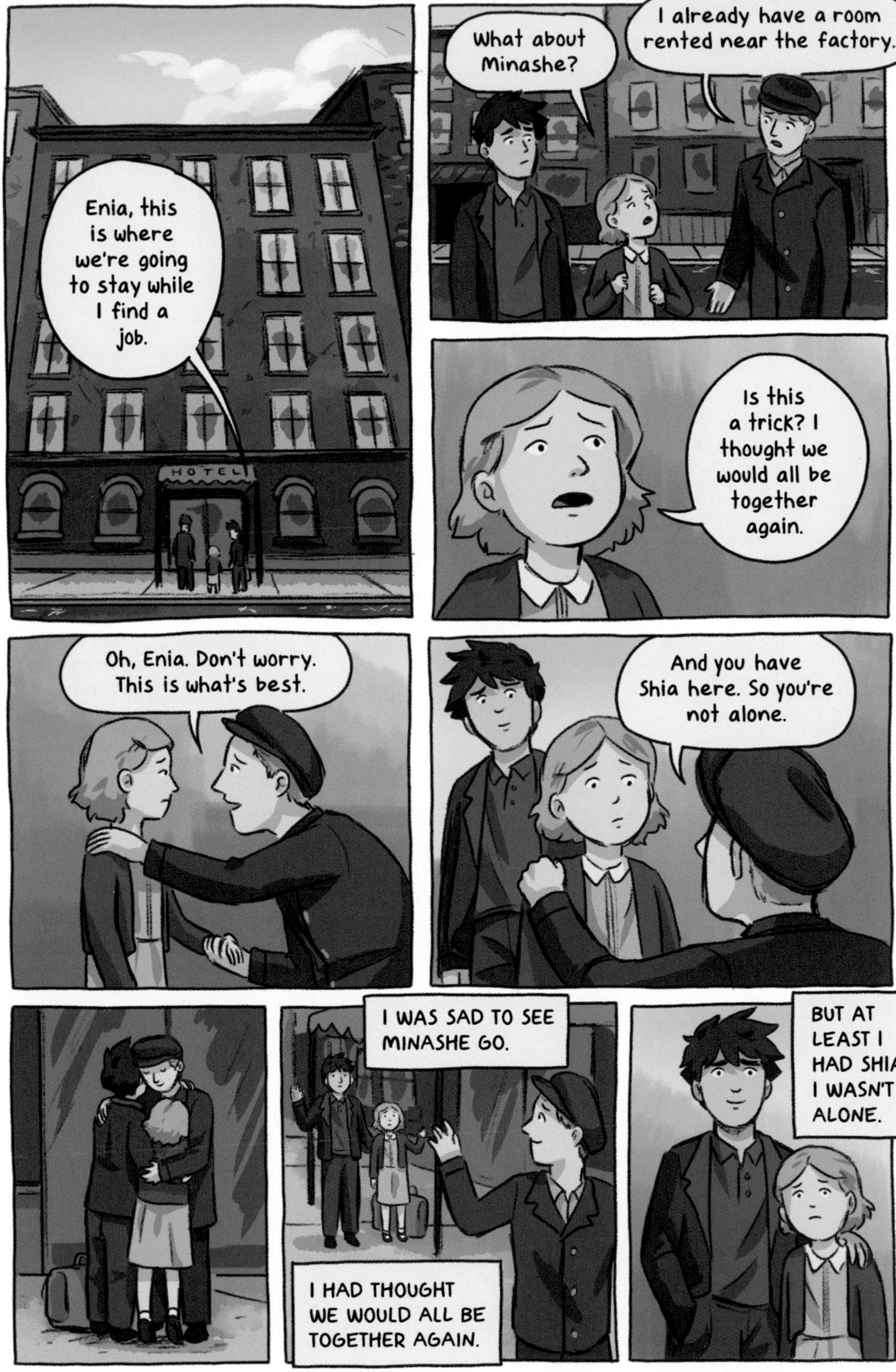
HOTEL
Enia, this is where we're going to stay while I find a job.
What about Minashe?
I already have a room rented near the factory.
Is this a trick? I thought we would all be together again.
Oh, Enia. Don't worry. This is what's best.
And you have Shia here. So you're not alone.
I WAS SAD TO SEE MINASHE GO.
I HAD THOUGHT WE WOULD ALL BE TOGETHER AGAIN.
BUT AT LEAST I HAD SHIA. I WASN'T ALONE.

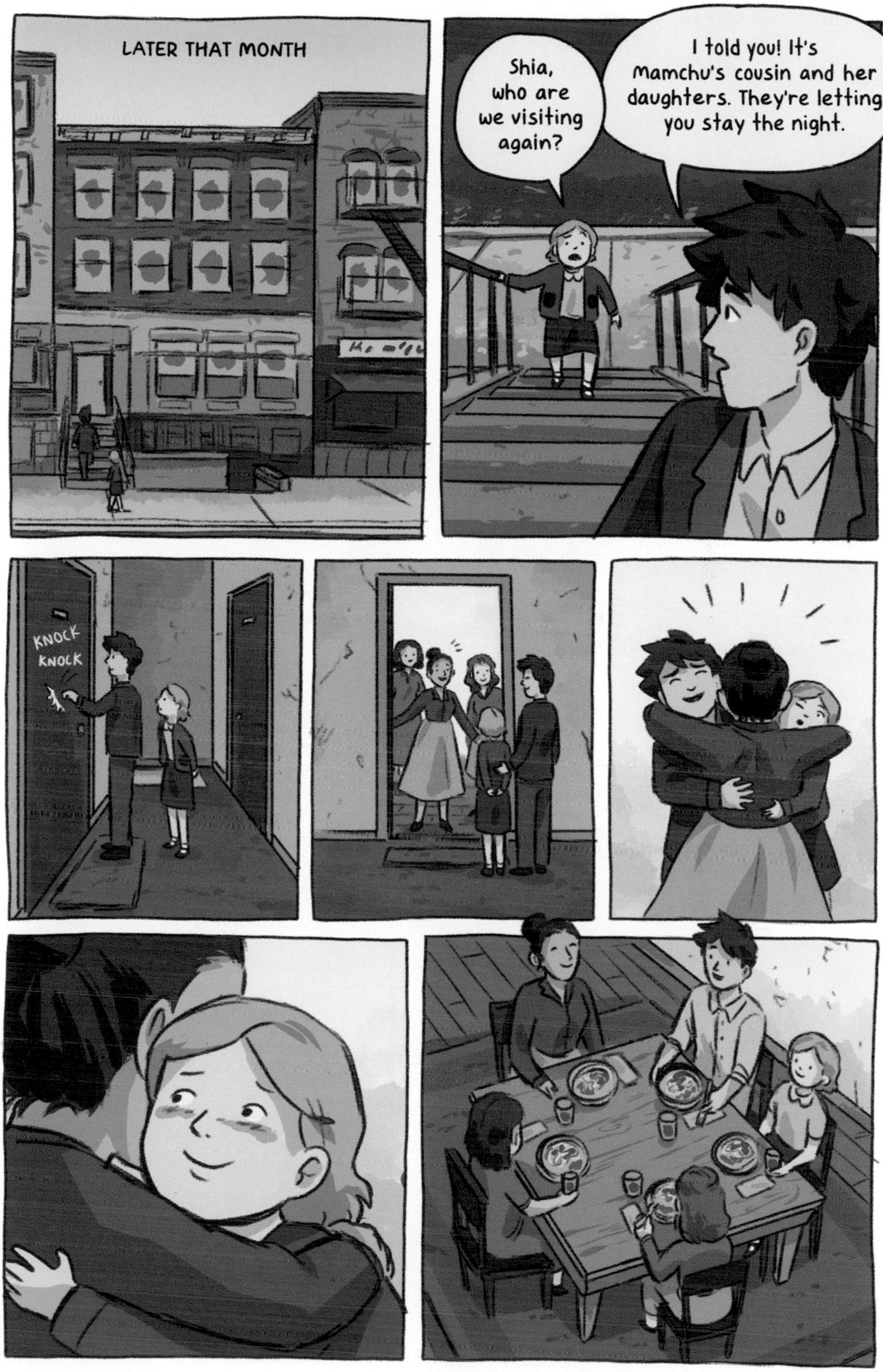
LATER THAT MONTH
Shia, who are we visiting again?
I told you! It's mamchu's cousin and her daughters. They're letting you stay the night.
KNOCK KNOCK

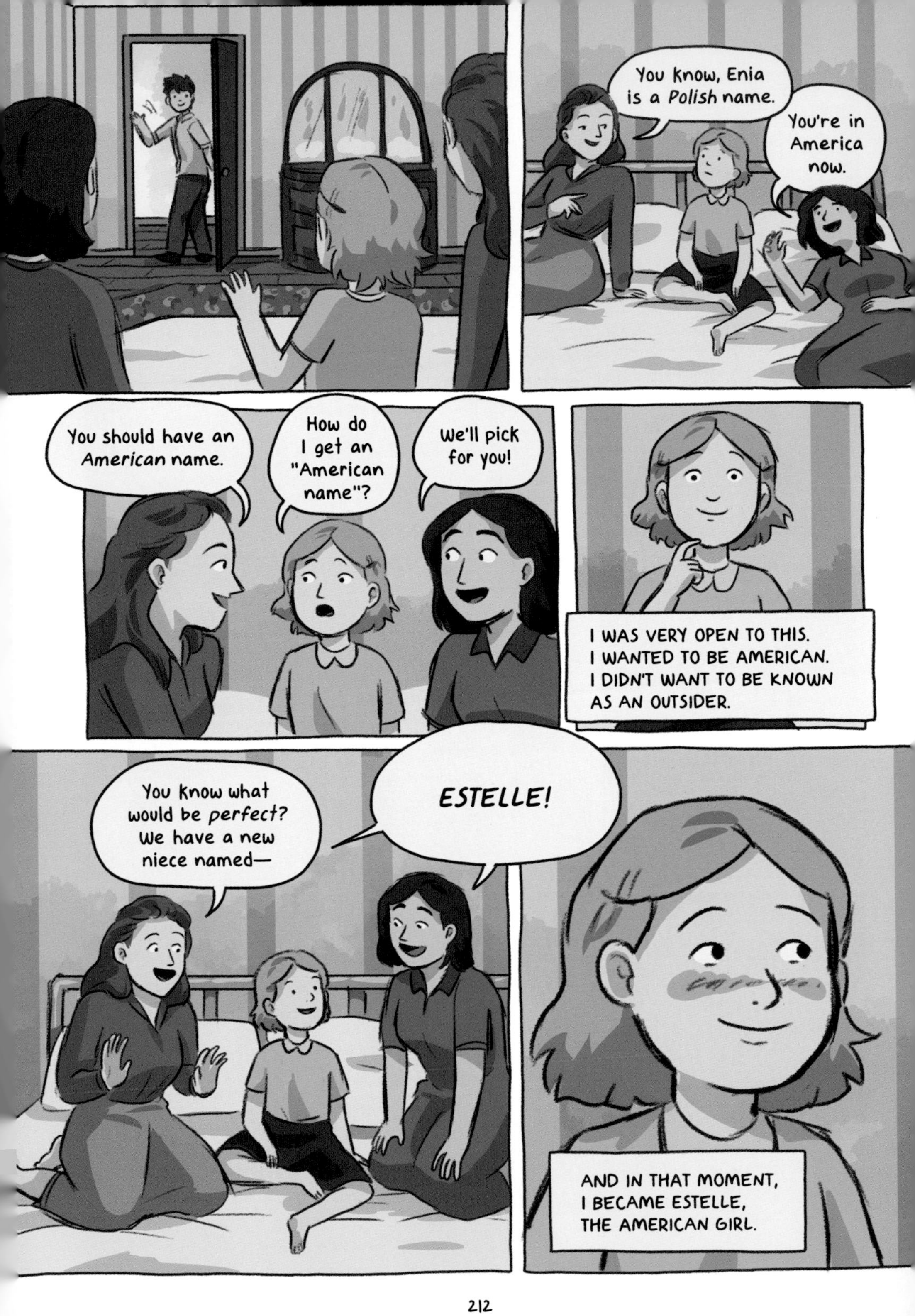
You know, Enia is a *Polish* name.
You're in America now.
You should have an *American* name.
How do I get an "American name"?
We'll pick for you!
I WAS VERY OPEN TO THIS. I WANTED TO BE AMERICAN. I DIDN'T WANT TO BE KNOWN AS AN OUTSIDER.
You know what would be *perfect*? We have a new niece named—
ESTELLE!
AND IN THAT MOMENT, I BECAME ESTELLE, THE AMERICAN GIRL.

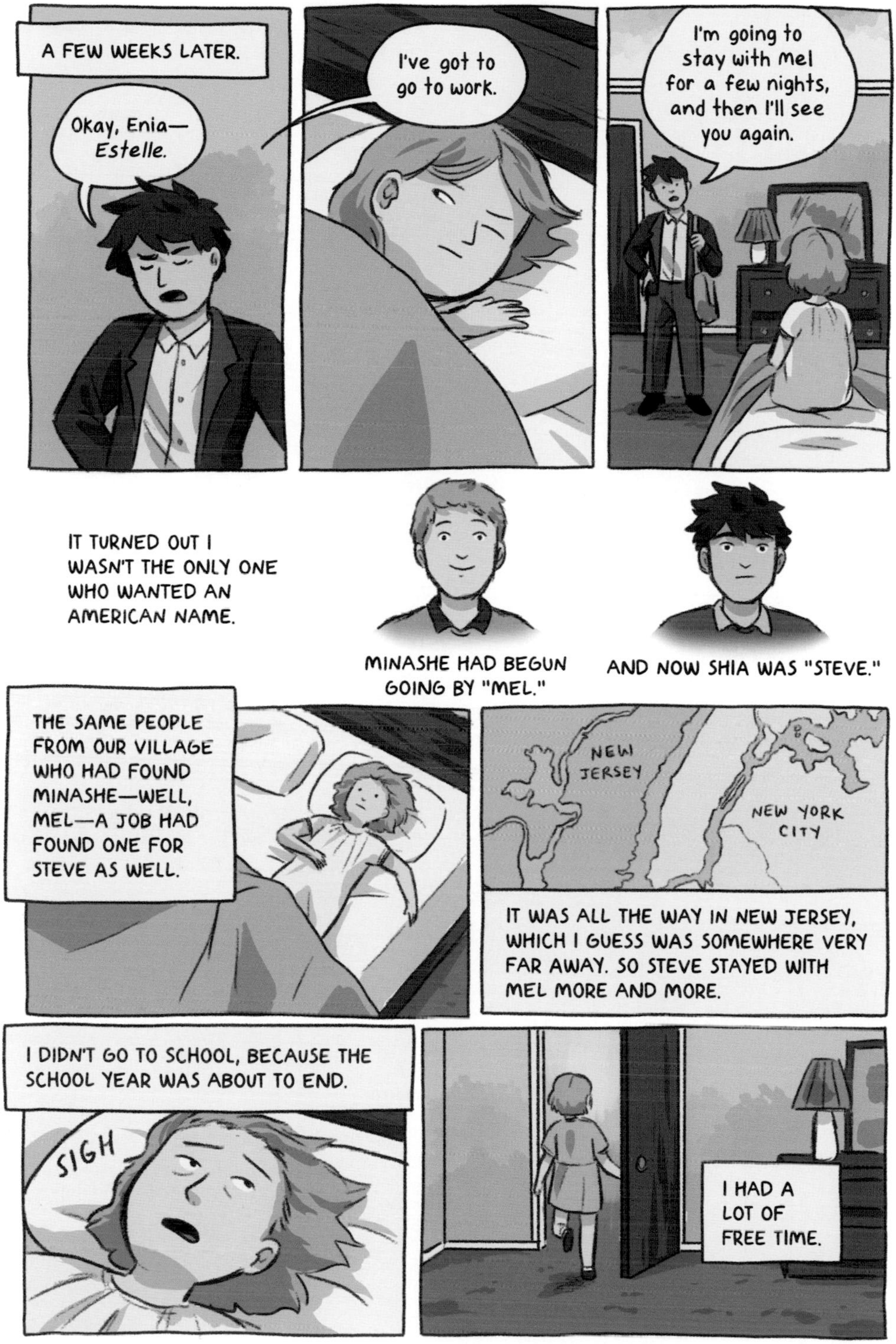
A FEW WEEKS LATER.
Okay, Enia—Estelle.
I've got to go to work.
I'm going to stay with Mel for a few nights, and then I'll see you again.
IT TURNED OUT I WASN'T THE ONLY ONE WHO WANTED AN AMERICAN NAME.
MINASHE HAD BEGUN GOING BY "MEL."
AND NOW SHIA WAS "STEVE."
THE SAME PEOPLE FROM OUR VILLAGE WHO HAD FOUND MINASHE—WELL, MEL—A JOB HAD FOUND ONE FOR STEVE AS WELL.
NEW JERSEY
NEW YORK CITY
IT WAS ALL THE WAY IN NEW JERSEY, WHICH I GUESS WAS SOMEWHERE VERY FAR AWAY. SO STEVE STAYED WITH MEL MORE AND MORE.
I DIDN'T GO TO SCHOOL, BECAUSE THE SCHOOL YEAR WAS ABOUT TO END.
SIGH
I HAD A LOT OF FREE TIME.

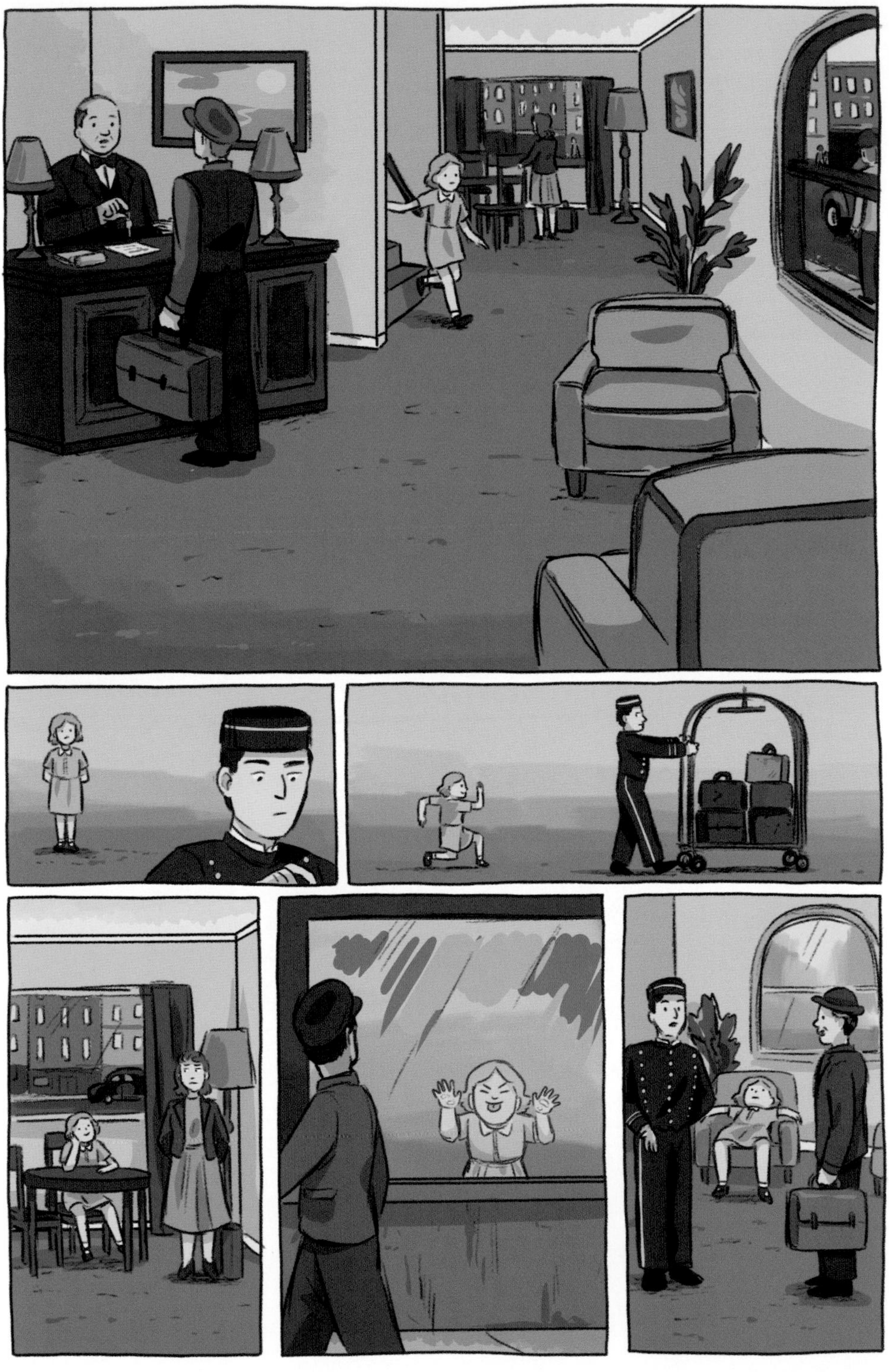

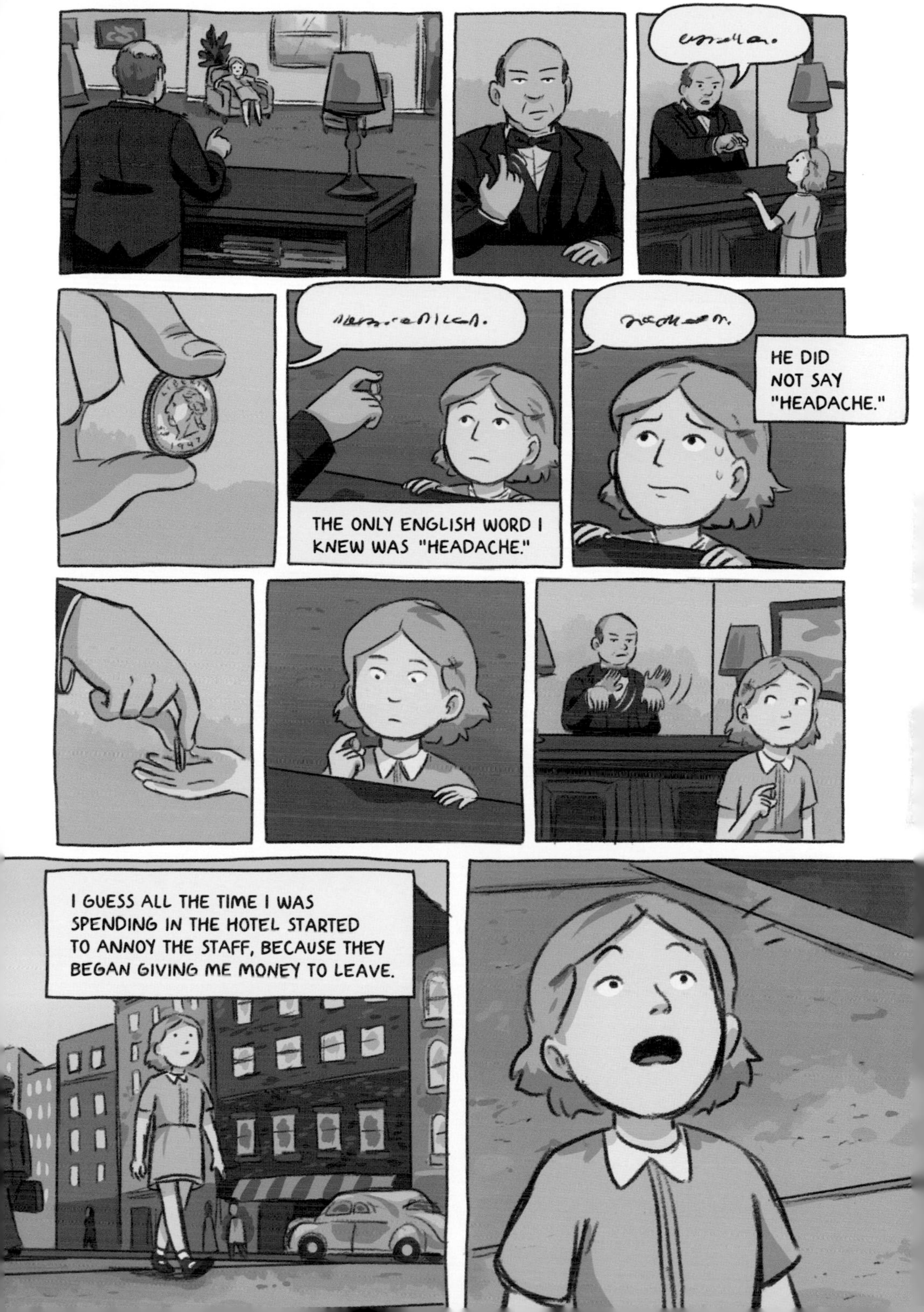
HE DID NOT SAY "HEADACHE."
THE ONLY ENGLISH WORD I KNEW WAS "HEADACHE."
I GUESS ALL THE TIME I WAS SPENDING IN THE HOTEL STARTED TO ANNOY THE STAFF, BECAUSE THEY BEGAN GIVING ME MONEY TO LEAVE.

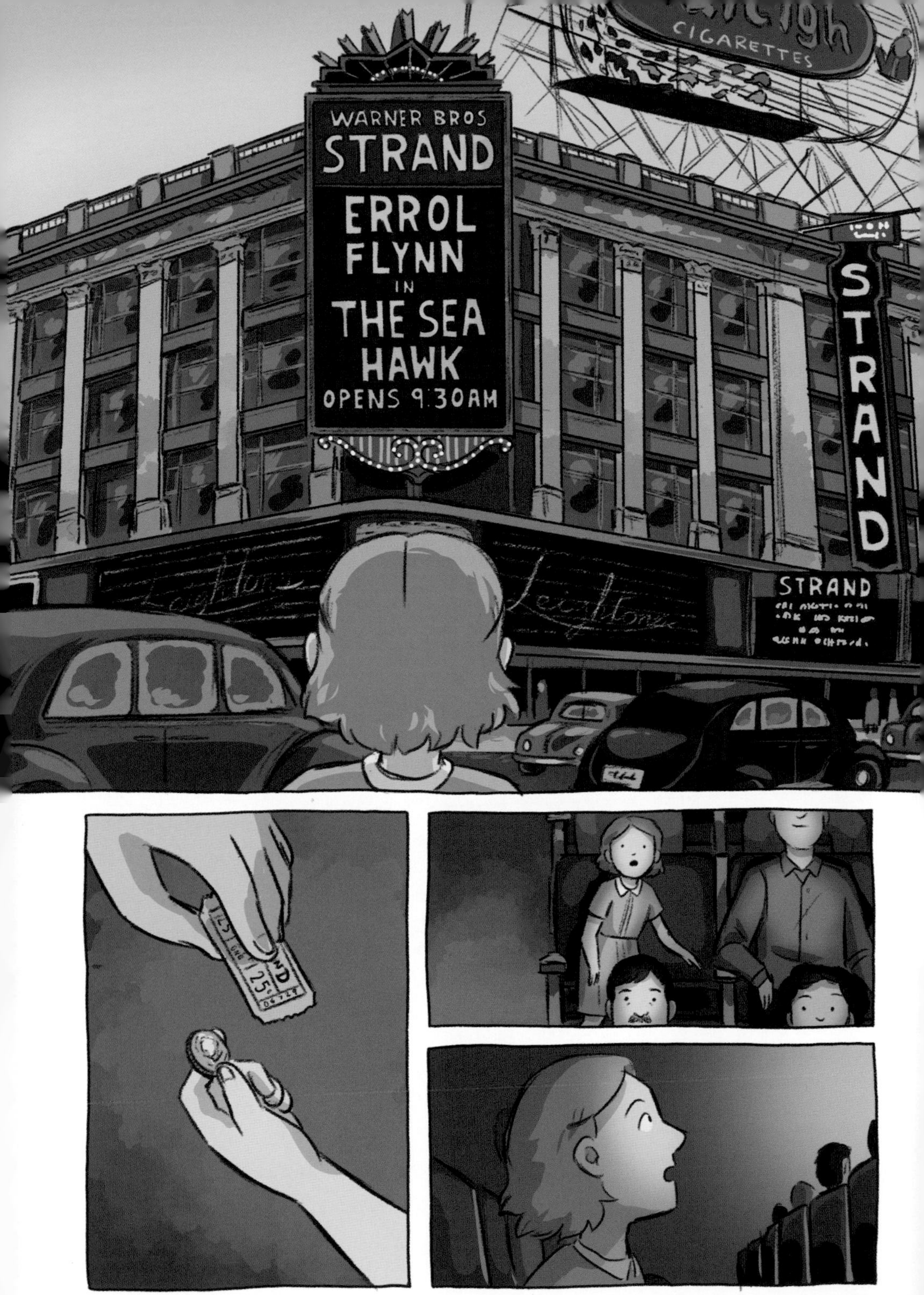
CIGARETTES
WARNER BROS
STRAND
ERROL FLYNN IN THE SEA HAWK
OPENS 9:30AM
STRAND
STRAND

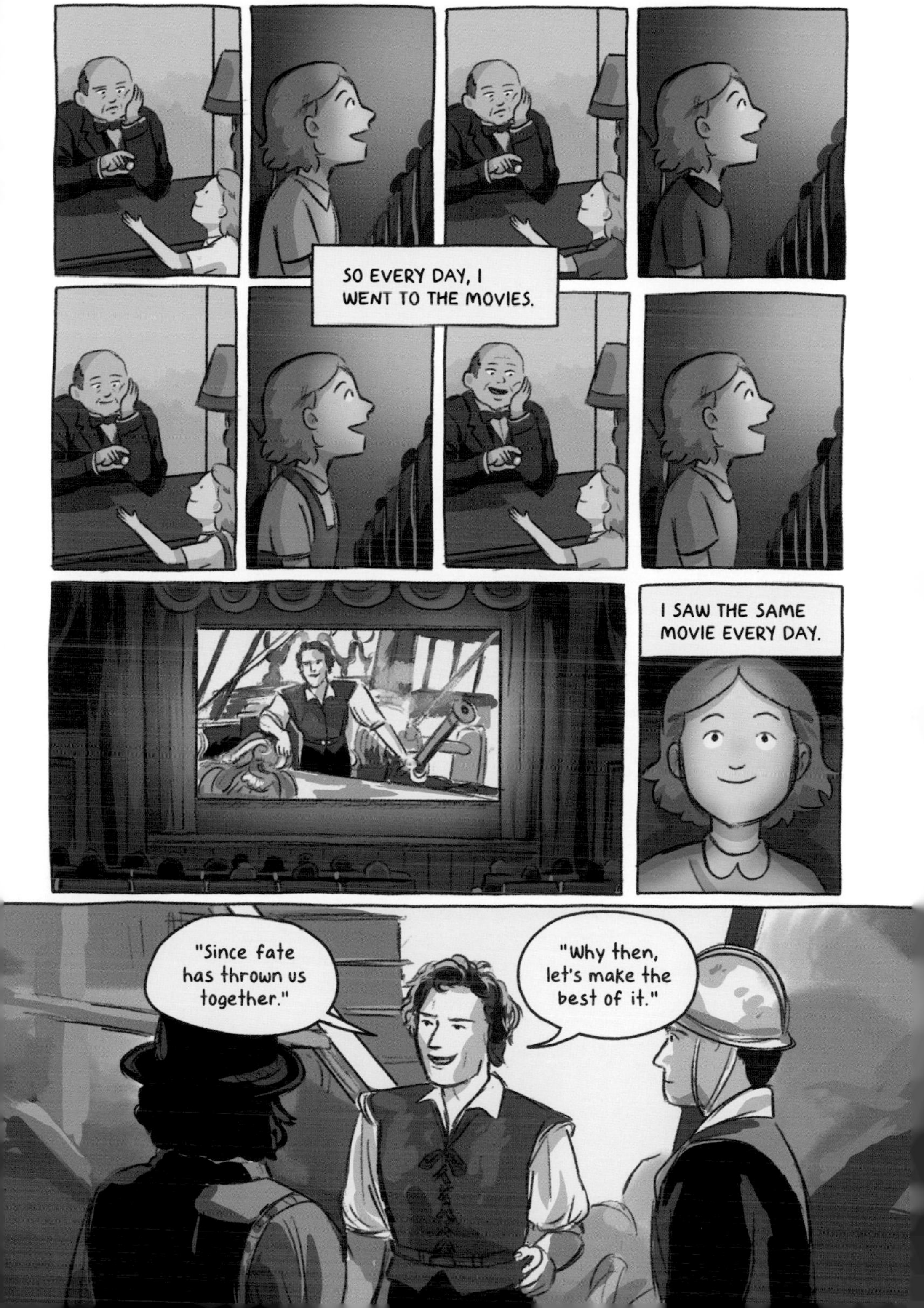
SO EVERY DAY, I WENT TO THE MOVIES.
I SAW THE SAME MOVIE EVERY DAY.
"Since fate has thrown us together."
"Why then, let's make the best of it."

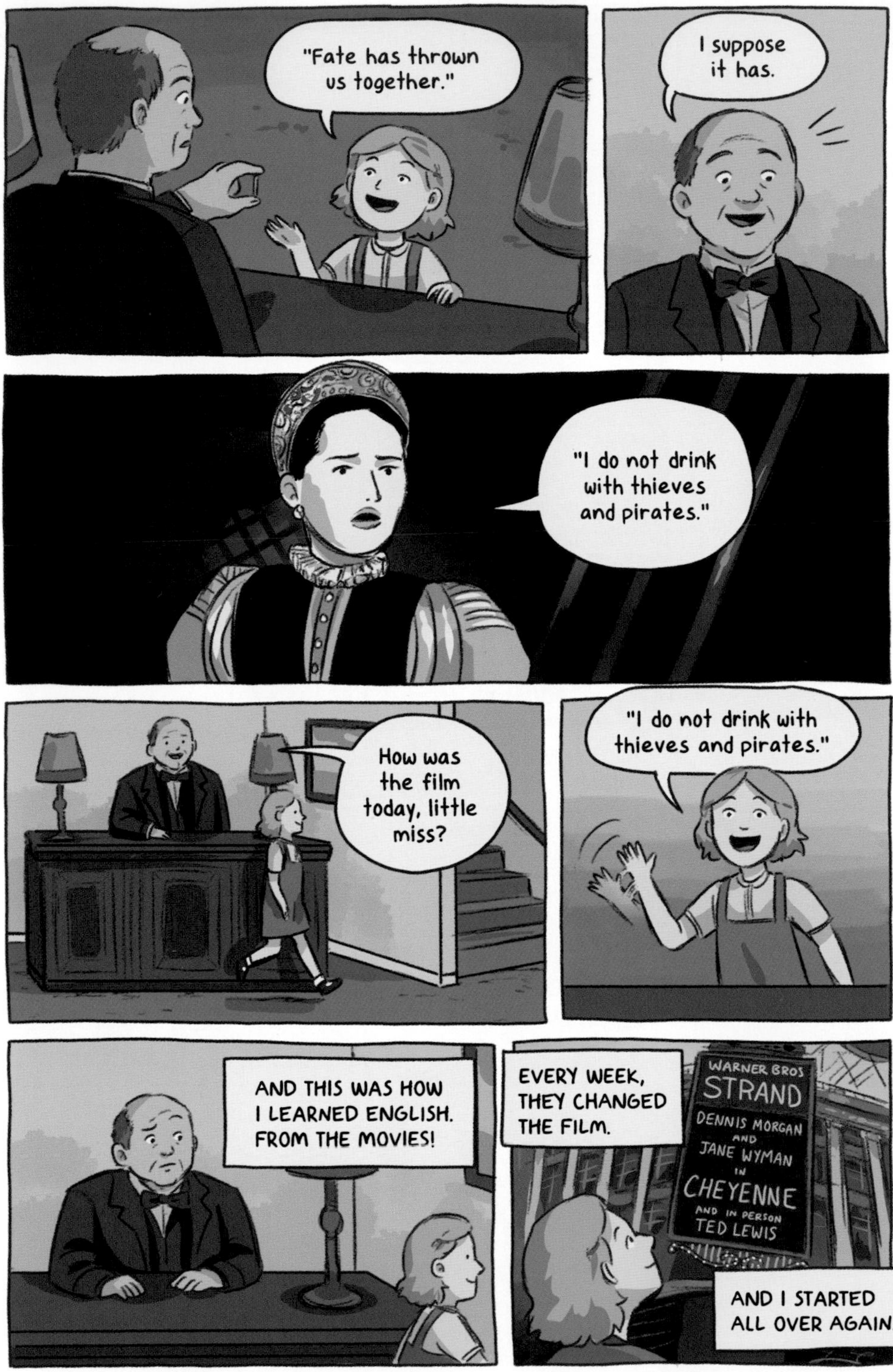
"Fate has thrown us together."
I suppose it has.
"I do not drink with thieves and pirates."
How was the film today, little miss?
"I do not drink with thieves and pirates."
AND THIS WAS HOW I LEARNED ENGLISH. FROM THE MOVIES!
EVERY WEEK, THEY CHANGED THE FILM.
WARNER BROS
STRAND
DENNIS MORGAN
AND
JANE WYMAN
IN
CHEYENNE
AND IN PERSON
TED LEWIS
AND I STARTED ALL OVER AGAIN.

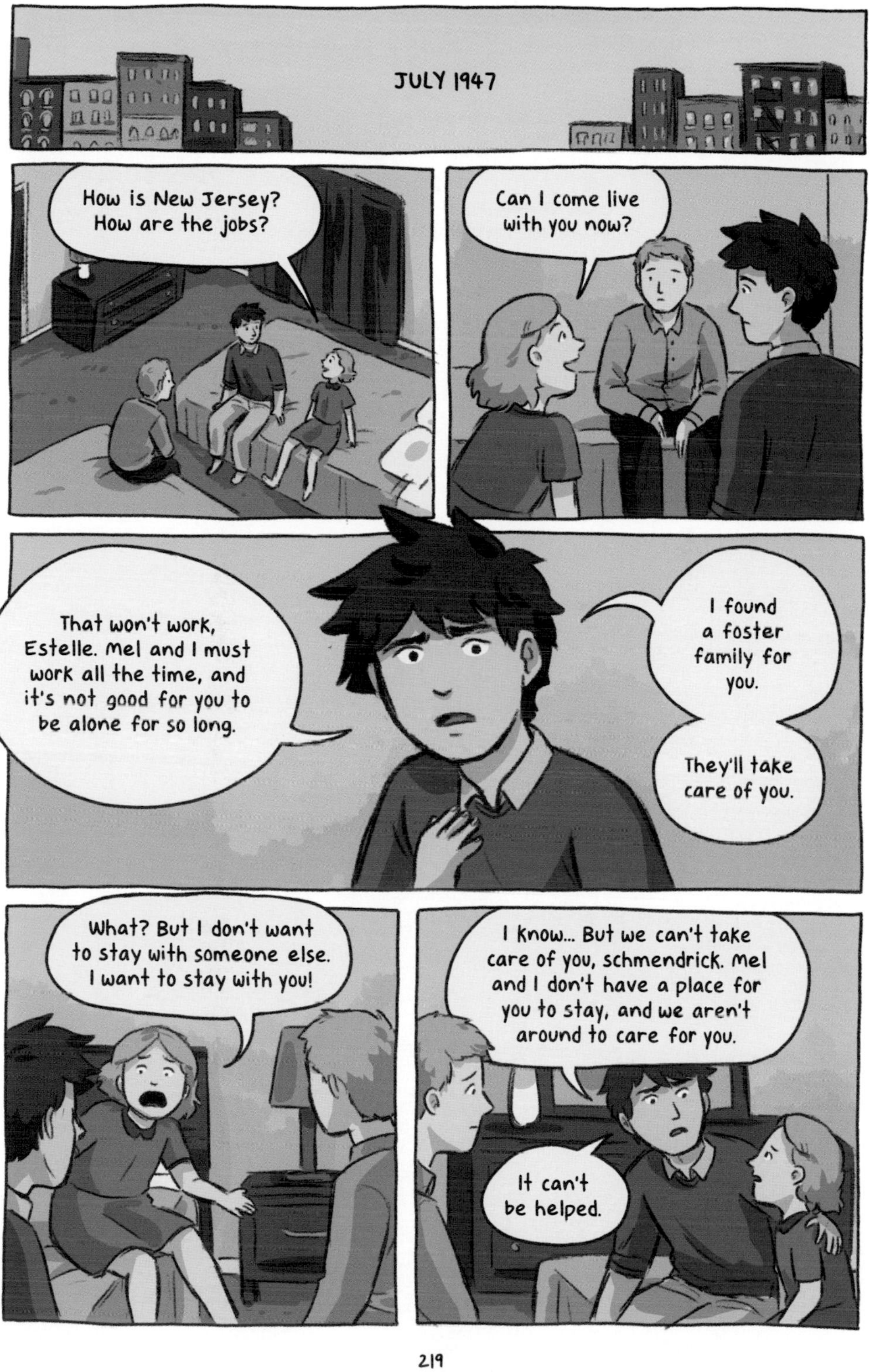
JULY 1947
How is New Jersey? How are the jobs?
Can I come live with you now?
That won't work, Estelle. Mel and I must work all the time, and it's not good for you to be alone for so long.
I found a foster family for you.
They'll take care of you.
What? But I don't want to stay with someone else. I want to stay with you!
I know... But we can't take care of you, schmendrick. Mel and I don't have a place for you to stay, and we aren't around to care for you.
It can't be helped.

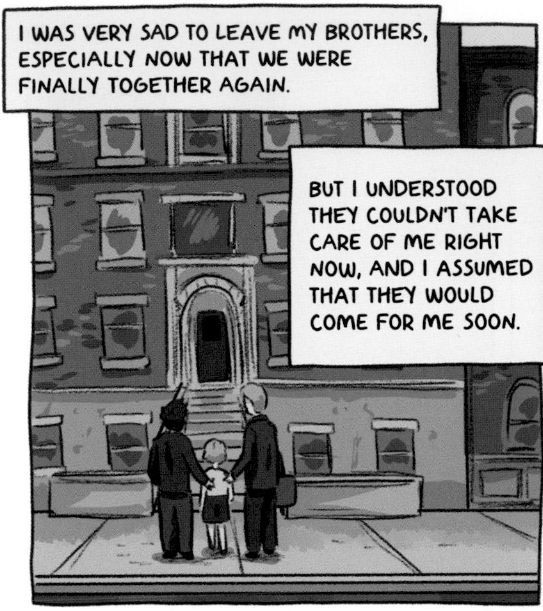
I WAS VERY SAD TO LEAVE MY BROTHERS, ESPECIALLY NOW THAT WE WERE FINALLY TOGETHER AGAIN.
BUT I UNDERSTOOD THEY COULDN'T TAKE CARE OF ME RIGHT NOW, AND I ASSUMED THAT THEY WOULD COME FOR ME SOON.

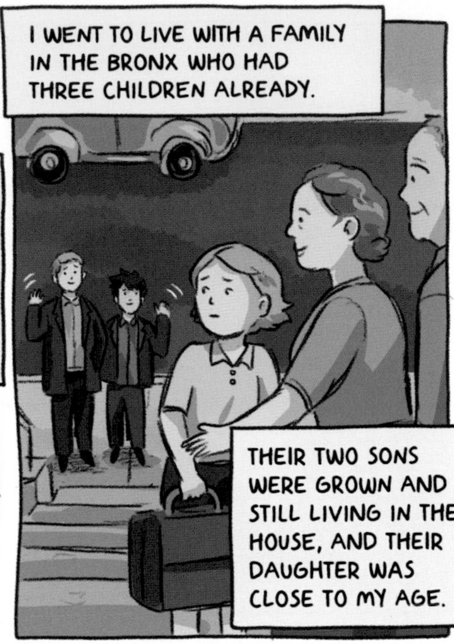
I WENT TO LIVE WITH A FAMILY IN THE BRONX WHO HAD THREE CHILDREN ALREADY.
THEIR TWO SONS WERE GROWN AND STILL LIVING IN THE HOUSE, AND THEIR DAUGHTER WAS CLOSE TO MY AGE.

THEN, AT ALMOST THIRTEEN YEARS OLD, I WENT TO SCHOOL FOR THE FIRST TIME IN MY LIFE.

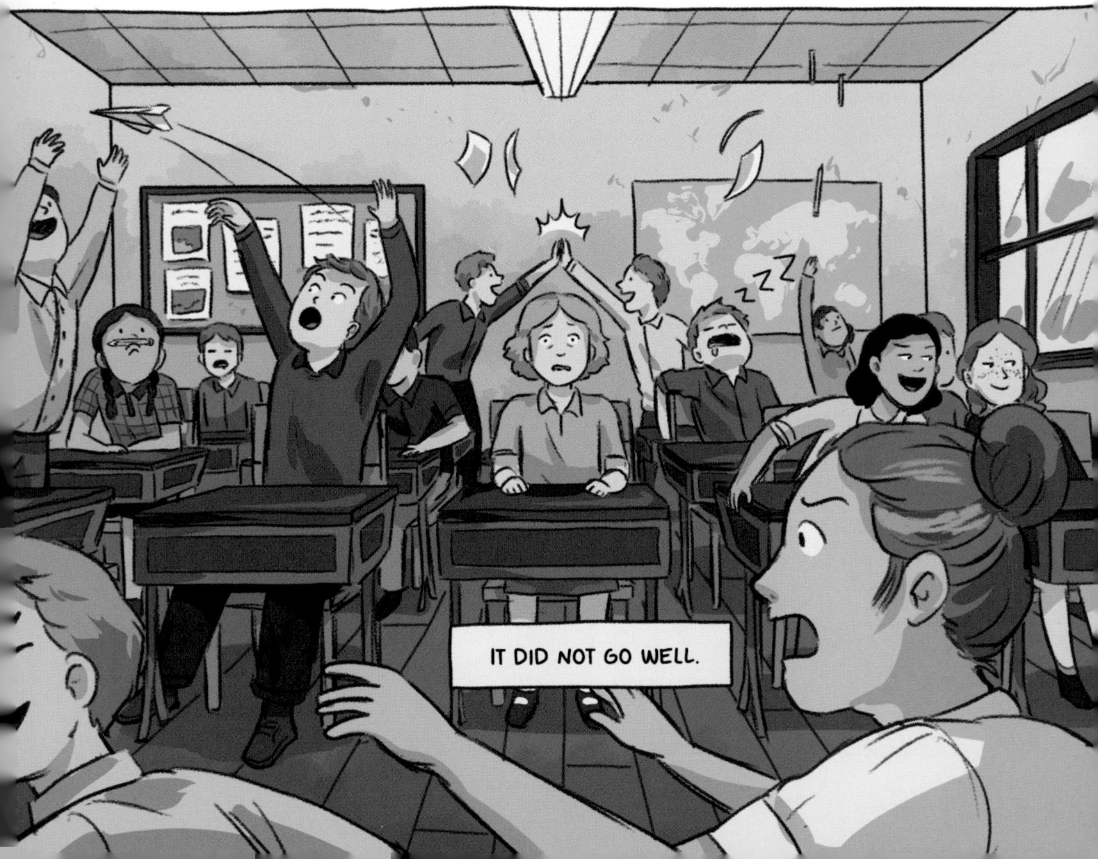
IT DID NOT GO WELL.

SEPTEMBER 1947
FIRST DAY OF
SCHOOL, SIXTH GRADE

Your first assignment will be on geography.

I'm passing out questions for you to study.

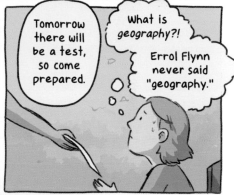

Tomorrow there will be a test, so come prepared.

What is geography?!

Errol Flynn never said "geography."

I SPOKE ENGLISH VERY WELL. BUT I STILL COULDN'T READ OR WRITE. I SPOKE POLISH AND YIDDISH (AND NOW ENGLISH), BUT I ONLY KNEW HOW TO WRITE A COUPLE OF THINGS IN YIDDISH—MY MOTHER HAD TAUGHT ME THAT—AND A COUPLE OF THINGS IN HEBREW—THE DP CAMP HAD TAUGHT ME THAT.

BUT NONE OF THAT WAS USEFUL IN THIS AMERICAN SCHOOL.

I HAD NO IDEA HOW TO DO THIS HOMEWORK. WHAT WAS GEOGRAPHY?

Can you help me with my work for school?

Not right now.

I'm busy.

SO I STAYED UP AND COPIED OUT THE QUESTIONS.

THERE WERE FIVE QUESTIONS.

On a map, what is the feature that indicates direction called?

What is the difference between latitude and longitude?

What rivers border Mesopotamia?

Describe the land of Mesopotamia.

the name of the writing ...potamia?

On a map, what is the feature that indicates direction called?

What is the difference between latitude and longitude?

What riv... ...Mesopotamia

Describe... Meso...

...at was the name o... ...n Mesopotami...

IT TOOK ME ALL NIGHT TO COPY THEM. I HAD NEVER WRITTEN LIKE THIS BEFORE!

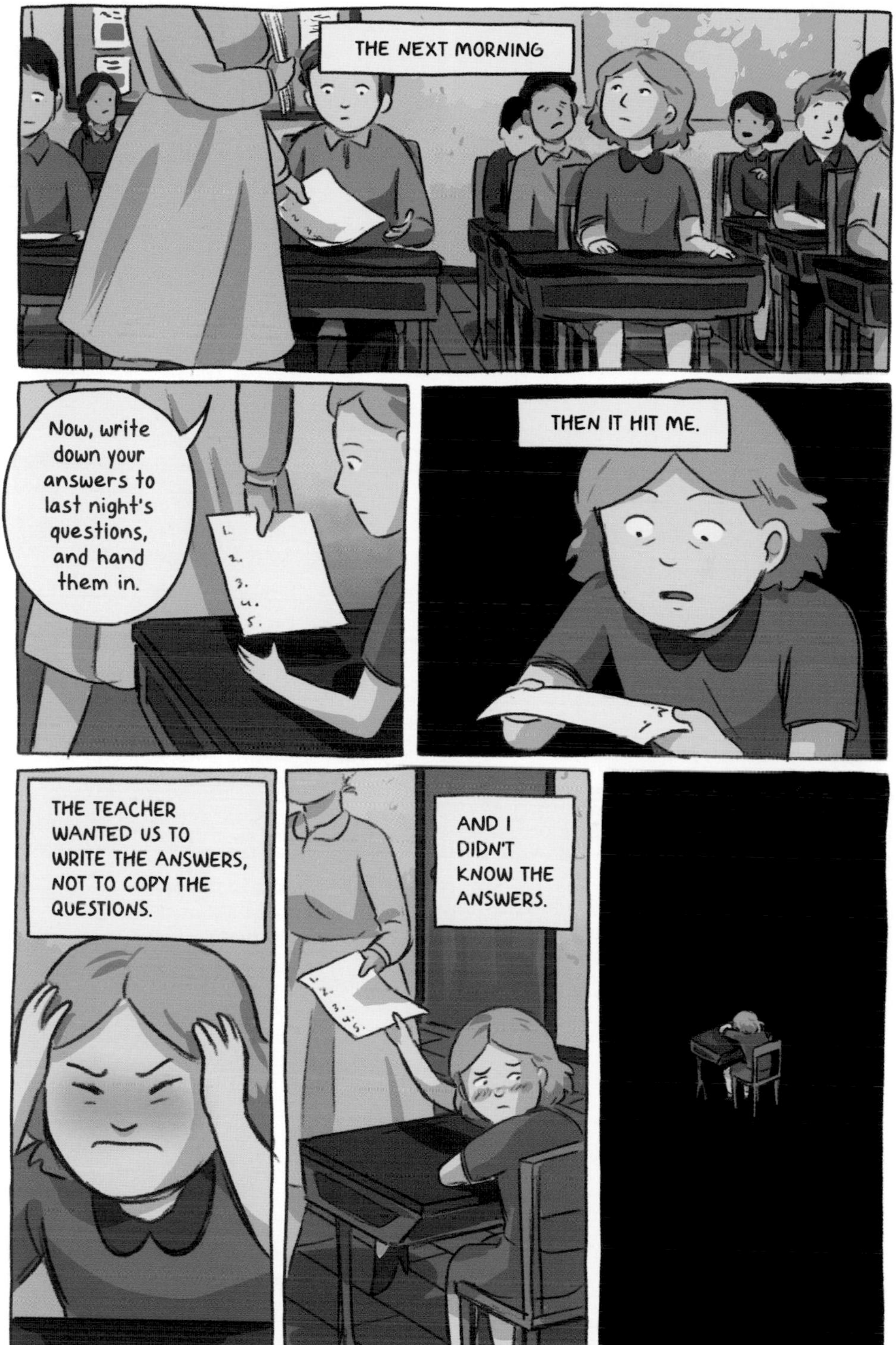
THE NEXT MORNING
Now, write down your answers to last night's questions, and hand them in.
1.
2.
3.
4.
5.
THEN IT HIT ME.
THE TEACHER WANTED US TO WRITE THE ANSWERS, NOT TO COPY THE QUESTIONS.
AND I DIDN'T KNOW THE ANSWERS.

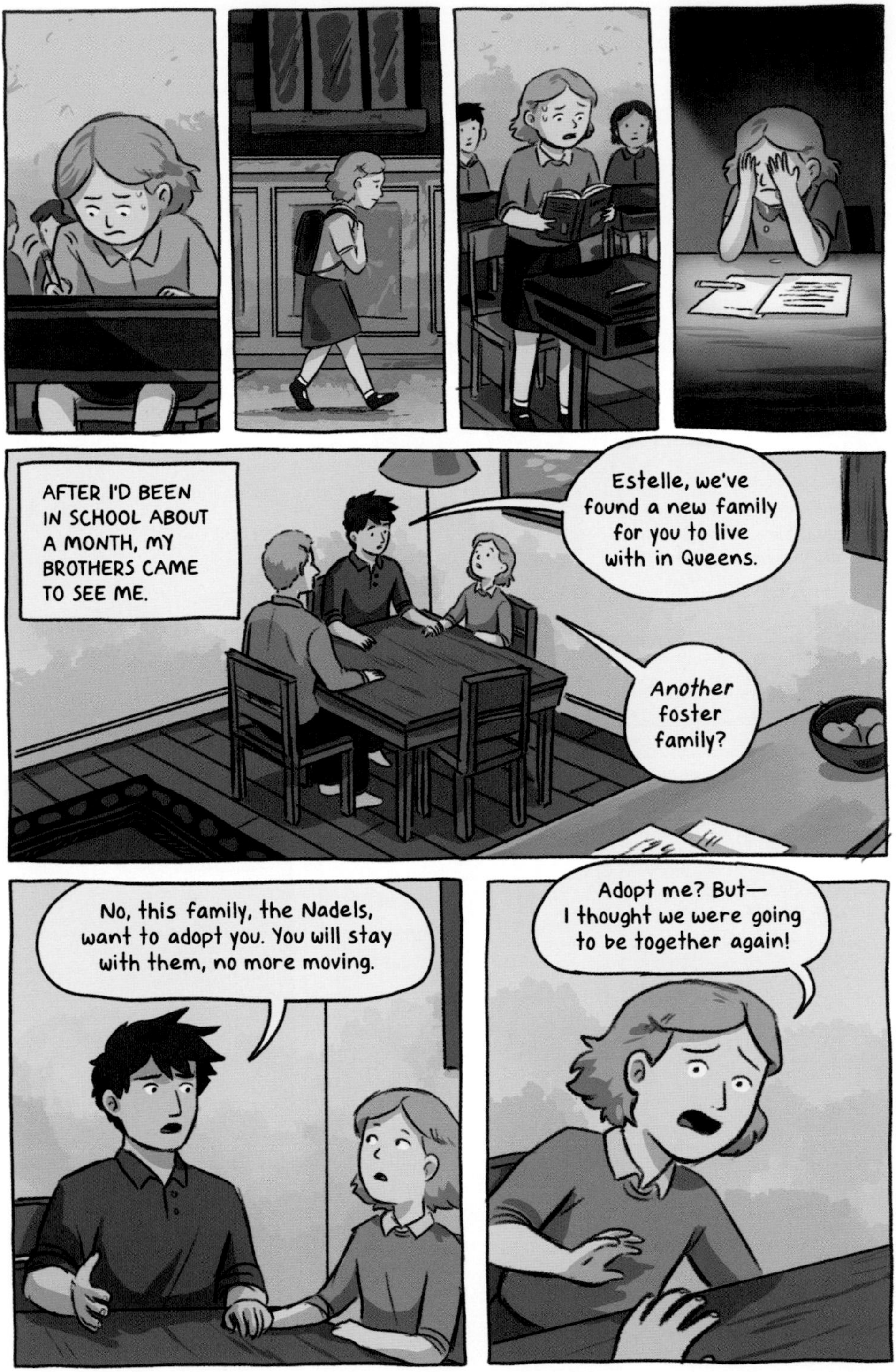
AFTER I'D BEEN IN SCHOOL ABOUT A MONTH, MY BROTHERS CAME TO SEE ME.
Estelle, we've found a new family for you to live with in Queens.
Another foster family?
No, this family, the Nadels, want to adopt you. You will stay with them, no more moving.
Adopt me? But— I thought we were going to be together again!

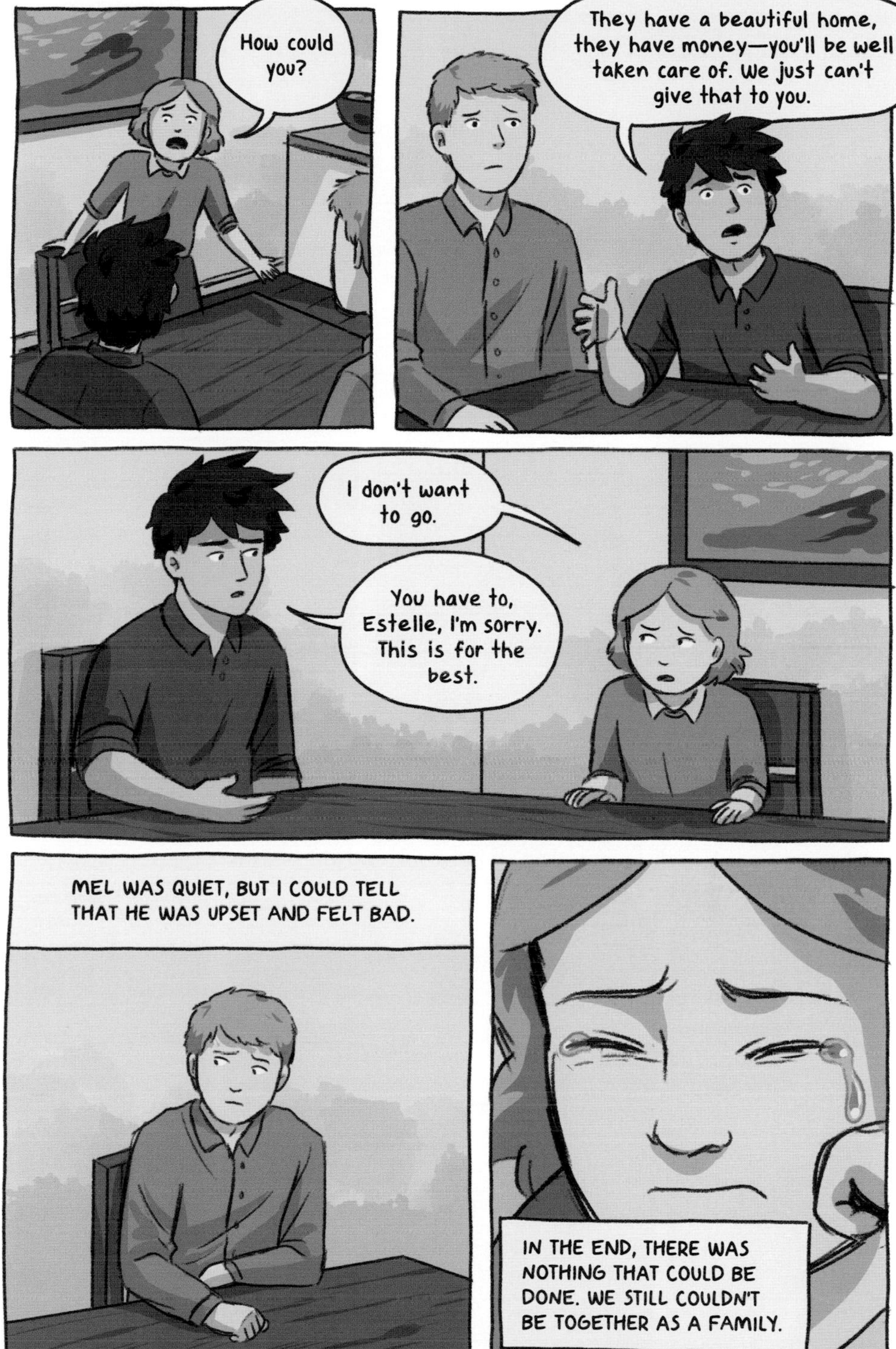
How could you?
They have a beautiful home, they have money—you'll be well taken care of. We just can't give that to you.
I don't want to go.
You have to, Estelle, I'm sorry. This is for the best.
MEL WAS QUIET, BUT I COULD TELL THAT HE WAS UPSET AND FELT BAD.
IN THE END, THERE WAS NOTHING THAT COULD BE DONE. WE STILL COULDN'T BE TOGETHER AS A FAMILY.

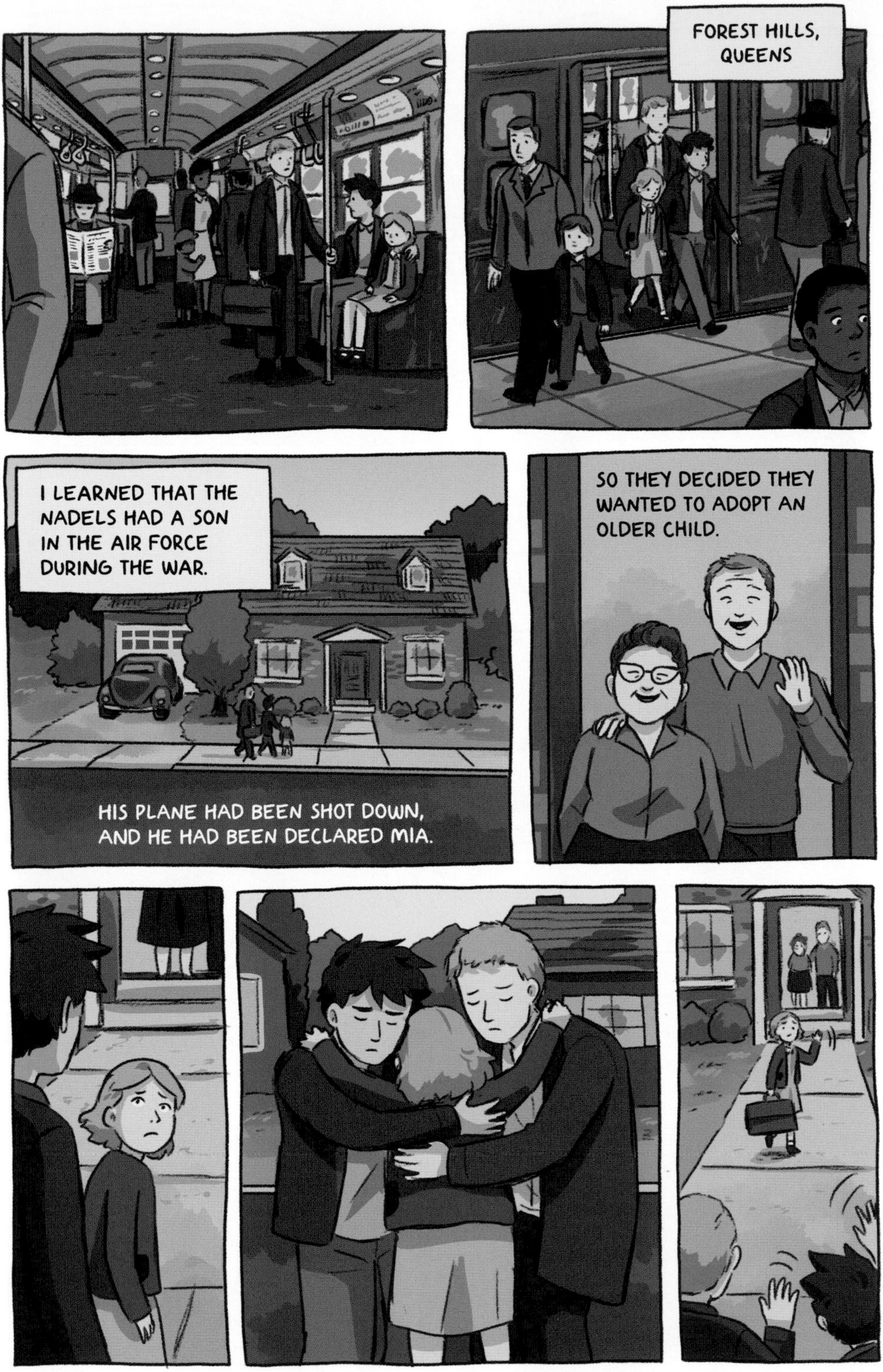
FOREST HILLS, QUEENS
I LEARNED THAT THE NADELS HAD A SON IN THE AIR FORCE DURING THE WAR.
HIS PLANE HAD BEEN SHOT DOWN, AND HE HAD BEEN DECLARED MIA.
SO THEY DECIDED THEY WANTED TO ADOPT AN OLDER CHILD.

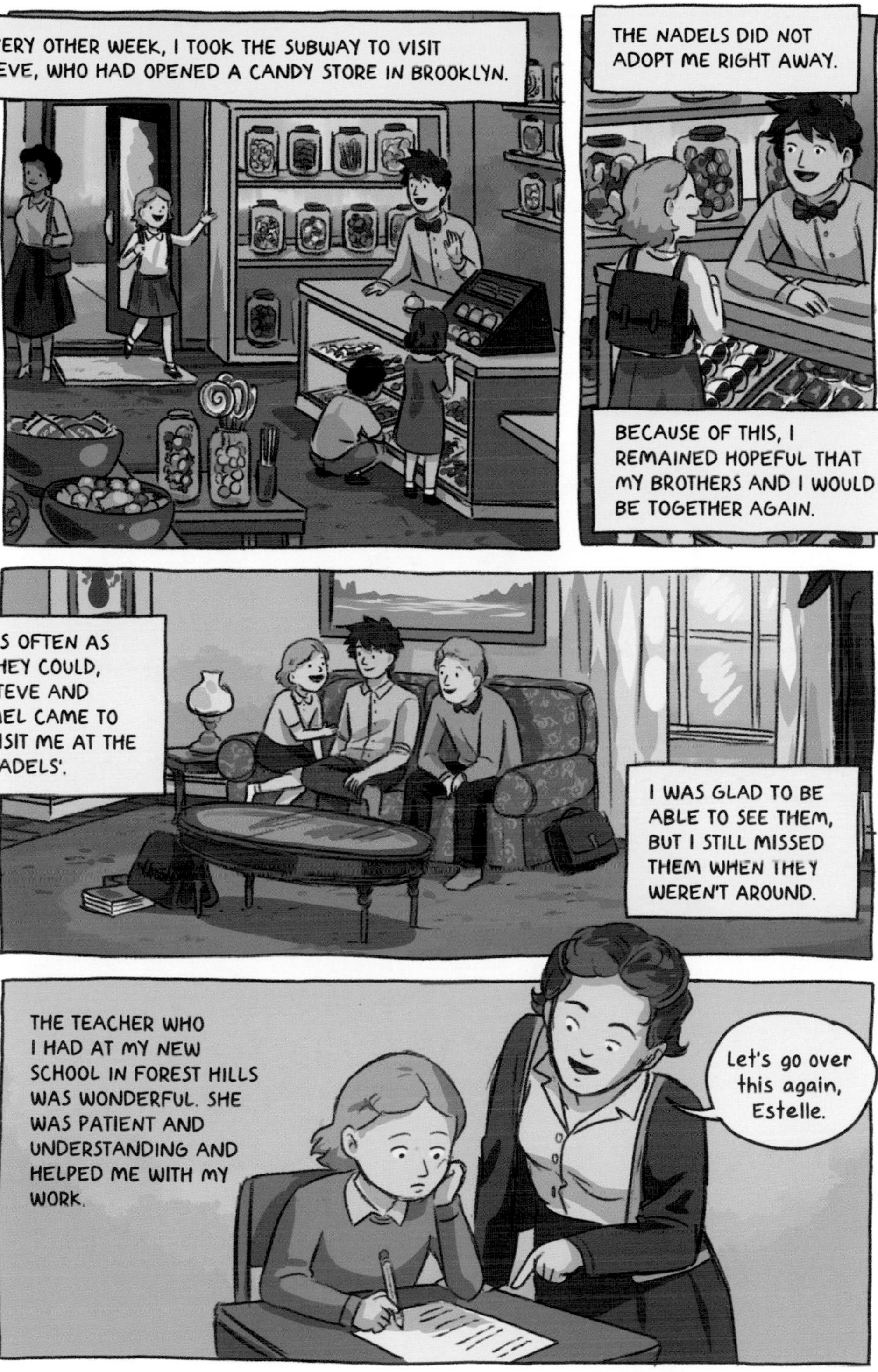
EVERY OTHER WEEK, I TOOK THE SUBWAY TO VISIT STEVE, WHO HAD OPENED A CANDY STORE IN BROOKLYN.
THE NADELS DID NOT ADOPT ME RIGHT AWAY.
BECAUSE OF THIS, I REMAINED HOPEFUL THAT MY BROTHERS AND I WOULD BE TOGETHER AGAIN.
AS OFTEN AS THEY COULD, STEVE AND MEL CAME TO VISIT ME AT THE NADELS'.
I WAS GLAD TO BE ABLE TO SEE THEM, BUT I STILL MISSED THEM WHEN THEY WEREN'T AROUND.
THE TEACHER WHO I HAD AT MY NEW SCHOOL IN FOREST HILLS WAS WONDERFUL. SHE WAS PATIENT AND UNDERSTANDING AND HELPED ME WITH MY WORK.
Let's go over this again, Estelle.

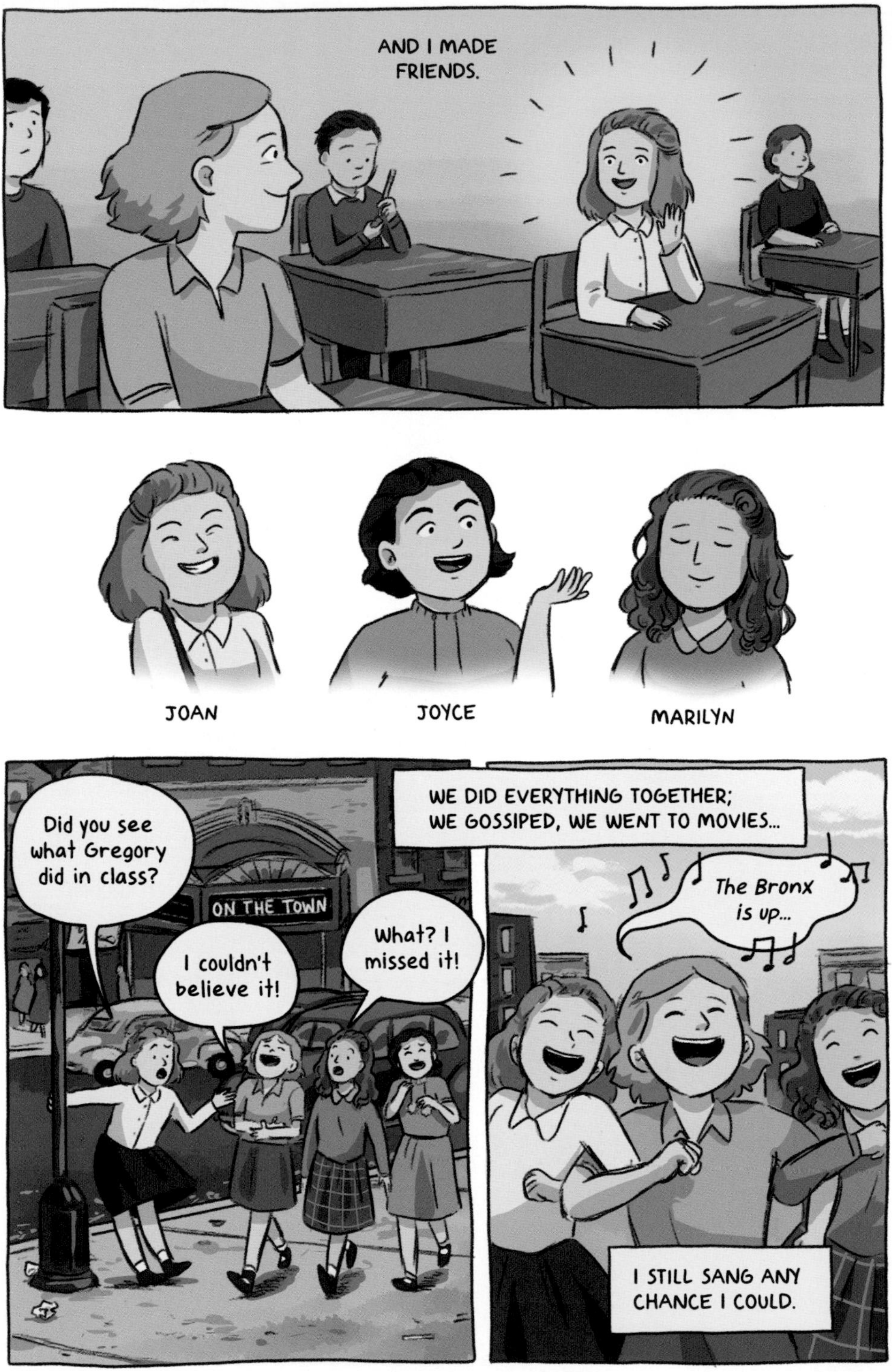
AND I MADE FRIENDS.
JOAN
JOYCE
MARILYN
Did you see what Gregory did in class?
ON THE TOWN
I couldn't believe it!
What? I missed it!
WE DID EVERYTHING TOGETHER; WE GOSSIPED, WE WENT TO MOVIES...
The Bronx is up...
I STILL SANG ANY CHANCE I COULD.

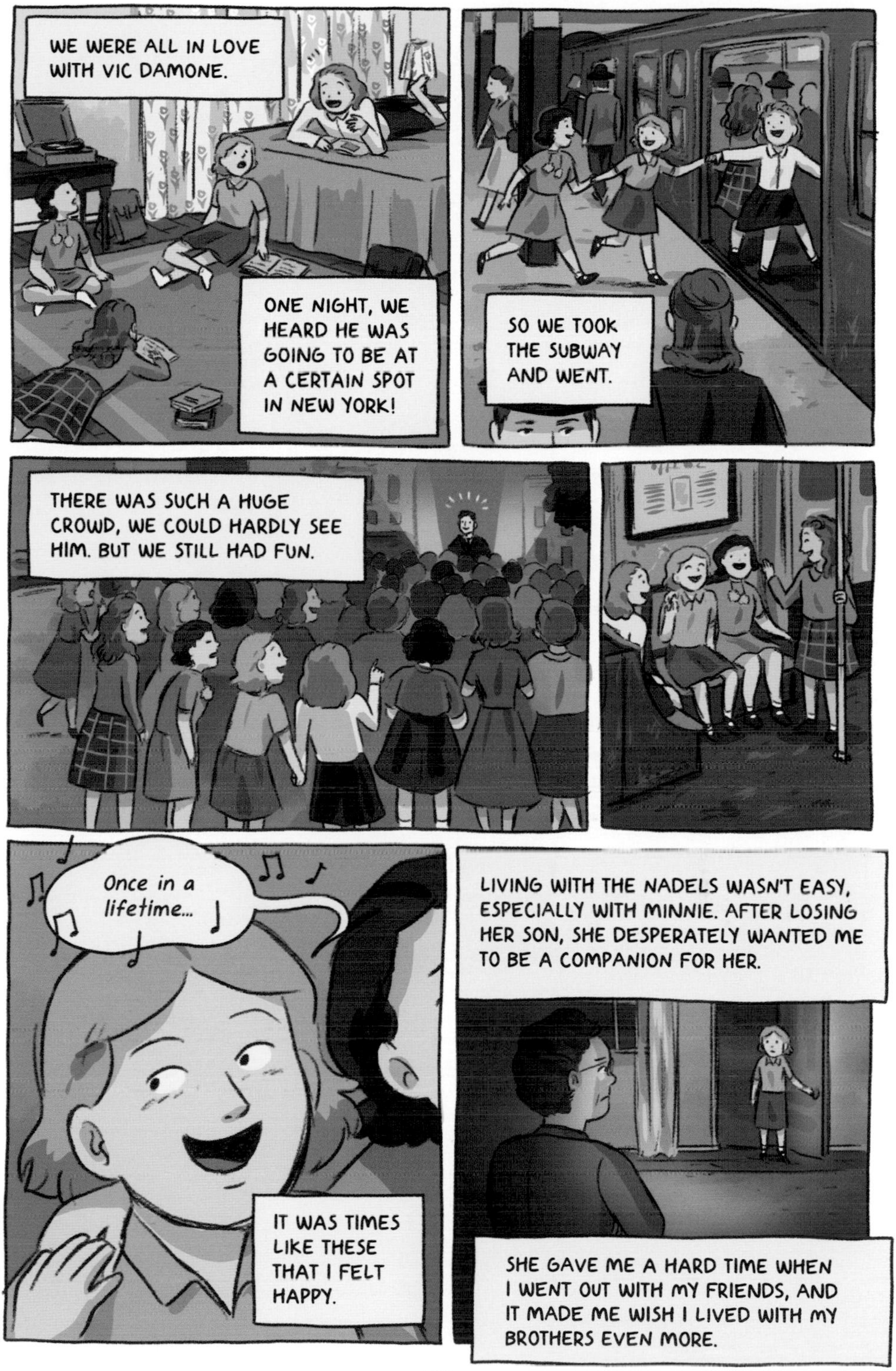
WE WERE ALL IN LOVE WITH VIC DAMONE.
ONE NIGHT, WE HEARD HE WAS GOING TO BE AT A CERTAIN SPOT IN NEW YORK!
SO WE TOOK THE SUBWAY AND WENT.
THERE WAS SUCH A HUGE CROWD, WE COULD HARDLY SEE HIM. BUT WE STILL HAD FUN.
Once in a lifetime...
IT WAS TIMES LIKE THESE THAT I FELT HAPPY.
LIVING WITH THE NADELS WASN'T EASY, ESPECIALLY WITH MINNIE. AFTER LOSING HER SON, SHE DESPERATELY WANTED ME TO BE A COMPANION FOR HER.
SHE GAVE ME A HARD TIME WHEN I WENT OUT WITH MY FRIENDS, AND IT MADE ME WISH I LIVED WITH MY BROTHERS EVEN MORE.

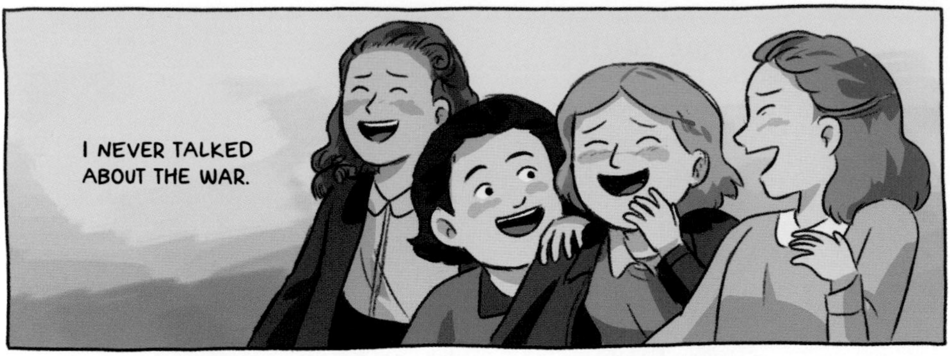
I NEVER TALKED ABOUT THE WAR.

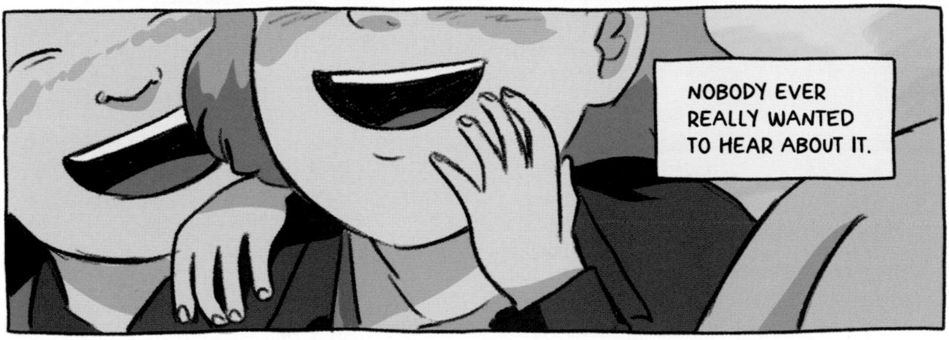
NOBODY EVER REALLY WANTED TO HEAR ABOUT IT.

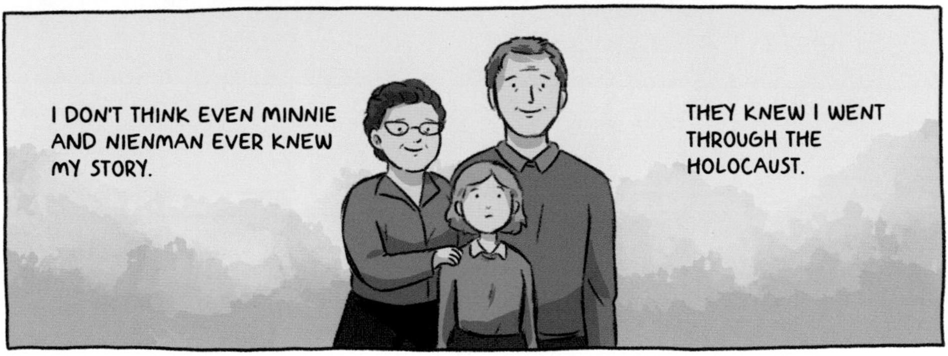
I DON'T THINK EVEN MINNIE AND NIENMAN EVER KNEW MY STORY.
THEY KNEW I WENT THROUGH THE HOLOCAUST.

BUT THAT WAS IT.

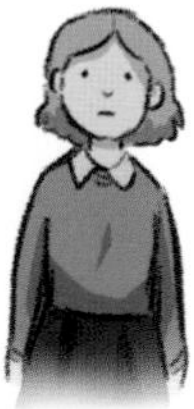

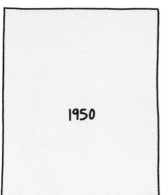

1950

DURING THIS TIME, STEVE GOT MARRIED TO A WOMAN HE'D BEEN SEEING NAMED ADELE.

AND MEL, NOW TWENTY-THREE, WAS DRAFTED INTO THE KOREAN WAR.

I'm going to miss you.

I'm going to miss you, too.

I wish I didn't have to leave.

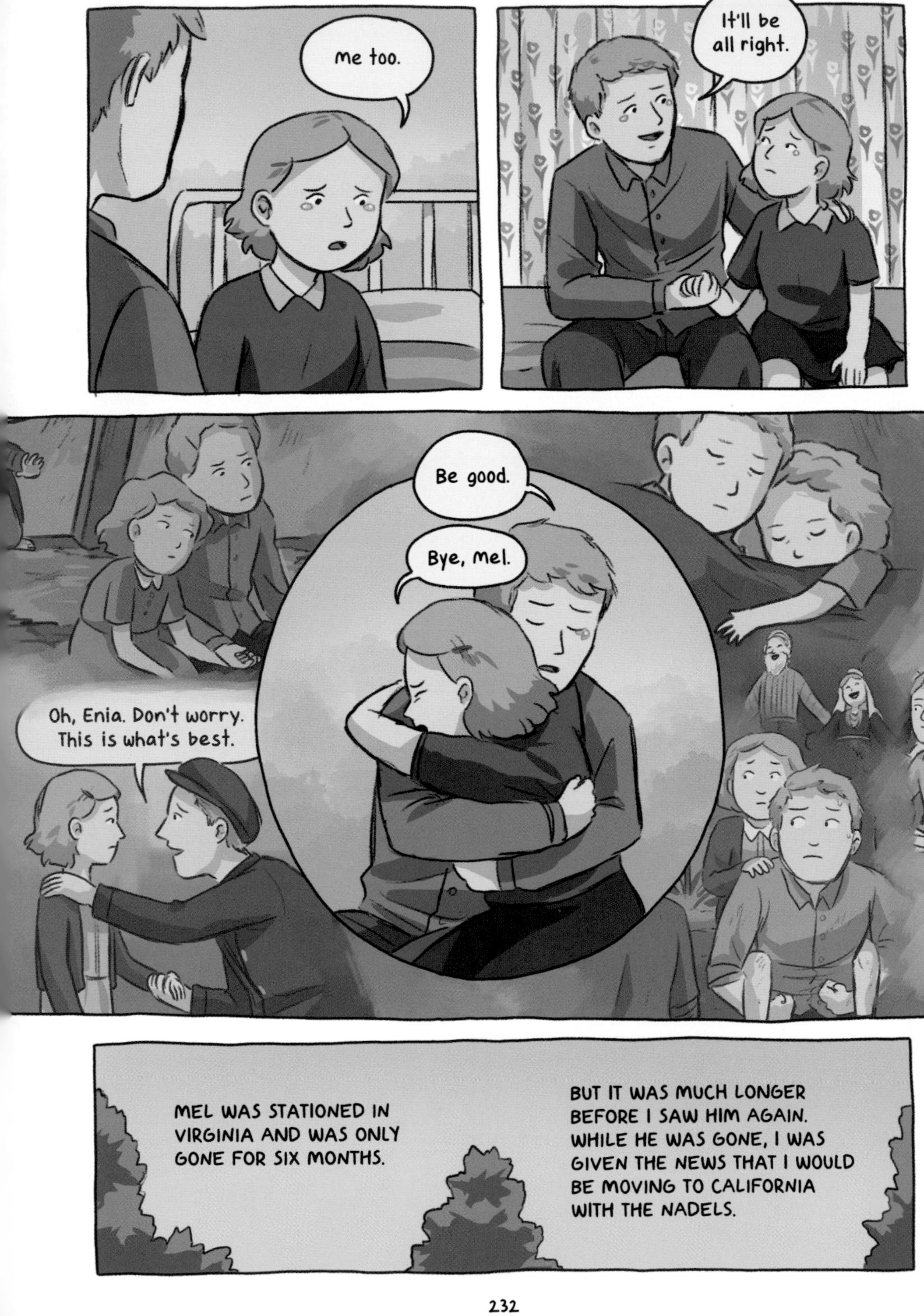
me too.
It'll be all right.
Be good.
Bye, mel.
Oh, Enia. Don't worry. This is what's best.
MEL WAS STATIONED IN VIRGINIA AND WAS ONLY GONE FOR SIX MONTHS.
BUT IT WAS MUCH LONGER BEFORE I SAW HIM AGAIN. WHILE HE WAS GONE, I WAS GIVEN THE NEWS THAT I WOULD BE MOVING TO CALIFORNIA WITH THE NADELS.

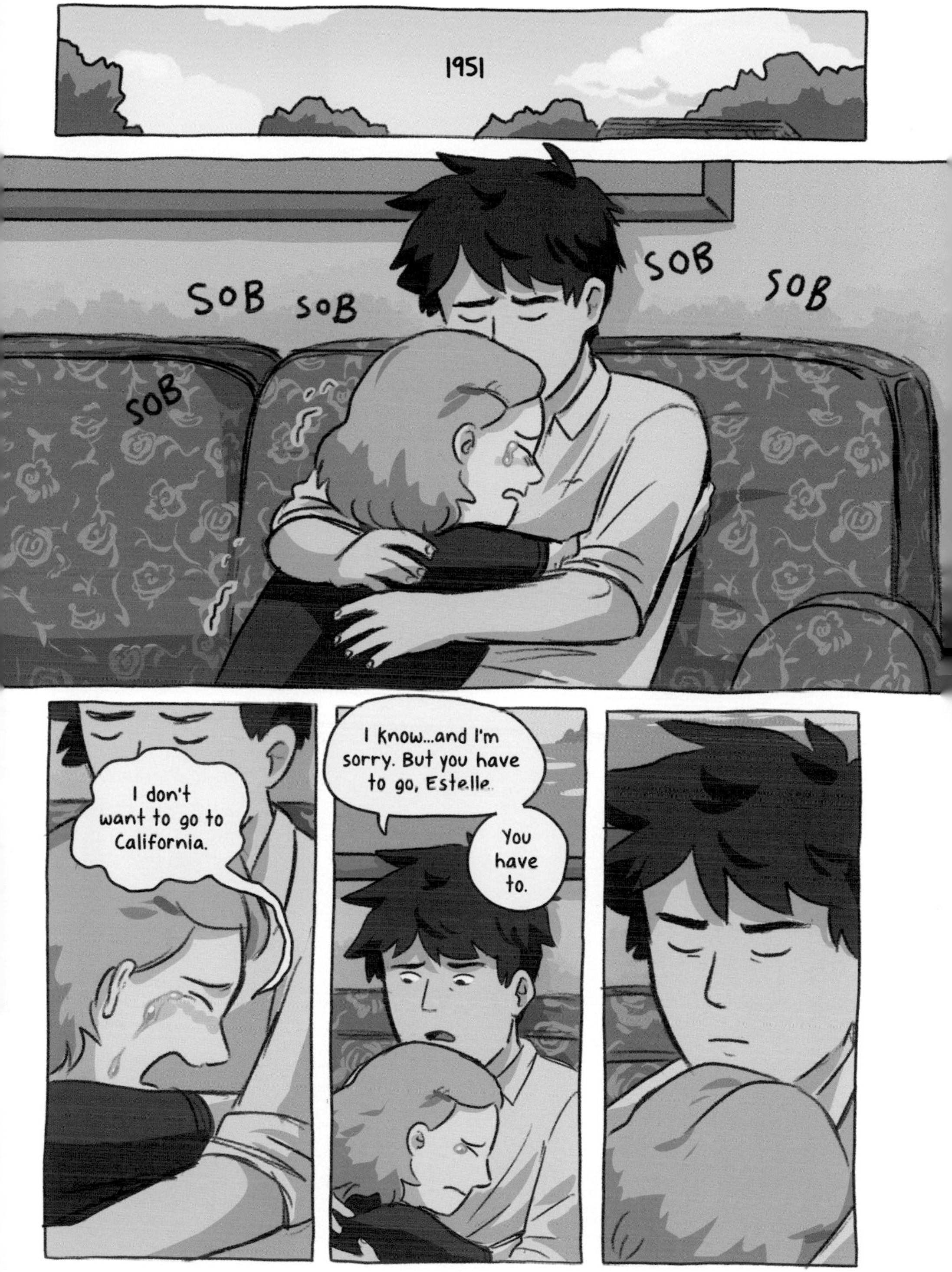

1951
SOB
SOB
SOB
SOB
SOB
I don't want to go to California.
I know...and I'm sorry. But you have to go, Estelle.
You have to.

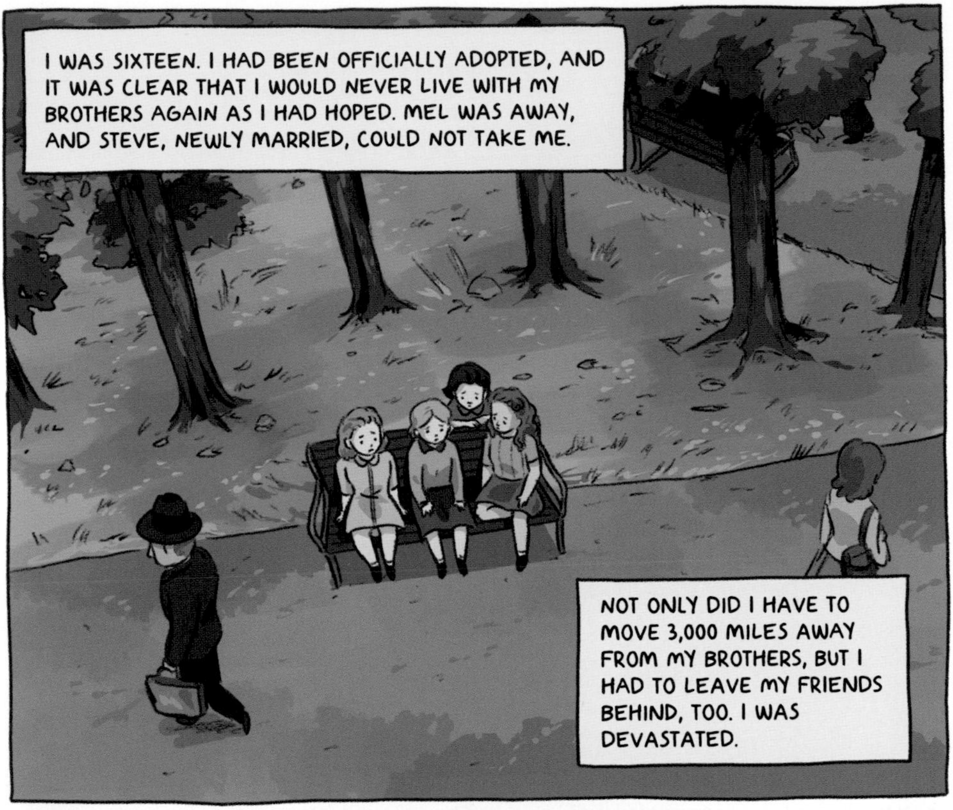
I WAS SIXTEEN. I HAD BEEN OFFICIALLY ADOPTED, AND IT WAS CLEAR THAT I WOULD NEVER LIVE WITH MY BROTHERS AGAIN AS I HAD HOPED. MEL WAS AWAY, AND STEVE, NEWLY MARRIED, COULD NOT TAKE ME.
NOT ONLY DID I HAVE TO MOVE 3,000 MILES AWAY FROM MY BROTHERS, BUT I HAD TO LEAVE MY FRIENDS BEHIND, TOO. I WAS DEVASTATED.

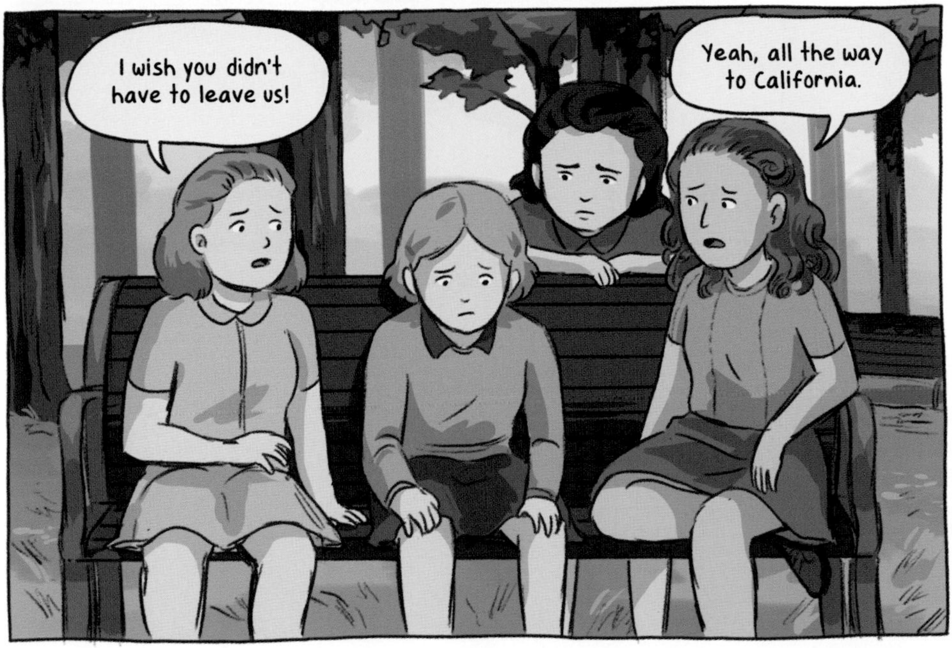
I wish you didn't have to leave us!
Yeah, all the way to California.

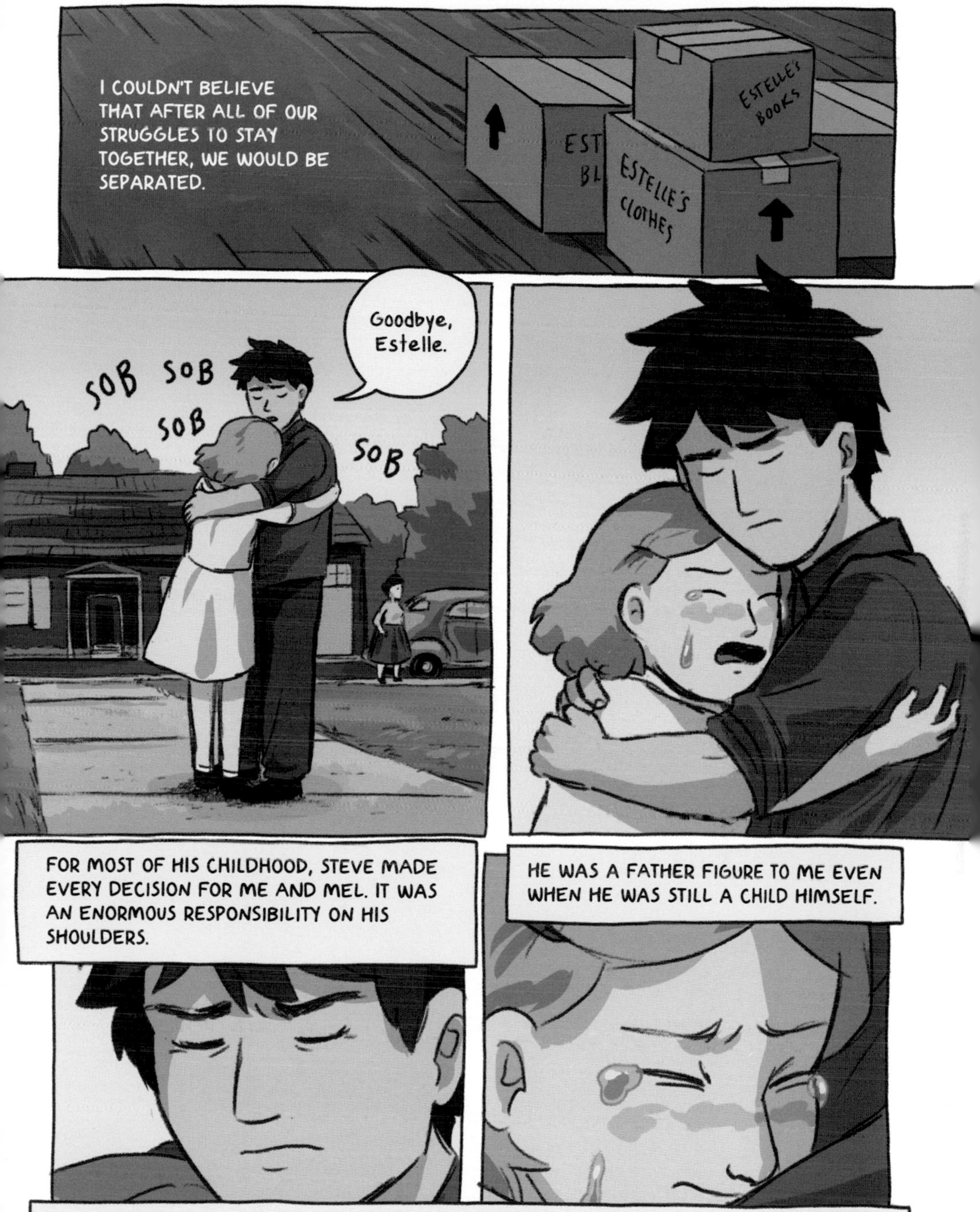
I COULDN'T BELIEVE THAT AFTER ALL OF OUR STRUGGLES TO STAY TOGETHER, WE WOULD BE SEPARATED.
ESTELLE'S BOOKS
ESTELLE'S CLOTHES
SOB SOB
SOB
SOB
Goodbye, Estelle.
FOR MOST OF HIS CHILDHOOD, STEVE MADE EVERY DECISION FOR ME AND MEL. IT WAS AN ENORMOUS RESPONSIBILITY ON HIS SHOULDERS.
HE WAS A FATHER FIGURE TO ME EVEN WHEN HE WAS STILL A CHILD HIMSELF.
I LATER UNDERSTOOD THAT CIRCUMSTANCES IN HIS NEWLY MARRIED LIFE MADE HIM FEEL HE COULDN'T TAKE CARE OF ME. BUT AT SIXTEEN, I FELT AS THOUGH HE HAD GIVEN ME UP—AS THOUGH HE HAD ABANDONED ME.

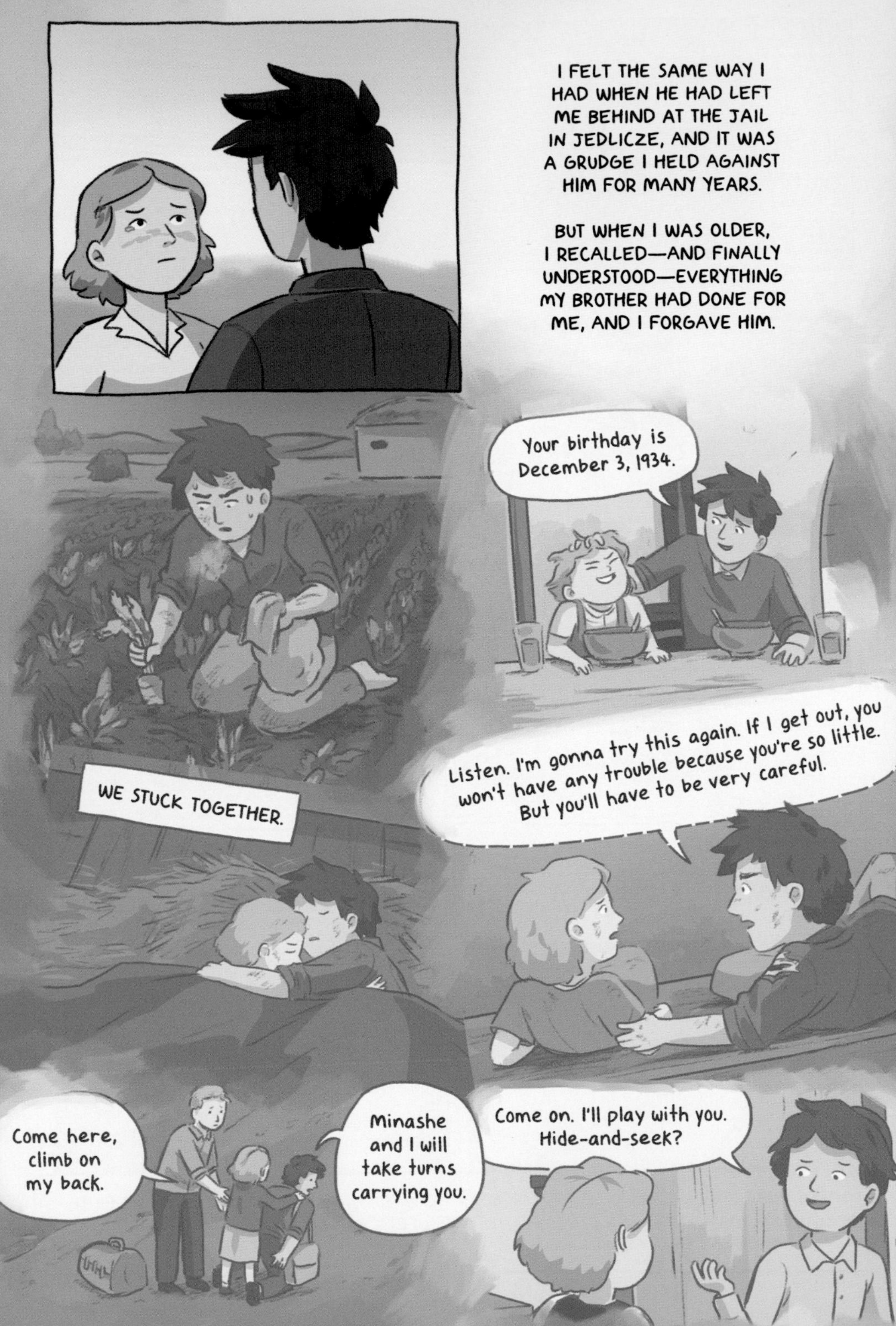
I FELT THE SAME WAY I HAD WHEN HE HAD LEFT ME BEHIND AT THE JAIL IN JEDLICZE, AND IT WAS A GRUDGE I HELD AGAINST HIM FOR MANY YEARS.
BUT WHEN I WAS OLDER, I RECALLED—AND FINALLY UNDERSTOOD—EVERYTHING MY BROTHER HAD DONE FOR ME, AND I FORGAVE HIM.
Your birthday is December 3, 1934.
WE STUCK TOGETHER.
Listen. I'm gonna try this again. If I get out, you won't have any trouble because you're so little. But you'll have to be very careful.
Come here, climb on my back.
Minashe and I will take turns carrying you.
Come on. I'll play with you. Hide-and-seek?

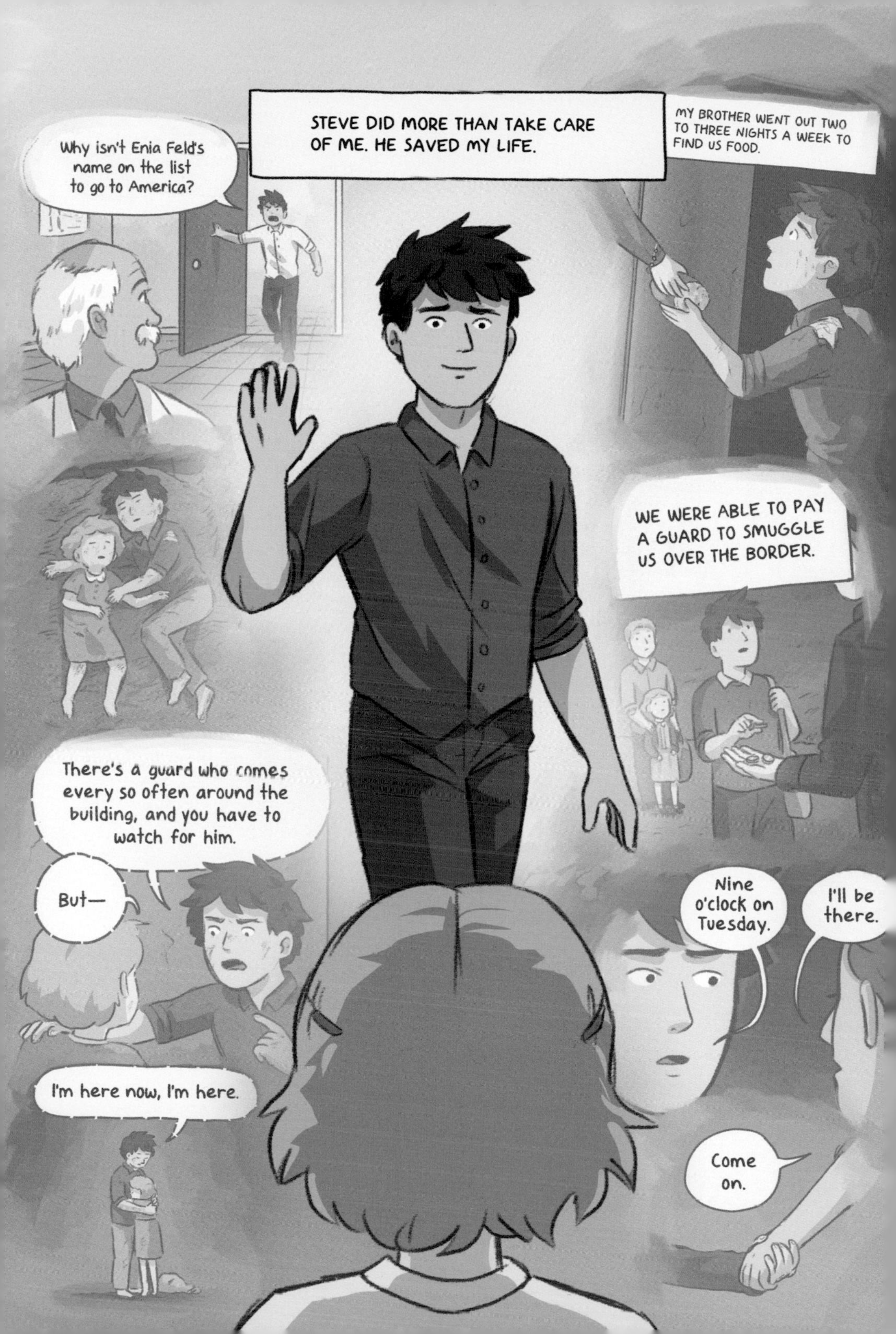

STEVE DID MORE THAN TAKE CARE OF ME. HE SAVED MY LIFE.
Why isn't Enia Feld's name on the list to go to America?
MY BROTHER WENT OUT TWO TO THREE NIGHTS A WEEK TO FIND US FOOD.
WE WERE ABLE TO PAY A GUARD TO SMUGGLE US OVER THE BORDER.
There's a guard who comes every so often around the building, and you have to watch for him.
But—
I'm here now, I'm here.
Nine o'clock on Tuesday.
I'll be there.
Come on.

PART 5:

THE GIRL
WHO SANG

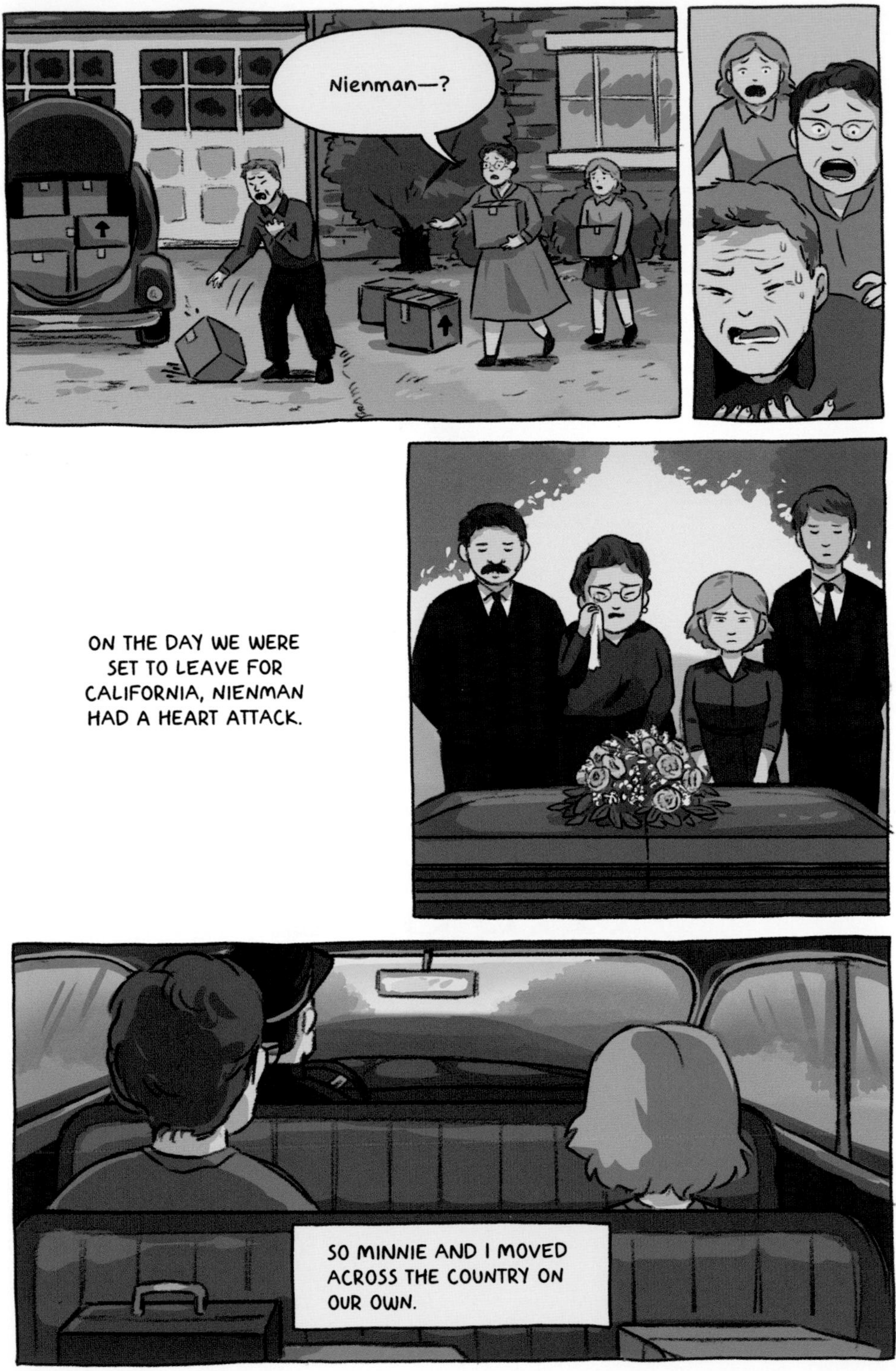
Nienman—?
ON THE DAY WE WERE SET TO LEAVE FOR CALIFORNIA, NIENMAN HAD A HEART ATTACK.
SO MINNIE AND I MOVED ACROSS THE COUNTRY ON OUR OWN.

I ENDED UP STAYING IN CALIFORNIA FOR FIFTY-THREE YEARS.

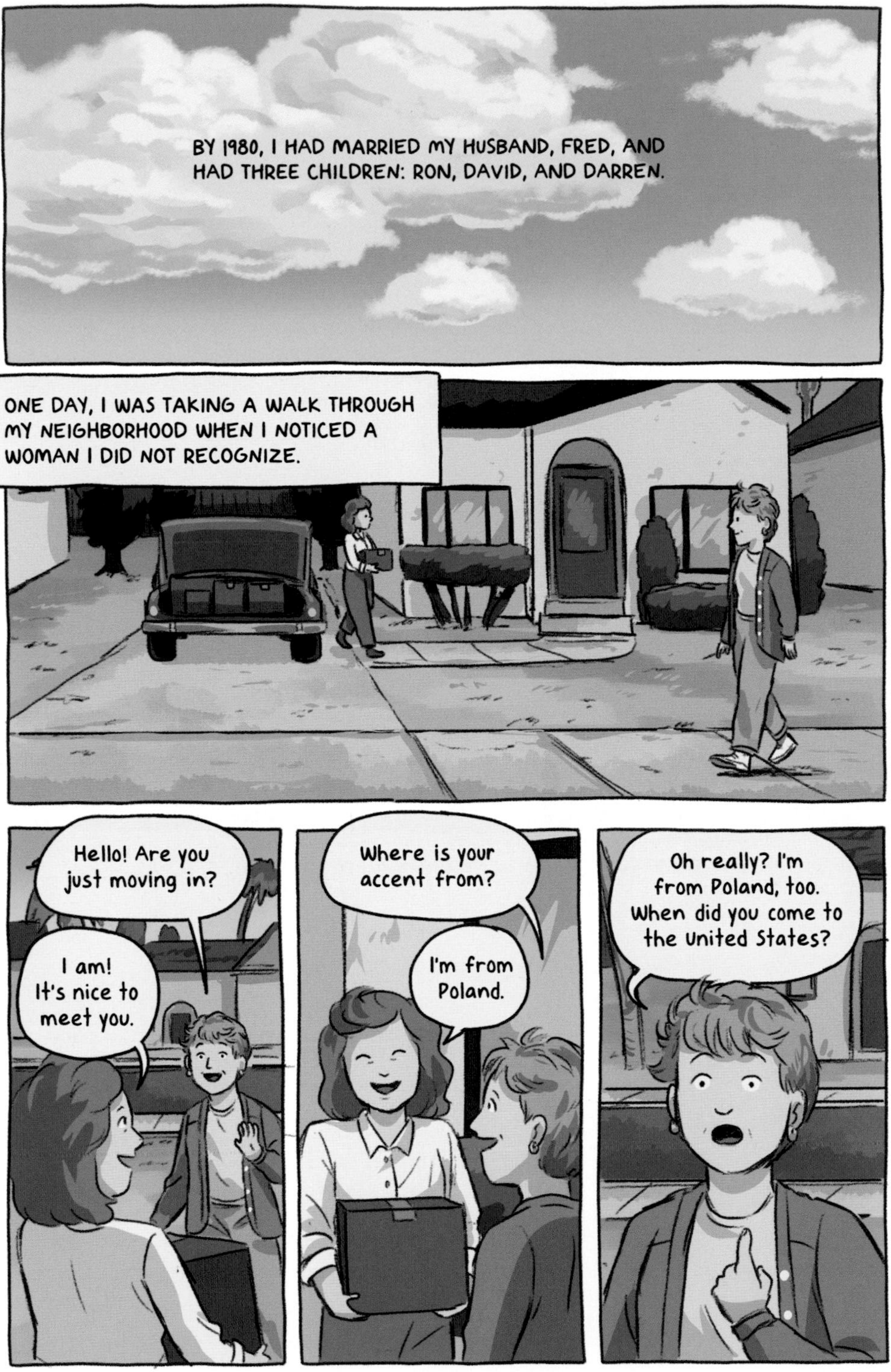
BY 1980, I HAD MARRIED MY HUSBAND, FRED, AND HAD THREE CHILDREN: RON, DAVID, AND DARREN.
ONE DAY, I WAS TAKING A WALK THROUGH MY NEIGHBORHOOD WHEN I NOTICED A WOMAN I DID NOT RECOGNIZE.
Hello! Are you just moving in?
I am! It's nice to meet you.
Where is your accent from?
I'm from Poland.
Oh really? I'm from Poland, too. When did you come to the United States?

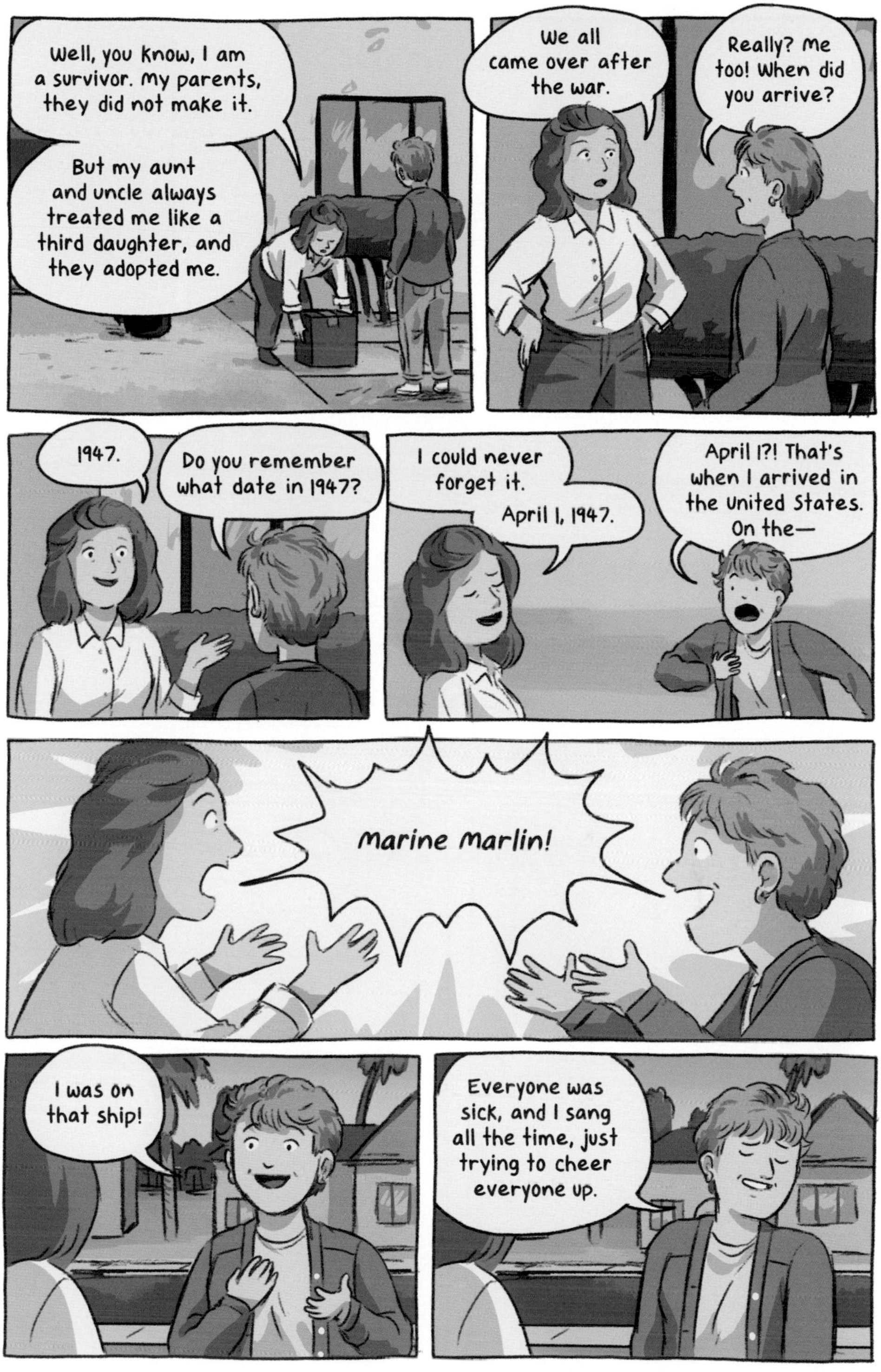
Well, you know, I am a survivor. My parents, they did not make it.
But my aunt and uncle always treated me like a third daughter, and they adopted me.
We all came over after the war.
Really? Me too! When did you arrive?
1947.
Do you remember what date in 1947?
I could never forget it.
April 1, 1947.
April 1?! That's when I arrived in the United States. On the—
Marine Marlin!
I was on that ship!
Everyone was sick, and I sang all the time, just trying to cheer everyone up.

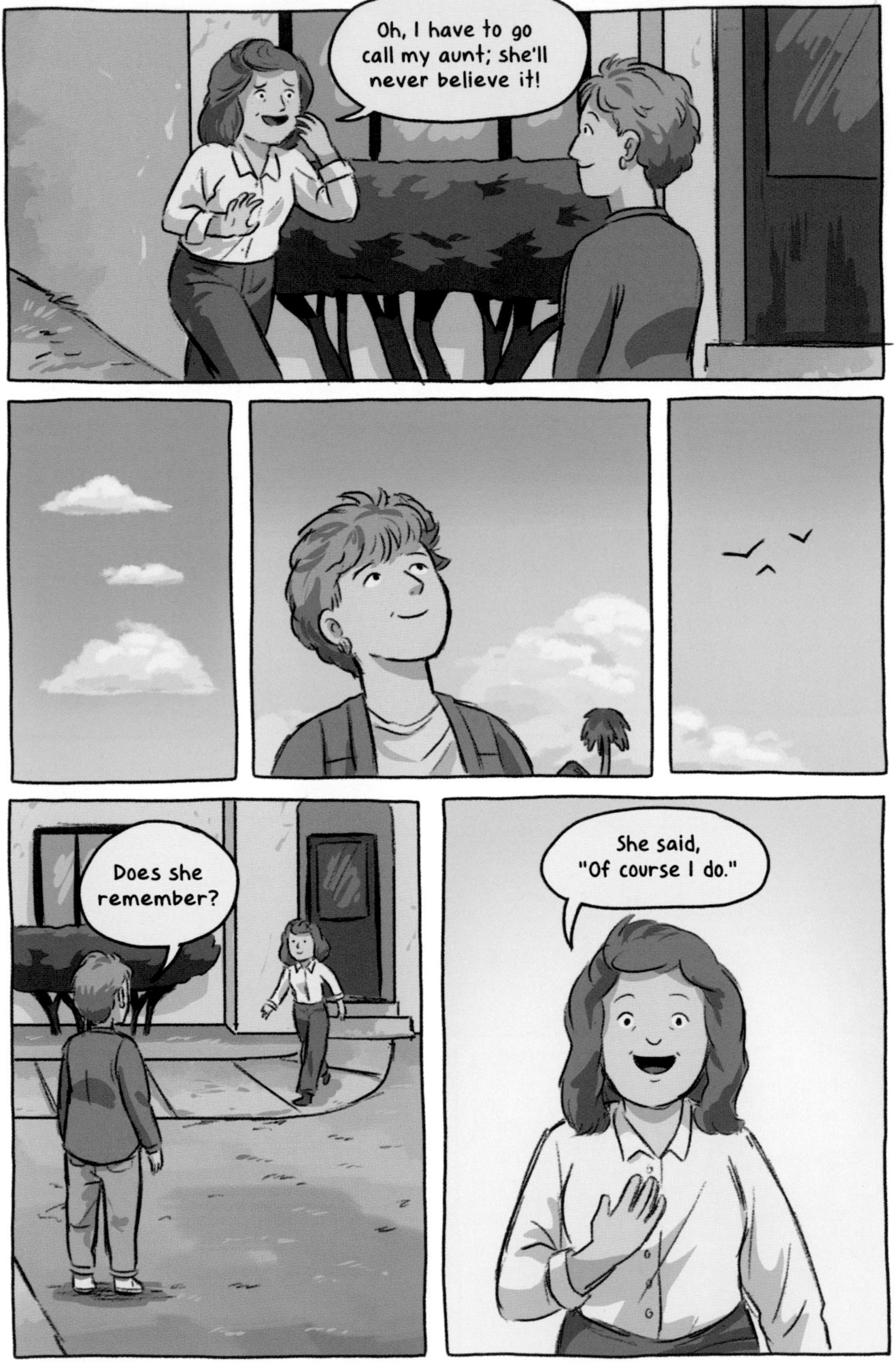
Oh, I have to go call my aunt; she'll never believe it!
Does she remember?
She said, "Of course I do."

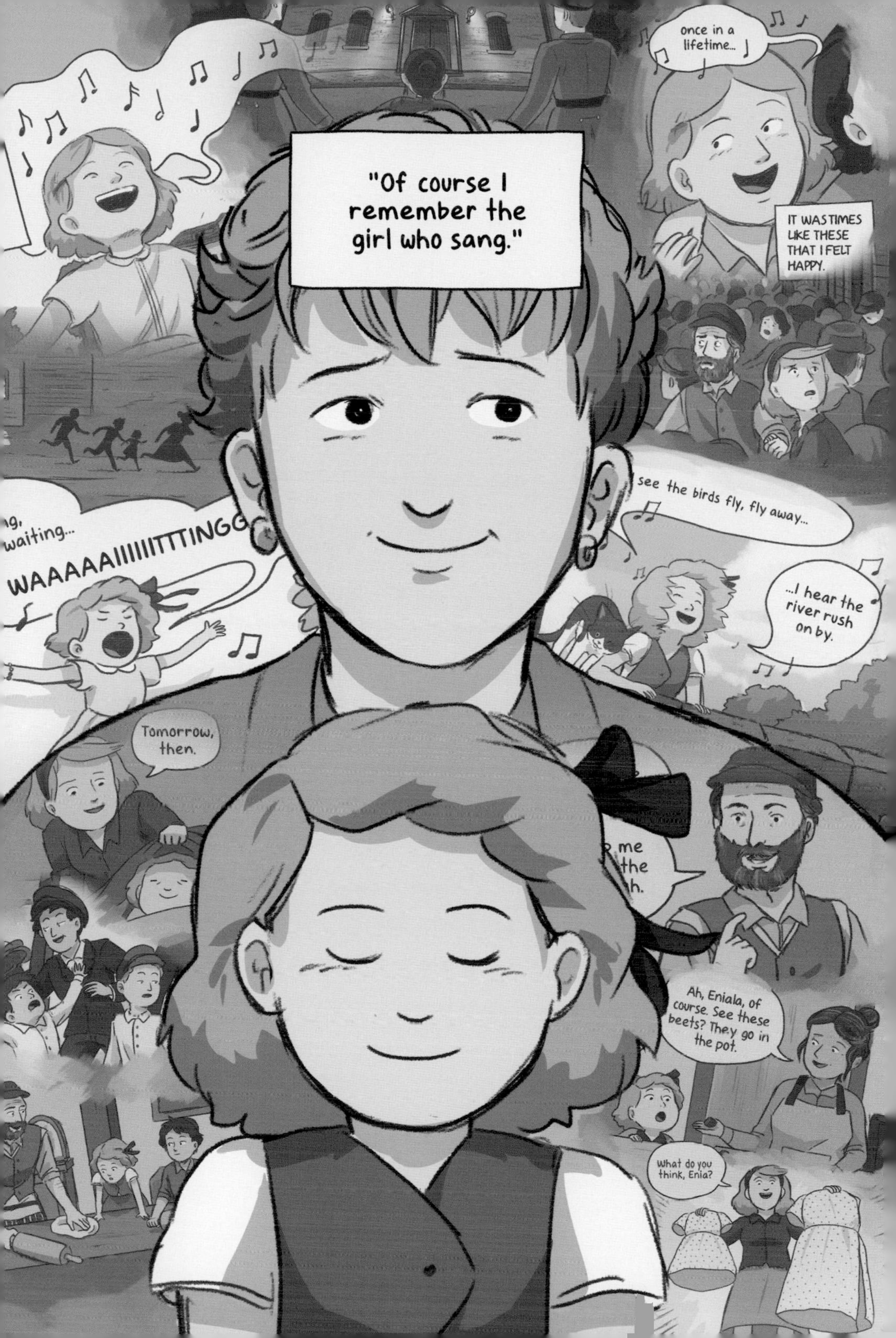
"Of course I remember the girl who sang."
once in a lifetime...
IT WAS TIMES LIKE THESE THAT I FELT HAPPY.
waiting...
WAAAAAIIIIIITTTINGG
see the birds fly, fly away...
...I hear the river rush on by.
Tomorrow, then.
Ah, Eniala, of course. See these beets? They go in the pot.
What do you think, Enia?

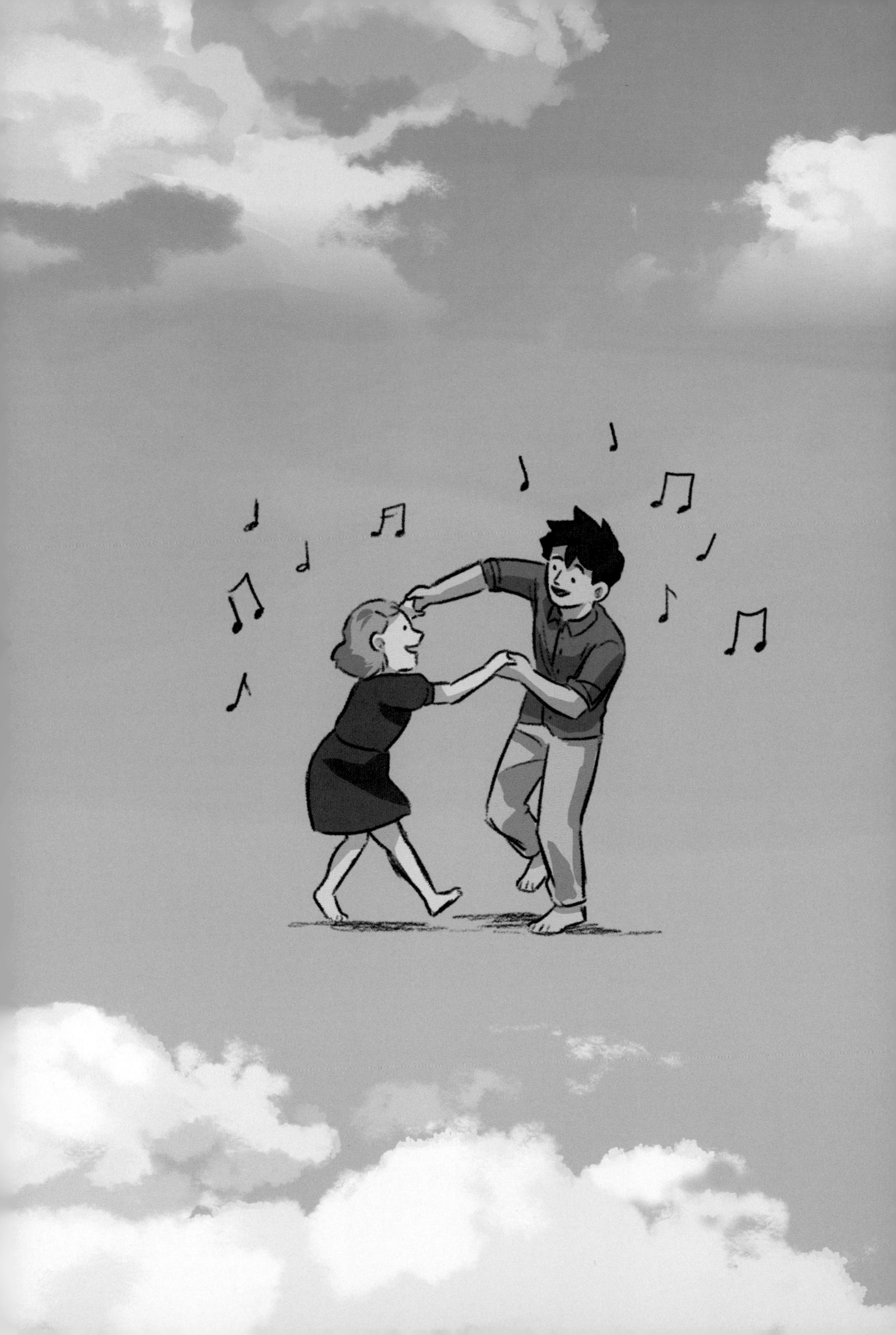

AFTERWORD

Emilia "Milcha" Wilusz and her parents, Jan and Maria Kurowski

Milcha and her family would continue to have an impact on Estelle's life. Several years after the war, Steve flew Milcha to New Jersey, and Estelle traveled from California to see her. Milcha had two sons: Jan and Tadeusz Wilusz. Tadeusz works as a professor at Krakow University of Economics, and he would visit Estelle, Steve, and Mel on his sabbaticals to the US and encouraged them to visit their old home in Poland, which they did in 1992. Today, he attends the International March of the Living* with Estelle.

During the March, Tadeusz talks to the students about his grandparents, emphasizing their generosity and kindness. Though they were poor themselves, they shared everything they had with friends and neighbors who had less, including Estelle and her family. They did not think about putting their own lives at risk. Tadeusz tells them, "They did not make sacrifices; they just did what they knew they needed to do."

Before leaving Poland in 1945, Estelle and her brothers gave their family's home to the Kurowskis, and their grandchildren and great-grandchildren still live there today.

Pudlina

When Estelle and her brothers returned to Poland, they learned from Pudlina's neighbors that she lived through the war and had gone to live with her son. Though they never saw Pudlina again, Estelle remembers her as "an amazing lady" and always wished they could have reconnected.

*A program that brings individuals of all ages and backgrounds to Poland and Israel to learn the history of the Holocaust and examine the origins of prejudice and intolerance.

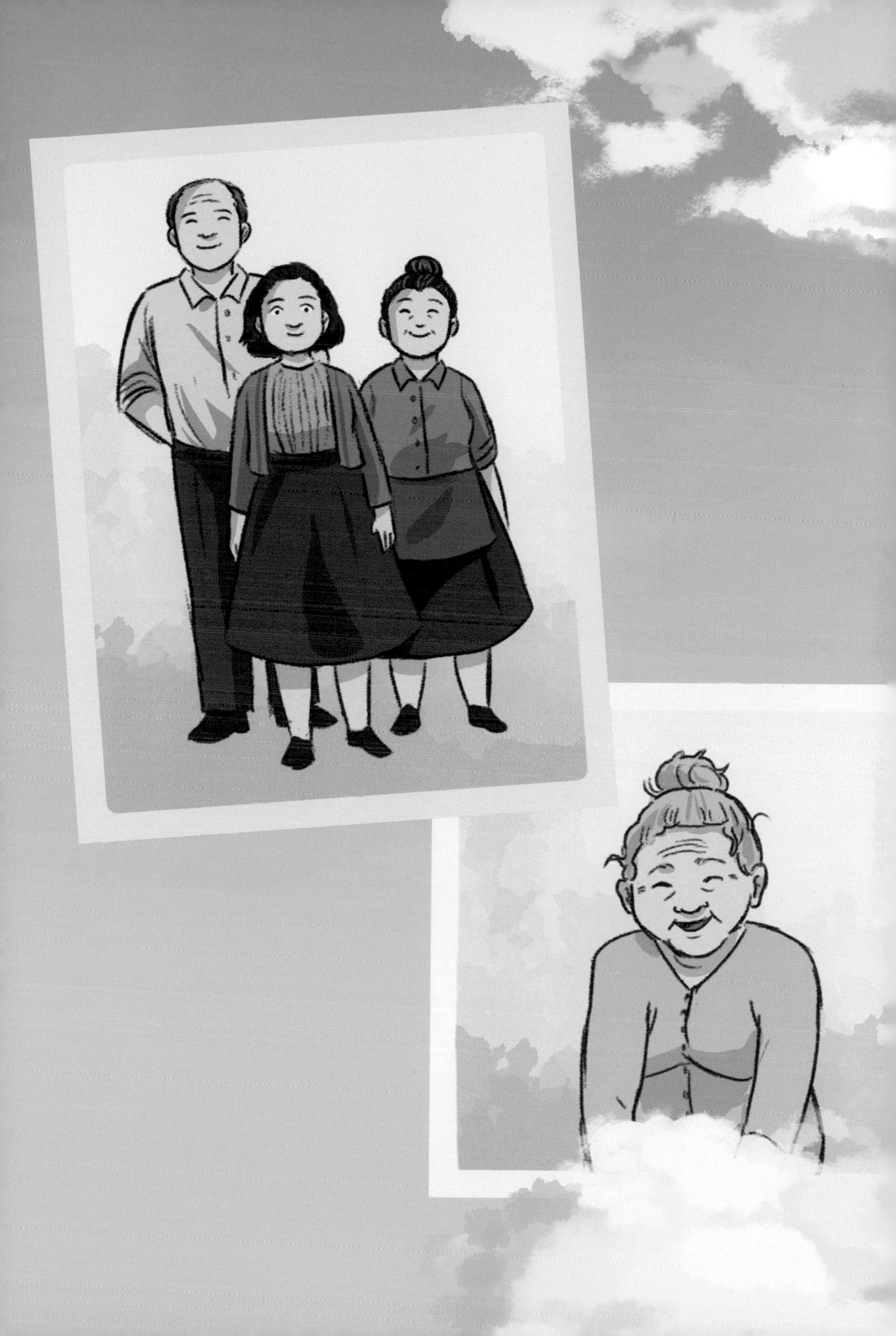

Mala

Years after Estelle and her brothers parted ways with Mala and Wujek Reiss in Romania, they learned that their uncle had another sister in Australia who had sent papers that would allow them to join her. But she hadn't sent papers for Estelle, Steve, or Mel.

Mala settled in Australia with her father and her aunt. She had three sons, Harry, Allan, and Steven, and five grandchildren. Estelle and Mala reunited twice after the war: first when Mala and her husband, Lester (Les), traveled to California for a bat mitzvah they all attended together, and again in 1992 when they returned to Poland to visit their old homes. Mala passed away in 2018 at eighty-seven years old.

Mel

Mel became a talented businessman and learned a great deal working at Rosenhan's Children's Dresses, his very first job in America. He later opened up his own factory in Perth Amboy, New Jersey, called Mel's Children's Dresses and became a millionaire from his business. Mel married his wife, Rose, in 1956 and had two daughters, Pamela and Michelle, and seven grandchildren. He passed away in 2016 at eighty-nine years old.

Steve

Steve continued to work at the candy store in Brooklyn before partnering with a friend to open a candy store of his own. Later, he joined Mel at his children's dress company.

In his thirties, Steve studied to become a cantor and sang for the High Holidays every year at different synagogues. Estelle recalls that her brother had "one of the most beautiful voices." Steve lived in New Jersey with his wife, Adele, and had two sons, Norman (Norm) and Irwin, and four grandchildren. He passed away in 2004 at seventy-eight years old.

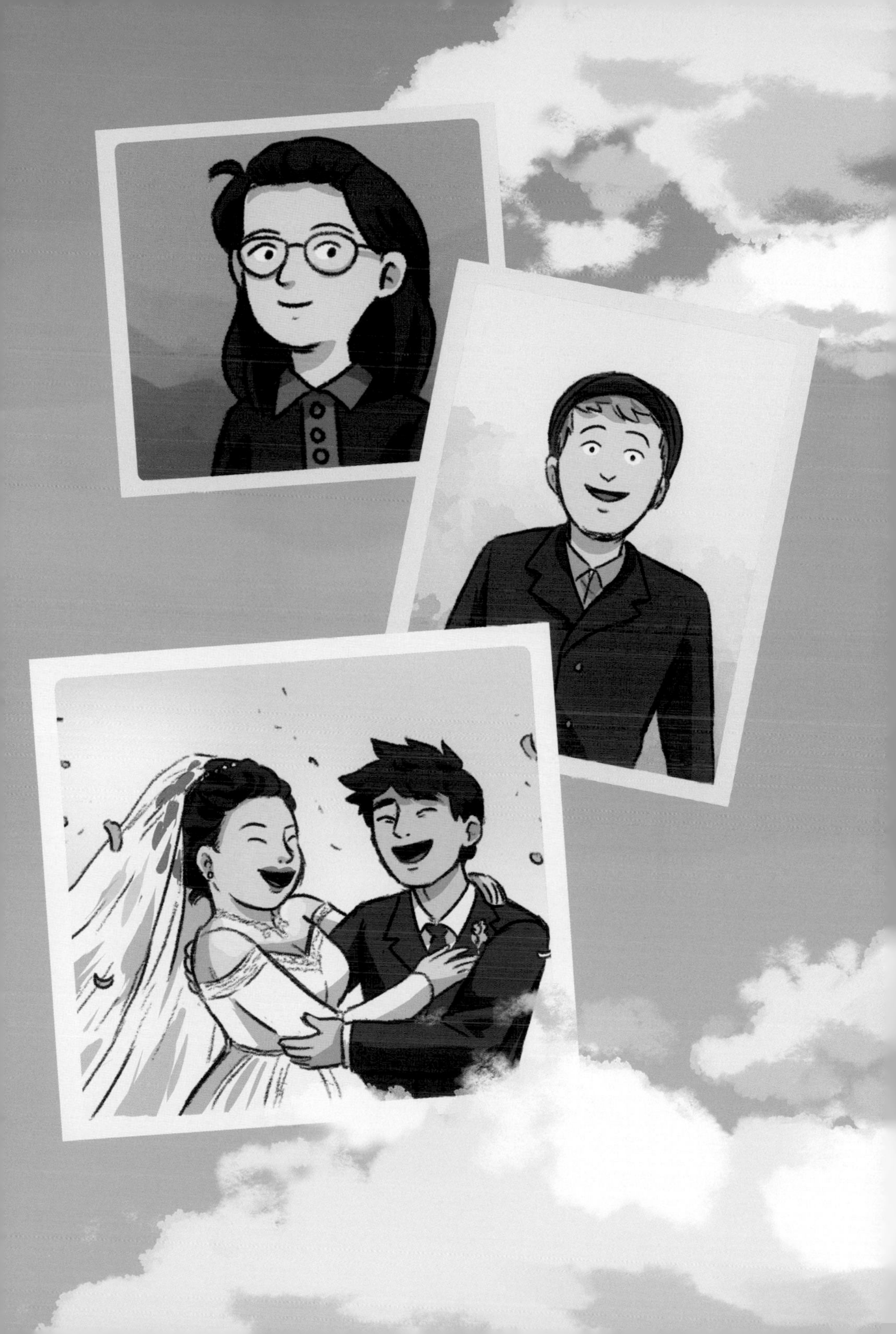

Estelle

After her move to California, Estelle and her brothers occasionally visited each other, maintaining their relationship as best as they could from so far away. In 1952, at seventeen years old, Estelle married Fred Nadel (no relation to Minnie and Neinman Nadel). They are still married today and have three sons and five grandchildren. When her youngest son was about eight years old, Estelle started her own jewelry business.

Estelle lived in California for fifty-three years before she and her husband retired to Colorado to be closer to two of their sons. She and Fred still live there today. Their eldest son, Ron, worked as a biology teacher in California and then as an IT manager at Lockheed Martin in Colorado before retiring. Her second son, David, is an accountant in Encino, California. And her third son, Darren, is an attorney in Colorado. Her daughter-in-law Michele is a PhD in psychology, and her daughter-in-law Hester was a special education teacher at a middle school in California, then a science program educator at the University of Colorado Boulder. She is now retired.

Estelle has never stopped singing, and has sung with various temples across Southern Californa, from Temple Emanuel in Beverly Hills to Valley Beth Shalom in Encino with famous conductor and composer Aminadav Aloni. Now in Colorado, she sings at Temple Sinai and with the Colorado Hebrew Chorale.

Today, Estelle tells her story to students at high schools and colleges around the country. She credits her daughter-in-law Hester Nadel with giving her the courage to speak.

She has also attended the International March of the Living as a speaker several times. The Bureau of Jewish Education in Los Angeles takes about two hundred high school seniors, twenty staff members, and six Holocaust survivors on the March every year to commemorate Holocaust Remembrance Day (Yom HaShoah). The three-kilometer March begins at Auschwitz and ends at Birkenau, the largest concentration camps built and operated by the Nazis during World War II.

Estelle continues to share her story, hoping to ensure the Holocaust is never forgotten.

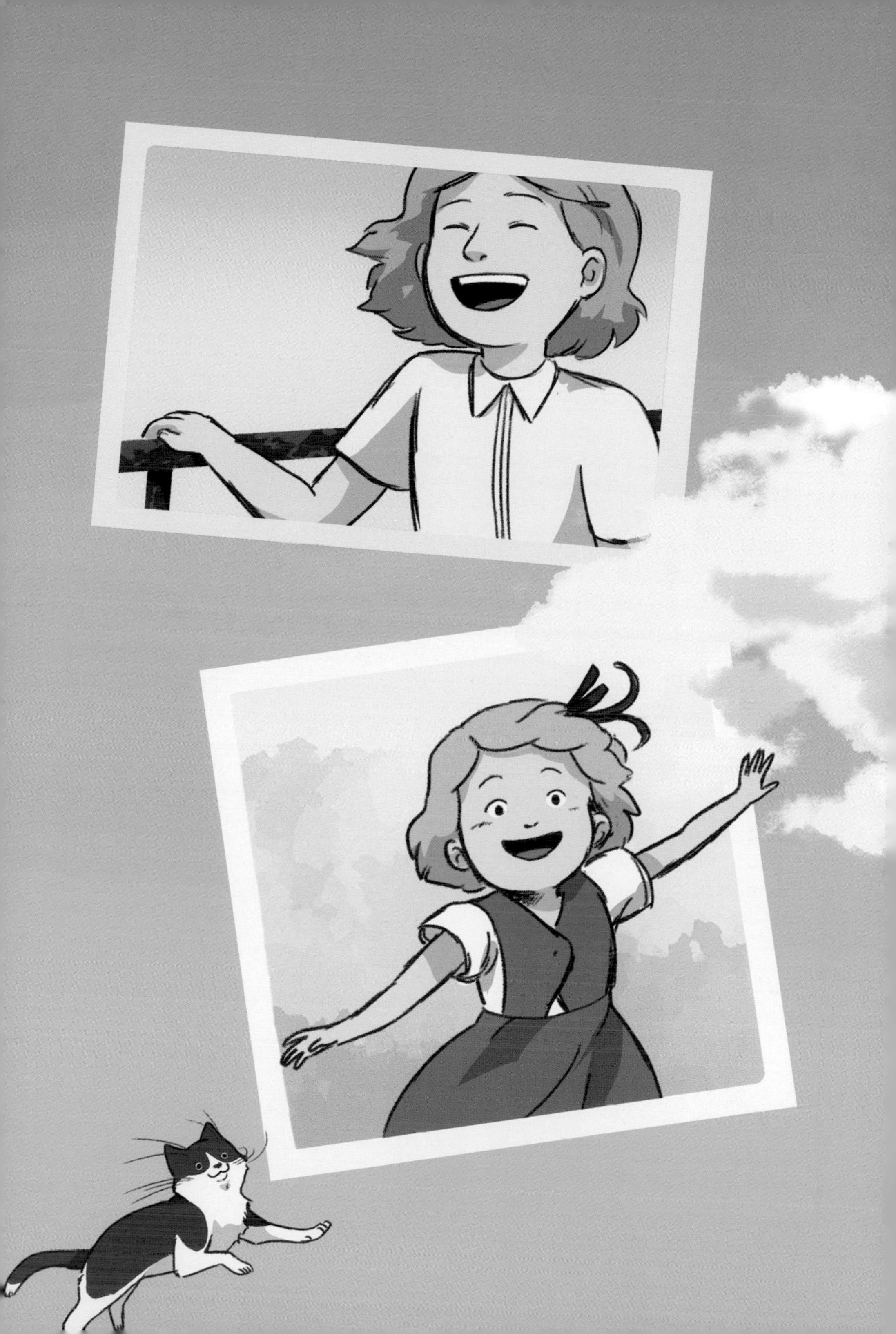

A NOTE FROM ESTELLE

It's true: I never stopped singing.

There was a time when I couldn't tell this story. When I first arrived in America, I just wanted to be American. I didn't want to be identified as a "Holocaust survivor." So I never spoke about it. I always kept it to myself.

Now, I often think about the people who helped us along the way. My brother Shia spoke to the jailer in Jedlicze shortly after we were liberated, and the jailer said that he had put us in the basement cell on purpose. He had hoped we would be able to escape out that window. And then there was, of course, Pudlina, who treated us as if we were her own children, and the Kurowskis, whose kindness and generosity will never be forgotten.

I'm not going to be here forever. Someday there will no longer be any Holocaust survivors still living. We will be gone. I want you, the young people, the next generation, to carry our stories on and someday tell your own children that, yes, you knew a Holocaust survivor. She was real. It really happened.

Love,

Estelle

A NOTE FROM SAMMY

My great-great-grandparents were Jews who came to America from many places in Eastern Europe, including towns in Poland less than an hour's drive from Estelle's hometown of Borek. They came to America long before World War II, and any family members who didn't leave Europe before the War likely perished. Because of my family history, I felt a great connection to Estelle's story and wanted to help bring her experiences and vision to the page. I was taught about the Holocaust from a very young age and want to continue those teachings with this book, especially now, during a time of such denial and misinformation.

It's been an incredible honor to illustrate Estelle's story and work so closely with her, especially as a Jewish person myself. I am thankful for the trust she and my editor, Mekisha Telfer, showed in allowing me to write additional scenes after interviewing Estelle. I've always dreamed of creating a graphic novel, and having my first one be a story as important, personal, and touching as Estelle's could not be more fulfilling.

With love,

BEHIND THE SCENES!

These were tests to decide what style of eyes we would use. None of these ended up being the final look! This was also before we decided to go with a pencil-texture for the lines.

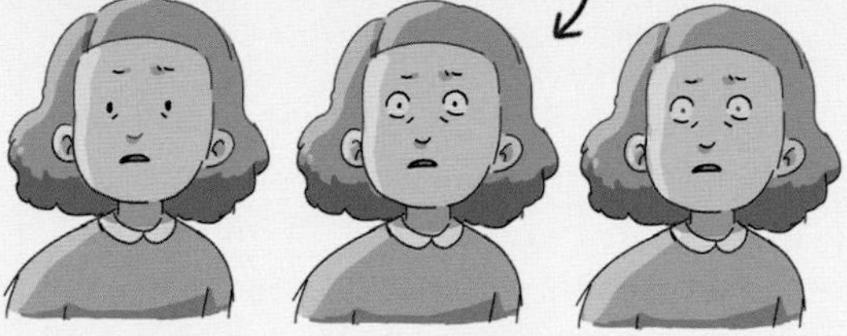

A sketch of Enia, Shia, and Minashe I did when figuring out how they would look at different ages.

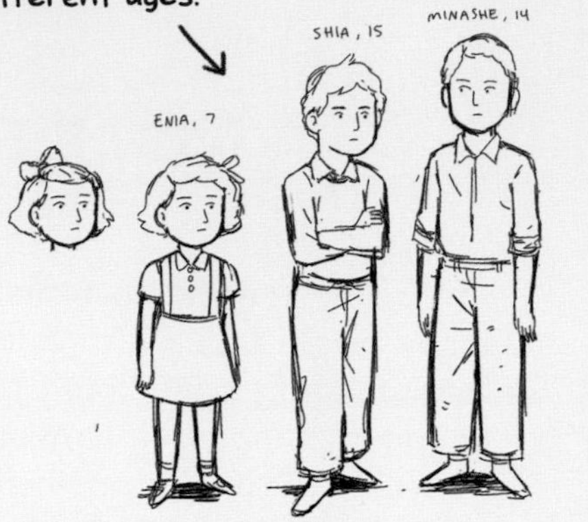

ENIA, 7
SHIA, 15
MINASHE, 14

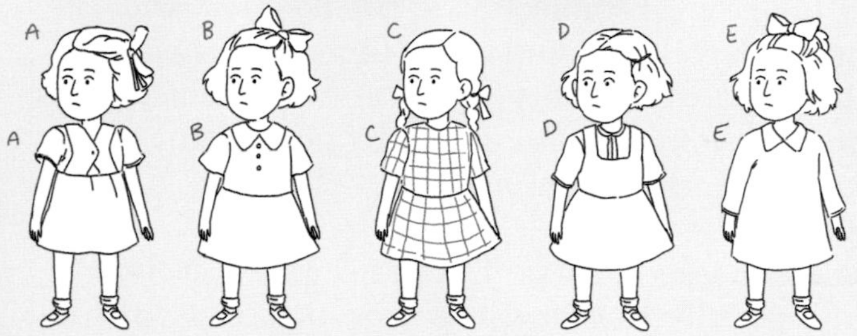

A
B
C
D
E

These are some early Enia drawings from when we were deciding on her clothing and hairstyle.

I drew layouts of the Kurowskis' barn and Pudlina's attic on notecards that I always kept at my desk to reference! They're similar but have differences that needed to be consistent.

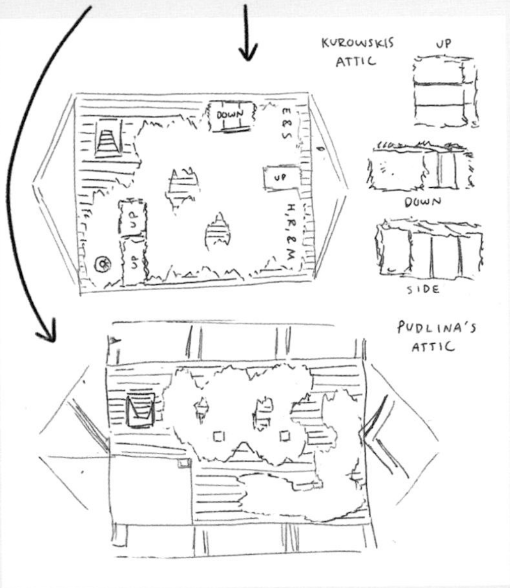

KUROWSKIS ATTIC
DOWN
E&S
UP
H,R,&M
UP
UP
UP
DOWN
SIDE
PUDLINA'S ATTIC

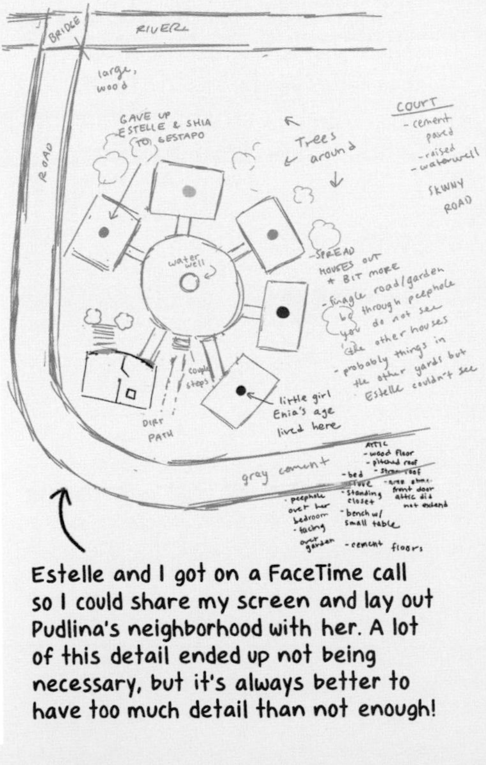

BRIDGE
RIVER
ROAD
large, wood
GAVE UP ESTELLE & SHIA TO GESTAPO
Trees around
COURT
- cement paved
- raised waterwell
SKINNY ROAD
water well
-SPREAD HOUSES OUT
* BIT MORE
- finagle road/garden
be through peephole
you do not see
the other houses
- probably things in
the other yards but
Estelle couldn't see
couple steps
DIRT PATH
little girl Enia's age lived here
gray cement
ATTIC
- wood floor
- pitched roof
- bed
- standing closet
- bench w/ small table
- cement floors
front door
attic did not extend
- peephole over her bedroom
- facing over garden

Estelle and I got on a FaceTime call so I could share my screen and lay out Pudlina's neighborhood with her. A lot of this detail ended up not being necessary, but it's always better to have too much detail than not enough!

Estelle provided a few photographs of different places, which I drew replicas of as panels whenever I could.

Photos of the village were sparse, so I used Estelle's photos, Google Street View, and other photographs of the Polish countryside and buildings to inform the backgrounds.

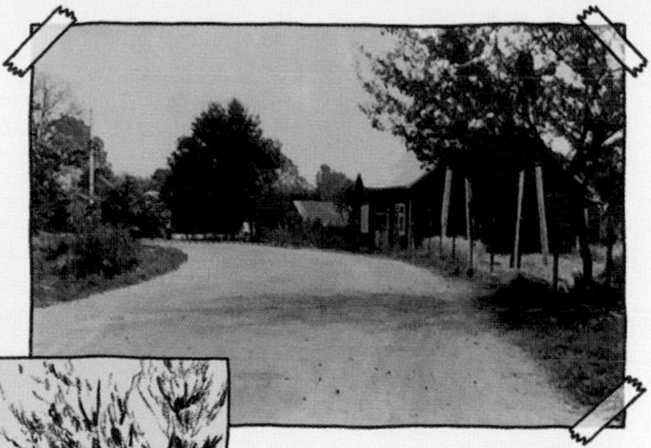

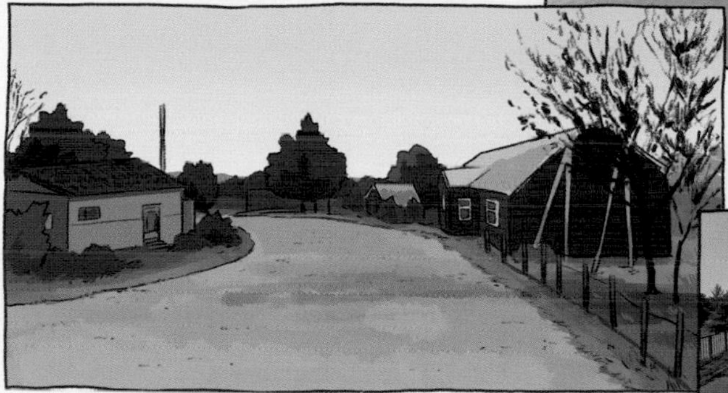

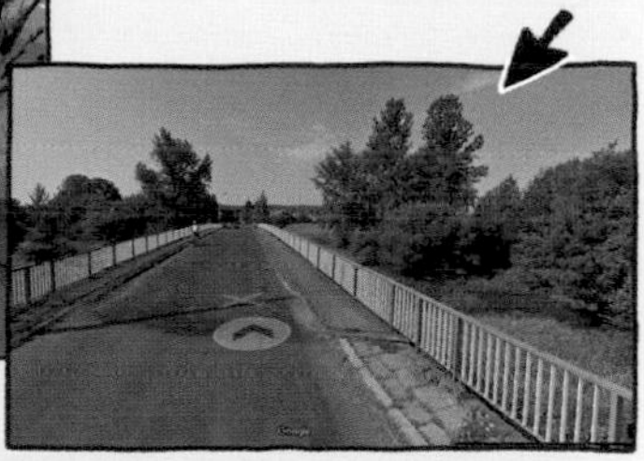

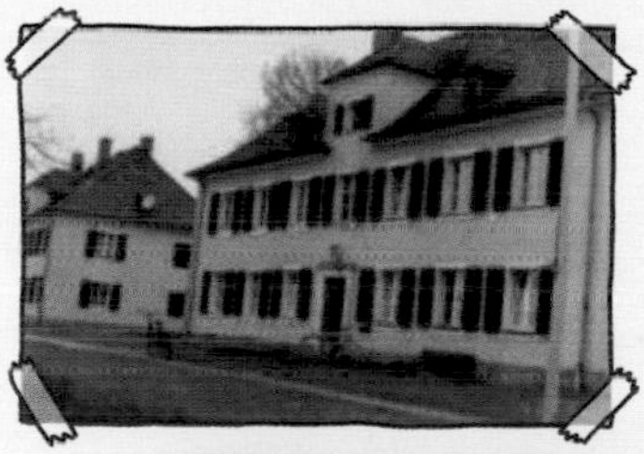

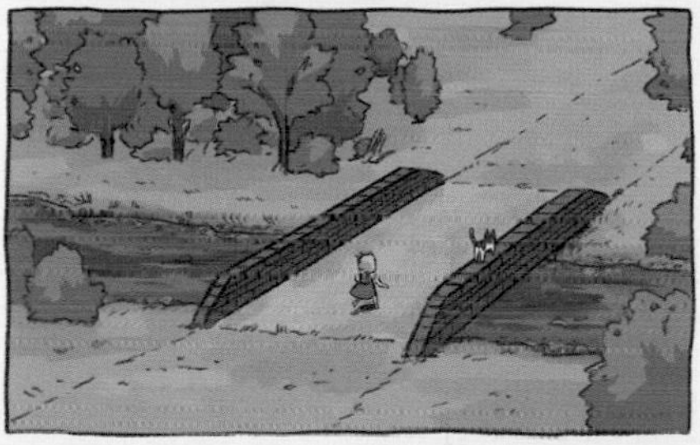

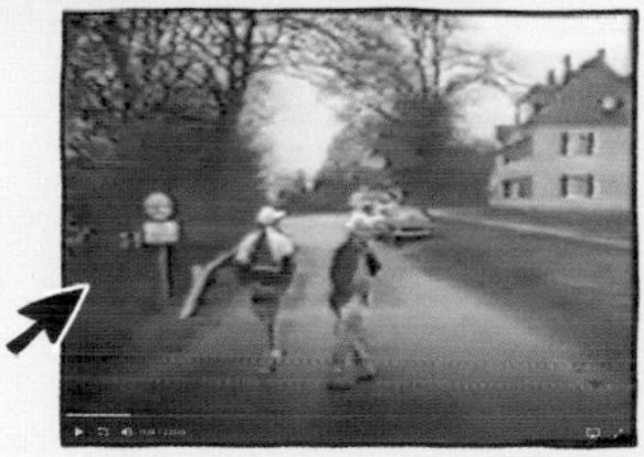

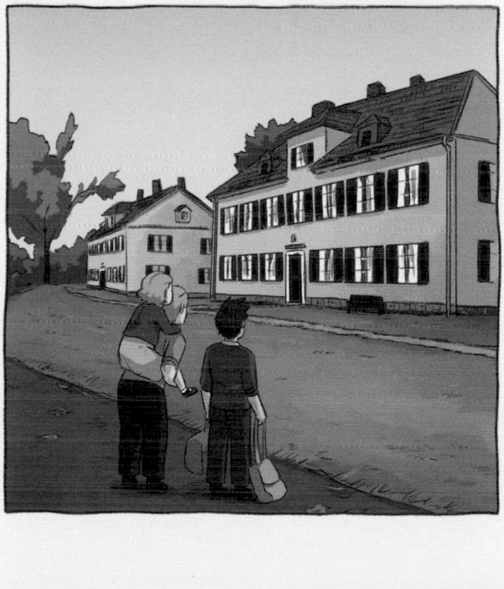

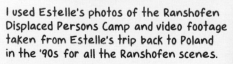

I used Estelle's photos of the Ranshofen Displaced Persons Camp and video footage taken from Estelle's trip back to Poland in the '90s for all the Ranshofen scenes.

Coincidentally, I happened to draw Shia and Minashe in almost the exact same spots as they stood in this screenshot decades later when revisiting.

HOW TO MAKE A COMIC PAGE

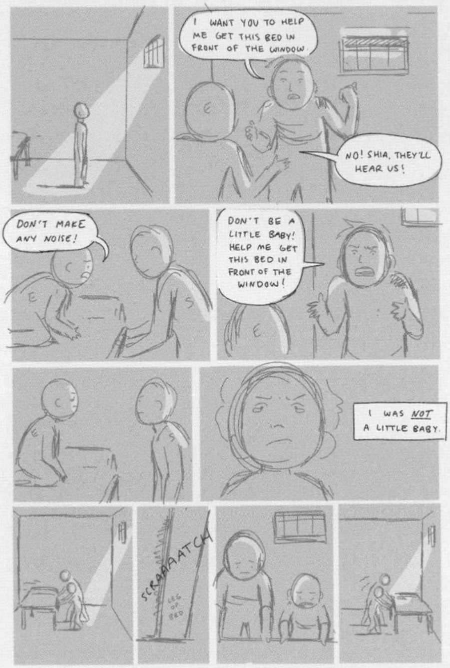
I WANT YOU TO HELP ME GET THIS BED IN FRONT OF THE WINDOW
NO! SHIA, THEY'LL HEAR US!
DON'T MAKE ANY NOISE!
DON'T BE A LITTLE BABY! HELP ME GET THIS BED IN FRONT OF THE WINDOW!
I WAS NOT A LITTLE BABY.
SCRAAAATCH
LEG OF BED

STEP 1: I began each page with the script in front of me and blocked out all the panels in colored boxes like this. I usually used blue when the scene was at night or in shadow, and I used yellow for daytime or brighter scenes.

STEP 2: After that, I wrote out the text and sketched in the figures and backgrounds, focusing on emotion, proportions, and composition rather than details. I also included some lighting cues to refer to during the coloring stage.

STEP 3: I started inking by typing out placeholder text. Then I traced the colored boxes by hand to make panels, went in to draw the backgrounds, and then drew the figures. All of the lines were drawn in a dark blue green.

I wanted to limit the use of straight line tools for this book in favor of the organic look of a hand-drawn line.

I used a straight line for some inorganic things like buildings (which you can see in this page) but always made sure it was balanced out with hand-drawn elements. I love a hand-drawn look in general, but it felt especially fitting for a story as personal and sentimental as this one.

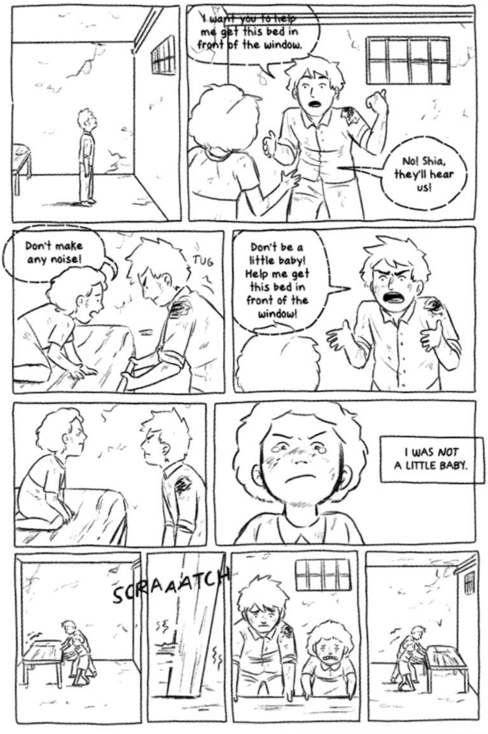
I want you to help me get this bed in front of the window.
No! Shia, they'll hear us!
Don't make any noise!
TUG
Don't be a little baby! Help me get this bed in front of the window!
I WAS NOT A LITTLE BABY.
SCRAAATCH

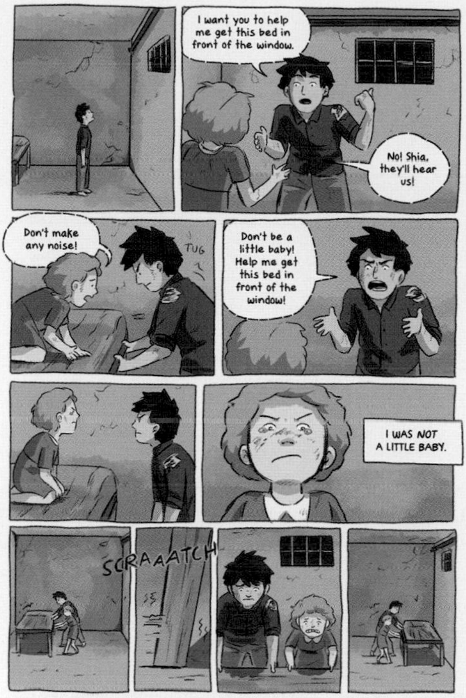
I want you to help me get this bed in front of the window.
No! Shia, they'll hear us!
Don't make any noise!
TUG
Don't be a little baby! Help me get this bed in front of the window!
I WAS NOT A LITTLE BABY.
SCRAAATCH

STEP 4: In the coloring stage, I cel shaded the figures and did a mix of cel shading and painting for the background. I also colored some linework (like Shia's wound on this page).

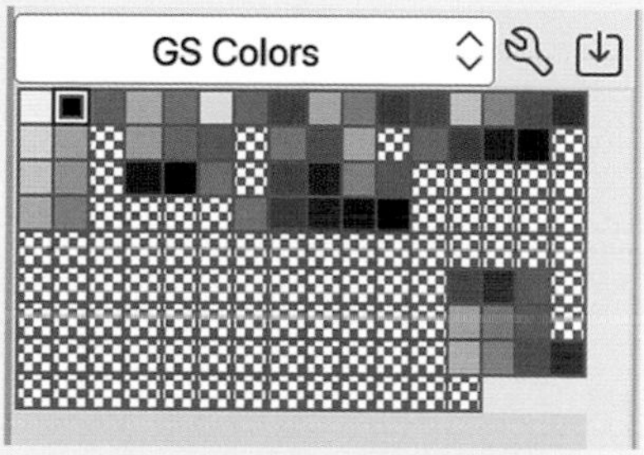
GS Colors

Here's my color palette I made for *The Girl Who Sang*! Mostly hair, skin, clothes, and common background colors, including the shadow color for each color.

STEP 5: Finally, I'd finish the page with atmospheric details like shadow and light!

The placeholder text changed to finalized text later, after multiple revisions.

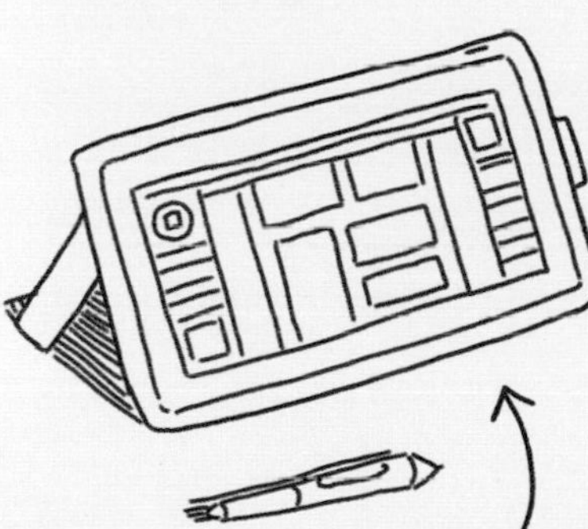

Everything was done on a Wacom Cintiq 16 in Clip Studio Paint!

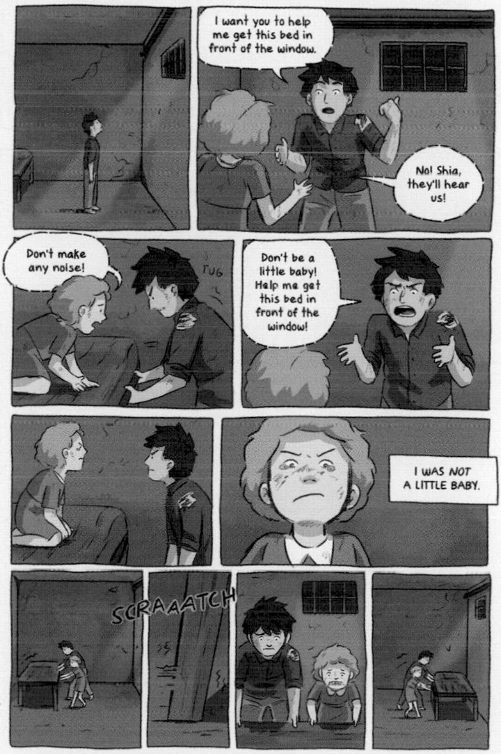
I want you to help me get this bed in front of the window.
No! Shia, they'll hear us!
Don't make any noise!
TUG
Don't be a little baby! Help me get this bed in front of the window!
I WAS NOT A LITTLE BABY.
SCRAAATCH

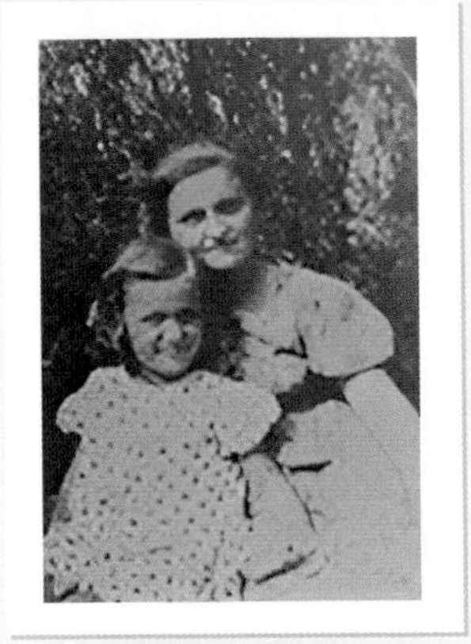

Estelle and her older sister, Sonjia

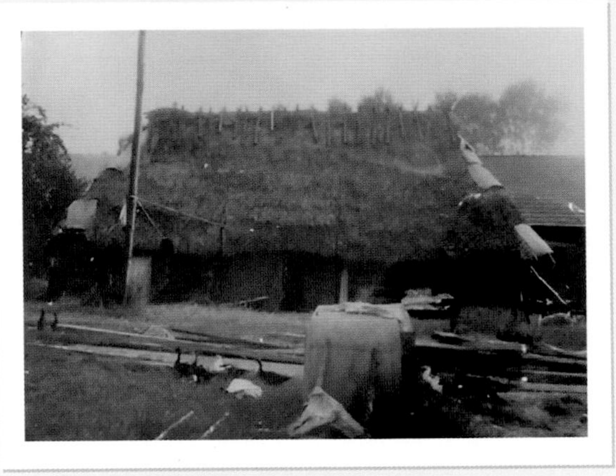

The Kurowskis' barn

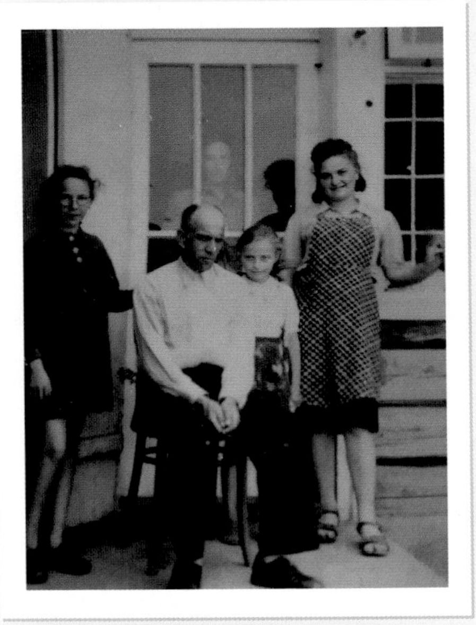

(Left to right) Mala, Wujek Reiss, Estelle, and Sonjia

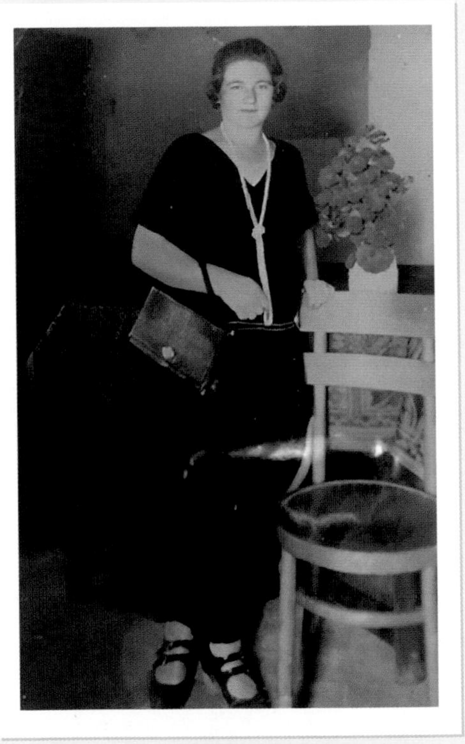

Tante Hinda

Shia (left) at Ranshofen
DP Camp, 1946

Minashe at Ranshofen
DP Camp, 1946

Enla and Minashe (front, left of center)
in a Ranshofen DP Camp performance

RESOURCES

In 1990, Steve's son Norman Feld interviewed Steve, Mel, and Estelle about their experience during the Holocaust in a recording titled "The Remembrance." And in 1992, at Tadeusz's urging, Estelle and her brothers took a trip back to Poland. Together, Estelle, Steve, Mel, and Mala, along with Steve's son Norman and Mala's son Allan, revisited their old homes, their town, and the most notable sites from their story. This trip was recorded by Norm in a video titled "Return to Europe." If you'd like to hear the full account from the siblings themselves, you can watch both "The Remembrance" and "Return to Europe" on the United States Holocaust Memorial Museum website.

Additionally, Estelle, Steve, and Mel have had their stories recorded by the USC Shoah Foundation. These recordings are housed in their Virtual History Archive and are available in Jewish museums around the world.

ACKNOWLEDGMENTS

I dedicate this book to Pudlina, to Maria and Jan Kurowski, and to their daughter, Emilia "Milcha" Wilusz Kurowska, for having the courage to save my aunt and uncle Reiss, my cousin Mala, my two brothers, and myself. They endangered their lives hiding us, and I will be forever grateful. I also dedicate it to Tadeusz Wilusz, Emilia's son, who urged us to return to Poland and to share our story.

—*Estelle Nadel*

To Estelle, for courageously continuing to educate students on the Holocaust, for your constant openness in answering my questions, and for always wanting to teach me as much as you can. Thank you so much for trusting me with your story and with your family's portrayals. You are an incredible woman, and I truly admire you. I also dedicate this book to my parents, Elissa and Chris, and my siblings, Jacob and Emmy, for your advice, encouragement, and endless emotional support. I love you!

And a special thank-you to Charlie Olsen, Mekisha Telfer, and Kirk Benshoff for all of your incredible support and guidance. Thank you so much!

—*Sammy Savos*

To Estelle, thank you for sharing your story.

—*Bethany Strout*